THE NEW TESTAMENT
AND
HELLENISTIC JUDAISM

1 - 01

CBD

.50

D1202887

Dedicated to   Nils Alstrup Dahl
                    Jakob Jónsson †
                    Aimo Nikolainen
                    Bent Noack
                    Harald Riesenfeld

A

THE NEW TESTAMENT
AND
HELLENISTIC JUDAISM

PEDER BORGEN
SØREN GIVERSEN

EDITORS

NYACK COLLEGE MANHATTAN

HENDRICKSON PUBLISHERS

Hendrickson Publishers, Inc.
P. O. Box 3473
Peabody, Massachusetts 01961-3473

ISBN: 1-56563-261-3

THE NEW TESTAMENT AND HELLENISTIC JUDAISM, edited by Peder Borgen and Søren Giversen © Aarhus University Press, 1995. Hendrickson Publishers' edition reprinted by arrangement with:

Aarhus University Press
Building 170
University of Aarhus
DK-8000 Aarhus C
Denmark
Fax (+45) 8619 8433

For the Hendrickson edition, Nikolaus Walter's article "Hellenistische Diaspora-Juden an der Wiege des Urchristentums" was translated into English by Doris Glenn Wagner.

This book may not be reproduced, in whole or in part, in any form (beyond what is permitted by copyright law) without the original publisher's permission. This applies particularly to reproductions, translations, microfilms, and storage and processing in electronic systems.

First printing — February 1997

Printed in the United States of America

Library of Congress Cataloging-in-Publication Data

The New Testament and Hellenistic Judaism /   edited by Peder Borgen and Søren Giversen.
   Papers read at a conference at the Faculty of Theology, University of Aarhus, Feb. 8–10, 1992.
   Includes bibliographical references and indexes.
   ISBN 1-56563-261-3 (pbk.)
   1. Bible. N.T.—Criticism, interpretation, etc.—Congresses. 2. Judaism—History—Post-exilic period, 586 B.C.–210 A.D.—Congresses. 3. Judaism—Relations—Christianity—Congresses. 4. Christianity and other religions—Judaism—Congresses. 5. Church history—Primitive and early church, ca. 30–600—Congresses. I. Borgen, Peder. II. Giversen, Søren.
BS2351.2.N46—1997
   225.6'7—dc21

96–52508
CIP

Preface

"The New Testament and Hellenistic Judaism" was the subject of a conference at the Faculty of Theology in the University of Aarhus from February 8-10, 1992, as one in a series of conferences held to celebrate the fiftieth anniversary of the establishment Theology as an independent Faculty.

Some of the conferences were arranged on a local basis, others as meetings of international academic societies. This conference was arranged by a group of New Testament scholars from the universities in Trondheim, Uppsala, Åbo and Aarhus, in cooperation with the Institute of New Testament at the University of Aarhus (now part of the Institute of Old and New Testament). This institute had the privilege of serving as the organizer and host of the conference.

The conference was made possible thanks to grants from different foundations. A very substantial grant from NOS-H, offered by the Nordic group of scholars mentioned above, was matched by the same amount from the Faculty of Theology in Aarhus; grants were also provided by the Aarhus University Research Foundation and the Danish Research Council for the humanities. We would like to express a warm thanks for this financial support, which made the conference possible.

The papers which follow were read at the conference. The editorial work has been financed by additional funding from NOS-H. The publication has been made possible by grants from the Danish Research Council for the Humanities, the Aarhus University Research Foundation and the Faculty of Theology. The editors, Professor Peder Borgen and myself, are very grateful for this support.

The conference papers were prepared for publication thanks to the efforts of my co-editor Professor Peder Borgen, who — when, I was hindered in this task by the serious illness of my wife, Inge Giversen, and her death on April 25th 1993 — took nearly all the burden upon himself. I wish to thank Professor Peder Borgen for this, just as I wish to thank Professor Borgen and the other members of the Nordic group: Professor Lars Hartman (Uppsala), Professor Karl-Gustav Sandelin (Åbo) and research fellow Per Jarle Bekken (Trondheim), both for their contributions to the conference as well as for the pleasant days when I took part in some of their annual meetings in Uppsala.

Aarhus, May 1994   *Søren Giversen*

Contents

Introduction

Peder Borgen

I

In his opening study *Søren Giversen* outlines the background and goals of this collection of essays on the theme "The New Testament and Hellenistic Judaism". An important aspect of the background is the fact that a substantial part of the New Testament is either written *in* the Jewish Diaspora or *to* members of the Diaspora — or written because of a relationship to the Jewish Diaspora.

In the relationship between Early Christianity and its Jewish context a central issue was the different views on the covenant. How did the Christians in the first two centuries AD understand the covenant? Also sources outside of the New Testament throw light upon this question, as for example the Epistle of Barnabas. Here the issue is sharply formulated: "But let us see whether this people (= the Christians) or the former people (= the Jews) is the heir, and if the covenant is for us or for them". The answer of the writer of the Epistle is that the covenant, the testament, of Jesus is the fulfilment of the Bible. In various ways the contributions in this volume illuminate this and related issues.

II

Thus, Hellenistic Judaism is primarily the Judaism of the Diaspora, in the Roman Empire outside of Palestine. Here, the most extensive collection of sources is found in the Jewish community of Alexandria. From these numerous texts, it is evident that there had been Jewish school activity in Alexandria at least two centuries before Philo's time. Therefore, Philo represents a long scholastic tradition. It is thus appropriate, at the beginning of this volume, to depict the religious life that is reflected in such Alexandrian Jewish texts as The Epistle of Aristeas, Aristobulus, Artapanus, Demetrius the Chronographer, Ezekiel the Tragedian, The Sibylline Oracles 3, The Book of Wisdom, and other sources. This is done by *Lars Hartman*, who examines how Bible study formed frames of references for the Jews and provided them with roles with which they could identify themselves in times of political or social pressures as well as in everyday life. Scripture formed people's way of looking at the world. This attitude towards Scripture was something which the Church later learned from Judaism.

III

Having the Alexandrian Jewish literature as a frame of reference, further discussion is needed on the relationship between Hellenistic Judaism and emerging Christianity. Hellenistic Judaism might be characterized as a kind of Judaism that has received the stamp of Hellenistic ideas, attitudes and way of life, to a large degree consciously, but partly unconsciously. It is a form of Judaism that has faced the challenge of its cross-cultural encounter with the Hellenistic surroundings. In some respects this characterization also applies to Palestinian Judaism, but some trends in the Judaism of the Diaspora are of special interest. According to *Nikolaus Walter*, the idea — stressed by Aristobulus and Philo and others — that the Torah is a universal Law for all peoples of the world, is of special importance as "mother womb" for the development of Christianity. This view made Judaism open to the whole of mankind and even included the idea that non-Jews might follow God's laws without identifying themselves with the "markers" of the Jewish nation. In this way, Hellenistic Judaism served as *praeparatio evangelica*, to use the phrase of Eusebius.

IV

In many cases, the dating and the nature of the sources pose great difficulties but also give important insights of value for New Testament interpretations as well as for the understanding of later stages in the history of Christianity. *Marinus de Jonge* draws the conclusion that since Jewish and Christian features are so closely interwoven in writings like "The Testament of the Twelve Patriarchs," they cannot be understood as Jewish writings. They primarily provide insights into the development of Christianity from its Jewish roots.

It is important that *James H. Charlesworth* draws magical texts into the discussion and in this way points to Jewish elements in popular religiosity inside and outside of Judaism. He states that he does not know of unedited texts predating AD 70 in which King Solomon, the Son of David, is called an exorcist. Using the tradition-historical method, he cautiously suggests that the later picture of Solomon as an exorcist mirrors an almost lost tradition that he controlled demons who caused illness and had the power to heal, and that this earlier tradition goes back to the time of Jesus. Such a conclusion opens up for a new interpretation of a New Testament passage, in casu of Mark 10.47.

V

When parts of the New Testament are examined against the background of Hellenistic Judaism and of the Graeco-Roman world in general, then the conclusions reached will sometimes have the emphasis on the way in which the texts reflect their Hellenistic surroundings, sometimes on the distinctiveness of the New Testament passages seen against such a background. The analysis of Mark's story of the empty tomb and the resurrection by *Adela Yarbro Collins* leads to the conclusion that it has received a formative influence from the Graeco-Roman cultural context: Mark affirms that Jesus, as body and soul, was translated from the grave to heaven. Thus the tomb was empty. This claim was quite similar both to the claim made by Jews (e.g. Josephus) that Enoch had been taken up to heaven, and also to the claims made in Graeco-Roman circles regarding the translation or apotheosis of heroes, rulers and emperors.

Yarbro Collins draws on Jewish and non-Jewish sources to throw light upon widespread notions in the Graeco-Roman world. Correspondingly, *Aage Pilgaard* draws on a wide range of sources to illuminate the idea of the divine man, *theios aner,* in the Graeco-Roman world. He then discusses the theory of some scholars that Mark's christology is decisively influenced by this figure. In his conclusion, he rejects such an interpretation: in their meeting with the pagan world and their traditions, Mark and the community to which he belonged, could adopt traits from traditions about pagan charismatic types, but a *theios aner* based on a specific pagan anthropology they did not adopt. They took their basic patterns from Old Testament-Jewish traditions, including Jewish apolcalypticism with its notion of creation/new creation, in Mark's text expressed by the term the Son of Man.

While Pilgaard focused on extra-Jewish notions, *Johannes Nissen* discusses the New Testament love command in relation to Hellenistic Judaism. As sources for Hellenistic Judaism he refers mainly to the Testament of the Twelve Patriarchs, the Epistle of Aristeas, and Philo. In the New Testament he places emphasis on the Synoptic Gospels, but the Gospel of John and other texts are also drawn into the discussion. Nissen sees the distinctive character of the New Testament love command in the following four points: 1) the combination of the two commandments; 2) the positive form of the "golden rule"; 3) the command to love one's enemies, and 4) Christ as the motivating power for the love command.

VI

Philo of Alexandria is a major representative of Hellenistic Judaism. A large body of his writings is preserved, and they are written before the middle of the first century after Christ. His expositions of the Pentateuch are commonly used to cast light on points in the New Testament. Their usefulness has been hampered by Philo's extensive use of allegorical interpretations and by his employment of philosophical and psychological ideas.

Several factors have contributed to a new situation with regard to the value of Philo for the study of the New Testament. First, as indicated above, scholars no longer regard the distinction between Palestinian Judaism and Hellenistic Judaism as a basic category for our understanding of Judaism. Instead, research is more focused on the differences within every Jewish community of some size, whether it was located in Palestine or in the Diaspora. Thus, Philo's writings reflect different situations and varying attitudes within Alexandrian Jewry, for example in relation to the pagan surroundings, e.g. the problem of polytheistic worship. Within this context, various uses of the Old Testament were at work. Paul's letters reflect corresponding situations. *Karl-Gustav Sandelin* draws on Philo's writings in order to throw light on the debate among scholars whether Paul in 1 Cor 10.1-14 argues against sacramentalism and over-confidence, or whether his main point is the injunction to shun idolatry.

Philo's writings and the Book of Baruch are utilized by *Per Jarle Bekken* in his analysis of the exegetical methods, forms and ideas expressed by Paul when using Deut 30.12-14 in Rom 10, and *Peder Borgen* calls attention to overlooked exegetical traditions about Hagar and Ishmael found in Philo's writings. Here, Hagar is seen as a proselyte and Ishmael represents an inferior form of Judaism. Against this background, new light is thrown on Paul's interpretation of Hagar and Ishmael in Gal 4.21-5.1. Although a gentile by birth, Hagar is a Hebrew by choice; similarly Mount Sinai, located in a pagan region, became the mountain of the God-given Law of Moses.

VII

A more general and wide-ranging use of sources from Hellenistic Judaism is found in the studies of *Niels Hyldahl* and *Niels Willert*. Hyldahl concentrates on Paul's Corinthian correspondence and defines the distinctiveness of Paul against the background of the conflict within the Corinthian Church itself. As a Jew, Paul had experienced the Hellenistic influence on Judaism both in Palestine and in the Diaspora. He was already a Hellenistic Jew before he became an apostle. A piece of Hellenistic philosophy had made its way from Alexandria to Corinth and found a place in Paul's Christian community there. Hyldahl thinks that Apollos represented this Alexandrian philosophy, while Paul in his response tries to subordinate this wisdom to the gospel which he preaches.

In his study of the catalogues of hardships in the Pauline correspondence, *Niels Willert* draws on material both from Hellenistic Judaism and from the wider Graeco-Roman world. Like Hyldahl, Willert reminds us that Paul was already living in the Hellenistic world before, as an apostle, he confronted himself with the challenges posed by its ideas, attitudes and behaviour. There has been a great research effort concerning the cultural background of the catalogues of hardships in Graeco-Roman philosophy, in Old Testament literature and in ancient Judaism. Willert emphasizes the influence from the Christian passion tradition in Paul's use of such catalogues. Paul, in urging an imitation of himself, joined the communities to the suffering of Jesus Christ. The earthly life of Jesus, including suffering and death, was much more important for Paul than normally asserted. Moreover, Paul understood his own suffering as a parallel to those Old Testament prophets who suffered persecution; through suffering, the eschatological quality of Christian life was maintained. Thus Willert joins the scholars who stress the distinctive character and attitudes of New Testament hardship catalogues, compared to their pagan and Jewish predecessors.

Finally, *Ole Davidsen*'s study on the structural typology of Adam and Christ, Rom 5.12-21, shows how linguistic methods can be applied to a Pauline passage within its Hellenistic context and illustrates the use of structural and semantic analysis with the purpose of giving precise formulation of the logic and the content of the passage.

The Covenant — theirs or ours?

Søren Giversen

The Covenant — theirs or ours? This important question, once asked and answered by Barnabas, was one of the questions discussed by the first Christians, and it is still one of the questions behind the general subject of this conference as indicated in its title: "The New Testament and Hellenistic Judaism".

This subject will be dealt with under the following four headings:

1. Eschatological apocalyptism in the Jewish Diaspora and the New Testament.
2. Philo and the New Testament.
3. The interpretation of the Old Testament in the Jewish Diaspora and the New Testament.
4. New Testament themes in the light of the Jewish Diaspora.

These four topics are, however, very closely connected, and each single paper, touches more than one topic, some of them indeed dealing with all four.

That the emphasis is laid upon the New Testament is clear — the words "New Testament" occur in all of the four topics which I have listed above. But the phrase "the Jewish Diaspora" is also important; it is found in three of them, while in a fourth, Philo, the most famous of all Diaspora Jews, is mentioned.

In this short opening address, I wish to take this as a starting-point for an outline of the background to this conference and of its goals.

In the first Christian generations, the Jewish Diaspora for a time also included a substantial part of the early Christian communities. We know this from Paul's letters and from the Acts. We read also how Christians, too, had to go into the Diaspora. An early case is perhaps mentioned in Acts 8.3-4. "As for Saul, he made havoc of the Church entering into every house, and haling man and woman committed them to prison. Therefore they, that were scattered abroad, went everywhere preaching the word." And in book II of his *Ecclesiastical History* Eusebius tells us that before the final siege of Jerusalem in the 60's AD, a substantial part of the Christian Community left the city and fled to Pella, east of the Jordan. Although the meaning — and veracity — of this information is sometimes disputed, we know from Origen that in his lifetime, Christians of Jewish origin still were living in the areas east of Jordan (Orig., *Com. in Joh.* 1.1.1).

Substantial parts of the New Testament were either written *in* the Diaspora or *to* members of the Diaspora — or written because of a relationship to the Jewish Diaspora. This is important as a background for the subject of this conference.

The eschatological apocalypticism in the Jewish Diaspora is of essential importance to an understanding of the message of the New Testament. How Philo, thanks to his exegesis of parts of the Old Testament, became important for the interpretation of the New Testament is an interesting topic. His exegesis of the Old Testament illuminates aspects of the exegesis of the Old Testament in the New Testament. And certain *themata* in biblical theology, found in the New Testament — the *Logos*, for example — are better understood when set in relief against the ideas of the Diaspora Jew Philo.

In a time like ours, one ought to be reminded that when, at the end of the eighteenth century, C.D. Moldenhawer created the catalogue of the Royal Library in Copenhagen, he placed the non-Christian Philo Alexandrinus as the first of the *Patres Graeci* — and with good reason. The main problem for Philo was the same as for the Christians: how should Holy Scripture be understood? For the Christians, before their own Christian literature came into existence, a word such as διαθήκη, *berit*, covenant, must have had special importance. In this single word the relation, the true relation between God and man was contained. The words of Jeremiah (31.31) about the New Covenant resounded in the ears of the Christians, who at the holy meal repeated this term in the words of Christ, as quoted by Paul in 1 Corinthians 11.25.

The word διαθήκη is discussed in Hebrews. Out of the 30 times the word is used in the New Testament, more than half of the examples are found in Hebrews. In Hebrews we have, perhaps, the first qualified Christian reflection on the meaning of this expression for biblical theology.

We are used to talking about the two διαθήκαι; the old and the new. We are influenced, naturally, by the words in Luke, in the Pauline letters, in Hebrews, and Acts. But we could also try to look at how, in the first two centuries AD, other Christians regarded the covenant. Their view of the covenant is influenced by their view of the LXX — and their view of the LXX is also influenced by what they thought of the covenant.

This single point is chosen to illustrate the problems we deal with at a conference like this one; the intention is not to provide a solution, but to delineate the situation of the first Christians.

Here, it would be tempting to look upon the Paschal Homily of Melito of Sardes, because in this Homily we find a clear exposition of what the exodus from Egypt meant: a type of the salvation by Christ in the New Covenant. I intend, however, to deal with this in a forthcoming publication and therefore I will concentrate on the Epistle of Barnabas.

The exegesis in the Epistle of Barnabas is, in a certain sense, a radical development of thoughts found in the Pauline writings and of ideas known from Hebrews — but on the other hand it has a much less receptive attitude towards the Jewish religion than Hebrews. It has been discussed whether the author was a Christian of Jewish or Non-Jewish descent. Although the text reveals the author's good insight into Jewish matters and Jewish traditions, it is probably not possible to draw any certain conclusions from this, because the text is probably compiled from already existing material, of a somewhat different kind. This is also the case in the long section, chapters 1 to 17. (I will not deal with the tradition about the two ways found in the chapters 18 to 20, nor with its obvious influence upon parts of chapter 20 or its relation to the *Didaché*.) In chapters 1 to 17, we find traces of different sources. In a number of cases we find the author, through his commentaries, acting as a good Bible-theologian. In fact, in some of his comments there are traces of *midrashes*. This is the case in *Barn*. 6.8-19; 7.3-11; 8.1-6 and also in some other sections. In other cases there are, as some scholars think, perhaps also traces of *testimonia*-collections. In *Barn*. 5,1ff, the author tries to show that Christ had to suffer and would rise again.

As said before, Barnabas acts as a good Bible-theologian and I wish to concentrate upon that. Two themes prevail in Barnabas chapters 1-17. The first is the preaching of Jesus as the Messiah, the second concerns the correct exegesis of the Law. Barnabas thus deals with two themes, both of the greatest importance to the early Christian communities in the Jewish Diaspora, and to the Christian church ever since.

It could seem strange to use Barnabas as the basis for an outline of the problem which this conference is dealing with, since the Epistle of Barnabas is not a part of the Canon. It is not so strange, however.

The Epistle of Barnabas contains many quotations from the Old Testament — altogether about a hundred, one quarter of which are from the Book of Isaiah. But there are only very faint reminiscences of New Testament writings. It is thus very difficult to show that the letter has used the canonical Gospels. (*Barn*. 4.14. "Many called but few chosen", could be a reminiscence of Matt 22.14, but it could also be taken from elsewhere).

The fact that the canonical Gospels are not used in the argumentation by a Christian as eager as Barnabas can only mean that his letter is old. And that we have an old Christian exegesis which, independently of the Gospels, tries to build a Christian Biblical Theology upon the Old Testament, is very important. We have thus, so to speak, an alternate source besides the Gospels to focus upon, when searching for the Christian understanding of the Old Testament.

The Epistle of Barnabas reminds us of Hebrews: a consistent mixture of exhortations and teaching. Its teaching tries to demonstrate that the Jewish understanding of the covenant was wrong and to teach the readers its correct sense: The Jews went wrong when they took Scripture literally. The true and correct understanding of the Holy Scripture is a spiritual or metaphorical one. Since the Jews did not understand the true sense of the Scripture, the Jewish cult was also misguided. The cult was not to consist of offerings of animals, cornmeal or incense, but of a righteous, humble way of life, just as fasting must consist of a life in righteousness and willingness to help other people.

Therefore, the Epistle of Barnabas attempts to show that neither the Jewish offering cult nor rules for human behaviour (such as the fast, the sabbath, the circumcision etc.) were required according to the Scripture; they were all based upon a misinterpretation of the Scriptures and therefore, the Jewish religion became idolatry. All these rules in the Scriptures should be understood in a way different from the usual Jewish interpretation.

This is followed by a series of discussions of particular subjects, such as Paradise, the Promised Land, types of baptism, the scapegoat and much more. These discussions end with the conclusion that the messianic texts are to be understood as describing Jesus as Christ.

Thus, overall, the author of the Epistle of Barnabas reaches a new under-standing of the old Christian explanation: God was against the cultic offerings; the correct offerings are righteousness and the praise of God from one's heart (*Barn.* 2); the self-destructive fast should be replaced by solidarity with the suffering people.

When the prophets speak about suffering, they speak about Jesus' suffer-ings (*Barn.* 5); the promise to the patriarchs means that the Christians have a hope (*Barn.* 6); the story about the scapegoat points ahead to Jesus (*Barn.* 7); the Jewish circumcision is abolished and is to be succeeded by a spiritual one, and the story about Abraham again points ahead to Jesus (*Barn.* 9); the dietary restrictions are not to be understood literally, but deal with moral questions (*Barn.* 10).

In the same way, it is explained what baptism means (*Barn.* 11), and the crucifixion is, according to the Scripture, the true way to the blessing (*Barn.* 12). That Joseph's youngest son was blessed before his older brother means that the Christian religion is to overthrow the Jewish religion (*Barn.* 13).

In 4.6-7 the Epistle of Barnabas raises the question of whether the covenant belongs to the Jews or to the Christians. Barnabas takes the problem up again in 13.1 and 14.4. In 13.1 he says: "But let us see whether this people (= the Christians) or the former people (= Jews) is the heir, and if the covenant is for us or for them".

Barnabas' answer is that Moses received the stone tables inscribed by the finger of the Lord's hand (*Barn.* 4.7, cf. Exod 31.18, 34.28), but when the Israelites turned to idols they lost the covenant before they got it, and Moses "cast the two tables from his hands" (*Barn.* 4.8). "And the covenant was broken in order that the covenant of Jesus the Beloved might be sealed in our heart in hope of his faith." (*Barn.* 4.8).

For Barnabas, the consequence is that there is only one covenant and that belongs to the Christians. Israel did not obtain the covenant at all, because Moses "cast the two tables away". The covenant thus belongs to the Christians.

But the main point for Barnabas in 4.6-7 is to give the Christians a warning: They risk losing the covenant if they behave as did the Jews.

Thus we have a clear message from the writer: the covenant, the testament of Jesus, is the fulfilment of the Bible. How this is to be understood and the consequences of this, will, I hope, be discussed at this conference. And — since I have used Barnabas — I will permit myself to welcome all of you to this conference with the *incipit*, the first words in the Epistle of Barnabas:

Hail, sons and daughters, in the name of the Lord who loved us, in peace.

Χαίρετε, υἱοὶ καὶ θυγατέρες, ἐν ὀνόματι κυρίου τοῦ ἀγαπήσαντος ἡμᾶς, ἐν εἰρήνῃ.

"Guiding the Knowing Vessel of your Heart":

On Bible Usage and Jewish Identity in Alexandrian Judaism

Lars Hartman

In 2 Tim 3.16 a member of the Pauline school counsels his reader to adhere to Scripture, for "it is useful for teaching, for reproof, for correction, and for training in righteousness". Throughout the centuries such an attitude has been typical of Christian Bible reading, and when teachers of homiletics have reflected on how to use Bible texts, they have proposed the principle of *usus quintuplex*, viz., the fivefold usage, as reflected in what a preacher could have to say about his text.

The above-mentioned attitude towards Scripture was something which the Church learned from Judaism. The Scripture was not only Law, not only the warrant behind the orthopraxy which helped to keep Jewish identity alive, both in Palestine and, not least, in the Diaspora. It also provided the material for defense against religious foes, for reflection on human conditions, for strengthening Jewish self-confidence, for comfort under social or existential pressure. There were several ways in which Scripture fulfilled these functions: learned studies, readings at the synagogue service, instruction of the children at home and in school, individual reflection etc. This life with the Bible could have the result that Scripture formed people's way of looking at the world, "guiding the knowing vessel of your heart" as a *hieros logos* expressed it.[1]

There is nothing revolutionary in drawing attention to the multifarious usage of Scripture mentioned in the preceding paragraph, nor in underlining its importance for forming and maintaining Jewish identity.[2] But to my knowledge, when scholars have focused on Jewish usage of the Bible, they have mainly been interested in particular elements and aspects of it. Thus, they — and I myself as one of them — have studied Jewish Bible usage as expressing or reflecting certain doctrinal, theological or ethical ideas, or (not least

---

1. The quotation is from Eusebius, *Hist. eccl.* 13.12.5; it belongs to a *"hieros logos"* from "Orpheus", cited by Aristobulus. Eusebius may, however, be wrong concerning Aristobulus' being the source; see N. Walter, *Der Thoraausleger Aristobulos* (TU 86; Berlin: Akademie-Verlag, 1964) 103-115, 205. I have used the edition *Fragmenta pseudepigraphorum Graece*, collegit A.M. Denis (PVTG 3; Leiden: Brill, 1978). The quotation is found on page 164 of this edition.
2. These aspects were stressed by G. Delling in his *Die Bewältigung der Diasporasituation durch das hellenistische Judentum* (Göttingen: Vandenhoeck & Ruprecht, 1987).

importantly) as relying on different hermeneutical presuppositions and using different expository techniques.[3]

In the following article, I will consider Jewish Bible usage from a slightly different perspective, viz. one more or less similar to the view contained in the *usus quintuplex*. I will, however, narrow down my scope and deal only with Alexandrian Judaism of the generations around the beginning of the Christian Era. How did its Bible usage serve to comfort, to refute, to correct etc.? Furthermore, I will dare to move on a general level, mixing examples from a dozen works by different authors writing in different genres.[4] I will look for references, open and hidden, to Scripture, and ask in what way they represent how Alexandrian Jews interpreted their situation and understood themselves

---

3. Instead of a detailed bibliographical note, allow me to refer to E. Schürer, *The History of the Jewish People. A New English Version* 2-3.1 (ed. G. Vermes and others; Edinburgh: Clark, 1979-1986) § 25 (Torah Scholarship), § 28 (Life and the Law), § 29 (Messianism), § 32. vi (Jewish Literature Composed in Hebrew or Aramaic: Biblical Midrash), viii.B (The Writings of the Qumran Community; Biblical Interpretation), § 34.2 (The Jewish Philosopher Philo; Philo's Philosophical Thought). These surveys also provide the reader with rich bibliographies. In addition see L. Hartman, *Prophecy Interpreted* (ConB, NT Ser 1; Lund: Gleerup, 1966) part 1; idem, "An Early Example of Jewish Exegesis: 1 Enoch 10.16-11:2," *Neot* 17 (1983) 16-26; D. Patte, *Early Jewish Hermeneutic in Palestine* (SBLDS 22; Missoula: Scholars, 1975).

4. Thus, I will use material from the following texts: *The Epistle of Aristeas*, Aristobulus, Artapanus, Demetrius the Chronographer, Ezekiel the Tragedian, The History of Joseph, Joseph and Aseneth, 3 and 4 Maccabees, Pseudo-Aeschylus, Pseudo-Phocylides, Pseudo-Sophocles, The Sibylline Oracles 3, The Book of Wisdom. I must admit that I have chosen these texts in a rather unsophisticated way, viz., by following the suggestions as to provenance by the scholars who have translated and to some extent commented the different texts in J.H. Charlesworth (ed.), *The Old Testament Pseudepigrapha 1-2* (London: Darton, Longman & Todd, 1983-85). In the following, I have largely used the translations provided in this edition. — For the expository techniques of some of these works see for Wis, G. Ziener, "Die Verwendung der Schrift im Buche der Weisheit," *TTZ* 66 (1957) 138-51. For *Sib. Or.* 3, see L. Hartman, *Prophecy Interpreted* (note 3) 91-94; D. Patte, *Hermeneutic* (note 3) 185-89. Furthermore, E. Schürer, *History* (note 3) § 33A, parts III-VII, where the authors are dealt with whose works have provided the material for this paper; for Aristobulus, see N. Walter, *Der Thoraausleger*, 129-41. For Philo see P. Borgen, "Philo of Alexandria," in *Jewish Writings of the Second Temple Period* (Compendia rerum Judaicarum II.2, ed. M.E. Stone (Assen: Van Gorcum, Philadelphia: Fortress, 1984) ch. 6, esp. 233-246; idem, "Philo of Alexandria. A critical and synthetical survey of research since World War II," *ANRW* II.21.1 (Berlin: de Gruyter, 1984) 98-154, esp. 117-137; R. Williamson, *Jews in the Hellenistich World: Philo* (Commentaries on Writings of the Jewish and Christian World 200 BC to AD 200; Cambridge: Cambridge University Press, 1989) 145-200.

in reading, and by reading, the holy texts.[5] In addition, I will exclude Philo, not because he would be irrelevant, but because Alexandrian Judaism is more than Philo and, of course, because one would otherwise all too easily be drowned in the Philonic sea; I believe that other texts provide us with sufficient material.

Above, I mentioned open and hidden Bible usage, which may call for some explanation. On the one hand, we encounter what we could call open usage of the Bible, i.e., explicit or evident quotations, references to Biblical stories, events, and statements etc.; a writer retells stories, perhaps embellishing them, or writes a new story with a point of departure in the Bible. Such an open usage is also represented by interpretative retellings, like Wisdom 10-19, where the exodus story is the subject of a kind of midrashic presentation. Furthermore, we encounter a few instances of interpretative answers to questions raised by oddities in the text, as well as an acrosticon in which the author interprets the initial letters of Adam's name as indicating the four cardinal points (*Sib. Or.* 3.24-26).

On the other hand, we may also speak of hidden usage, consisting of allusions, turns of phrase or echoes from distinct passages; the unknowing reader sees nothing particular in the present text. However, in the mind of the reader who is well versed in the Scripture, the echoes resound, and the texts receive additional nuances of meaning from the passages which are called to mind.[6] Such echoes also mean a usage of the Bible, or, rather they presuppose such a usage, sometimes even one which represents a particular understanding of these Bible passages. An example is *Sib. Or.* 3.719. The line is a rewording of Isaiah 2.3, according to which the nations shall say at some point: "Come, let us go up to the mountain of the Lord..., for out of Sion shall go forth the Law and the word of the Lord from Jerusalem." So the Sibyl makes the Gentiles say: "Come, let us send to the temple...and let us all ponder the Law of the Most High God". The rewording depends on an interpretation which adapts the words of Isaiah to the Diaspora situation, and the attentative reader hears not only the Sibyl, but also how she agrees with the divine promise in Isaiah, understood in a particular way.

We may also think of another, particular type of hidden Bible usage, viz., one where there is no doubt that the idea expressed is taken from the Bible, but not from one single, easily defined passage. Instead several passages say the same thing or a couple of passages have together inspired the statement made

---

5. To be clear in terms of the author-text-reader relationship: let us assume that the authors were doing something of this sort when writing their texts, *and* that the Bible usage in the texts had a similar effect on the reader.
6. Of course there is always that risk that we hear too much or too little in the text. I have tried to apply a systematic approach in L. Hartman, *Prophecy Interpreted* (note 3), and idem, *Asking for a Meaning* (ConB, NT Ser 12; Lund: Gleerup, 1979).

in the later text. One example of the last-mentioned phenomenon is *JosA* 8.11, in which Joseph is said to pray for Aseneth's conversion, saying: "number her among your people that you have chosen before all things came into being (καὶ συγκαταρίθμησον αὐτὴν τῷ λαῷ σου, ὃν ἐξελέξω πρὶν γινέσθαι τὰ πάντα)."[7] His words contain echoes from the Psalms: 32.12 (LXX): "the people which he chose as a heritage for himself (λαὸς ὃν ἐξελέξατο εἰς κληρονομίαν ἑαυτοῦ)" and 73.2 (LXX) "remember your congregation, which you created from the beginning (ἐκτήσω ἀπ' ἀρχῆς)".

When we now put our hands to the task before us, let us first consider some examples of how Scripture was used to remind the reader of something very fundamental to Jewish religion, viz., that *the Jews were a chosen people*. Above, we came across the echo from Ps 32.12 (LXX), where the Biblical expressions were applied to the Egyptian Aseneth, a future proselyte; the prayer was that she would be counted among the chosen people. The same idea is expressed in a rather astonishing manner a little further on in the same romance. There (*JosA* 28.1) we are told how some of Joseph's brothers attack their Egyptian sister-in-law. When their plans are thwarted, their reaction is: "the Lord fights against us for Aseneth". This is not simply a sudden insight of some people who have acted wickedly. As a matter of fact it is an echo from Exod 14.25, where the Egyptian army is confused by God in the Red Sea and the soldiers exclaim: "Let us flee from before Israel, for the Lord fights for them against the Egyptians". Is not this a subtle way of underlining how radically the true convert and proselyte is numbered as one of God's chosen people — and of how he or she should consider the new status?[8] We may recall how Philo emphasized that a pious proselyte is far better than a reluctant Jew (*Spec.* 1.51-55; *Praem.* 152).

In Wisdom 14-15 the vanity of idolatry is presented as a root of immoral life and thus contrasted to true religion. As one of its adherents the author directs himself to God saying: "we are yours" (15.2). Both this clause and its context — "you are slow to anger and govern everything in mercy" (15.1) — are echoes of Exod 34.6-9 in its LXX version, i.e., from the chapter which describes how the covenant was made: "we shall be yours" (34.9). The author — and his understanding reader — direct themselves to God, using God's own words on the making of the covenant. This means reinforcing the fundamentals of religious self-consciousness quoting the strongest thinkable authority, God himself.

Furthermore, according to 3 Macc 6.3, the high priest Eleazar prays that the Jews will be saved from the king who plans to execute them. He refers to earlier examples of how God has rescued his people from its enemies, but

---

7. Thus according to ms A.
8. Cf. G. Delling, "Einwirkungen der Sprache der Septuaginta in 'Joseph und Aseneth'," *JSJ* 9 (1978) 29-56, 45.

begins by characterizing the Jews as "the people of your sanctified lot (μερίδος ἡγιασμένης σου λαόν)". In doing so, he silently reminds God and, above all, those who listen to his text, of what Scripture said concerning the favoured position of God's own people (e.g., Deut 32.9. "Jacob, his people, became the Lord's lot — ἐγενήθη μερὶς καὶ λαὸς αὐτοῦ ᾿Ιακώβ"). Modern scholars do well in reminding ourselves that these examples reflect more than theoretical doctrine; they also reveal something of existential and fundamental importance to Jewish assurance: the Jews were different from other people; the only real God was on their side, and they on his.

One aspect of God's choice of his people was that *God had entered into contact with them in giving them his Law.* Accordingly, to study the Law meant to enter into contact with God. In *Sib. Or.* 3.584-85 we note a pride in this fact: "to them alone did the great God give wise counsel and faith and excellent understanding in their breasts" (cp. Deut 4.6 and 6.6). However, it also brought with it a duty to learn it and to abide by it, studying it. In a fragment containing the phrase that is used in the title of this paper, this duty is mentioned. Eusebius quotes Aristobulus as the source, but it seems to be secondary.[9] Anyway, the author makes Orpheus command, in a *hieros logos*: "Look to the divine word, study it closely (προσέδρευε) guiding the knowing vessel of your heart."[10] The fact that the immediate context contains echoes from Deut 6.4 makes it probable that we should hear Deut 6.6 in the background: "these words which I command you today, shall be in your heart and in your soul" (LXX). In Deut 6.7 the ideal was depicted in this way: "you shall teach them (the words of God) diligently to your children" (similarly Deut 11.19). It is of course hard to know how far the commandment was upheld in Alexandrian Jewish families, but Philo also stresses its importance.[11] Other texts in our collection indicate a similar attitude: 4 Macc 18.10 refers to the teaching given by a father to his seven sons, and Ezekiel the Tragedian, when rewriting the story of Moses, adds something not found in Exodus when he lets Moses' mother "declare all things to me (Moses) concerning my father's God and race" (34-35).

Given the view that in the Scriptures God entered into contact with His people, it is no surprise to find that in the literature we are now considering, *the ways of thinking of and characterizing God* are often inspired by wordings from the Bible. Thus Aseneth states that Joseph's God is "a jealous God" (*JosA* 11.7). The discerning ear hears how the attribute quotes the development of the first commandment in the Decalogue (Exod 20.5-6; Deut 5.9-10). Aseneth, however, also refers to a hearsay that God is "a compassionate and long-suffering and pitiful and gentle" God (*JosA* 11.10). The same trained ear realizes that

---

9. N. Walter, *Der Thoraausleger*, 103-15, 205.
10. Eusebius, *Hist. eccl.* 13.12.5 (*Fragmenta*, ed. Denis, 164).
11. Philo, *Spec.* 4.141-42. See also Josephus, *Ag. Ap.* 2.204.

what the repentant Gentile woman has heard is the manner in which God describes himself before making the covenant at Sinai (Exod 34.6).[12]

The Sibyl, too, knows how to talk of God in a manner which is concordant with Scripture: when she introduces her oracle by calling on "the heavenly one", she also calls him the one "who has his throne established on the cherubim" (Sib. Or. 3.1-2; cp. for example Pss 80.1; 99.1).[13]

Pseudo-Aeschylus, although presented as the classical Attic poet, appears to be well versed in the Law when he talks of God, actually gathering a whole series of hidden references to the Bible: God is mysterious and ungraspable, he says — "at times he appears as fire ... sometimes as darkness. He is similar to beasts, to wind, cloud and lightning, thunder and rain ... Hills, earth, the enormous depth of the sea and the lofty heights of mountains quake, when they behold the terrible eye of the Master" (Clem. Al., Strom. 5.14.131.2-3).[14] The motifs are mainly taken from the description of the theophany on Sinai in Exodus 19, but also from other passages.[15] The author is faithful to what the old texts tell him about Israel's God, but he is also eager to safeguard his Jewish identity by avoiding or preventing a gross understanding of the ways in which God's appearance is described in the Law: God is mysterious and ungraspable. Thus "Aeschylus" not only tacitly refers to the Law, but also consciously interprets it. Probably this safeguarding was directed not only against adversaries from outside but also intended to calm the critical mind of the Jew who pondered the Law. Adherents of the usus quintuplex would have termed the usage one of teaching and instruction.

Of course God's unity is often stressed. "Aristobulus" quoted the already mentioned hieros logos as a proof: "there is an old saying about him: 'he (i.e., God) is one'...he comes in company with love and hate, and war and plague and weeping pain, and there is no other." The Jew with a knowing ear caught the echoes from Deut 6.4 (the beginning of the Shema', "the Lord, our God, is one") and from Deut 4.34-35 (on God's deeds over against the Egyptians).[16] In a polytheistic environment it should have an encouraging effect to learn that also Gentile sages had been prepared to accept this "old saying" that God is one. Neither should we forget that a passage like the one quoted could serve as a weapon in apologetic.

In a similar manner the classical Greek author Sophocles is quoted, proclaiming things an educated Jew could recognize from his Bible. Thus Sophocles is quoted as saying "God is one, who fashioned heaven and the

---

12. See also, e.g., Wis 15.1. As a matter of fact, Aseneth's prayers in JosA 11-13 are saturated by Biblical turns of phrase, not least in the clusters of divine attributes.
13. See also Sib. Or. 3.17 (Exod 33.20; Judg 13.22), 20 (Ps 33.6).
14. Fragmenta, ed. Denis, 161-62.
15. Exod 13.21; 20.18; Judg 5.4-5; Ps 68.8-9.
16. See also Sib. Or. 3.629.

broad earth" (Clem. Al., *Strom.* 5.14.113.2).[17] Behind the iambic trimeter, we easily recognize the beginning of the Shema' (Deut 6.4) but also the very first verse of the Bible: "In the beginning God created heaven and earth".

Knowing the one and only God was something to be proud of. But sometimes pride is replaced by *polemic*. Or maybe rather by a defensive polemic, for monotheism was still something queer, accepted only by a minority. One weapon was ridicule, and thus the irony of Second Isaiah recurs in many variations in our material, e.g., in Wis 13.11-19. "some skilled worker in wood fells with his saw a convenient tree ... a useless piece ... he takes and carves ... he shapes it ... into the image of a human being ... he fixes it on the wall, securing it with nails...". The author builds on, *inter alia*, Isa 44.13 (LXX), which says: "the carpenter chose a piece of wood, put it up, shaped with glue, and gave it the form of a man and the beauty of a man, in order to put it up in his home." And when Solomon is said to continue saying that the idols "do not see, nor breathe or hear or walk" (Wis 15.15), the faithful Bible reader may have thought that the royal author might have learnt from his father, for in the Psalms he found the same expressions (Pss 113.13-15; 134.16-17 LXX). Expressed differently: the prophecy placed weapons in the hands of the believers,[18] or (with the term from the list of the fivefold uses) Scripture served for refutation, in these cases, of idolatry. And, again, a refutation probably not only for the reason, but also one needed by a disturbed heart.

The Jews, having the privilege of being informed by God himself, could boast of the superior *morality of the Jews*. The proofs of this in 4 Maccabees are taken from the laws which govern Jewish life; according to this author's view they embody reason, and, accordingly, a life in obedience to them is a life according to reason. Thus the commandment not to covet one's neighbor's wife etc. (Exod 20.29) is interpreted as an example of how reason controls all desire (4 Macc 2.5; we recognize the author's favourite point of view). Similarly the exhortations to lend to the needy, even if the year of release is near (Deut 15.9), and not to gather the last of one's harvest (Lev 19.9-10) demonstrate how reason quenches natural tendencies (4 Macc 2.8-9). It even masters enmity, which is illustrated by the Law's order that one must not cut down the trees of one's enemy (Deut 20.19) and its commandment to raise his donkey if it falls (Exod 23.4-5; 4 Macc 2.14). One may label this use of Scripture a form of teaching, but it has a propaganda effect against non-Jews — or not-yet-Jews; however, it should also have a refutating effect on Jews who tended towards laxity, and a comforting or instructing one against others.

Sib. Or. 3.218-47 likewise praises the Jews for their high moral standards, and readers versed in the Torah easily recognize that the standards mentioned

---

17. *Fragmenta*, ed. Denis, 162.
18. See also *Sib. Or.* 3.13-16 (Isa 40.18-38), 586-90 (Isa 44.8-20; Ezek 8.10), 605-607 (Isa 2.18-20; 31.7), 629 (Isa 43.11).

in the passage are those of the Law. But in spite of the echoes from, notably, Leviticus 19, the examples given are not especially Jewish, except for the refusal to engage in astrology and soothsaying (according to passages like Deut 4.19 etc.; Lev 19.31 etc.). Thus, what the Law requires is very respectable, and the Sibyl confirms this by saying the same things as the Torah, although in epic hexameter.[19]

One aspect of Jewish morality was that their law laid down certain forms of behaviour in *ritual matters*, including such questions as permitted and forbidden food. In the Hellenistic world these regulations could be the object of much scorn, and of suspicion as well. On the Jewish side, it took some resolve to maintain them. One essential fucntion of Scripture-reading was to find justification for these rules. In *Ep. Arist.* (144) the high priest defends the Law before the king saying, i.a., "do not take the contemptible view that Moses enacted this legislation because of an excessive preoccupation with mice and weasels and such creatures." Implicitly, the text refers to the regulations concerning precisely such things in Lev 11.29. The mocking objection is not necessarily that of an imagined outsider; also in a Jewish mind this sort of doubtful objection could make itself heard.

In the apologetic speech mentioned in the preceding paragraph, the high priest also argues that the rules reflect the highest rationality; they have symbolic meanings. Thus, the carnivorous birds are forbidden food, because man must not be like them but should be generous and righteous (*Ep. Arist.* 146-47). Since the author is of the opinion that the Law conforms to natural reason (143), the consequence is that the regulations, although they have a symbolic meaning, must be respected in their literal meaning as well:

---

19. See also *Sib. Or.* 3.573-600, where, however, the OT echoes are less evident. — Something similar could be said of the sentences of Pseudo-Phocylides. The book is enigmatic, however: is it an exponent of some kind of Jewish propaganda, has it anything to do with "god-fearers", or had it an inner-Jewish purpose to prevent Jews from sliding too far away? (see, e.g., the discussion of P.W. van der Horst in Charlesworth, ed., *Pseudepigrapha* 2, 565-66). Anyway, *Ps-Phoc.* 1-41 proclaims sentences which clearly represent, i. a., a florilegium from Exodus 20 and Leviticus 18-19, adding counsels from Wisdom tradition. Furthermore *Ps-Phoc.* 175-206, on marriage and chastity, contains evident echoes from Lev 18.8, 22-23; 20.11, 15-16; Exod 22.16, 19; Deut 27.21. Nonetheless in the contents not much is particularly Jewish; monotheism is presupposed but not defended, but the stand over against homosexual behavior is derived from Lev 18.22 and could be regarded as typically Jewish. — In this connection we may also recall the common Jewish way of explaining similarities between Jewish rules and laws or customs among Gentiles: the others, viz., Plato, Orpheus, etc., had learnt from the Jewish lawgiver, Moses: "it is evident that Plato imitated our legislation" (Aristobulus; Eusebius, *Hist. eccl.* 13.12.1; *Fragmenta*, ed. Denis, 221- 222); see also Eusebius, *Hist. eccl.* 13.12.4 (*Fragmenta*, ed. Denis, 223), Artapanus, Eusebius, *Praep. evang.* 9.27.4 (*Fragmenta*, ed. Denis, p 188), Philo, *Mos.* 2.8-27, and Josephus, *Ag. Ap.* 2.168.

"everything being governed by one supreme power" (143). Do we hear a quiet refutation of more "liberally" minded Jews, as well as a subtle support for those who stay loyal to tradition, strange as it may seem?[20]

When defending the sabbath commandment Aristobulus (Eusebius, *Praep. evang.*, 13.12.9-14)[21] refers to nature: sabbath observance is ordered by God in conformity with Wisdom (reference is made to Prov 8.22-31), but also according to a sevenfold principle of cosmos. Under the text resound not only the sabbath commandment but also echoes of the creation tale (Gen 1.3-5, 14-18; 2.2-3) and the aforementioned Prov 8.22-31. In addition, both Homer and Hesiod are said to have learnt from "our books" about the holiness of the seventh day. Again, in this case the text superficially appears to be directed at readers outside Judaism. But read within the Jewish community, it can be reassuring: the rules, by which one diverges from the standards of the surrounding human community, are in accordance with the system that governs the whole cosmos — as testified both by Scripture and by the authorities of Greek antiquity.

This may be the place to mention that some of our authors explicitly or implicitly eliminate *difficulties in Scripture* or answer questions which the study of it may raise. Thus, Ezekiel the Tragedian makes the concept of God somewhat more acceptable than it appears in the Exodus story: it is not God who "passes by", sparing the first-born Israelites; instead, the fearsome angel (159) or death (187) does so. In a similar way Aristobulus (Eusebius, *Praep. evang.* 8.10.8-17)[22] argues against an anthropomorphic reading of Scripture: God's "hand" (Exod 13.9; 3.20; 9.3) stands for his power. Aristobulus refers to Exod 19.11, 18, which mention God's coming down upon Sinai, and bluntly states that there was no descent by God to Sinai. Secretly, he uses Exod 3.2 (on the burning bush) as a help: the fire of the theophany (19.16-18) consumed nothing and the trumpet blasts did not originate from any trumpets, but "God manifested his majesty, which is throughout all things". Aristobulus dedicated his book to king Ptolemy, and even if it be regarded as apologetic in character,[23] it seems realistic to assume that such apologetics had a function *intra muros* as well. To me, the fact that the argument is taken from Scripture supports such an assumption.

The indoor Jewish reader — or rather, listener — might also need explana-

---

20. P. Borgen, "Philo of Alexandria " (*Jewish Writings*) (note 4), 260-62, discussing how Philo apparently knew of people who defended a "spiritual" interpretation of the Law leaving the practice aside. Cp. also the defense of Eleazar against Antiochus, 4 Macc 5.25.

21. *Fragmenta*, ed. Denis, 224.

22. *Fragmenta*, ed. Denis, 219-21.

23. A.Y. Collins (Charlesworth, ed., *Pseudepigrapha* 2, 834), but N. Walter (*Der Thoraausleger*, 134) is more doubtful on this matter.

tions of oddities in the holy texts.[24] Thus Demetrius the Chronographer (Eusebius, *Praep. evang.* 9.29.16)[25] explains where the Israelites got the weapons they are presupposed to have in Exod 17.8-13, where their fight with Amalek is reported. Furthermore, why did Joseph prosper for nine years without sending for his father (Gen 46.31-34)? Demetrius' answer is that Jacob had a profession which was despised among the Egyptians (Eusebius, *Praep. evang.* 9.21.13).[26] Such dealings with the texts show that reverence did not exclude curiosity.

Another usage of Scripture means that Biblical passages, through open or hidden references, are used to *describe or interpret one's human status*. The mother of the martyred brothers in 4 Macc 18.7-8 characterizes herself by alluding to Genesis: she was a chaste woman, created by God (Gen 2.22), and did not fall like Eve (Gen 3.1-7). The Book of Wisdom refers to man as God's image,[27] created for immortality (2.23; Gen 1.27), and alludes to Gen 2.7 in stating that God breathed vital spirit into him (15.11). Pseudo-Phocylides 106 seems to combine the two Genesis passages — man's spirit is (a loan from God[28] and) God's image. Furthermore Wisdom 2 interprets Gen 3.1-2 on the serpent's conversation with Eve: the passage is understood to say that through the Devil's envy death entered the world (2.24). Human relations to the rest of creation are understood in the light of Gen 1.26 and Ps 8.7: the human race rules over it, but, the author continues, it shall be done "in holiness and justice" (Wis 9.2-3). When things like these are taught from Scripture, it is not only a matter of teaching or doctrine, but it also means giving the human being a place in God's creative plan, thus deepening and strengthening his or her identity.

The *situation of individual characters* in our books can likewise be interpreted through scriptural allusions. Thus, in Aseneth's prayer for acceptance, echoes resound from turns of phrase from, above all, the Psalter, where the phrases are found on the lips of the righteous under pressure. Some random examples: "rescue me from my persecutors" (*JosA* 12.6; Ps 7.2), "deliver me from the mouth of the lion" (*JosA* 12.11; Ps 22.22); "my lips are as a potsherd" (*JosA* 13.9; Ps 22.16). Also in Wisdom, the lot of the righteous is often depicted with colours from the Psalter, but, additionally, also from Isaiah. For example: the righteous perish, "but they are in peace" (Wis 2.3; Isa 57.2); "after a brief chastisement they will be treated well, because God tested them" (Wis 3.5; Isa 54.7-8). Both Isa 57.2 and 54.7-8 deal with the distressed people of God. Many

---

24. On the form of *quaestiones et solutiones* see P. Borgen, "Philo of Alexandria" (*ANRW*)(note 4), 135-37.
25. *Fragmenta*, ed. Denis, 179.
26. *Fragmenta*, ed. Denis, 177.
27. Also *Sib. Or.* 3.8.
28. Similarly Wis 15.16.

features in the description of the righteous in Wis 2.12-18 are also found in Ps 88.21-28 (LXX):[29] he is God's servant (Wis 2.13; Ps 88.21), God is his father (Wis 2.16; Ps 88.27), and he is God's son of whom he will take care (Wis 2.18; Ps 88.27-28).

The God who had made himself known to his people was the God both of the forefathers and of the Alexandrian Jew around the beginning of our era. So *history* was not just something past but also, and even more so, something *always topical*.

First, there is the aspect of propaganda and of strengthening Jewish self-confidence. For easily understandable reasons, the story of Joseph appears to have been of particular importance to Alexandrian Jews. Thus, the romance of Joseph and Aseneth combines a love-story with the glorification of a convert and praise of Joseph. To the Jewish minority, it must have been a silent triumph to think of the respected Jewish administrator in the Egypt of ancient times. A similar pride may lurk behind the History of Joseph, and, as well, behind the notice in Wis 10.14. that wisdom gave Joseph "the sceptre of a kingdom and authority over his despotic masters".

The stories about Moses and the Exodus, too, must have had a special ring to Egyptian Jews. The Exodus story was rewritten as a drama or as a monody by Ezekiel the Tragedian. Wisdom 10-19 commented on it with parallel applications to the righteous and wise and to the wicked and idolaters of the reader's own time. The same stories were also reported and partly commented on by Demetrius the Chronographer. Artapanus, finally, seems to have presented Moses as the great miracle-worker in a novel which retells the Exodus story.[30] All these instances probably had not only the function of serving as propaganda or defense, stressing the great history of this despised part of the Alexandrian population. They were also, maybe even more so, intended to strengthen the minds of the Jews themselves. There was not only awareness of the past, but also comfort to be gained from such teachings.

Sib. Or. 3.248-58 briefly retells the story of the Exodus and the Lawgiving. It continues (258-85) by referring to the blessings and curses of Deuteronomy 28-30, which were to come over Israel depending on its obedience to the Law. It is done in such a way that the warnings are evidently applied to the Jew

---

29. See G. Ziener, "Verwendung" (note 4), 139-40. I would not make a point of the circumstance that the Psalm is said to deal with "David, my servant" (v. 4), as if the wise identified himself with the Messiah. Apparently our author has only understood the psalm in the same manner of recognition as when pondering other texts concerning the righteous in trouble. Cp. also J. Jeremias, "παῖς θεοῦ" TWNT 5 (1954), 676-713, 682-83, suggesting that Isa 53 is echoed several times in Wisdom's description of the righteous and wise in chapters 2-5.

30. Artapanus also felt obliged to defend Moses' behavior: his killing of the Egyptian man according to Exod 2.12, took place in self-defense (Eusebius, *Praep. evang.* 9.27.18; *Fragmenta*, ed. Denis, 171).

who read or heard the Oracles, telling him what would occur if he did not keep to the Law.[31] The story of the past has the morale: "But you, remain, trusting in the holy laws of the great God" (*Sib. Or.* 3.283-84).

Describing or referring to the *virtues of the fathers* may have had the same purposes, although sometimes with even greater stress on the effect on Jewish minds. Using the terminology of the *usus quintuplex*, we could talk of comfort and of instruction. Again, Joseph is in high esteem. Chaste, he resisted the invitations of Potiphar's wife (cf. *JosA* 7.3-4). Similarly, the writer of 4 Maccabees considers that this story demonstrates how Joseph's reason mastered sensualism (2.1-2).

4 Maccabees is dominated by the topic that one must be faithful to the Law. Thus, in 2.17 Moses is mentioned as an example of a moderation guided by reason — we remember this idiosyncrasy of the author — which is demonstrated when he quenches his anger against Dathan and Abiram (Num 16.23-30). The author also recalls the episode of 2 Sam 23.13-17 where David fights his thirst. The story is taken to illustrate how reason should fight passions (4 Macc 3.6-18).[32] Isaac is said to have been reasonable when he was brought to the altar as a sacrifice (Gen 22.7,15). When the author claims that Isaac was ready to give himself up for piety's sake (4 Macc 13.12), he brings forward another theme which is important to him; in this way other figures are also held up as examples of the uncompromising fight unto death for the Law. Thus, the three young men in the fiery furnace (4 Macc 13.9; Dan 3) are mentioned as an example. Towards the end of the book, the martyred brothers' mother gives a speech in which she not only repeats the two previously mentioned examples but also refers to Abel, slain by Cain (Gen 4.8), to the imprisoned Joseph (Gen 39.7-23), to the zealous Phineas (Num 25.7-13) and to Daniel among the lions (Dan 6) (4 Macc 18.11). The passage has sprung from a mind to which it is natural not only to live according to Scripture's ordinances but also to feed on what it has to narrate, and it presupposes that the reader understands it in a similar mood.

Much milder than 4 Maccabees in its exhortative usage of Biblical heroes is the Book of Wisdom. It refers to Henoch as an example of God's saving the righteous (4.10-11; Gen 5.24). It is, however, done in such a subtle way that only one who knows his way in Genesis realizes that the author is adding Henochian color to his general talk of wise and righteous people: the righteous pleased God, and, living among sinners, he was taken away,[33] so that evil

---

31. Actually Deuteronomy 28-30 have played a salient role in Jewish literature of our era. See L. Hartman, *Asking for a Meaning* (note 6), 152-53 for further references.
32. With similar applications the author praises Moses (4 Macc 2.17; cp. Num 16.23-30), Jacob (4 Macc 2.19; cp. Gen 49.7), Aaron (4 Macc 7.11; cp. Num 16.45-50).
33. εὐάρεστος θεῷ γενόμενος ... μετετέθη; Gen 5.24. εὐηρέσησεν Ἐνὼχ τῷ θεῷ ... μετέθηκεν αὐτὸν ὁ θεός.

would not warp his mind. Here, comfort and cautious instruction are given to Wisdom's disciples.

A sheer *edifying exposition* of the text, especially of the exodus story, is found in Wisdom. Thus, e.g., in Wis 16.5-15, the story of Num 21.6-7 on the serpents receives the following comment: "they were troubled for a short time as a lesson (εἰς νουθεσίαν; Wis 16.6) ... they were bitten to remind them of your words, and quickly they were saved ... your all-healing word, O Lord, cured them" (16.11-12).

The manna miracle (Exod 16.14-15; Ps 77:24-25; LXX) receives a similar comment (Wis 16.20-21): "your sustenance showed your sweetness towards your children".[34] And that the manna melted away at sunrise (Exod 16.21) showed "that we must rise before the sun to give you (i.e., God) thanks and pray to you when light begins to dawn" (Wis 16.27-28). These few examples demonstrate how the author of Wisdom helped his audience to make features of the Torah topically edifying and comforting. Using the *quintuplex usus* terms we could call it instruction and/or comfort.

The two prayers in 3 Maccabees, by the high priest Simon and by Eleazar respectively, reveal how the pious Jew could reflect on *God's saving acts and promises in the past*. Such acts could form a *basis for a hope of salvation in the present*. Thus Simon (2.4-12) mentions the punishments sent over Pharao (Exod 5-12; 14.21-31) and how "those who believed in you" were saved from the sea. Furthermore he reminds God of his promise, when the Temple was sanctified, to hear the prayers of his people (1 Kings 8.33-53).

In the same manner Eleazar in 3 Macc 6.1-15 lists God's saving acts during the Exodus, and, furthermore, how Sennacherib and his hosts were shattered (2 Kings 19.35); he mentions the three men in the fiery furnace (Dan 3), and Daniel among the lions (Dan 6), as well as Jonah in the sea monster (Jonah 1.17-2.9). All of the examples, except the last one, remind the reader of the situation in which 3 Maccabees posits Eleazar's prayer, viz. a wicked king threatening God's chosen. So, at the turning point of the prayer, Eleazar summarizes and applies the earlier part of the prayer: "So now, you who hate insolence, full of mercy, protector of all, manifest yourself swiftly to those of the people of Israel who are outrageously treated by the abominable and lawless heathen" (6.9). The prayer concludes with a quotation from Lev 26.44. "'not even when they were in the land of their enemies have I neglected them.' So bring it to pass, Lord" (3 Macc 6.15). This is, of course, where the Alexandrian Jew felt he was: in the land of his enemies, and the verse from Leviticus was understood as a valid promise for himself. Evidently, the Biblical texts are here allowed to teach and to comfort.

---

34. It is hard to resist the thought that Ps 33.9-10 (LXX) has contributed to the wording: "taste and see that the Lord is good", although the LXX reads χρηστός in Ps 33 and γλυκύτης in Wis 16.

When authors found moral support and comfort in God's saving acts of the past, these acts also meant *fighting the enemies*. The latter motif can, however, dominate in such a way that no saving effect is mentioned, only the punishment of the enemy. Thus Scripture could strengthen the Jews who were, or felt themselves to be, oppressed: God would revenge them and punish the wicked. Such is the case in 3 Macc 2.4-5, which refers to the fate of the wicked people at the Flood (Gen 6.4-7.7) and in Sodom (Gen 19.24) — neither Noah nor Lot is mentioned. Wis 4.18 functions in a similar way, in that Psalter language is applied to the wicked crowd: God laughs at them, as in Pss 2.4; 37.13; 59.9.[35] Furthermore, *Sib. Or.* 3.357-62 uses biblical phrases to describe the wicked Rome: she is a virgin drunken from marriage to many suitors, and she will be cast from heaven to earth. Behind, we recognize echoes from Jer 25.27; 48.26; Isa 14.13-16, which denounce the idolatrous Israel, the arrogant Moab and the wicked mistress Babel, respectively.

In the material discussed so far, we have seen how Scripture delivered substance and marrow to Jewish religious life in the present: here, teaching on religious and human fundamentals was found, Scripture concerned both basic beliefs and morality, and could serve both for refutation and for instruction and discipline. But it also furnished the believer with tools for interpreting and expressing different situations and feelings, especially under various kinds of pressure, including the hope of deliverance from present pressure. It remains to ask how the Bible was read with reference to the future: what hope is there for the individual after death, and where is history leading.

As far as "individual eschatology" is concerned, Wisdom reflects a belief that the righteous can expect immortality of their souls after death. This hope is probably also expressed with Bible passages as a hidden support: "their souls are in God's hands" (Wis 3.1; cp. Deut 33.3 LXX: "all the sanctified ones are under your hands"). In Wis 3.7-8 the picture of their coming glorification is possibly inspired by Dan 12.3 ("the wise shine like the luminaries") and 7.18, 24 (the kingdom of the saints).[36]

In *JosA* 8.9 Joseph prays for Aseneth: "let her enter your rest which you have prepared for your chosen ones", which echoes Ps 94.11 (LXX; cp. Heb 3.7-4.13). The author has understood the line from its context. The passage in the Psalm says "they will not enter my rest", which refers to the wilderness generation. To them are contrasted the "we" of the Psalm, who confess, "we are the people of his pasture" (v. 7). So, by implication, they will enter the rest. In the light of, i.a., *JosA* 22.13, which speaks of "her place of rest in the

---

35. Also, e.g. Wis 5.14, echoing Ps 1.4.
36. See H.C.C. Cavallin, *Life After Death. Paul's Argument for the Resurrection of the Dead in I Cor 15. Part I. An Inquiry into the Jewish Background* (ConB NT Ser. 7:1; Lund: Gleerup, 1974) 127.

highest", the expression seems to refer to a heavenly existence with God after death (or, possibly, after her initiation as a proselyte[37]).

In the martyrdom perspective of 4 Maccabees, the author of the book presents a collection of scriptural passages which support the idea that immortality awaits the righteous after death.[38] In 17.18-19 Deut 33.3 is explicitly quoted: "all the sanctified ones are under your hands" (cp. above Wis 3.1), and in 18.14-19 the father of the seven martyrs is said to have taught them passages like the following: "the fire will not burn you" (Isa 43.2); "he is a tree of life to those who do his will" (Prov 3.18); "shall these dry bones live?" (Ezek 37.3; implied answer is "yes"!); "I kill and I make alive" (Deut 32.39).

These passages in 4 Maccabees reflect a conscious quest for biblical support for the belief in (the soul's) immortality after death. The martyrs' mother who quotes the passages indirectly suggests that they should be well known to any pious Jew, although the collection rather smacks of a school midrash. The Bible usage has led to results that shed the light of hope and comfort over the faithfulness of the oppressed. But indirectly it must also have contained an admonition to stand fast.

In order to find anything concerning so-called general eschatology, i.e., a hope or expectation concerning *where history was heading*, we must turn to *Sib. Or.* 3. There the author usually only refers to biblical texts in a hidden way, and the allusions are mainly to passages in the prophets, who are obviously understood to have spoken of the end time. Thus "heaven and earth will be rolled up like a scroll" (3.82) in the catastrophes of the end. Clearly Isa 34.4 has contributed. Furthermore, in *Sib. Or.* 3.660-97 the eschatological attack on the Temple, which is followed by the judgment, is consistently painted with features from Ezekiel 38-39 (Gog and Magog).[39] The picture of the blessed state of salvation in *Sib. Or.* 3.702-31 is also full of Biblical allusions, e.g., God is a wall of fire (706; Zech 2.5), the nations say, "Come, let us fall to the ground and entreat the immortal king, the great eternal God" (*Sib. Or.* 3.716-17; Ps 95.6). Here, we also encounter the expression of a hope for the conversion of the Gentiles: they say "come, let us send to the temple ... and let us all ponder the Law of the Most High God" (719). The line is inspired by Isa 2.3. So it is no surprise to encounter a confession of the converting heathen, "we erred from the path of the Immortal" (*Sib. Or.* 3.721), which sounds like Isa 53.6 etc. (where the people speak who have despised God's servant). A little further on, the situation in the kingdom of God is described: "from all the earth they will bring incense and gifts" (*Sib. Or.* 3.772), behind which we recognize Isa 60.6. The same Isaiah, but also other texts resound in *Sib. Or.* 3.785-95. "rejoice, O maiden, and be glad, for he who created heaven and earth has given you eter-

---

37. Thus, H.C.C. Cavallin, *Life After Death*, 157-58.
38. H.C.C. Cavallin, 116-26, esp. 121-22.
39. See L. Hartman, *Prophecy Interpreted* (note 3), 91-94.

nal joy. He will abide in you and will be for you an immortal light" (Zech 2.10; Isa 12.6; 60.1.19). And lastly: Then "wolves and lambs will graze together in the mountains" etc., a scene that is inspired from Isa 11.6-9 and 65.25 and then developed.

In this case, also, there is an interpretation behind the use of the texts, viz. a conviction that they deal with a new, not-this-worldly situation in which God reigns without resistance from evil. (This can be claimed notwithstanding the fact that the book consists of several collections or oracles from different times).[40] The situation is one in which the Jews feel certain that they live the righteous life, worshipping the only true God. But they do so as a small group under the cultural pressure of a political and cultural world-power. It is all the more important to the reader that the finale looks forward to "the judgment and dominion of the great God" (784). Thus, oracles to the Greeks conclude with the exhortation (740) "serve the great God so that you may have a share in these things" (i.e. in the salvation of the sons of God). Similarly in 763-64 "worship the Living One. Avoid adultery..."; and in 808, before the Sibyl's conclusion: "all must sacrifice to the great King".

Before coming to an end, I want to make two observations concerning the usage of the Bible of which we have caught some glimpses. The first observation may be illustrated by a quotation from the Christian Apocalypse of John. There, the author describes a deviant group of Christians by associating them with Jezebel, "who claims to be a prophetess, and who by her teaching lures my servants to commit adultery and to eat food which has been sacrificed to idols" (Rev 2.20). In this verse, Scripture is used to provide ammunition for attacking co-religionists who are viewed as apostates. Although there appear to have been members of the Alexandrian Jewish community who slid away from Jewish practice,[41] I cannot think of any clear example in the works under consideration, in which Scripture has been used to interpret this circumstance, attacking the apostates and so reinforcing the steadfastness of the remaining faithful. It might be unfair to draw any positive conclusions from this circumstance, since, to such a large extent, the types of literature adduced are genres which do not easily lend themselves to internal polemics. Although in *Sib. Or.* 3 such a thing would have been possible, nothing of the sort is clearly stated, nor is Scripture used for such a purpose. The author of 4 Maccabees could even have cited the Jezebel example as a warning or as a negative way of characterizing an apostate, but he did not. The Book of Wisdom, on the contrary, touches rather lightly on the different cases of grumbling and opposition within the Exodus generation (11.8-9, 16.2,5-6; 18.20-25). In the last-mentioned passage it says: "also the righteous were touched by death, and destruction struck a multitude in the wilderness, but the

---

40. See J.J. Collins in Charlesworth, ed., *Pseudpigrapha* I, 354-361.
41. See Philo, *Mos.* 1.31; P. Borgen, "Philo of Alexandria" (*Jewish Writings*)(note 4), 257.

wrath did not last long" (referring to Num 16.41-49 on the grumbling against Moses and Aaron and the ensuing plague).[42] Certainly, nothing is encountered that reminds one of the later Rabbinic judgment that among the generations which will have no share in the world to come is the one of the wilderness (m. Sanh. 10.3 etc.). Actually, Paul is much harsher than his Alexandrian fellow-Jews, when, in 1 Cor 10.10, he applies Num 16.41-49 to the Corinthians.

The other observation is also a negative one: we have not encountered any clear example of so-called typological interpretation. Actually Professor L. Goppelt in his classical Typos argued concerning "Hellenistic Judaism" that it "lacked any attempt at a typological understanding of Scripture" and that this had to do with "a spiritual Grundhaltung of this current of Judaism which was related to that of Philo".[43] Certainly characters and events of the past were regarded as some kind of patterns which were applicable in later times. 4 Macc 15.11 thus praised the mother of the seven martyrs in this way: "like the ark of Noah, carrying the universe in the cataclysm ... enduring the waves, so did you, guardian of the Law, buffeted by the passions, persevere." Certainly Jacob, Joseph, Moses, etc. are brought forward as examples of virtue, and Abel, Isaac, Daniel, etc. as examples of faithfulness. But what is told of them is not understood as a prophecy in narrative form of a coming salvation (or, for that matter, judgment). Similarly, in Wisdom the exodus events are understood as illustrations of God's attitude to his elected people according to the covenant. When in 3 Maccabees examples of God's saving acts in the past are brought forward as the basis for a prayer that God should act in a similar way in the present crisis, we seem to be closer to a way of thinking in which the past forms models of what to expect from God in the future. When, however, future "eschatological" judgment and salvation are foreseen, prophetic statements of the Bible underlie the text (Sib. Or.), but we see no allusions to, for example, the Flood or to Sodom or to Exodus 15 (the destruction of Pharao's army). Neither is, e.g. the manna a type of anything in the expected kingdom of God (cp. 2 Bar 29.8),[44] nor is an expected Savior painted in colors from Moses or David.[45]

This seeming lack of a fully developed "typological" interpretation in the texts we have studied may be more than a coincidence. But if it is representative, the confrontation between the first generations of Christian Jews and

42. Cp. 4 Macc 7.11.
43. L. Goppelt, Typos. Die typologische Deutung des A.T.s im Neuen (BFCT 43; Gütersloh: Mohn, 1939) 66-67.
44. Cp., though, JosA 16.14. the honey prepared in the heavenly paradise, which seems to be the same as the manna, and which is to be the food of the elect in heaven.
45. Given the present context in Sib. Or. 3, I find it difficult to follow J. Nolland in his essay, "Sib. Or. III.265-94, an Early Maccabean Messianic Oracle," JTS 30 (1979) 158-166. Cp. L. Goppelt, Typos, 34-47.

Jewish Jews of the Diaspora in Alexandria must have meant complications of which we may not have thought. For although both parties regarded the Bible as an authority and both of them used it in partly the same ways, nevertheless the Christian typological exegesis meant advancing a step further than the Jewish Jews were wont to go.[46]

I have now covered the ground I intended. I have read the texts through other spectacles than those we usually don when studying the usage of the Bible by Jewish or Early Christian authors. We have caught some glimpses of how Bible study formed frames of reference for these Jews and of how it provided them with roles with which they could identify themselves, in times of political or social pressure as well as in everyday life. It was hardly the case that every Alexandrian Jew always regarded the world through the filter of an applied Bible. But neither have those authors whose Bible use we have considered here formed a closed elite, who alone knew how to speak and think in such terms. In "looking to the divine word" they presumably also made the Bible "guide the knowing vessel of the heart" of their fellow-Jews. They could have subscribed — with their own presuppositions — to that which the early Christian writer wrote, whom I quoted at the beginning of this essay: "all Scripture inspired by God is profitable for teaching, for reproof, for correction, and for training in righteousness" (2 Tim 3.16).

46. Cp. L. Goppelt, *Christentum und Judentum im ersten und zweiten Jahrhundert* (Gütersloh: Bertelsmann, 1954) 157: from 70 and even more so after 135, the Jewish understanding of Scripture changed: "Atl. Worte, die in den Tagen Jesu allgemein messianisch verstanden wurden, werden nun auf Erscheinungen der Geschichte Israels zurückbezogen und gleichzeitig die Unverbrüchlichkeit des Gesetzes und der Erwählung Israels stetig betont". If our material is representative, it indicates that in Alexandria this change hardly had to take place, since the attitude Goppelt assumed for the time after the revolts against Rome existed there already earlier.

Hellenistic Jews of the Diaspora at the Cradle of Primitive Christianity[1]

Nikolaus Walter

Primitive Christianity originated in Judaism. This statement, which is undoubtedly correct, has two sides. On the one hand, it says that Christianity grew out of Judaism, where it is rooted. Given the person of Jesus, the Jew from Nazareth, and his first disciples, it is impossible to conceive of Christianity any other way. On the other hand, however, the statement also says that primitive Christianity developed *out of* Judaism, that from a given point on it no longer belonged to Judaism, no longer allowed itself to be looked upon as an aspect, a branch, a faction, or a group within Judaism. Of course, within early Christianity there was also a branch, closely tied to the person of James, the "brother of our Lord", which emphatically did want to remain within Judaism. It directed its preaching of Jesus as Messiah only to Jews and, whenever non-Jews converted, demanded that they be circumcised, that is, that they take on Jewishness as a prerequisite for becoming disciples of Jesus. This was "Jewish Christianity" in the narrow sense of the term, which then finally also broke off contact with that branch of primitive Christianity which was open to Gentiles.[2] This latter branch, on the other hand, which more and more as a matter of course accepted also Gentiles into the church of Jesus, without requiring that they become Jews, proved in the long run to be the only faction within primitive Christianity that would influence world history. By the second century AD this faction's tie to Judaism was already hardly recognized by outsiders (but cf. Celsus!), going completely unrecognized—being rather considered "Gentile"—by a Judaism which in the meantime had become centered on the rabbinic tradition.

Using the term "Gentile Christianity" for this branch of primitive Christianity is, however, problematic. It can be confusing in that it can lead one to believe that one is dealing with a totally different Christianity, a Christianity of "Gentile" origins which had no essential or original ties to Judaism, a Christianity, therefore, which to a certain extent represented a completely new phenomenon

1. Translated from the German by Doris Glenn Wagner.
2. A differentiated attempt to describe what the name "Jewish Christianity" could mean historically has been offered by C. Colpe ("Das deutsche Wort 'Judenchristen' und ihm entsprechende historische Sachverhalte"[1978] in *Das Siegel der Propheten* [Arbeiten zur neutestamentlichen Theologie und Zeitgeschichte 3; Berlin: Institut Kirche und Judentum, 1990] 38-58, esp. 46-51). I have tried to describe my own use of the term more or less exactly.

emerging from paganism. And in fact "Gentile Christianity" has occasionally been understood in this way, and its "creator" Paul either praised or blamed. However, such an understanding is mistaken. This branch of primitive Christianity — from which the Christian church developed as a new, independent entity — also has its origin in Judaism. Jews were present at its beginning also, and precisely Jews who were tied to the "fathers", to the inheritance, of Israel — not "apostates".

I. The Two Groups of Jesus' Disciples in Jerusalem — and the "Hellenists"

When and how did primitive Christianity become an entity in its own right, first still within, but then outside of, "standard" Judaism? What made Christians distance themselves from "Judaism", or what caused "standard" Judaism to exclude them (in distinction, for example, from the Qumran community, which emerged as a protest group *within* Judaism, but which never became an entity alongside of or outside of Judaism but rather eventually died out as a Jewish group)? What was, and would in the end remain, uniquely Christian about primitive Christianity?

Evidently it was *not* only the confession of Jesus as Messiah. "Christians" cannot simply be defined as "messianic Jews". To be sure, confessing as Messiah Jesus of Nazareth, who had been crucified at the instigation of the Jews, brought followers of Jesus into a certain conflict with "normative Judaism" (cf. the prohibition to speak in Acts 4 and 5); but it still allowed them to remain a Jewish group. So also Rabbi Akiba, in spite of his failed proclamation of Simon bar Kosiba as the "Star-of-Jacob" Messiah, continued to be recognized as a significant rabbi in the rabbinic tradition. And when around the end of the first century the curse of the *minîm* was introduced in the *Eighteen Benedictions*, it did not refer *exclusively* to the followers of Jesus. Nonetheless, they were certainly included since precisely only that branch of primitive Christianity that at that time still understood itself as a group completely *within* Judaism, namely, as "Jewish Christianity", was in view.

The name *Christianoi*, on the other hand, occurs in Acts 11.26 in a context in which Christians had stepped outside the boundaries of the Jewish people of God not only incidentally and rather unintentionally, but also consciously and *deliberately*. That is, this move had become by that time an integral part of the missionary (and thereby also of the theological) *program* of that faction of primitive Christianity (Acts 11.20).

The post-Easter Jesus tradition maintained that, in his works, *Jesus* only exceptionally (Luke 7.1-10 par.), and even against his will (Mark 7.24-30), extended membership in the *basileia tou theou* even to non-Jews. It also maintained, however, that, with his questioning of ritual purity thinking (Mark 7.1-23 — with a certainly historical core in Mark 7.15), Jesus had created the theological presuppositions for stepping outside Israel's boundaries (Mark certainly placed 7.1-23 before 7.24-30 intentionally).

Peter, according to Luke's account (Acts 10 and 11.1-18), had to undergo a very intensive learning process in order first of all to understand for himself, and then also to be able to explain to "apostles and brothers" in Jerusalem, that the reception of "Gentiles" into the church of Jesus was in accord with God's will (Acts 11.1). In any case, the author Luke is fully aware of the explosiveness of this decision (from the perspective of Jews *and* Jewish Christians!) — it was not for nothing that he spent a chapter and a half justifying it; but historically one can question whether the "historical Peter" himself in fact already completely internalized such a new vision (his behavior in the so-called "Antioch conflict", as reported in Gal 2.11-14, gives rise to questions in this regard).

Then, however, Jewish preachers of the message about Christ — Diaspora Jews from Cyprus and Cyrene — decided in Antioch to preach the gospel also to the "Hellenists" (here, therefore, in all probability Greek-speaking Syrians) and thereby bring them without preconditions into the church of Jesus. This obviously amounted to a revolutionary innovation for the disciples in Antioch as well, since up to that time Jesus Christ had been preached only to Jews (of the Diaspora) (11.19-20). Soon it was clear that the groups which had grown in this manner represented something new in the history of primitive Christianity, so that this group could no longer be integrated into the Jewish Diaspora in Antioch, "so that in Antioch the disciples were for the first time called 'Christians'" (Acts 11.26). These preachers of Christ with the new "program" are linked by Luke, at least indirectly, to the group around Stephen which had been driven from Jerusalem (Acts 11.19).

It is generally recognized today that historically speaking the group of "seven" linked with *Stephen* was not (as Luke would have us understand it in Acts 6.1-7) established by and subordinate to the "twelve apostles" around Peter, but was rather an independent, autonomous group which was active in evangelism and in social ministry and which also differed from Peter's group in its theological perspective. All that Luke reports about them from Acts 6.8 onward confirms this, and especially the different treatment of the two groups by "official" Judaism: While one group (those around Peter) came away with a mere prohibition to speak, the other very quickly — after Stephen was put to death for his distinctive preaching of Christ — had to flee Jerusalem for their lives (Acts 8.1, 4; 11.19). This group must have formed very soon after Pentecost, and naturally it had a link with Peter and the other disciples of Jesus; however, what type of link this was and generally how Stephen's group came into being can no longer be reconstructed. What Luke knows about these things he presumably gathered from the (oral?) tradition of the Antioch church; the beginnings of this group that formed around Stephen were evidently no longer completely clear even for him. (Already he appears to have believed that the conflict over the care of widows from the Diaspora was an *internal* conflict among Jesus' disciples in Jerusalem — one should presumably understand Acts 6.1 in this manner, even if that is not clearly stated; in my opinion,[3] this is historically incorrect.) While, therefore, the beginnings of this group within the Jesus movement are unclear, considerably more can be said about the group's background: they are "Hellenists" and, therefore, according to Luke's terminology, non-Greeks (e.g. Jews or even Syrians) whose everyday language was Greek. Here (in Acts 6), then, they were Greek-speaking Jews who had returned home to Jerusalem from the Diaspora and who, by that time, also had their own synagogues there (Acts 6.9).

Although in New Testament research the Jesus group around Stephen is generally referred to simply as "the Hellenists", this surely does not correspond to Luke's use of the term. This incorrect terminology is the cause (or perhaps a result?) of the opinion that Acts 6.1 refers to dissension among Jesus' disciples in Jerusalem — but this cannot be inferred from the text; rather, one should think of a disagreement (between the Aramaic-speaking majority and the Greek-speaking minority of Jews in Jerusalem) in which Stephen's group became involved. According to Luke's terminology, "Hellenists" are all non-Greeks who speak Greek, for example, also Antiochian Syrians (if the reading of Acts 11.20 according to Nestle-Aland[26] is correct). But in any case the term also refers to Diaspora Jews who had a completely different attitude toward the Torah, the temple, and even Jesus than did Stephen's group, as is evident from Acts 6.9-10, where Stephen, along with his comrades, must engage in rancorous debate (here, of course, one does not find the expression "Hellenists"), and likewise from Acts 9.29, where Paul must argue in the same manner with "Hellenists".

---

3. That this was in fact not a conflict between followers of Jesus of different languages, but rather one having to do with different language groups within the Jewish community of Jerusalem itself, was already presumed and argued before my investigations ("Apostelgeschichte 6.1 und die Anfänge der Urgemeinde in Jerusalem", NTS 29 [1983] 370-393) by N. Hyldahl (*Udenfor og indenfor. Sociale og økonomiske aspekter i den ældste kristendom* [Copenhagen: Gad, 1974]). A hypothesis of his own regarding the origin of the circle of disciples around Stephen has been put forward by K. Löning ("Der Stephanuskreis und seine Mission", in *Die Anfänge des Christentums* [ed. J. Becker et al.; Stuttgart: Kohlhammer, 1987] 80-101, esp. 84-86). Regarding the history of research on this issue, see in addition: H.-W. Neudorfer, *Der Stephanuskreis in der Forschungsgeschichte seit F.C. Baur* (Gießen: Brunnen, 1983).

II. What is "Hellenistic Diaspora Judaism"?

We have just seen hints that there was obviously no such thing as "standard" Hellenistic Judaism, that is, Judaism as a monolithic entity with a unified understanding of the basis of Judaism and its essential theological "contents". Can one nevertheless speak of a general "profile" of Hellenistic Judaism — or can one describe it only as a pluralistic "palette"?

Of course, the answer to this question is already partially determined by the manner in which one defines the expression "Hellenistic Diaspora Judaism". If one employs a rather precise and therefore narrow definition (as I intend to do), one must also admit at the same time that in the Diaspora outside of Palestine a "Hellenistic" Judaism also existed which did not conform to our narrow definition, that therefore a much broader spectrum of Jews lived in the Diaspora than the Judaism I would like to call "Hellenistic" (in the narrower sense).

My definition refers to a Judaism whose own thinking has been — in part unconsciously, but to a large degree quite consciously and knowingly — shaped by Hellenistic thinking and a Hellenistic ethos or "worldview"; a Judaism which consciously took part in the intercultural encounters of late antiquity, not refusing in any way to do so; a Judaism which was therefore not only exposed, in a more or less strong and more or less unperceived way, to the general Hellenistic influences of the era, and so was subordinated to them, or on the other hand expressly kept itself apart from them and (when possible) untainted by them. I am therefore concerned with *one* particular way of preserving a particular religious and national identity while living in foreign parts, *one* of several possibilities which on the surface, under certain circumstances, may be contradictory.

Above all, I am here disregarding the question regarding Hellenistic influences on Palestinian Judaism — and certainly without at all denying such influences. Evidently, after a phase of extensive openness to Hellenistic influences in the Jewish homeland, primarily among the leading stratum of temple priests, who aspired to attain Hellenistic citizenship for themselves in Jerusalem,[4] a general swing of the pendulum began at the time of, and under the influence of, the Maccabees. Of course, this did not mean that politics, trade and commerce, daily living, and religious art (architecture, the minting of coins, and also plastic art) could, in the long run, truly be free of Hellenistic influences.[5]

---

4. Cf. in this regard the standard work of M. Hengel, *Judentum und Hellenismus. Studien zu ihrer Begegnung unter besonderer Berücksichtigung Palästinas bis zur Mitte des 2. Jh. v. Chr.* (WUNT 10; Tübingen: Mohr, 1969); [Engl. trans.] *Judaism and Hellenism. Studies in Their Encounter in Palestine during the Early Hellenistic Period*, 2 vols. (Philadelphia: Fortress, 1974).

5. For example, in the sense of the "puristic" concepts of S. Safrai (see in this regard G. Mayer, "Zur jüdischen Geschichte", *ThR* 55 [1990] 1-20, esp. 4-5, 10, 16-19).

Later even the rabbis themselves were unsuccessful in completely barricading themselves against Hellenization, in spite of the fact that this effort was more or less elevated to the level of a political program.[6]

I am rather thinking primarily of the Judaism in Alexandria, since there the sources for "Hellenistic Judaism" in that narrower sense are surely the most accessible and, for me in any case, the most familiar. Basically no texts — apart from a few inscriptions — have been preserved for us from other centers of the Jewish Diaspora in the Hellenistic-Roman world (to say nothing at all of Babylonia), so that we can hardly know precisely how Jews thought e.g. in Antioch or Tarsus, in Ephesus or Athens, or even in Rome.

However, even with respect to Alexandria one must naturally make distinctions. Without doubt it is clear that neither Philo of Alexandria nor even his older brother, the alabarch (arabarch) Alexander, who made a large donation to the Jerusalem temple, simply represented the intellectual and cultural status and the religious attitude of the several hundred thousand Jewish inhabitants of Alexandria, much less the additional hundreds of thousands of Jews of the surrounding area, even as far as Leontopolis with its Jewish temple. A few things about other groupings and parties can be gathered from Philo's writings. He himself evidently sympathized with the so-called Therapeutae, that exclusive, evidently highly cerebral and secretive, Essene-type religious community. He also once referred to the so-called Allegorists, who like himself (and Pseudo-Aristeas before him) interpreted the cultic and ritual regulations of the Torah allegorically, but who also went further and claimed it was unnecessary to keep these laws — for which Philo rebuked them. But surely all of these groups represent only a thin, intellectually oriented elite; and one may well wonder[7]

Cf. again M. Hengel, *The "Hellenization" of Judaea in the First Century after Christ* (Philadelphia: Trinity Press International, 1989), as well as my review of the work in *TLZ* 118 (1993) 394-396.

6. Cf. still the work of R. Meyer, *Hellenistisches in der rabbinischen Anthropologie* (BWANT 74; Stuttgart: Kohlhammer, 1937), as well as S. Lieberman, "How Much Greek in Jewish Palestine?" in *Biblical and Other Studies* (A. Altmann, ed.; Cambridge, Mass., 1963), 123-141; idem, *Hellenism in Jewish Palestine* (2nd ed.; New York: Jewish Theological Seminary, 1962), esp. 47-82 and 100-14. More reserved in this regard is L.H. Feldman, "How Much Hellenism in Jewish Palestine?", HUCA 57 (1986) 83-111.

7. For example, Y. Amir, "Die messianische Idee im hellenistischen Judentum", *Freiburger Rundbrief* 25 (1973) 195-203; cf. also M. Hengel, "Messianische Hoffnung und politischer 'Radikalismus' in der 'jüdisch-hellenistischen Diaspora': Zur Frage der Voraussetzungen des jüdischen Aufstandes unter Trajan 115-117 n. Chr.", in *Apocalypticism in the Mediterranean World and the Near East* (D. Hellholm, ed.; Tübingen: Mohr, 1983) 655-686 (Hengel here concerns himself primarily with Book V of the *Sibylline Oracles*).

how many synagogue-goers would have really been pleased with, or would even have understood, Philo's Sabbath-day homilies on biblical texts.

Nevertheless it is known that Philo was also a "man of political action" — against his inclination, of course, since such activities disturbed his academic, exegetical deskwork (*Spec.* 3.1-6), yet with full engagement and in no way without risk. In other words, his intellectual-elitist attitude did not at all result in an aloofness to, or withdrawal from, the world.[8]

Yehoshua Amir and others have, on the other hand, referred primarily also to the Jewish elements in the collection of *Sibylline Oracles*,[9] which could serve as documentary evidence for a very different, and presumably much more popular, type of Alexandrian Judaism. Even here, however, one should make the qualifying observation that those who produced the *Oracles* (over a period of several centuries) must also in any case have enjoyed a Greek education which enabled them to compose, more or less with ease and finesse, hundreds of hexameters in the language of Homer, or rather the language of the pagan Sibylline proverbs which they had before them. This also is therefore in a certain sense authentic Hellenistic Judaism — although it is linked to a completely different intellectual-religious stance than, for example, Philo. In spite of intensive cultural contact with the Hellenistic educational system, dominant here is a rather uncouth attitude of rejection vis-à-vis the "Gentiles", that is, above all, probably vis-à-vis their "godless" governing authority. Eschatological hope is, to some extent, very concretely political; and it aims at a new aeon, conceived as a terrestrial reality, that will follow all the catastrophes that have been prophesied for the tyrannical powers. Philosophical and transcendental spiritualizing is quite foreign to the authors of Book 3 (second century BC) through Book 13 (third century AD). Is it Jews in Alexandria who here express their hate and their hope in hexameters? Or — as J.J. Collins suspects at least for Book 3 — is it Jews in the circle of Onias (IV), who fled to Egypt, that is, perhaps Jews who settled in Leontopolis around the middle of the second century BC?

---

8. Cf. e.g. H. Hegermann, "Das griechischsprechende Judentum", in *Literatur und Religion des Frühjudentums* (ed. J. Maier and J. Schreiner; Gütersloh: Mohn, 1973) 328-368; idem, "Philon von Alexandrien," ibid., 353-369, esp. 366-368 ("Philon als Mann der politischen Praxis").

9. Apart from the works mentioned in footnote 7, cf. also D.S. Potter, *Prophecy and History in the Crisis of the Roman Empire: A Historical Commentary on the Thirteenth Sibylline Oracle* (Oxford: Clarendon, 1990) (on Book 13 of the Sibylline Oracles as evidence from the third century AD); as well as the comprehensive summaries of J.J. Collins, *The Sibylline Oracles of Egyptian Judaism* (SBLDS 13; Missoula: Scholars Press, 1974) and idem, "The Development of the Sibylline Tradition" (ANRW II: 20/1; Berlin: de Gruyter, 1987) 421-459; and his commentary to the Sibylline Oracles in: *The Old Testament Pseudepigrapha*, 1 (ed. J.H. Charlesworth; Garden City, N.Y.: Doubleday, 1983) 317-472, esp. 322-323, 354-357.

In any case, we may easily imagine that thoughts and end-time expectations of this type met with greater approval — particularly in times of Ptolemaic repression — in the wider circles of Egyptian Judaism than did the highly intellectual allegories of a Philo. Be that as it may, it is still remarkable that even such prophecies made use of literary techniques taken from Greek tradition, which means that authors and readers alike were familiar with such traditions.

In any case, today we are beginning to understand more clearly than we did twenty-five years ago the significance of the fact that an intensive and actively appropriated Hellenistic education among Alexandrian Jews was present not only in Philo's time, but rather already a good two hundred years earlier. If the oldest Jewish Sibylline verses come from the middle of the second century BC, at the same time, or somewhat later, a certain *Ezekiel* nevertheless wrote his drama about Moses and the Exodus out of Egypt in a language spiced as much with phrases from Aeschylus and Euripides as from its main source, the Septuagint. Also before or around 100 BC the *epic poet Philo* wrote an epic poem on Jerusalem which still today offers experts on Hellenistic epic literature some philological nuts that are hard to crack even after one has recognized the stylistic borrowing from Rhianus of Bene or Apollonius of Rhodes (both from the third century BC).[10] These texts, preserved in fragments of the Hellenistic Roman Alexander Polyhistor's book *On the Jews* that were transmitted by Eusebius, were naturally already known a hundred years ago, particularly since in 1874/75 Jacob Freudenthal had dedicated some of his exemplary studies to them, and Emil Schürer had treated them appropriately in his standard work.[11] Nevertheless, outside of this framework they

---

10. Regarding Ezekiel the tragedian, J. Wieneke has already given careful evidence for his knowledge of the Greek writers of tragedy (*Ezechielis Iudaei poetae Alexandrini fabulae quae inscribitur EXAGWGH fragmenta* [Münster: Aschendorff, 1931]); cf. then B. Snell, "Die Jamben in Ezechiels Moses-Drama", *Glotta* 44 (1966) 25-32, and, more recently, H. Jacobson, *The Exagoge of Ezekiel* (Cambridge: Cambridge University Press, 1983) 24-25. With regard to the relationship shown between the epic poet Philo and the Hellenistic epic of Apollonius of Rhodes, as well as the epic of Rhianus of Bene, we are indebted to a work by J. Atwell and J. Hansen, which unfortunately has remained unpublished (seminar paper; Cambridge, Mass., 1970); cf., in this regard, N. Walter, "Fragmente jüdisch-hellenistischer Epik" (JSHRZ 4:3 [ed. W.G. Kümmel; Gütersloh: Mohn, 1983] 141-142).

11. J. Freudenthal, *Alexander Polyhistor und die von ihm erhaltenen Reste jüdischer und samaritanischer Geschichtswerke* (Breslau: Skutsch, 1874/1875); E. Schürer, *Geschichte des Jüdischen Volkes im Zeitalter Jesu Christi*, vol. 3 (Leipzig: Hinrichs, 1909) 497. Cf. my translation into German in JSHRZ (ed. W.G. Kümmel; Gütersloh: Mohn, 1974-) 1:2 and 3:2 and 4:3, as well as the translations into English by H. Attridge and others in: *The Old Testament Pseudepigrapha*, vol. 2 (ed. J.H. Charlesworth; Garden City, N.Y.: Doubleday, 1985) 781-919.

were given little consideration for several decades, especially since the classical philologists of those decades labeled these products from Hellenistic times as everything from "bombastic and affected" to "stupid" and "inferior".[12] Only within the course of the new evaluation of Hellenistic literature in general and Hellenistic poetry in particular did one learn to see that these Hellenistic Jewish authors were also simply living up to the expectations of their times and, within the framework of their contemporary culture, did not look too bad.

That is true also for popular literature, a few fragments of which, dating possibly from around 100 BC, have in part likewise been preserved only through Alexander Polyhistor and Eusebius, for example, *Artapanos*, the author of a fantastic novel about Moses, or the anonymously transmitted romance *Joseph and Aseneth*, or the *Testament of Job*. Still within the realm of popular literature are also the synagogue sermons *On Samson* and *On Jonah*, which were preserved only in Armenian translation and later published in Latin by B. Awgerean (1826) and in German by F. Siegert (1980).[13] With the "Treatise on Reason as the Master of the Passions", known as *4 Maccabees*, we find a mixture of popular philosophy with the pious martyrological novel. To this genre one could also assign the Hellenistic variant of Enochic apocalyptic in the *Slavonic Apocalypse of Enoch*

12. According to E. Schürer (see footnote 11 above), the verses of the epic poet Philo were "a true insult to Greek prosody" and his diction was "bombastic and affected to the point of incomprehensibility" — one must admit that there was some truth in this statement regarding incomprehensibility, since, given their linguistic compactness, the fragments are too short to be clearly interpretable. However, even that belongs to the style of the "modern" Hellenistic epic of that day. The Jewish *Sibylline Oracles* were labeled in a lump as "inferior" by F. Blass (in *Die Apokryphen und Pseudepigraphen des Alten Testaments* [ed. E. Kautzsch; Tübingen: Mohr (Siebeck), 1900], 2, 180). One may perhaps make such judgments from the perspective of literary aesthetics; for us, however, the *Sibylline Oracles* are highly important for our knowledge of the inner diversity of Hellenistic Judaism.

13. F. Siegert, *Drei hellenistisch-jüdische Predigten*, vol. 1, *Übersetzung aus dem Armenischen und sprachliche Erläuterungen* (WUNT 20; Tübingen: Mohr [Siebeck] 1980); see also now vol. 2, *Kommentar nebst Beobachtungen zur Vorgeschichte der Bibelhermeneutik* (WUNT 61; Tübingen: Mohr, 1992). One of the three sermons in volume 1 ("Über die Gottesbezeichnung 'wohltätig verzehrendes Feuer'" [On the designation of God as "beneficent consuming fire"]) is in style and content so similar to Philo's homilies that it could well be taken for a product of Philo himself; thus F. Siegert, *Philon von Alexandrien: Über die Gottesbezeichnung "wohltätig verzehrendes Feuer" (De Deo)* (WUNT 46; Tübigen: Mohr [Siebeck], 1988), with a retroversion of the Armenian text into Greek, as well as a commentary. There then remain two sermons (and a fragment) of an otherwise unknown author, which for this reason are of great interest, since they acquaint us with another variety of biblical interpretation in Hellenistic Judaism.

(also known as 2 *Enoch*), as well as the pseudepigrapha with their various attempts to put Jewish-Hellenistic theology or ethics, in verse form, into the mouths of some classical Greek authors — this also is in any case an expression of Jewish efforts toward intercultural contact, of the Jewish attempt to find a place in the intellectual landscape of Hellenistic culture, but without surrendering Jewish identity.[14]

One may disagree concerning details regarding the meaning of each of these pieces of literary evidence. I myself have been concerned with two things. First, I wanted to show that, as a representative of Jewish Hellenism, Philo in no way stood alone, that he rather had behind him a long prehistory of approaches to Hellenistic education within Alexandrian Judaism. Furthermore, I wanted at least to point out the considerable range of relationships between Alexandrian Judaism and Hellenistic education and literature (to this should be added at least a sketch of the ties to various types of Hellenistic philosophy), in order to elucidate to some degree the intellectual background of Hellenistic Judaism at the time of the birth of primitive Christianity.

It is important at this point to state that the Hellenistic Judaism of the Diaspora in turn established "branches" in Jerusalem. This Judaism, now "reimported" into the Jewish homeland, evidently in spite of its "return home" did not (or could not) simply give up the form it had taken in the foreign context. Rather, even here, it remained "Hellenistic" Judaism (and that to a degree far exceeding the general level of Hellenization, which even in Jerusalem no one could evade). If one can therefore speak generally of a "Hellenized" Judaism even in Jerusalem, then the term "Hellenistic Judaism" means more to me than the simply passive state of submission to the generally prevalent influences of the epoch. In any case, at the time of primitive Christianity (of course, even already at the time of Jesus), there were synagogues in Jerusalem where, at the very least, Greek was the most commonly spoken language, though surely much more of a genuine Hellenization could be felt. Acts 6.9 indicates — surely reliably — that in Jerusalem there were two or even five synagogues of "foreigners" of the Diaspora (of "Libertines" [?], Cyrenians, and Alexandrians; and of Cilicians and Asians), which meant that there were communities, organized according to nationality, of Jews from North Africa and Asia Minor.[15] (We can

---

14. Cf. my introductory remarks in JSHRZ (see above footnote 10) 4:3 (1983) 175-181.
15. Cf. (with additional bibliographical information) W. Schrage, *TWNT* 7.835-836 [Engl. trans., *TDNT* 7.835-836]. According to A. Weiser, Luke thought of "at least three synagogues of different compatriot groups" ("mindestens drei landsmannschaftlich verschiedene[n] Synagogen"); Weiser understands the "Libertines" or "Freedmen" to be returnees from Rome (*Die Apostelgeschichte, Kapitel 1-12* [ÖTK 5/1; Gütersloh: Mohn, 1981] 172). Of course, this tripartite division is more difficult to substantiate on the basis of the wording in the text than a bi- or

here leave open the question of whether the synagogue of the Libertines had something to do with the Theodotus synagogue inscription, dated around AD 100, or whether "Libertines" was a copyist's error for "Libyans", which would fit well in the context with the names of other North African regions. In any case, there was a Jewish Diaspora in Libya.) Luke calls those related to such synagogues of returnees from the Diaspora "Hellenists" and expresses thereby the notion that these people, though non-Greeks, speak Greek and are therefore also more closely tied to Hellenistic culture than to their Jerusalem environment.

Presumably this inability of the returning Jews to reintegrate fully into the situation of the motherland[16] is reflected also in the conflict regarding the care for Hellenistic Jewish widows living in Jerusalem, who had no social support system (Acts 6.1) — that conflict which, in my judgment, was not peculiar to the church of Jesus' disciples, but was rather generally reflected in the "social network" of Jerusalem and now challenged Jesus' followers among the "Hellenists".[17] That by that time there could have already been in the Jesus movement any independent organizing of social relief work at all is rather improbable, given the fact that the first disciples of Jesus were completely tied to the larger Jewish "community". In the tradition of the Jesus people of Antioch, this was obviously remembered as the first case of organized independence on the part of their group.

Be that as it may, the image of the "Hellenists" in Jerusalem that is found in Acts 6.(1-)8-14, as well as in Acts 9.26-29, confirms once again from the Jerusalem perspective, so to speak, that the Greek-speaking Diaspora Jews had by no means been shaped by a single, unified theology. Stephen, as *one* such "Hellenist" and as the intellectual leader of a group of like-minded people, was engaged in a severe conflict with other "Hellenists" — precisely those members of refugee synagogues, among whom there were certainly also Alexandrians — over the question of relativizing the temple cult and the law, a conflict which ultimately led to his death (in any case, Luke does not present the matter as if it had to do with the "Hebrews" of 6.1, who conceived the killing of Stephen). And the same is true somewhat later regarding Paul, who now, as a Christian, follows in the wake of Stephen's group and must contend forcefully with other

pentapartite division. Also for this reason it seems to me quite plausible that, with regard to the "Libertines", we are dealing with a mistake in the transmission of the text (see above).

16. Even at the present there are parallels; one thinks, for example, of the Turks who, after residing for decades in European countries, return to their homeland and are completely at home neither there nor here, since they speak the language of their host country better than Turkish and have also become somewhat estranged from their native customs, although they still consider themselves Turks.

17. See above footnote 3.

"Hellenists" both in Damascus (Acts 9.22) and in Jerusalem (9.29) — presumably with people who represented the same position that he as a Pharisee had stood for prior to his conversion to Christianity and because of which he, at that time, had endeavored "to destroy" the "church of God" (Gal. 1.13 etc.). Later, he himself encountered such bitter hostility during his missionary activities in Asia Minor; more than once he came close to being killed (Acts 9.29-30; 20.3; 21.27-30), avoiding death only by fleeing (9.30) or by altering his route of travel (20.3), and finally by placing himself under Roman protection (21.31-36; cf. generally in this regard 2 Cor 11.22-33; 6.4-10 etc.). Particularly instructive is Acts 21.27-30 (and 23.12-15), since from these verses we learn that the Diaspora Jews from Ephesus, who are in Jerusalem at the same time as Paul (and not by accident, as we may infer from Acts 20.3!), had with sharp criticism observed (not to say hounded) his activities in Ephesus, and now waited in Jerusalem for the chance to kill him, whose work they could only regard as the preaching of apostasy from the genuine worship of God. It is irrelevant whether these Diaspora "colleagues" spied on Paul on behalf of Jerusalem authorities or whether they acted out of personal religious zeal[18] — in Jerusalem they reported his cult- and Torah-relativizing activities (which were evident as soon as he conferred upon Gentiles membership in the people of God without requiring circumcision or other Torah observances) and by so doing imperiled his life. All of this should, within this context, serve only to substantiate once again the internal diversity of Hellenistic Diaspora Judaism.

Just as Paul, prior to his call to bear witness to the gospel of Christ, was, according to his own self-description, a Pharisee in the strictest sense (Phil 3.4-6) and yet, at the same time, an outstanding master of the Greek language (as his letters clearly indicate),[19] so were surely also the Alexandrian Jews basically loyal to the Torah and in that sense "orthodox" Jews. (To what extent they were also "orthoprax" in the Pharisaic or even later rabbinic sense of Torah observance, is difficult to say; however, their *doxa*, their fundamental position, was faithfulness to the Torah.) This is as true for *Philo* as for the writers of the *Wisdom*

18. In my opinion, even in the case of the preachers agitating against Paul in Galatia, one must take into consideration that the concerned Jews were non-believers in Christ who reproached Paul for going only halfway (and thereby, as they claimed, already betraying the foundation of Judaism), while they now wanted to steer the Pauline mission into the direction of winning converts in the only way that was possible for their way of thinking, namely, by insisting on the additional requirement of the observance of the law. Cf. N. Walter, "Paulus und die Gegner des Christusevangeliums in Galatien," in *L'Apôtre Paul. Personnalité, style et conception du ministère* (A. Vanhoye, ed.; BETL 73, Louvain: University Press, 1986) 351-356.

19. Cf. M. Hengel, "Der vorchristliche Paulus", *Paulus und das antike Judentum* (ed. M. Hengel and U. Heckel; WUNT 58, Tübingen: Mohr [Siebeck] 1991) 177-293.

of Solomon and of 3 and 4 *Maccabees*, as well as for the various authors of the Jewish *Sibylline Oracles*. And yet their attitudes toward their non-Jewish neighbors differ considerably — depending, naturally, on how they found themselves treated by their non-Jewish neighbors.

The *Sibylline Oracles* demonstrate, as already mentioned, a rather harsh rejection of the Gentiles, for whom they hold only the desire for eschatological annihilation. Just as emphatically do 3 and 4 *Maccabees* distance themselves from their surroundings, particularly from the Hellenistic rulers. Whether, on the other hand, the *Wisdom of Solomon* is referring primarily to Gentiles when it denounces the godless and the blasphemers, or whether it rather means primarily apostate Hellenistic Jews, does not seem clear to me (Wisdom's commonly noted rather "individualistic" perspective on salvation and eschatological hope could point to the latter possibility). And still the author avoids clearly revealing his Jewish identity to the reader (if one considers the present title of the book to be not original but rather a heading taken later from 9.1-12); he operates "stylistically and conceptually with the tools of international education common to the Hellenistic world"[20] and would apparently like to present his book to the Hellenistic reader as "generally understandable" literature — a peculiar mixture of strict loyalty to the Torah and constant readiness to suffer for the Torah's sake, combined with intellectual openness to the world, with the unambiguous claim that the Torah contains the true, divine wisdom for *all* human beings.

Such a tendency is even more evident, however, in other Jewish-Hellenistic authors, especially where Greek philosophy is quite plainly considered to be dependent on Moses, that greatest of all human philosophers — thus already around 150 BC in *Aristobulos*.[21] Already underlying such a view is the thesis that the Torah has fundamental significance not only for the one chosen people, but for all peoples, all humanity — and not as a document in which Gentiles would find for themselves only rejection and scathing divine judgment. When addressing the Ptolemy (presumably Ptolemy VI Philometor; at least the literary framework addresses the Ptolemy, though this may be a fiction) and thereby simultaneously all educated persons, Aristobulos proposes that the Torah be considered the property of all humanity and given a "proper", acceptable philosophical interpretation — without expecting or even desiring that anyone should for this reason become a Jew. The pseudonymous *Letter of Aristeas*, whose ostensibly non-Jewish author wishes to represent precisely the model of a

---

20. D. Georgi, "Weisheit Salomos", JSHRZ 3:4 (Gütersloh: Mohn, 1980) 391.
21. Aristobulos is by no means, however, the first or only early Jewish-Hellenistic author who represented this way of thinking; cf. N. Walter, *Der Thoraausleger Aristobulos* (TU 86; Berlin: Akademie-Verlag, 1964) 43-51.

non-Jew enthusiastic about the Torah, presents itself similarly. And over a hundred years later *Philo*, above all, presents himself, with the same intensity, both as an expositor of the divine Torah *and* simultaneously as a thinker who can deal in a sovereign manner with elements of Hellenistic culture (e.g. he often cites the Greek "classical writers"). For him, the completion of the divinely inspired translation of the Hebrew Torah into Greek is an auspicious day to be celebrated annually, first of all, of course, for the Jews of Alexandria, but also just as much for (Greek-speaking) humanity as such (*Mos.* 2.12-44). This generous opening of the Torah for *all* human beings (the exact opposite of the later rabbinic view, according to which it was a dark day for Israel when the translated Torah — fortunately only the *written* Torah! — was made available to Gentiles) is remarkable, particularly in view of the fact that Philo had experienced, in all its severity, the attack upon the Alexandrian Jews by their Greek compatriots and Roman rulers (see above). Should one say that, in defense, Philo made "a preemptive retreat forwards"? I think that he himself would not agree with this.

To this palette of Hellenistic Jews loyal to the Torah must still be added, for example, the *Therapeutae*, so highly regarded by Philo, with their Torah piety colored strongly by liturgy and meditation and with their obviously profound intellectualism (*Contempl.*), whereas on the other hand we have the so-called *Allegorists*, whom Philo rebuked because of their "thoughtlessness" (*Migr.* 89-90). These were liberals, so to speak, presumably characterized by an intellectualism similar to that of the Therapeutae, but holding the opinion that only the allegorical, "spiritual" sense of the Torah should still be considered essential, while they appeared to have felt that following the Halacha in everyday, practical matters was an unnecessary separation of themselves from their surroundings, so they did not follow it. Philo's rejection of their behavior does not, in my opinion, speak against the fact that his own intellectual stance with respect to Torah interpretation was not really remote from theirs at all; however, he does in fact seem to shy away from surrendering signs of Jewish identity visible also to outsiders. (Of course, it remains difficult to say exactly how far Philo's own "orthopraxis" went in daily life; one can hardly deduce more than hints even from passages such as *Mos.* 2.21-22, which are concerned with keeping the Sabbath.)

It would further enrich the palette if there had indeed been a charismatic-Jewish, Torah-based missionary movement aggressively active in Gentile areas, as has been claimed, for example, by Dieter Georgi.[22] But the question regarding

---

22. D. Georgi, *Die Gegner des Paulus im 2. Korintherbrief* (WMANT 11; Neukirchen-Vluyn: Neukirchener Verlag, 1964) 83-187; [Engl. trans.] *The Opponents of Paul in Second Corinthians* (Philadelphia: Fortress, 1986) 83-228.

active, organized, planned, and executed proselytizing by Torah-observing Judaism does not appear to me to be clearly answerable. Matt 23.15 gives evidence, first of all, for the time around the end of the first century; the verse could almost reflect, from an Antiochian perspective, the anti-Pauline campaign to Judaize Gentile-*Christian* churches in Asia Minor and Greece (as far as Rome?). The validity of the verse would then reach back to the middle of the first century; however, this Jewish mission would then, in either case, already be a result of primitive Christian mission, not its preliminary stage or its model. In any case, what can be drawn from Matt 23.15 sounds to me specifically related to Paul's polemic against his opponents in Galatia (Gal 5.1-10).[23]

III. The Significance of Hellenistic Judaism for the Formation of Primitive Christianity

The sketch just given indicates that Hellenistic Diaspora Judaism — just like Judaism in the homeland, by the way — was not monolithic but rather exhibited a variety of different views within the common framework of preservation of Jewish identity in a foreign context, a variety which admittedly, due to insufficient source materials, can be described exactly neither in total nor in detail, but which nevertheless can be approximately deduced from various hints in the sources.

But if one cannot reduce the tendencies and aspirations of Hellenistic Judaism to a common denominator, then neither can the effect of this Judaism on the formation of primitive Christianity be described in a unilinear fashion.

1.

From the presentation in Acts one can recognize, at points directly and at other points (as also in Paul's letters) indirectly, that certain groups — even and especially ones from Hellenistic Diaspora Judaism, namely, groups holding strictly to the Torah and being loyal to the temple, for whom in addition to Torah and temple as the foundation of Judaism also the uniqueness of Israel among and over against the "nations" was an indispensable aspect of their Jewishness — became actively hostile to primitive Christianity, which was taking shape and spreading out over the Gentile world, as soon as it became clear that Christian preachers, who were normally Jews, relativized (or

---

23. Cf. above footnote 18. Still, some scholars continue to presuppose a programmatic and actively pursued proselytizing mission carried on by (Diaspora) Judaism both before and simultaneous to the missionary activities of primitive Christianity, thus e.g. D. Georgi (see previous footnote), but also C. Bussmann, *Themen der paulinischen Missionspredigt auf dem Hintergrund der spätjüdisch-hellenistischen Missionsliteratur* (Europ. Hochschul-Schriften XXIII 3; 2nd ed.; Bern: H. Lang, 1975).

appeared to relativize) that foundation and called into question its universal and eternal validity or even proclaimed it "abolished".

As we have seen, there was such active opposition from the time of Stephen on; it accompanied Paul from the moment of his conversion to Christianity, through the entire time of his missionary activities in Asia Minor and Greece, to his arrest in Jerusalem and Caesarea and, beyond that, presumably all the way to Rome — where we, admittedly, know nothing about the precise circumstances which led to his death. However, it seems clear to me that, primarily during the final phase of his ministry, he was opposed by an active propaganda campaign which followed him everywhere and tried to torpedo his founding of Christian churches or subsequently transform them into communities of Jewish proselytes. Once again we should remember that such opposition grew out of the same attitude which had made Paul, before he became a Christian, an enemy of the Jesus churches founded by the missionaries of Stephen's group. There is therefore no reason to be surprised by the active hostility of certain Jewish factions over against the kind of missionary activity practiced precisely by Stephen's group and then by Paul.

2.

On the other hand, however, there was evidently *one* faction of Hellenistic Diaspora Judaism which, after joining the earliest disciples of Jesus, continued to develop their own line of thinking, which had been set into motion by a (positive) coming to terms with Hellenistic education: the group around Stephen, led by the "seven" (Acts 6.5). They had formerly perhaps held the view, not yet fully formulated, that faithfulness to Torah and temple potentially separated Judaism from the rest of humanity; but they had nevertheless already come to the conclusion that, if the Torah were indeed of divine origin, it must properly belong to all human beings created by God. Now, following the post-Easter encounter with Jesus' disciples and driven by the impulse of Jesus' message, which had been transmitted to them, they developed their view — appealing to Jesus' message — to the point that they programatically verbalized and hotly debated (Acts 6.9-10) a relativization of Torah and temple worship (as a way of salvation not necessary for all people). This relativizing was interpreted by the other side as a blasphemous betrayal of the foundation of Judaism.

It is clear that the motives here tacitly presumed to underlie this development, which led the entire Jesus movement a step beyond the position held by Peter and Jesus' original disciples, are and must remain hypothetical. However, the result corresponds in any case to the picture which — when one asks the necessary critical questions — emerges from the account of the prehistory and early history of the Antioch church utilized by Luke in Acts 6.1-15, 7.54-59, and 11.19-26. For even if Luke emphatically states that the accusations raised against Stephen (Acts 6.11-14) are false allegations, something Luke wants to support by the speech he attributes to Stephen (Acts 7 — it is presumed with good reason that the essential parts of this text originated in Hellenistic Jewish circles), it is nevertheless obvious that this group around Stephen has different emphases in its proclamation of Jesus as the Christ than did the original disciples around Peter. Since, however, the tendency toward a fundamental relativizing of Torah and temple, as represented by Stephen, is perhaps not directly traceable to Jesus of Nazareth and his original disciples, it seems most reasonable to consider as the background of Stephen's group that Diaspora Judaism which was characterized by an openness to the world and a positive relationship to universal Hellenistic culture, and which on its own initiative had already reflected on how to overcome the dichotomy between the belief in One God for all humankind and the nationalistic and particularistic effect of every kind of Torah propaganda that simultaneously adhered to the claim that the Torah was given to Israel alone. Because, for example, circumcision and the strict keeping of the Sabbath — the best known and most visible marks of Judaism in classical antiquity — could not be required of every "Gentile", there inevitably arose the tendency to relativize these and other exclusivist Torah regulations which opposed the transformation of faith in the God of Israel into a new kind of "world religion". And, on the other hand, it is easy to understand that Jews who did not share the presuppositions of these Hellenistic men looked upon them as apostates from the faith of their fathers and therefore reacted with vigorous hostility — as did also Paul in the beginning.

The Hellenistic Jewish-*Christian* followers of Stephen now explicitly elevated and made central what was only potentially present in the spontaneous openness of Jesus and his first disciples. The Hellenistic Jews who joined the Jesus movement saw in Jesus' devotion to the religious outcasts and the degraded *among* the Jewish people (and only occasionally, at the fringe, also beyond the borders), the triggering impulse for the notion, which was already latent in them, that God's devotion to all of his creatures among all peoples cannot end with the national and ritual-cultic boundaries of the One People, chosen and distinguished by means of the Torah, but, to the contrary, must rather genuinely benefit all human beings in like manner and by the same "right" — and must therefore be made known also to all through missionary preaching.

In my opinion, it is remarkable that not even Luke gives the impression that this view — which was fundamental for his writings — had already been fully present and transformed into missionary activity from the beginning of earliest Christian proclamation. He rather presents the reader with a developmental process which plays itself out in numerous stages: personal (Peter, Stephen, Philip, Barnabas, Paul), geographical (Jerusalem, surroundings, Samaria, Cyprus, Antioch, etc.; the ambiguous status of Damascus remains striking), and according to human groups (Jews, "God-fearers", Gentiles). Also the last mentioned is once again, and with greater differentiation, presented in Acts 11.19-26: the followers of Stephen, who were driven from their home in Jerusalem, come to Phoenicia, Cyprus, and Antioch, where in the beginning they speak only to Jews; only then do Diaspora Jews from Cyprus and Cyrene, who have newly been won to the Christian faith, enter into mission work there and complete the next step (which then, so to speak, required still another boost out of Hellenistic Diaspora Jewish circles): they begin with the proclamation to the Hellenistic non-Jews of Antioch. It is my opinion, as already suggested above, that Luke here generally follows the outlines of the accounts he received from the church in Antioch — that church which first called itself "Christianoi" (or was so called) because it could no longer be integrated into the Jewish synagogue community.[24]

IV. "Praeparatio evangelica"

Considering the consequences to world history of the onslaught of this contingent of primitive Christianity, then one can probably speak without exaggeration of the literally epoch-making significance of Hellenistic Judaism (or more precisely, that contingent within Hellenistic Judaism which was open to humanity) for primitive Christianity and thereby for Christianity, the later (Gentile Christian) church, as a whole.[25]

---

24. The discussion regarding an "Antiochian source", accessible to Luke, should not and cannot be continued here. Basically, I consider the position represented, for example, by A. von Harnack, as correct; but I leave open the question whether the "Antiochian source" should be thought of as a coherent, composed literary work or rather as (oral or written) individual traditions.

25. The article by P. Borgen, "The Early Church and the Hellenistic Synagogue" (ST 37 [1983] 55-78), which, according to its title, would appear to be closely related to our present contribution, approaches the subject, however, from a different perspective; Borgen is concerned, on one hand, with analogies regarding the relationship between Hellenistic synagogues and, on the other hand, primitive Christian churches (in the environment of Jewish Diaspora) vis-à-vis the culture and everyday world of Hellenism, particularly its religious environment. He supposes that primitive Christian churches oriented their behavior primarily according to the behavior of the Diaspora synagogue toward the proselytes or according to the behavior demanded by the proselytes, though, of course, not without certain differences.

In one of his major works, to which he gave the title *Euangelikē proparaskeuē*, Eusebius described God's preparation for the Christian faith God through the Old Covenant — especially also by utilizing evidence from Greek-speaking Judaism; he was convinced that herewith he was tracing a redemptive line of God's movement in history. Referring to this, Martin Hengel and Hermann Lichtenberger have,[26] in my opinion rightly, spoken of the *praeparatio evangelica* which Hellenistic Judaism performed for primitive Christianity and thereby for the Gentile church. That is, Hellenistic Judaism thought through (or at least began to think about) the possibility of relating that revelation of God, given to the people of Israel in the Torah, to all humanity, and certainly not with the intention of "Judaizing" humankind by intensive proselytizing (as a certain variation of the notion of "the pilgrimage of the nations to Zion"), but rather by understanding the Torah as universal law (that is — to express it in the terms just used — in the sense of a cosmic extension of "Zion"), neglecting those references in the Torah which constitute, so to speak, Israel's national mark of distinction among the "nations". This represents quite considerable preparation accomplished by Hellenistic Judaism, a genuine "praeparatio" for the proclamation of the Christian gospel to all nations, as it appears in the Gospel of Matthew (which most probably came from Antioch) in the final and programmatic words of the risen Lord to his disciples, where it was made their responsibility (Matt 29.18-20). I believe that the pre-Pauline Gentile mission, and then also Paul's mission to the Gentiles, cannot be fully described factually without these preparations by Hellenistic Jews, unless one wants to set aside a clearly nameable component of the dawning history of the Christian church.

Concluding Remarks

Not without reason have I in the foregoing presentation put aside the role of the translation of the Hebrew text into Greek, that is, the role of the *Septuagint* in its original sense (meaning only the Pentateuch), as well as its more complete form (encompassing the entire "Old Testament" of the early church). Of course, the entire development of Hellenistic Judaism as such is conceivable only against the background of this translation — a unique intellectual achievement, since one is dealing with the first compact (even if not done at one go) translation of a comprehensive corpus of literature from an oriental into an "occidental" language. It is controversial, however, to what extent this translation itself should be considered already a part of the process of the Hellenization of Jewish thinking.

---

26. M. Hengel and H. Lichtenberger, "Die Hellenisierung des antiken Judentums als Praeparatio Evangelica", *Humanistische Bildung* (1981), Heft 4, 1-30.

In my opinion, the translation of the Torah into Greek *as such* (and then also of the other Hebrew writings) should not be considered evidence of the process of the Hellenization of Alexandrian Judaism. On one hand, contemporary research again, more than in previous times, considers it possible that this translation was set into motion by the Ptolemies, therefore initiated more or less for administrative and political reasons, in order to enable the *ethnos* of Jews in Alexandria to live according to the "laws of the fathers" — laws, however, which then had to be accessible also to non-Jews, for example, to administrative officials, in the Greek language.[27] On the other hand, one can perhaps say — for example, along with Robert Hanhart[28] — that the Septuagint is the truest possible rendering of the Torah into the Greek language, a rendering which has no other aim than to reproduce the contents of the Torah as precisely as possible, though now in Greek. (Admittedly, already the grandson of Jesus Sirach, in the prologue to his translation of his grandfather's proverbs, makes it clear to his readers that that is an unattainable ideal, whereas, on the other hand, Alexandrian Jews such as Aristobulus and Philo have no doubt that this rendering corresponds exactly to the original text.) In any case, it is true that the Greek *nomos* aims to be precisely the *nomos* of the Greek-speaking Alexandrian *Jews*, the *nomos* of a Judaism bound to the Sinai covenant, the Torah, and divine election.

In practice, nevertheless, Hellenisms were unavoidable right from the start. One need only think of the rendering of the Hebrew name for God in Exod 3.14. Less obviously Hellenistic, on the other hand, is the Septuagint's tendency (though by no means consistently carried through) to avoid anthropomorphisms, since very similar phenomena can also be observed in contemporary and later Palestinian exegesis and in the Targums. And, for example, the mention of the ibis among the unclean animals (Lev 11.17; Deut 14.16) indeed shows that the translators keep their contemporary environment in view; but this does constitute "Hellenization". Of course, the longer the process of translation took, as it extended beyond the Torah to the remaining writings, the more one must reckon with genuine Hellenistic features. In this regard, one should make precise distinctions from writing to writing, and that means from translator to

27. Thus e.g. E. Bickerman, "The Septuagint as a Translation" [1959], *Studies in Jewish and Christian History*, I (Leiden: Brill, 1976) 167-200 (esp. 171-175), as well as — with reference to Bickerman — K. Schubert, *Die Kultur der Juden, I: Israel im Altertum* (Handbuch der Kulturgeschichte; Wiesbaden: Athenaion, 1970) 120, 141-143.

28. Of the numerous pertinent articles by R. Hanhart I here name: "Fragen um die Entstehung der LXX", *VT* 12 (1962) 139-163, and "Die Bedeutung der Septuaginta für die Definition des 'hellenistischen Judentums' ", *Congress Volume Jerusalem 1986* (ed. J.A. Emerton; VTSup 40; Leiden: Brill, 1988) 67-80.

translator; the relevant research has already borne much fruit.[29] However, no-where in the Septuagint can one recognize a tendency among the translators to abandon the national identity of Judaism in favor of a universal application of the translated Torah.

Still, once this translation was available, it set some of its readers and interpreters on the way to an intellectual opening to the "Gentiles", the more so as these persons occupied themselves with Greek thinking and allowed themselves to be enriched by it. And to this extent even the Septuagint itself, as translation, already participates in the triggering of this later process which was so important to primitive Christianity.

For precisely this reason the inclusion of the Septuagint (henceforth in the wider sense of the word) in the biblical canon of the Christian church is logical and essential, particularly if the Christian church does not want to forget, or even disavow, its original ties to the people of God of the Hebrew Bible. It is not clear, on the other hand, why there was an effort after the fact in the third century, initiated primarily by Jerome, to harmonize the scope of the Christian Bible, or rather its Old Testament section, with the canon of the contemporary Hebrew Bible, which had in the meantime been fixed. (To harmonize meant, in this case, to reduce.) This harmonization made rabbinic decisions regarding the size of the canon (which for the rabbis was centered completely on the Torah) the measure also for the scope of the Christian canon.[30] And what applies to the scope of the canon is applicable, to the same or an even greater extent, to the language: the Christian church must recognize the Greek Torah and the Greek text of the remaining writings as being at least as "canonical" as the Hebrew text, as surely as the latter — for the majority of Old Testament writings — is and remains the "original text" in the philological and historical sense and, as such, naturally continues to be relevant also for Christian exegetes and theologians.

That Judaism, and thereby also Jewish theology, thinks differently regarding this question, goes without saying. It did not participate in that step toward opening itself to the "Gentiles", or more precisely put, after AD 70, during its own "formative" phase, it reversed the step and emphatically blocked it for centuries. The clearest evidence for this blocking out of any further Hellenization and

---

29. Cf. the survey of research by E. Tov, "Die griechischen Bibelübersetzungen", *ANRW II 20/1* (Berlin: de Gruyter, 1987) 121-189, esp. 135-151; as well as Tov's "The Septuagint", *Mikra. Text, Translation, Reading and Interpretation of the Hebrew Bible in Ancient Judaism and Early Christianity* (M.J. Mulder, ed.; CRINT 2:2; Assen, 1988) 161-188.

30. On this cf. also my article "'Bücher: so nicht der heiligen Schrift gleich gehalten ... '? Karlstadt, Luther — und die Folgen", *Tragende Tradition* (Festschrift M. Seils, ed. A. Freund, U. Kern and A. Radler [Frankfurt: P.Lang, 1992], 173-197).

openness to the "Gentiles" is the complete elimination of the Septuagint and all Jewish literature written in Greek from the process of tradition in Judaism. If it had not entered into the process of tradition of the Christian church, it would have practically disappeared without a trace; even from the works of Josephus, who can only to a certain extent be considered a "Hellenistic" Jewish author in the strict sense, only an abbreviated Hebrew summary of his writing, done by Hegesippus (4th cent.) and the so-called Josippon (10th cent.), and similar chronological works would have remained known — but even these would have no longer been possible without the Christian transmission of Josephus.

That this loss to inner Jewish tradition was neither inadvertent nor accidental, but rather the result of a conscious decision, is evident in rabbinic tradition itself, which was conscious of the fact that the Greek translation of the "scriptures" ultimately tended to open up to the "nations" the traditions of Israel. Rabbi Jehuda b. Shalom, who was active in Palestine around 370 (that is, during the progressive Christianization of the Roman Empire), handed down the following Haggada (P^{e}siqta Rabbati 5$^{(14b)}$): Moses desired that the Mishnah also be given to him *in written form* (as the Torah had been); God refused to do this because he anticipated that the gentiles (!) would then translate also the Mishnah into Greek (and thereby take it away from Israel); they would then say that the Israelites were not the true Israel. Rather, they would say (because they already had the Greek translation of the Torah): We are (the true) Israel; we are the children of God. And Israel will then have only *one* piece of opposing evidence on which to base its case, namely, the oral tradition of the Mishnah entrusted to them alone, which they have not shared with the "nations".[31] According to this perspective of a rabbinic scholar from the fourth century, the oral Torah is the only remaining guarantor of Israel's identity, since the written Torah, which could be and actually was translated into Greek, has become the universal property of the "nations" — in reality, of the Christian churches. The day the Greek translation of the Torah was completed, which was celebrated annually by Alexandrian Judaism as an auspicious day, now had become a day that called Jewish identity into question, an ominous day.

---

31. Cf. [H.L. Strack and] P.Billerbeck, *Kommentar zum Neuen Testament aus Talmud und Midrasch*, 1 (Munich: Beck, 1922) 219-220. Cf. also the rabbinic verdicts on the Septuagint from the *Sepher Tora* (1 § 8) and from the appendix to the early rabbinic scroll on fasting (*Megillat Ta'anit*, 13), in P.Billerbeck, 4 (Munich: Beck, 1928) 408 or 414.

The so-called Pseudepigrapha of the Old Testament and Early Christianity

M. de Jonge

1. The problem

Much has been written on the Pseudepigrapha of the Old Testament, particularly about those which are thought to be of Jewish origin. They have been studied as sources for the history and thought of Judaism in the time between 200 BC and AD 100. They have especially been used as witnesses to the diversity of Judaism in that period – and, of course, also to throw light on the origins of the Jesus movement and early Christianity. The Pseudepigrapha were thus studied as Jewish writings, though transmitted by Christians (just as the writings of Philo and Josephus); sometimes interpolated by the Christians or redacted more thoroughly, sometimes also seemingly free from contamination. Scholars were confident that they could reconstruct the original Jewish texts with the help of customary text-critical and literary-critical methods, and then use those "original" documents for historical investigations into the ideas of Judaism in the period around the beginning of the common era. Forty years of study of the Testaments of the Twelve Patriarchs have made me aware of the many pitfalls encountered by scholars who want to pursue the track leading backwards from one particular document, which has come down to us because Christians thought it worth while to copy it, to a possible early Jewish text underneath it, or at least to Jewish material incorporated into it. In a separate essay I have described the road to be followed in the case of the Testaments, and the various aspects of the transmission of this type of literature by Christians. The situation will be different in the case of other Pseudepigrapha of the Old Testament, but it is clear that certain questions will always crop up. Hence, I shall briefly summarize my findings in the case of the Testaments at the end of this introductory essay.

The so-called Pseudepigrapha of the Old Testament have to be read primarily as writings transmitted by Christians throughout many centuries. They were transmitted because copyists regarded them as important, and were of the opinion that they could function meaningfully in the communities for which they copied them. Transmission clearly presupposes the enduring relevance of what is transmitted. In early Christianity as well as in the Middle Ages, and even later, Christians all over the Christian world were interested in narratives, wisdom books, psalms, apocalypses, testaments etcetera centering around figures known from the Old Testament (I use this term deliberately in this connection, and do not speak about the Jewish Bible). Are we able to say anything more about their importance, and about the nature of their authority? Only when we understand the function of these writings in the circles in which they were transmitted, the questions connected with the provenance of the material involved, and with the possible Christian adaptation of it, may be answered satisfactorily. So much is clear: much careful analysis has to be carried out before a particular pseudepigraphon can be used as a source for our knowledge of early Judaism or of Christianity in the first century.

2. Recent contributions to the study of the problem

A number of older studies of the problem in hand have been reviewed by G.B. Coleman in his "The Phenomenon of Christian Interpolations into Jewish Apocalyptic Texts: A Bibliographical Survey and Methodological Analysis".[1] He gives extensive bibliographical information (until 1970) for the Apocalypse and the Testament of Abraham, The Life of Adam and Eve (Apocalypse for Moses), the Greek Apocalypse of Baruch, 1 and 2 Enoch, 4 Ezra, the Ascension of Isaiah, the Sibylline Oracles and the Testaments of the Twelve Patriarchs. In another chapter he analyses the problem expressed in the title of the Ascension of Isaiah, the Parables of Enoch (1 Enoch 37-71) and the Testaments of the Twelve Patriarchs; the other writings mentioned are only discussed very briefly. In a brief but important final chapter Coleman emphasizes the impossibility of distinguishing between "Jewish" and "Christian" elements; next he stresses that in all cases the writings were read by Christians as writings meant for Christians; finally, he reminds us of the necessity to apply redaction criticism and to ask for the "life-situation" presupposed in the document; at the same time he wants to continue the search for Jewish origins.

Of great value is Robert A. Kraft's programmatic article "The Multiform Jewish Heritage of Early Christianity" of 1975,[2] followed in the next year by a contribution "Reassessing the 'Recensional Problem' in Testament of Abraham " to a volume Studies in the Testament of Abraham edited by George W.E. Nickelsburg.[3] First of all Kraft emphasizes that we should use the terms "Jewish" and "Christian" as neutrally as possible, taking into account the great variety in Judaism and Christianity during the first centuries of the common era. We should also consider the possibility that for certain persons the distinction between "Christian" and "Jewish" was not very relevant — at least

---

1. Ph.D. Diss. Vanderbilt, 1976 (available through University Microfilms).
2. It appeared in J. Neusner (ed.), *Christianity, Judaism and other Greco-Roman Cults* FS Morton Smith (Leiden: E.J. Brill, 1975), 3, 174-99.
3. SBLSCS 6 (Missoula, Mont.: Scholars Press, 1976) 121-37. See also Kraft's study on a related problem "Christian Transmission of Greek Jewish Scriptures: A Methodological Probe," *Paganisme, Judaïsme, Christianisme. Mélanges offerts à Marcel Simon* (ed. A. Benoît; Paris: de Boccard, 1978), 207-26.

in certain respects. Although the so-called Pseudepigrapha of the Old Testament were transmitted as literature for Christians, characteristically Christian interests and ideas were not always in evidence. "Apparently the orientation of the various Christian users was flexible enough to allow some sort of positive status to these materials without causing serious conflict with 'Christian' ideas".[4] In many cases it is difficult to decide whether transmission entailed copying, redaction, interpolation or even composition. These processes may not even be mutually exclusive. Certainly we may never assume that "Christian" interest always betrayed itself by leaving "Christian" traces. "It should not be assumed that a document composed or compiled by a Christian will necessarily contain characteristically 'Christian' tenets."[5] The evidently Christian elements are usually found in "messianic" texts. "Some Christians seem to have felt it important to have 'predictive' texts (especially apocalyptic) in which aspects of the career and function of their messiah were somehow noted, even if only cryptically or in passing".[6] In many instances, however, Jewish and Christian ideas ran parallel. Homiletic and liturgical texts (of a various nature, think especially of prayers) could be used in Jewish and Christian communities; the same applies to parenetic material. Moreover, Kraft asserts, "many Christians still looked for a future eschatological / apocalyptic consummation, and thus helped maintain a continuity with similar pre- and non-Christian Jewish interests."[7] He also reminds us that the Greek form of the Jewish Bible was transmitted by Christians without Christian adaptations worth mentioning, at least as far as the earliest form of text is concerned. Also many pseudepigrapha were transmitted over a considerable period of time without noticeable adaptation (see e.g. the Ethiopic Enoch cycle). Other writings were redacted only superficially or interpolated in only a few places (here Kraft mentions the Testaments of the Twelve Patriarchs — wrongly, in my opinion). We also find cases of thorough reworking of Jewish material and incorporation into Christian compilations without loss of a "Jewish" flavour. As examples are mentioned the Adam-Eve cycle transmitted in various forms in different Christian circles, the Ascension of Isaiah and the Sibylline Oracles. In connection with this last collection Kraft says: "The overtly Christian portions are themselves quite diverse in content and origin, and the total work provides an excellent example of how some types of literature were not 'authored' in any normal sense of the word, but evolved in stages over the years."[8]

Finally, we should remember that a considerable number of fragments

4. "Jewish Heritage", 179-80.
5. "Recensional Problem", 135.
6. "Jewish Heritage", 180.
7. "Recensional Problem", 136.
8. "Jewish Heritage", 184-85.

from Hellenistic-Jewish authors have only come down to us because Eusebius of Caesarea copied them for his Praeparatio Evangelica, composed in the beginning of the fourth century. Of course, shorter quotations and allusions are also found in the works of other Christian authors. Kraft has very cogently demonstrated the necessity of systematically studying "Jewish" literature transmitted through Christian channels as part of the "Christian" heritage. Much more study should be devoted to this problem than it has received so far. There is yet another aspect of this complex matter to which he attracts our attention: In Christian circles this material circulated in a Greek form — often lost, and then only recoverable through ancient versions dependent on it — but it seems likely that it existed earlier in Hebrew or Aramaic.[9] But who translated it, and when and where? All along there must have been intensive contacts between Hebrew or Aramaic and Greek speaking Jews, but how the writings of interest to us were translated, we do not know. Moreover, as he remarks elsewhere, it is extremely difficult to distinguish between translation Greek and "biblical" Greek that Christians considered suitable for this type of literature.[10] Not to mention the fact that certain sections incorporated in a writing may indeed go back to Semitic sources, whilst the rest may have been composed in a language inspired by the Greek Bible.

In 1986 Kraft received support and approval from Michael E. Stone in a clear article called "Categorization and Classification of the Apocrypha and Pseudepigrapha."[11] His position is brought out very clearly in the following statement:

Documents for which there is no independent early corroboration or other compelling evidence can no longer just be used, with no more ado, as sources for Judaism of the Second Temple period. Indeed, some of them are undoubtedly just that; others, I am sure, are reworkings of Jewish documents or traditions from that period and contain material of extraordinary importance for the study of Judaism and Christian origins. The position here being maintained is not nihilistic; it is a call for greater methodological sophistication, while making no presuppositions as to the results thus obtained. Indeed, it is reasonable to think that the antiquity of some works will be confirmed, while others will be shown to incorporate Jewish sources or traditions. Nonetheless, before the Pseudepigrapha and similar writings are used

---

9. "Jewish Heritage", 194-96.
10. "Recensional Problem", 127-35.
11. *Abr-Nahrain* 24 (1986), 167-77. See also his "The Metamorphosis of Ezra: Jewish Apocalypse and Medieval Vision", *JTS* n.s. 33 (1982), 1-18, now in M.E. Stone, *Selected Studies in Pseudepigrapha & Apocrypha with Special Reference to the Armenian Tradition* (SVTP 9; Leiden: Brill, 1991), 359-76. Compare also R.A. Kraft, "'Ezra' Materials in Judaism and Christianity," *ANRW* II.19.1 (Berlin, 1979), 119-36.

as evidence for that more ancient period, they must be examined in the Christian context in which they were transmitted and utilized.[12]

J.H. Charlesworth, the editor of two well-known volumes, *The Old Testament Pseudepigrapha*[13] has shown himself an advocate of an inclusive definition of that term. His collection includes no less than fifty-two writings plus a long supplement with fragments of lost Judaeo-Hellenistic works. In the introduction to his first volume he writes: "the Pseudepigrapha must be defined broadly so as to conclude all documents that conceivably belong to the Old Testament Pseudepigrapha" . He says that they "almost always were composed either during the period 200 BC to AD 200 or, though late, apparently preserve, albeit in an edited form, Jewish traditions that date from that period" (p. xxv). One would expect him to be particularly interested in the complicated and variegated history of the transmission of these pseudepigrapha. Yet we find comparatively little on that subject in his introductory book *The Old Testament Pseudepigrapha and the New Testament*.[14] In the section on "Dating the Evidence" (pp. 31-46) we find a number of relevant remarks, but the reader who wants to know whether particular passages reliably portray ideas current in early Judaism and therefore may be used for a better understanding of early Christianity, does not receive sufficient guidance. He hears that a number of the writings are too late, and receives a long list of clearly pre-Christian documents. He is told that the tradition history of writings only preserved in Slavonic languages has been extremely complex, and that also other writings are Christian in their present form. Relative certainty of pre-Christian origin is provided by quotations in early Christian writers (beginning with the author of the Epistle of Jude), extant fragments in early papyri and, of course, the presence of Hebrew or Aramaic fragments of these documents (or of writings related to them) among the Qumran scrolls. The final answer is that one may use the pseudepigrapha for a better understanding of the New Testament documents, but that the New Testament scholar "needs to be guided constantly by a specialist in this vast expanse of documents, sources, Jewish interpolations, Jewish redactions, later Christian interpolations, and Christian redactions" [15]. An earlier article, called "Christian and Jewish Self-definition in Light of the Christian Additions to the Apocryphal writings" deals, as the title indicates, with only part of the problem involved.[16] Here, Charlesworth excludes the documents preserved only in Slavonic languages, those that are clearly

---

12. "Categorization", 172-73.
13. (Garden City, New York: Doubleday) 1983-1985.
14. SNTSMS 54 (Cambridge: Cambridge University Press, 1985).
15. Op. cit., p. 44.
16. It is found in E.P. Sanders, A.I. Baumgarten and Alan Mendelson (eds.), *Jewish and Christian Self-definition II. Aspects of Judaism in the Graeco-Roman Period* (London: SCM, 1981), 27-55.

Christian, and those which have received little significant addition. In the end he is left with five documents that have received considerable Christian additions: Hellenistic Synagogal Prayers (as transmitted in the Apostolic Constitutions),[17] the Testaments of the Twelve Patriarchs, Martyrdom and Ascension of Isaiah, 4 Ezra (in its Latin version transmitted together with chapters 1-2 and 15-16, both Christian documents) and the Sibylline Oracles. Although he realizes how difficult the exact delineation of Christian additions from the period after AD 70 is, he nevertheless sees no problem in analysing them with the purpose of finding out how they functioned in efforts of Christians to determine their own stand vis-à-vis Judaism. These additions help us to see how early Christianity achieved "normative self-definition" in an variety of ways. However, "as the canon took shape and became normative in the Christian communities, the Christians who depended on the 'apocryphal' books were eventually moved to the fringes of triumphant Christianity. Their own interpolations and expansions provide us with a rare glimpse into their ideas. We receive a significant reminder of the existence of non-normative Christianity". [18] Charlesworth's approach is limited in purpose and method. He takes for granted that we are able to distinguish Christian additions in originally Jewish writings; he analyses changes without taking into account how much was transmitted without change. A positive point is his attempt to do justice to the non-normative elements in Christian "self-definition" but, in the end, his contribution does not offer much help in our present search.

G.N. Stanton's article "Aspects of Early Christian-Jewish Polemic and Apologetic",[19] on the other hand, opens interesting perspectives. He stresses the point that contacts and polemic between Christian and Jewish groups did not end after AD 70. He points to Justin's Dialogue with Trypho, and especially to chapter 108 in that document where he discovers a "Sin-Exile-Return pattern", a form often used in the apocalyptic passages in the Testaments of the Twelve Patriarchs. Stanton also finds it in Matt 23.38-39, the final verses of the harangue against the scribes and the Pharisees in Matthew, and he demonstrates how this pattern serves Christian apologetic against Judaism. The pattern underlines the continuity in God's intention and in his actions, it leaves room for Israel's refusal to accept Jesus as Messiah, but also for final repentance of at least some in Israel. Also in the Testaments of the Twelve Patriarchs we find severe criticism of the leaders of Israel, especially the priests, with, at the same time, the desire to stress the continuity and connection in the persons of the patriarchs, the fathers of Israel. The same approach is found in Stanton's

---

17. See also D.A. Fiensy, *Prayers alleged to be Jewish. An Examination of the Constitutiones Apostolorum* (BJS 65; Chico, Ca.: Scholars Press, 1985).
18. Charlesworth, op.cit., p. 77.
19. *NTS* 31 (1985), 377-92; see now his *A Gospel for a New People. Studies in Matthew* (Edinburgh: T.& T. Clark, 1992) 232-55.

earlier article "5 Ezra and Matthean Christianity in the Second Century."[20] Stanton regards 5 Ezra as a writing very much influenced by the Gospel of Matthew, with the replacement of Israel by a new people of God as its main theme. It is an apologetic document that explains why the secession from Israel took place, and tries to support the Christian group concerned in persecution. Nevertheless the continuity between this group and Israel receives attention. "This suggests a community primarily concerned to establish its continuity with Israel in spite of a recent final rupture for which a thorough explanation has to be found."[21]

Georg Kretschmar, in a tantalizingly short section of his very informative article "Die Kirche aus Juden und Heiden. Forschungsprobleme der ersten christlichen Jahrhunderte",[22] describes the group of writings under discussion as "crypto-Christian" and connects these documents with a broad movement of Jewish Christianity (not to be identified with any of the Jewish-Christian groups mentioned by heresiologists), eventually going back to the Hellenistic-Jewish Christianity of New Testament times (see e.g. the Epistle of James). As an example, Kretschmar mentions the Testaments of the Twelve Patriarchs which must have received their present form in a Christian group that chose to express its convictions in words ascribed to fictitious authors known from the Old Testament; the message about Christ is given by them in the form of veiled promises, understandable only to the initiated. In this group of writings all emphasis is on the continuity in the history of salvation, whatever literary genre one may prefer. Besides the Testaments pursuing the Wisdom tradition, there is the Ascension of Isaiah for which the apocalyptic form was chosen.

Kretschmar emphasizes that crypto-Christian texts of this type serve, in fact, as additions to the Holy Scriptures of Israel, taken over in the canon of the Christian Church. They should be studied together with the so-called NT apocrypha, and subsumed under the category of "Christian apocryphal writings", as the editors of the Series Apocryphorum of the Corpus Christianorum have suggested.

3. Some special studies

The studies referred to above are nearly all of a more general nature. In the present much shorter section I want to mention a number of studies devoted to individual writings. Besides the Testaments of the Twelve Patriarchs

---

20. *JTS* n.s. 28 (1977), 67-83; see now *A Gospel for a New People*, 256-77.
21. "5 Ezra," 77-78. At the end of his article Stanton mentions the Nag Hammadi Gospel of Peter, a writing that, in his view, is also thoroughly Matthean.
22. In J. van Amersfoort and J. van Oort (eds.), *Juden und Christen in der Antike* (Kampen: Kok, 1990), 9-43; on this question especially pp. 31-35. Another article in this collection relevant to our enquiry is R. van den Broek, "Juden und Christen in Alexandrien im 2. und 3. Jahrhundert," 101-15.

particularly the Lives of the Prophets, 5 Ezra and the Ascension of Isaiah have received attention in recent times. A complete documentation in view of a thorough study of all aspects of the Christians transmission of this type of literature is urgently needed. David Satran of the Hebrew University, Jerusalem has dealt with the Christian transmission of the Lives of the Prophets, e.g. in his contribution "Daniel: Seer, Philosopher, Holy Man" to the volume *Ideal Figures in Ancient Judaism* which appeared in 1980.[23] He tries to prove that the Lives of the Prophets introduce us to the world of monastic asceticism; Daniel adopts the features of the Byzantine holy man. "This is the atmosphere of the passage in Vitae Prophetarum concerning Nebuchadnezzar's repentance. Daniel has prescribed an ascetic diet for the atoning king comparable to that which a monk would take on as a penitential discipline during the Lenten period.[24] Satran, who wrote a dissertation entitled *Early Jewish and Christian Interpretation of the Fourth Chapter of the Book of Daniel*,[25] is about to publish a comprehensive study of the Lives of the Prophets with the title *Biblical Prophets in Byzantine Palestine. Reassessing the Lives of the Prophets*[26].

Much attention has been paid lately to the Ascension of Isaiah. The theory that it is a Christian composition incorporating Jewish material has been revived lately, mainly by Italian scholars.[27] The most recent monograph is A. Acerbi, *L'Ascensione di Isaia. Cristologia e profetismo in Siria nei primi decenni del II seculo*.[28] The author dates the Ascension of Isaiah between AD 100 and 130, and thinks it originated in prophetic circles in Western Syria. A second recent publication is R.G. Hall, "The Ascension of Isaiah: Community, Situation, Date

23. Edited by John J. Collins and George W.E. Nickelsburg, SBLSCS 12 (Chico, Ca.: Scholars Press, 1980) 32-43.
24. Op.cit., 40.
25. Ph.D. Diss. Hebrew University (Jerusalem, 1985) see especially Chapter 8 "The Lives of the Prophets. The 'Vita' of Daniel and Early Byzantine Religiosity", 335-82.
26. It is to appear in the series "Studia in Veteris Testament Pseudepigrapha". See also my study of some Christian elements in the Lives of the Prophets, "Christelijke elementen in de Vitae Prophetarum", *NedTTs* 16 (1961-62), 161-78.
27. See also B. Dehandschutter, "Judentum-Christentum. Das Problem der frühchristlichen Apokalypsen", *Archivio di Filosofia* 53 (1985), 261-66, and J. Verheyden, "L'Ascension d'Isaïe et L'Evangile de Matthieu. Examen de AI 3, 13-18", *The New Testament in Early Christianity. La réception des écrits néotestamentaires dans le christianisme primitif* (ed. J.-M. Sevrin; BETL 86; Leuven: University Press 1989), 247-24. For older studies see G.B. Coleman (note 1), 146-81.
28. Studia Patristica Mediolensia 17 (Milano: Vita e Pensiero, 1989). See also his *Serra lignea. Studi sulla fortuna della Ascensione di Isaia* (Roma: AVE, 1984), and Antonio Acerbi et al., *Isaia, il Diletto e la Chiesa. Visione ed esegesi profetica cristiano-primitiva nell' Ascensione di Isaia* (ed. M. Pesce, Teste e Ricerche di Scienze Religiose 20; Brescia: Paideia, 1983). See noe also E. Norelli, *Ascension du Prophéte Isaïe* (Turnhout: Brepols, 1993).

and Place in Early Christianity."[29] Hall, too, argues that the Ascension of Isaiah stems from a Christian prophetic school in the beginning of the second century, in conflict with other similar schools.

Essential for a proper assessment of 5 Ezra is now Theodore A. Bergren's dissertation *Fifth Ezra. The Text, Origin and Early History*.[30] A few years ago, his *Doktorvater* R.A. Kraft contributed a stimulating essay "Towards Assessing the Latin Text of '5 Ezra'. The 'Christian' Connection" to the *Festschrift* for Krister Stendahl.[31] In it he drew attention to the fact that "the value of the various claims about origin, authorship, date, provenance and 'message' of 5 Ezra is severely compromised by uncertainties about the text".[32] There are two groups of textual witnesses, a "French" and a "Spanish" one, the first of which has generally been followed in the editions and commentaries. According to Kraft (and Bergren), the Spanish text-type is nearer to the original than the French one; in this they follow the assessment of M.R. James.[33] According to James, the Spanish text-type is more clearly Christian than the secondary French one; the latter not only writes better Latin, but also tries to sound more Jewish. Kraft is not sure; he writes: James's suggestion that the complicated Latin textual situation in 5 Ezra preserves evidence in SA (representatives of the French type, dJ) of Christian de-Christianization of a would-be 'Jewish' text is exciting, and deserves close scrutiny. My own tentative conclusion is that he is wrong in this instance (but not necessarily for every other writing as well), and that the MEC type of text (the Spanish one, dJ) can be understood better as a relic of pre- or non-Christian 'Judaism' in its broader sense.[34] In a recent article Bergren tried to demonstrate this in the case of 5 Ezra 1.38 'Iam, pater, aspice cum gloria et vide populum venientem ab oriente'.[35] Because of the phrase "from the East" it is difficult to find a characteristic Christian "ideological setting", many parallels point to an

29. *JBL* 109 (1990), 289-06. See now also D. Lührmann, "Alttestamentliche Pseudepigraphen bei Didymos von Alexandrien", *ZAW* 104 (1992) 231-49.

30. SBLSCS 25 (Atlanta, Georgia: Scholars Press, 1990).

31. George W.E. Nickelsburg and George W. MacRae (eds.), *Christians among Jews and Gentiles. Essays in Honor of Krister Stendahl on His Sixty-fifth Birthday* (Philadelphia: Fortress Press, 1986 = *HTR* 79 [1986]), 158-69.

32. Op.cit., p. 159.

33. In his introduction to R.L. Bensly, *The Fourth Book of Ezra* (TextsS 3/2.; (Cambridge: Cambridge University Press, 1895); see #6 "The text of the additional chapters", xliv-lxxviii.

34. Op.cit., 167.

35. *JBL* 108 (1989), 657-83. See also his contribution "Christian Influence on the Transmission History of 4, 5 and 6 Ezra" to a forthcoming collection of essays, *Jewish Apocalyptic in Early Christian Literature*, edited by J.C. VanderKam; and compare P. Geoltrain, "Remarques sur la diversité des pratiques discursives apocryphes. L'exemple de 5 Esdras", *Apocrypha, le champ des apocryphes. La fable apocryphe 2* (Turnhout: Brepols, 1992), 17-30.

originally Jewish context. Bergren regards 5 Ezra in its present form as Christian, but concludes that in this verse we have a case of borrowing and adaptation on the part of Christians. "The employment of Jewish themes and motifs within 'Christian' settings represents one of the fundamental formative dynamics of Christian origins, and such motifs form much of the foundation of early Christian ideology".[36] All problems related to the provenance of 5 Ezra have now been treated in Bergren's dissertation, on the basis of a detailed study of the primary sources resulting in a critical edition of the Latin text.

4. The Testaments of the Twelve Patriarchs

In conclusion, it may be useful to mention a number of issues that proved to be important in the study of the Christian transmission of the Testaments of the Twelve Patriarchs; for details the reader is referred to my separate study on the topic.[37]

a. The Testaments (and other writings) have come down to us because in different periods scribes were interested in them and regarded them as relevant. Studying their transmission we have to work our way backward, from the Middle Ages to the period in which they originated. It is important to know why such writings were transmitted and how they functioned in the life of Christian communities. In the case of the Testaments we know that, in the thirteenth century, Bishop Robert Grosseteste had them brought to England and translated them into Latin, because he wanted to make abundantly clear to the Jews and all possible other adversaries of the true doctrine that salvation is to be expected exclusively from Jesus Christ and from the true Church that abides by Scripture. We have many marginal notes in the medieval Greek manuscripts; particularly frequent is the gloss περὶ χριστοῦ. We also get a glimpse of their use (in a Dutch translation, made from Latin and known from fifteenth century manuscripts) in circles of the Modern Devotion. In an epilogue, the person responsible for this translation says: "Here end the sermons and the testaments of the twelve patriarchs children of Jacob the patriarch which they made at the very end of their lives in which they narrate a part of their lives with a variety of good examples and teaching which they taught to their children and commanded them to practise". Somewhat later, in the sixteenth century, the Testaments were probably used (in an other translation) in the chiliastic movement of David Joris.

---

36. Bergren, op.cit., 682.
37. See M. de Jonge, "The Transmission of the Twelve Patriarchs by Christians", *VC* **47** (1993), 1-28.

b. Study of the textual history proper and textual criticism are essential to determine the shape and the date of the archetype of the existing witnesses. In the case of the Testaments (as, no doubt, also in the case of other writings) it is important to examine the transition from uncial to minuscule script in the Byzantine empire in the ninth century. It is likely that the Testaments were transcribed twice; hence the archetype of our textual tradition must go back beyond the ninth century. The Armenian version of the Testaments is of importance in this respect; unfortunately its date cannot yet be established with certainty.

For other pseudepigraphical writings earlier witnesses of (at least part of) the text are known, in Greek, Latin, Coptic or Syriac. This may alter the situation considerably, though in the case of fragments we must be careful in extrapolating from the part(s) to the entire document. The same applies in the case of quotations in early Christian and Byzantine authors.

c. It is necessary to investigate the evidence for a non-Christian transmission of a document or parts of it. The finds of fragments at Qumran have proved important in some cases, e.g. that of Enoch and that of Jubilees. For the Testament of Levi the situation is clearly complicated. This Testament goes back to a Vorlage (in Greek, or Aramaic) akin to the Levi document of which fragments have been found at Qumran, in the Cairo Genizah and even (in Greek) in additions to the text of T. Levi in the eleventh century MS Athos, Koutloumous 39. We should speak of parallel transmission in Jewish and Christian circles (with an interesting, and so far unexplained, contact in the case of the Greek manuscript just mentioned or one of its ancestors).

d. The history of the transmission of the Testaments between the third and the eighth centuries cannot be followed in detail. From a short quotation in Origen's Homilies on Joshua we may conclude that he attributed at least some authority to the Testaments and that they existed in the beginning of the third century. On the basis of parallels with other authors from the last half of the second century and the beginning of the third (Justin, Irenaeus and Hippolytus) it is likely that they came into being at the end of the second century. Their exact contents at the time remain unknown; a number of passages may later have undergone interpretation or redaction, and we may keep in mind Robert Kraft's remark about "evolving" literature, but an exact delineation of later elements is completely impossible. This also applies to the variegated Christological passages, in view of the great diversity in Christological approaches in early Christianity before (in at least certain circles) standards of orthodoxy were maintained. Moreover, the Testaments purport to be the last words of the sons of Jacob, who are portrayed as announcing, from their own perspective, what would happen in the future, including the coming of the Saviour.

e. The Testaments assume continuity in the history of salvation. Their author(s) took the Jewish scriptures very seriously, and concomitant Jewish traditions were readily adopted. Tradition critical investigation of parallel material, in Jewish and Christian writings, is very important for a better understanding of the contents of the Testaments and of their functioning in early Christianity. Equally relevant is comparison with the ways in which Old Testament passages were treated in early Christian commentaries. As an example one may mention Hippolytus's commentary on Gen 49 and Deut 33. This does not yield many direct parallels but shows that to Hippolytus and his readers Jesus was to be connected with Levi as well as with Judah.

f. The Testaments give, first and foremost, ethical instruction – influenced by the Psalms and the Wisdom books of the LXX; the Cynic-Stoic philosophical tradition and early Christian sources offer many parallels. In the field of ethics there has been a considerable measure of continuity between Hellenistic Judaism and certain circles in early Christianity. Many utterances in the Testaments are Jewish as well as Christian, and at the same time acceptable to Hellenistic fellow-citizens of Jews and Christians.Of special importance are statements by Justin, Irenaeus and Tertullian concerning the faith of the patriarchs and their obedience to God's commandments in the time before Moses, and the concentration on the two commandments (love of God and love of one's neighbour) as summary of the Decalogue after the coming of Jesus Christ — in fact bypassing the law of Moses considered as meant only for Israel and only for a limited period. To these pre-Mosaic patriarchs belong the sons of Jacob, who in their testaments could formulate what was essential for the true service of God, in their own period and in the time after Jesus Christ, whose coming they announced. Their message is important for Christians, as well as for Jews; it is the twelve tribes of Israel that are addressed in the Testaments.

g. Viewed against the background of what has just been said, the function of the Testaments of the Twelve Patriarchs in early Christianity becomes clear. They formulate how in the time after Jesus Christ God's commandments have to be obeyed, indeed what was God's intention throughout the history of salvation. For Israel, too, it is this obedience that really matters; this is the message contained in the summons by the fathers of the twelve tribes, who also announce the salvation in Christ to Israel. The author(s) of the Testaments was/were clearly anxious about the fate of Israel; he/they wanted to urge the Jews to accept the message of Jesus Christ and to let themselves be persuaded by it. To this end he/they strikingly chose the form of a parenetical tract rather than that of a polemic, apologetic or missionary writing.

5. Conclusion

This is, of necessity, only an introductory essay, and the survey in section 4 was concerned with only one pseudepigraphon of the Old Testament. Yet it has become clear, I hope, how important detailed study of these pseudepigrapha, as writings transmitted by Christians for Christians, is for a better understanding of these documents. Continued study is likely to result in an increasingly differentiated picture of the relations between Jews and Christians belonging to various streams in Christianity in the second and third centuries — and probably also later, in the period after Constantine when Christianity took up a central position in the Roman Empire.

The Son of David: Solomon and Jesus (Mark 10.47)

J.H. Charlesworth

What is the meaning of Bartimaeus' cry to Jesus: υἱὲ Δαυὶδ 'Ιησοῦ, ἐλέησόν με? Who does he think Jesus is?

According to Mark 10 a blind man named Bartimaeus calls out to Jesus υἱὲ Δαυὶδ 'Ιησοῦ, ἐλέησόν με, and then again υἱὲ Δαυὶδ, ἐλέησόν με. He calls on Jesus to restore his sight. The pericope is not easy to understand, and commentators have for centuries customarily interpreted Bartimaeus' exhortation as a recognition of Jesus' Messiahship. The purpose of this essay is to question this exegesis and to raise another possible approach to, and interpretation of, Bartimaeus' cry.

If Mark thought that Bartimaeus was announcing that Jesus was the Messiah, then in light of his tendency to have Jesus silence the confession that he is the Messiah, why does he not have Jesus exhort silence.[1] If, however, Bartimaeus was claiming that Jesus possessed the miraculous powers of Solomon, then we should explore the possibility that the healing is contextually grounded in the narrative and makes sense in the assumed historical setting. This conclusion will have to be built upon the demonstration that Solomon was considered not only the paradigm of the wise man, and not only an exorcist (as is so clear from the Testament of Solomon and other early Jewish traditions), but that he was able to heal someone who was blind.

New Perspectives and Methods

With the abundance of new perceptions into the origins of Christianity some methods and conclusions need modifying and sometimes altering. The new perceptions derive from the increase in literary data that antedate the Bar Kokhba Revolt (AD 132-135). In the sixties, when we considered the Old Testament Pseudepigrapha we usually meant 17 documents, but now we frequently mean at least 65. Then we examined about 12 Dead Sea Scrolls, but now well over 400.

---

1. See W. Wrede, *The Messianiac Secret* (trans. J.C.G. Greig; Greenwood, S.C.: Attic, 1971); C. Tuckett, ed., *The Messianic Secret* (Issues in Religion and Theology 1; London: SPCK, 1983).

In the 1960s, archaeologists held out little hope of finding something significant from the first century AD by which to reconstuct the Herodian and later periods. The last twenty years have alterred that perception. Our understanding of Jerusalem and Lower Galilee have been considerably altered;[2] and this reevaluation is primarily due to unexpected archaeological discoveries.[3]

Hand in glove with the vast amount of realia now available from the time of Hillel and Jesus, and Johanan ben Zakkai and Mark, is the improvement to the historical critical method. Most importantly, is the world-wide recognition that sociology is essential in historical reconstruction. Most importantly, the sensitivity to anthropological and social phenomena found in the works of Max Weber[4] and Emile Durkheim[5] have opened our eyes to what has been before us for almost 2,000 years. In particular Weber's model of the charismatic has profoundly shaped our understanding of the Moreh has-sedek and Jesus of Nazareth,[6] and Durkheim's concept of purity has helped alter us to the social crisis caused by the heightened demands for purification and extended limits of danger that is so obvious form the time of the writing of the Temple Scroll up until the time of the Great Revolt of 66 to 70.[7]

The documentary evidence has forced us to recognize that we can no longer assume, or claim, that many Palestinian Jews were looking for the coming of the Messiah.[8] There is a consensus that we know about only three messianic Jewish groups that antedate AD 70: the group founded by the Moreh has-sedek (which began around the middle of the second century BC), the group who used the psalmbook called the Psalms of Solmon (which dates from the second half of the first century BC and was centered in Jerusalem), and the

---

2. E.M. Meyers and J.F. Strange, *Archaeology: The Rabbis & Early Christianity* (Nashville: Abingdon, 1981) 24, 48-49.

3. See N. Avigad, *Discovering Jerusalem* (New York: Thomas Nelson, 1983); A. Negev, ed., *The Archaeological Encyclopedia of the Holy Land* (New York, London: Prentice-Hall, 1986, 1990 [3rd ed.]); J.H. Charlesworth, *Jesus Within Judaism: New Light from Exciting Archaeological Discoveries* (ABRL 1; New York: Doubleday, 1988).

4. See especially the series titled *Max Weber Gesamtausgabe*, edited by H. Baier, et al., and published by J.C.B. Mohr (Paul Siebeck).

5. E. Durkheim, *The Elementary Forms of the Religious Life* (trans. J.W. Swain; New York: Free Press, 1915, 1965).

6. See especially Charlesworth, "The Righteous Teacher and the Historical Jesus: A Study of the Self-Understandings of Two Jewish Charismatics," *Perspectives on Christology*, ed. W. Weaver (Nashville: Exodus, 1989) 73-94.

7. Fruitful in developing a sociologically informed recreation of life in Jerusalem when the Temple was the focal point of purity and danger are the sociological insights published by M. Douglas in *Purity and Danger* (London, Boston: ARK, 1966,1984).

8. See the studies in Charlesworth, ed., *The Messiah* (Minneapolis: Fortress, 1992).

Palestinian Jesus Movement (which began in the first half of the first century AD and was centered in Galilee and then apparently moved to Jerusalem). Hence, the approach to Christian origins needs to be refined from the possible distortions of reading back into pre-70 Palestinian Judaism the messianic fervor found in the earliest kerygma. Even titles, or terms, which the New Testament authors assumed to be messianic may not have had a messianic denotation during the time of Hillel and Jesus. The present paper helps to illustrate this point by looking at Mark 10.46-52, "The Healing of the Blind Bartimaeus."

Translation and Philological Observations

Here is my translation of Mark 10.46-52:

And they came to Jericho,[9] and when he, his disciples, and a large crowd were leaving Jericho,[10] Bartimaeus the Son of Timaeus,[11] a blind beggar, sat beside the road. And hearing that (the commotion concerned) Jesus of Nazareth,[12] he began to cry out and say,[13] "Son of David, Jesus, have mercy on me." And many rebuked him (urging him) to be silent. But he cried out more (vociferously): "Son of David, have mercy on me." And stopping Jesus said, "Call him." And they called the blind man, saying to him, "Take heart, arise, he calls you." Then[14] throwing off his mantle, as he sprang up[15] he came to Jesus. And answering him,[16] Jesus said, "What do you want me to do for you?" And[17] the blind man said to him,

---

9. This opening phrase is omitted by Vaticanus.
10. The maverick text of Codex Bezae, and some other witnesses substitute for this phrase "there with"; perhaps they considered the phrase redundant.
11. Why does the Greek have the unusual order "the Son of Timaeus, Bartimaeus"? Is emphasis placed on "the Son of Timaeus"; and if so, does that indicate that this unknown person was prominent in or around Jericho?
12. What is this noun articular? It cannot be unnatural in Greek; no Greek scribe omits it. Many witnesses change the noun to an adjective. Apparently the scribes of Codexes B, D, and others, found an articular noun awkward.
13. Some early and important witnesses change the vocative υἱέ to the nominative υἱός; here and in v. 48 minuscule number 28 shows a later propensity: κύριε υἱός.
14. The connective is the mild adversative δέ?
15. Note the lack of a connective before "springing up"; the asyndetic contiguity seems to denote that he was casting off his mantle as he was springing up.
16. This is a well-known Semitism; Bartimaeus has not asked Jesus anything.
17. Greek δέ.
18. Gk. ἀναβλέπω; apparently we are being told that Bartimaeus has not been blind from birth (as is the case with ἄνθρωπον τυφλὸν ἐκ γενετῆς in John 9.1). A strictly philological or etymological approach to New Testament Greek can be misleading; the literary and social context of a pericope is obviously a key to unlocking the

"Rabbouni, to see again."[18] And Jesus[19] said to him, "Go, your faith has saved you." And immediately he saw again and followed him on the way.

This pericope elicits numerous questions. In the order in which they appear, here are the most impressive one:

Why Jericho?

Does the ὄχλος ("crowd, mob") function narratively like the Greek chorus?

What is the meaning of the Semitisms: Bartimaeus son of Timaeus, "began to cry out and say," Jesus son of David, Rabbouni (changed by some Greek scribes to κύριε ραββί), "stopping said" (v. 49)?

Is it significant that Bartimaeus was a "blind beggar"?

Is "Jesus" a title? And why is it found only in the first cry from Bartimaeus?

Is "Son of David" a title? What does it mean? Are the variants to it significant?

Is ἐλέησόν με a formula shaped by Jesus' earliest followers?

What is the meaning of Bartimaeus' cry?

Why is the cry "Son of David" repeated?

Who are the "many" and why do they rebuke him?

Is this an example of the Marcan secrecy motif?[20]

Is "θάρσει, ἔγειρε, φωνεῖ σε" formularic?

If Bartimaeus could not see, how could he spring up and come to Jesus? Did he know where to go because of Jesus' voice? The story is ambiguous here; is that intentional?

How is the man healed?

Does not σέσωκεν ("has saved") denote that this story is unhistorical and about faith?

intended meaning. The Gk. ἀναβλέπω does mean "receive sight again". The Gk. βλέπω, "to see" (perhaps "to see" for the first time), colors the narrative of John 9 (esp. in vss. 15, 19, 21, 25 in which it appears) even though ἀναβλέπω is used in v. 11 (and it does not mean only "receive sight again" but also "obtain sight," and in a Johannine sense "to look up" to the ἄνω (the framework of John's narrative is cosmic: ἄνω and κάτω). The author of John, unlike the author of Mark (or his source), is playing with the spiritual meaning of "seeing"; he and his community were apparently fond of *double entendre* (see the Odes of Solomon, and the Semitic sources antedating John).

19. Why is the noun articular?

20. The so-called messianic secret cannot be said to originate with Mark. It is grounded in the Jewish traditions that the Messiah will be announced by God alone, and in his own time and way (see esp. Pss. Sol. and 4 Ezra). The doublet in Matthew to the Bartimaeus pericope contains an exhortation to silence placed on the lips of Jesus and not paralleled in Mark: "And Jesus sternly charged them (the two blind men) saying, 'See that no one knows (it)'" (Matt 9.30).

How is the man healed?

Does not σέσωκεν ("has saved") denote that this story is unhistorical and about faith?

Is "and *followed* him on *the way*" a theological motif, and is there then a link between vv. 46 and 52? Does the appearance of εὐθύς (v. 52) not betray the editorial reworking of Mark?

All these questions, and those that spin off from them, cannot be explored, let alone answered, in one essay. These questions help us see the dynamics of the pericope, if our focus is on the questions involved in trying to ascertain the meaning behind Bartimaeus' implied concept of Jesus. What did he mean when he called Jesus "Son of David"? This cry is found not only in Mark, but also in Luke (18.38), and in each verse parallel to Mark 10.47 in Matthew's doublet, Matt 9.27 and Matt 20.31.

Son of David: The Messiah

The focus of the questions listed above are Bartimaeus' outcry to Jesus, "Son of David." It appears twice in the pericope. The customary exegetical approach to this passage indicates that the cry, "Son of David," acknowledges the messiahship of Jesus. Assuming that it is a messianic title, and convinced of Marcan redaction Rudolf Bultmann[21] concluded that the pericope was "a late formulation".

Ezra P. Gould, in the ICC commentary on Mark, was convinced that "*Son of David* is a distinctly Messianic title, ..." He claimed that this messianic cry, "reflects the sentiment of the multitude, who mean to make this a triumphal progress to Jerusalem, though as yet they are preserving a policy of silence."[22]

Even though Mark places Jesus' triumphal entry into Jerusalem immediately after the Bartimaeus pericope, Gould's exegesis is remarkable. He contends that Bartimaeus' cry defines the sentiment of the crowd, although they are explicitly said to urge him to be silent, and after he shouts "Son of David." C.S. Mann more recently concludes that the "phrase is broadly 'messianic' ... ."[23]

Far more critical scholars continue to perpetuate the contention, which was never fully researched, that Bartimaeus calls on Jesus as the Messiah. Hugh Anderson, for example, notes that "Jesus, Son of David" does not appear elsewhere in Mark, and that "Son of David" is "here simply a messianic title."[24] He offers the opinion that "Mark may have seen a connexion between

21. R. Bultmann, *History of the Synoptic Tradition*, (trans. J. Marsh; New York, London: Harper, 1963 [revised edition]) 213.
22. E.P. Gould, *Gospel According to Mark* (ICC; Edinburgh: T. & T. Clark, 1897) 204.
23. C.S. Mann, *Mark* (Anchor Bible; Garden City, New York: Doubleday, 1986) 422.
24. H. Anderson, *The Gospel of Mark* (London: Oliphants, 1976) 258.

the designation Son of David here and the messianic fervour of the people on the entry into Jerusalem in 11.9-11."[25] While Anderson may be on the right road to understanding Marcan redaction and theology, an attempt to understand the theology of Mark must not mislead us from searching for the meaning of Batimaeus' cry and recognizing the possibility that Mark did not understand this dimension of the traditions he obviously received, since the pericope does not orginate with him, as the doublet in Matthew (20.29-34; 9.27-31) and the traditional elements, especially the Semitisms, prove.[26]

Bartimaeus wants Jesus to heal him; he replies to Jesus' question, τί σοι θέλεις ποιήσω with the words ραββουνί, ἵνα ἀναβλέψω. It is not likely that he thought Jesus was the Messiah, because there is no early tradition that depicts the Messiah as a healer or attributes to him the function of healing.[27] Is it possible that "Son of David" denoted Solomon, David's son through Bathsheba, and the third king of Israel? Clearly, any study of Jesus' miraculous deed must study the cosmology, demonology, and magic of the ancients.[28]

Son of David: Royal Genealogy

Is it possible that Bartimaeus was only acknowledging that Jesus was of Davidic descent, or according him honor and respect?[29] The counter-claim that Davidids were not known to exist in first-century Judaea is now disproved by the recovery in 1971 of an ossuary from the environs of Jerusalem; the inscription refers to "belonging to those from the house of David" (*shlby dwd*), and it dates from the first half of the first century BC.[30] Davidic families existed in Jerusalem before the destruction of the Temple and on the 20th of Tammuz they brought to the Temple altar the wood offering of the priests (see m. *Ta'an.* 4.5 and t. *Ta'an.* 3.5).

25. Anderson, *Mark*, 259.
26. Matthew and the communities of the Palestinian Jesus Movement can — and did — add Semitisms to the Jesus traditions; but I am not convinced that Mark is characteristically one who adds Semitisms. I am more persuaded that the Latinisms are from him or his own community.
27. See the articles in *The Messiah* (ed. J.H. Charlesworth, et al.; Minneapolis: Fortress, 1992).
28. M. Smith concluded that Jesus probably "did use magical methods," and that the New Testament stories "have usually been shaped by knowledge of magical practices." Smith, *Jesus the Magician* (New York: Harper & Row, 1978, 1981) 152.
29. See the comments by C.E.B. Cranfield, *The Gospel According to St. Mark* (Cambridge: Cambridge University Press, 1963).
30. See D. Flusser's insights in *Jesus' Jewishness* (ed. Charlesworth; New York: Crossroad, 1991) 157-59 and plate 19.

Son of David, Jesus: Joshua Ben Peraḥyah

Did Bartimaeus employ a title, "Jesus," or "Joshua," when he called out υἱὲ Δαυὶδ 'Ιησοῦ, ἐλέησόν με? An alleged healer named Joshua ben Peraḥyah, who lived in the latter half of the second century BC and the beginning of the first century BC,[31] studied in Jerualem under Yose ben Joezer of Zeredah and Yose ben Johanan, and is quoted in *Pirke Abot* 1.6.[32] In rabbinic traditions he is not described as a healer.

This "Jesus"[33] is called "the healer" (*'sy'*) in Aramaic incantation texts.[34] I am dubious that magical charms, and indications that Joshua Ben Peraḥyah performed exorcisms,[35] help us understand the words ascribed to Bartimaeus. Perhaps all Bartimaeus acknowledged was Jesus' name, which was not a title. Nevertheless, I do think we should entertain further questions.

Do the incantation texts indicate that Jews in the environs of Jerusalem, in Jericho in particular, revered Joshua ben Peraḥyah as a healer, who worked in and around Jerusalem? Did they accord him supernatural powers, such as exorcisms, and was he considered one who was apocalyptically inspired or

31. In rabbinic traditions he is said to have fled to Alexandria to escape the persecutions of Pharisees by Alexander Yannai (Jannaeus). See the important articles by M.D. Herr, "Joshua ben Perahyah," in *Encyclopaedia Judaica* 10 (1971) 284-85. At the beginning of this century rabbinic experts sometimes placed the persecution of Joshua ben Perahyah during the time of John Hyrcanus. See J.Z. Lauterbach, "Joshua b. Perahyah," in *The Jewish Encyclopedia* 7 (1904) 295 and J.Krengel, "Josua ben Perachja," in *Jüdisches Lexikon* 3 (1929) cols. 362-63.

32. M. *Abot* 1.6, "Joshua b. Perahyah said: Provide thyself with a teacher and get thee a fellow[-disciple]; and when thou judgest any man incline the balance in his favour." H. Danby, *The Mishnah* (Oxford: Oxford University Press, 1933) 447.

33. Joshua ben Peraḥyah is probably "Rab Jesus bar Perahia" mentioned in CBS 16086 (= no. 32 in Montgomery).

34. CBS 2922 = no. 17 in Montgomery and no. 13 in Isbell. See J.A. Montgomery, *Aramaic Incantation Texts from Nippur* (University of Pennsylvania; The Museum Publications of the Babylonian Section 3; Philadelphia: University Museum, 1913); C.D. Isbell, *Corpus of the Aramaic Incantation Bowls* (SBL Dissertation Series 17; Missoula, Mont.: Scholars, 1975). Montgomery no. 17 is the most important incantation text for understanding the tradition that Joshua ben Peraḥyah was a renowned healer (see line 12. *dyhwsh' bn prwhyh 'sy'*. The noun *'sy'* probably means "the healer" (as Mongomery translated it [191]) and not "savior" (as Isbell translated it [49]). The Aramaic *'sy'* derives from the verb *'sy*, which means "to be well," and the noun denotes "healer," "physician" or "surgeon." This term, *'sy'*, has loomed large, as scholars know, in the discussion of the etymology of the "Essenes," who were accorded healing powers. For "saviour" I would expect *parôqâ*, which means "redeemer" in Jewish Aramaic (cf. Christian Syriac, *parôqâ* ["Saviour," "Deliverer"]). For other texts referring to Joshua ben Perahyah, see also Montgomery no. 8 = Isbell no. 12, Montgomery 9 = Isbell no. 15, and Montgomery no. 32 (not in Isbell).

35. CBS 16086 = no. 32 in Montgomery (not in Isbell).

influenced?[36] If so, then it is easy to see why, in rabbinics,[37] he was thought to be associated with Jesus of Nazareth. If this association was possible in later times, in the Talmudim, then it is not inconceivable in the first century, perhaps even by a blind man in Jericho. These speculations need further refining and in-depth exploration. It is not impossible that a Bartimaeus called out to Jesus and associated him with a certain renowned healer who bore the same name; but, what is not impossible is far from what looms probable from careful historical scrutiny.

Son of David: Solomon

Is it conceivable that Bartimaeus, whether in historical or narrative context, was heralding Jesus of Nazareth as a Solomonic figure, that is one who possessed the healing powers of Solomon? Solomon was considered a wise man at an early date, and to him were attributed numerous writings in Israel's Wisdom Literature, namely Proverbs, Song of Songs, and the Wisdom of Solomon.

He was also considered an exorcist, and this tradition is well attested, especially in the magical incantation bowls from Nippur, and in the Testament of Solomon. The 40 bowls found at Nippur, which contain incantations, date from about AD 600, or earlier.[38] In Nippur Incantation CBS 9012 (= Montgomery 34) we find the following tradition (lines 7-8):

Charmed and sealed is all sickness (*kwlh byshwt'*) that is in the body of (*bpgrh*) Mihrhormizd bar Mâmî, in his house,[39] his wife, and his sons, and his daughters ... and

---

36. See CBS 16086 = no. 32 in Montgomery, esp. lines 7-8 (not in Isbell).
37. See y. *Hag.* 2.2, *Sanh.* 6.8; b. *Sanh.* 107b = *Sota.* 47a.
38. C.H. Gordon dated them to shortly before or after AD 600. Gordon, *Adventures in the Nearest East* (London: Phoenix, 1957) p. 161. G. Vermes, et al., report that upon "the basis of stratification, the bowls can be assigned to c. AD 300-600." See E. Schürer, *The History of the Jewish People in the Time of Jesus Christ*, ed. G. Vermes, et al. (Edinburgh: Clark, 1986) vol. 3.1, 353.
39. The fear of demons entering a house and killing or causing sickness to those in it was a real fear for all who believed, with the author of the Testament of Solomon, that there were demons who did such things; note *T. Sol.* 7.5, Lix Tetrax states, "I slither in under the corners of houses during the night or day." The corners of houses is where magical incantation bowls, turned upside down to entrap demons, were placed; see Montgomery, *Aramaic Incantation Texts from Nippur*, 40-42. Montgomery draws attention to an inscription that announces the demons are bound and sealed "in each one of the four corners of the house," and concludes that "we have to do with a species of sympathetic magic, the inverted bowls symbolizing and effecting the repression and suppression of the evil spirits" (42). The incantation bowls, the Testament of Solomon, and the New Testament pericopes present evidence of a widespread and ancient fear of demons causing illness.

by the seal of King Solomon son of David (*wb'yzgth dshlymwn mlk' br dwyd*).[40]

Two ideas in this incantation are extremely important for our present research, focused on Bartimaeus' exhortation to Jesus of Nazareth.

First, bodily sicknesses are prevented (perhaps cured) by Solomon. The noun *byshwt* means "wickedness," but when combined with *pgr*, "body," and seen in light of the cognate noun, *bîsh*, which means "bad," or "sick,"[41] the context of this incantation is to appeal to Solomon to heal, or protect from sickness, those mentioned. Other Aramaic incantations indicate that in no. 34, lines 7-8, we are confronted with ancient formulae.[42]

Second, Solomon is given a title: "son of David." It is possible to translate "the seal of King Solomon son of David" as follows: "the seal of Solomon, the King, Son of David."[43] Here, "Son of David" is clearly a title. It appears repeatedly also in the Testament of Solomon; note Solomon's command to Asmodeus: "I am Solomon, Son of David" (5.10).

Solomon's powers as an exorcist are well known.[44] Is he described in early hellenistic texts as a "healer"? I know of none. I also do not know of Jewish pre-70 texts in which he is called an "exorcist." His exorcisisms are narratively described in the Testament of Solomon.[45] Sickness and illness is caused by demons; and the demons are controlled by Solomon.[46] Note the following excerpts, highlighting Solomon's powers over demons who cause sickness. Ornias, who causes a boy to grow thin (and be sick), who strangles humans, and causes great pain (2.2), is controlled by Solomon (7.1-2). Onoskelis who strangles men is commanded and controlled by Solomon (4.1-12). A

---

40. Translation mine. For text see Montgomery, 231.
41. See Midrash Rabbah to Ecclesiastes 4.6 and the Palestinian Talmud of Baba Mesi'a 1.60c.
42. See Isbell No. 48 (= Gordon B), according to which demons are sealed, and humans protected, "with the signet-ring of King Solomon the son of David, who worked spells on male demons and female liliths" (for text and translation see Isbell, p. 110). Also see Isbell no. 50 (= Gordon E), according to this text a household is sealed "with the signet-ring of King Solomon the son of David, ... Blessed art Thou, YHWH, God of Israel" (for text and translation see Isbell, 114). For Gordon B and E, see C.H. Gordon, "Aramaic Magical Bowls in the Istanbul and Baghdad Museums," *Archiv Orientální* 6 (1934) 319-34, 466-74.
43. See *T. Sol.* 3.3, "Solomon the King summons you."
44. L. Ginzberg rightly points out that Solomon ruled over all creatures, including demons and spirits. See Ginzberg, *The Legends of the Jews* (Philadelphia: Jewish Publication Society, 1968) esp. 4, 142-44 and 6, 289. See the legends represented in "Solomon," *Legends*, 4, 125-76.
45. I am indebted to D. Duling and his work on the *T Sol.* in *OTP* 1.
46. *T Sol.* prologue, *T Sol.* 12.4-5, 13.7, 15.24, esp. 18.41. Ironically a demon named Lix Tetrax, who causes problems relating to fire, is also a healer of "the day-and-a-half fever" (7.6-7).

headless demon, named "Murder", who attacks ten-day-old infants, "inflames the limbs, inflicts the feet and produces festering sores" (9.6) is commanded by Solomon (9.7). A demon, "The Lion-Shaped Demon," who prevents people from recovering from disease (11.2), is sentenced and controlled by Solomon. A demon, who is a three-headed dragon and *blinds* children (τυφλῶ τὰ παιδία) in the womb (12.2), and who causes deafness and dumbness, is sealed and commanded by Solomon (12.4-5). A demon named Obyzouth is the one who causes *eye injuries* (13.4), is controlled by Solomon (13.7).[47]

The most important passage for our purposes of understanding, if Solomon was perceived as only an exorcist or was also conceived as one who could heal a person, especially one who was blind like Bartimaeus, is the Testament of Solomon, chapter 18. Here is an epitome of this section with a focus only on the illnesses caused by the demons:

demon's name	physical sickness it causes
Ruax	head aches
Barsafael	pains on the sides of heads
Artosael	*eye* damages
Oropel	sore throats
Kairoxanondalon	hearing
Sphendonael	tumors
Sphandor	weakens shoulders, deadens hand nerves and paralyzes limbs
Belbel	hearts and minds
Kourtael	attacks bowels
Metathiax	kidney pains
Phobothel	tendons
Leroel	chills, shiverings, sore throats
Soubelti	shivering and numbness
Katrax	inflicts incurable fevers
Ieropa	stomach convulsions
Mardero	incurable fevers
Rhyx Nathotho	knees
Rhyx Alath	coup in infants
Rhyx Audameoth	cardiac pain
Rhyx Manthado	kidneys
Rhyx Aktonme	ribs
Rhyx Anatreth	gas and burning in the bowels
Rhyx Enautha	minds and hearts
Rhyx Axesbuth	diarrhea and hemorrhoids
Rhyx Hapax	insomnia

47. Solomon controls a lecherous spirit by "the sign of the cross" (17.4); in its present form this passage is Christian and it is not easy to discern Jewish traditions behind it.

Rhyx Anoster	hysteria and bladder pains
Rhyx Physikoreth	long-term ilnesses
Rhyx Aleureth	swallowing
Rhyx Ichthuon	tendons
Rhyx Achoneoth	sore throats and tonsillitis
Rhyx Phteneoth	"the evil eye"[48]
Rhyx Mianeth	rotting flesh

The list is impressively extensive. Most importantly, all these demons, and therefore the sicknesses reputedly caused by them, are controlled by none other than Solomon. The purpose of listing and describing the demons and the sicknesses is to clarify that Solomon controls what ails humanity (18.41-42). Indeed, the purpose of the Testament of Solomon was written to inform "the sons of Isreal," of the power of demons and the means by which they are controlled (15.14). In twentieth-century language that seems to mean that the author of this pseudepigraphon wants his readers to know that the origins of sicknesses is known by the wise Solomon, and he knows the means for healing each sickness. While Solomon is not hailed as a "healer," it is unrepresentative of the language and world-view of the traditions in the Testament of Solomon to conlcude that he was only an exorcist and not a healer. It is thus conceivable that Solomon was considered not only an exorcist but also a healer.

The Testament of Solomon is too late and too heavily redacted by one or more Christians to be used to describe Solomonic legends in Judaea in the first half of the first century AD. If Solomon was celebrated as an exorcist or healer in pre-70 Judaism, then it is impressive that this perspective is reflected neither in the apocryphal passages that celebrate Solomon,[49] nor in the Psalms of Solomon.

It would be equally unwise to ingore the traditions preserved in this writing. Although it is probably a third-century writing, perhaps from Alexandria, the traditions preserved in it in many passages obviously antedate the origins of Christianity and help us obtain some insights into the fears, fantacies, and faith of the average person in the early first century AD.

The Jewish Aramaic incantation texts, even though they are also late, are an independent witness to the lore of the ancients; they help us perceive what may well have happened in Judaea. An important parallel to Jesus' healing of Bartimaeus is found in the Mandaic incantation texts, but they are far too late

---

48. I include this notation for inclusiveness and because it is impossible to exclude the effect of magic (the evil eye) on physical maladies.
49. Sir 47.13, 23; 2 Macc 2.8, 9, 10, 12; 1 Esd 1.3, 5; 5.33, 35; 4 Ezra 7.108; 10.46; 4 Macc 18.16; *Sib. Or.* 11.80-103.

to help us considerably.[50] Jesus heals Bartimaeus without touching him and by merely speaking. Words are accorded magical powers in many cultures, especially those which are primitive. In the Mandaic incantation texts we find a formula, the angels are exhorted to heal by words: "... you are a healer (*'sy'*) who heals (*dm'sy'*) maladies by the word (*bml'l'*)."[51]

Solomon was accorded magical powers long before the dates given to the incantation texts. The early date of this idea seems confirmed by the Apocalypse of Adam, which contains traditions from the early centuries AD.[52] This pseudepigraphon, in 7.13, refers to Solomon and his army of demons. This idea is very close to many passages in the Testament of Solomon.

The Greek Magical Papyri conceivably also confirm an ealier date for the traditions that Solomon controls demons who cause sicknesses. Papyrus IV, which dates from the fourth century AD, contains a charm that is attributed to Solomon.[53] However, it is too late and too ambiguous to be of significant help in understanding Bartimaeus' cry.

The New Testament documents are our most important source for assessing the meaning of Bartimaeus' words. Matthew is clearly from the first century. In Matthew, Solomon is portrayed as a wise man (Matt 12.42) and a wealthy person (Matt 6.29). His name was commemorated in the Temple, in the portico to the east (John 1.23). But Solomon is not called a healer in the New Testament. As far as I know there is no reference to Solomon as a "healer" in the Jewish pre-70 Jewish pseudepigrapha, nor in the Old Testament Apocrypha, Philo, or Josephus.

Perhaps our reflections are too myopic. The key may be found in passages in which the phrase "Son of David" is found. As C. Burger demonstrated in *Jesus als Davidssohn*,[54] the application of the title "Son of David" to Jesus appear almost always within stories of healing. And as U. Mauser demonstrates, in his *The Peace of the Gospel*,[55] seven sections in Matt contain the title "Son of

---

50. According to E.M. Yamauchi, the earliest texts are from around AD 400 (no. 22), the religious texts postdate the eighth century, and the magical bowls are from about 600. See his *Mandaic Incantation Texts* (American Oriental Series 49; New Haven: American Oriental Society, 1967) 2.

51. See 7.22-24, 8.43-45, 18c.2-5, 19.15-16, 26.16. For texts and translations, see E.M. Yamauchi, *Mandaic Incantation Texts*.

52. See G. MacRae's comments in *OTP* 1,708.

53. For the text, see K. Preisendanz, *Papyri Graecae Magicae: Die Griechischen Zauberpapyri*, 2 vols. (ed. A. Henrichs Stuttgart: Teubner, 1973-1974) vol. 1, 102-104. For the English transtlation by W.C. Grese, see *The Greek Magical Papyri in Translation* (ed. H.D. Betz; Chicago: University of Chicago Press, 1986) 55-56.

54. C. Burger, *Jesus als Davidssohn: Eine traditionsgeschichtliche Untersuchung* (FRLANT 98; Göttingen: Vandenhoeck & Ruprecht, 1970) esp. 170.

55. U. Mauser, *The Peace of the Gospel* (Louisville: Westminster/Knox, 1992). I appreciate Professor Mauser discussing his book with me, as I prepared this paper for publication.

David," and six of these are healing stories (9.27-31, 12.22-24, 15.21-28, 20.29-34, 21.1-11, and 21.14-16). Why is Jesus hailed as the "Son of David" who heals? In assuming that this is a messianic title have we become blinded to possible Solomonic meanings?

This possibility is perhaps increased by an examination of Matthew 12.22-23, which is independent of and not parallelled in Mark. According to Matthew 12, Jesus heals a man possessed of a demon; he is blind and dumb. When it is obvious that the demonaic is healed πάντες οἱ ὄχλοι exclaim, "Can (μήτι) this be the Son of David?" The Greek particle μήτι may indicate a negative answer is expected, or it may indicate that they do not know what answer seems most likely. Matthew' text will not allow us to conclude that the crowd thought Jesus was to be seen in terms of Solomon; but, it may indicate that "the Son of David" as healer and one who could exorcize a blind man and enable him to see was a concept accepted as possible by first-century Palestinian Jews.

Perhaps the meaning of Matt 21 will shed some light on our search. Jesus' triumphal entry into Jerusalem was of special importance to Matthew. The traditions he preserves are of great signifiance for us, since the crowd (ὄχλοι) shouts, "Hosanna to the Son of David!" (Matt 21.9). After Jesus allegedly heals the blind and the lame in the Temple, children cry out, "Hosanna to the Son of David!" (Matt 21.15). If the Messiah was not thought to heal, then what are the meanings of these exclamations?

More questions are raised by our observations. The claim that Jesus was of the house of David was an early aspect of the kerygma and liturgy, as the pre-Pauline tradition in Romans 1.3-4 clairifies; but then we are led to the most important observation, as expressed by Burger, "dass sich im gesamten Stoff der Evangelien keine Überlieferung zum Thema Davidssohn findet, die mit einiger Sicherheit auf Jesus selbst zurückgeführt werden könnte."[56] And so, we ask with more insight, what were the intentionalities behind the claim that Jesus was the "Son of David"? Obviously, different Jews, representing the various groups within Judaism of Jesus' day, would have felt free to express, perhaps narratively, their own perceptions. Paul is our first witness, and he indicates that he has inherited the title "Son of David."[57]

---

56. Burger, *Jesus als Davidssohn*, 165.
57. I am indebted to Bent Noack for many insights; especially now I think of his "TESTE PAULO: Paul as the Principal Witness to Jesus and Primitive Christianity," in *Die Paulinische Literatur und Theologie: Anlässlich der 50.-jährigen Gründungs-Feier der Universität von Aarhus* (ed. S. Pedersen; Teologiske Studier 7; Aarhus: Aros, 1980) 9-28; esp. 22-23.

Conclusion

It is evident that Mark 10.46-52 elicits many questions from the exegete. If the Messiah was not perceived as a healer, or would perform healing functions, then it is unlikely that Bartimaeus, who wanted to regain his sight, hailed Jesus as the Messiah. If the traditions about Solomon as an exorcist mirror a lost tradition that he understood the art of healing and was accorded the powers to heal, and if these traditions date from the time of Jesus, then we can raise the possibility that Bartimaeus was thinking of Jesus as a healer, after the order of Solomon. Bartimaeus may have linked traditions in the Solomonic cycle with the traditions about the healer, Joshua Ben Peraḥyah, who was hailed as a great healer in Judaea.

Mark's use of this story is not clear. If he thought about the exhortation of Bartimaeus as a messianic confession, then his handling of this tradition departs from his usual tendency and the so-called Messianic Secret. As C.E.B. Cranfield stated, if "Son of David" is to be understood as a messianic title, and if it was intended that way by Bartimaeus and "understood in that sense by the crowd, it is remarkable that Jesus apparently did nothing to silence him — contrast viii.30."[58] I have little doubt that one of the reasons Mark recorded this tradition is because of his apocalyptic eschatology; in the End-of-time God will come (*'elohîm hû yābô*), then "the blind man's eyes shall be opened" (*'z tpgḥnh 'yny 'iwrym* Isa 35.4-5). Perhaps the link between Mark 10 and Isa 35.4 is obvious because of the concept of how God shall "save" (*ysh'* in Isa 35.4 and σῴζω in Mark 10.52). Perhaps it was Mark, or an early Christian, that brought out this link with scripture, since Jesus' injuction — "Go your way; your faith has made you well" — seems out of context with the simple story told and is in line with Marcan theology. As Anderson points out, "For Mark the emphasis in the story is not on the *healing* as such (no action or healing word of Jesus is mentioned) but on the response of faith to God's call in Jesus ... through blind eyes are opened and true fellowship becomes possible."[59] The truth in this exegesis seems confirmed by the way Mark has ended the story: "And immediately (εὐθύς) he received his sight and followed (ἠκολούθει) him on the way (ἐν τῇ ὁδῷ). It should be obvious that these terms reveal the hand of the early Christian community and of the redactor Mark.

The most important result of the present report of research is that we have become — once again — aware of the truncated view caused by a purely christological approach to traditions in the New Testament. We dare not assume that what would become messianic symbols, terms, and titles possessed such meaning before the middle of the first century AD. By struggling with issues

---

58. C.E.B. Cranfield, *St. Mark* 344.
59. Anderson, *Mark*, 259.

arising out of Mark's account of Bartimaeus' healing we are thrust back into the context of the Marcan text, and into the hellenistic world of about AD 30 to 70. If we are convinced that Bartimaeus was not hailing Jesus as Messiah, we are far from convinced that he was hailing him as Solomon. We grow more sensitive to the perplexities and possibilities inherent in studying Marcan traditions.

In conlusion, what did Bartimaeus mean when he called out to Jesus, υἱὲ Δαυὶδ Ἰησοῦ, ἐλέησόν με? If this episode reflects a historical event, perhaps in Jericho, whether in actuality or in verisimilitude through Mark's narrative, then there are several possible ways of discerning an answer. The first is that we will never know and every attempt will be frustrated by the inability of discussing the claim with Bartimaeus and the complexity, incompleteness, and lateness of our sources.

Second, it is possible, but unlikely, that Bartimaeus was hailing Jesus as the Messiah. He clearly wanted to be healed, but we have no evidence that the Messiah was perceived as a healer in Palestine before AD 70. Yet, this conclusion seems to be the dominant one chosen by the commentators on Mark 10.

Third, Bartimaeus' call υἱὲ Δαυὶδ may simply acknowledge Jesus' royal genealogy. This possibility can no longer be dismissed since we know about Davidids living in Jerusalem during the time of the alleged encounter between Bartimaeus and Jesus. Two objections loom large against opting for this solution to the question what Bartimaeus may have meant by the words υἱὲ Δαυὶδ. First, critical scholarship has raised serious questions about Jesus' Davidic lineage. Where we find it in the New Testament, and related literature, it appears linked with the confession that Jesus is the Messiah and therefore must be of Davidic desecent.[60] Secondly, this option is insensitive to the narrative in which the words, which may well be an invocation, are couched. That is, Bartimaeus wants to be healed, and any solution to the question of what he meant by υἱὲ Δαυὶδ should attend to the relation between such words and the need for healing.

Fourth, attention must be turned not only to the words, υἱὲ Δαυὶδ, but also to Ἰησοῦ, ἐλέησόν με. Bartimaeus surely wanted to be cured of his sickness and to see again. Does he simply call out Jesus' name, or is it a title? We have no criteria by which to discern the one from the other. If Ἰησοῦ is a title, and if it is associated with a known healer, then it is conceivable that Bartimaeus is linking Jesus with the famous magician and healer, named Joshua ben Perahyah, who lived in Jerusalem and was famous not only for his healings but also for his altercation with Alexander Jannaeus in the first third of the first century BC. This possiblity appears remote to me; and it certainly does not help us understand the most problematic words, namely υἱὲ Δαυὶδ.

---

60. See the informed discussion in R.E. Brown, *The Birth of the Messiah* (Garden City, New York: Doubleday, 1977) 66-70.

Fifth, by attending to the full narrative, the call υἱὲ Δαυὶδ 'Ιησοῦ, ἐλέησόν με me, and to the healing of Baritmaeus' blindness, we are confronted with the most probable answer. Taken literally "son of David" would be Solomon. While we are far from any certainty, I am convinced that the most probable explanation of Bartimaeus' υἱὲ Δαυὶδ is some Solomonic denotation. We possess traditions that may well derive from the first century AD, in which Solomon is hailed as an exorcist who controls demons and the sickness, including blindness, they cause. It is conceivable, but surely in need of further research and discussion, that Bartimaeus called to Jesus, hailing him as one who like Solomon possessed miraculous powers of healing. We have not endeavored to discern whether this conclusion leads us to an historical context or a pre-70 narrative context.

Our research has opened our eyes to the complexity of the hellenistic world, and the insights it provides in guiding our exegesis of New Testament texts. In this endeavor we are reminded of the great professors who have taught here in Aarhus,[61] especially Poul Nepper-Christensen, who opened our eyes to the Jewishness of Matthew,[62] Søren Giversen, and Johannes Munck. The latter renowned scholar revised his work on Acts at Princeton while a Visiting Professor of New Testament at Princeton Theological Seminary.[63] The crossing of continents in our day remind us to be wary of constructing barriers in the hellenistic and Roman world, and refusing to allow what was believed in Nippur to inform us of what may have occurred in Jericho.

61. The Faculty of Theology at the University of Aarhus is internationally celebrated for pioneering research into the background of early Judaism and early Christianity. See especially the following: B.S. Hansen, [ed.], *Religionshistorie ved Aarhus Universitet 1960-1985* (Aarhus: Institut for Religionshistorie, 1985).

62. See P. Nepper-Christensen, *Das Matthäusevangelium: Ein Judenchristliches Evangelium?* (Acta Theologica Danica 1; Aarhus: Universitetsforlaget, 1958). Nepper-Christensen's words and insights of the fifties proved to be precursors of the best research of the eighties and nineties. I find that his words were similar to those in the founding of *Explorations* (see his p. 9. "... die Christen und die Juden getrennte Wege gingen und es nach und nach klar wurde, dass das Christentum und Judentum sich grundsätzlich voneinander unterschieden.")

63. See Elisabeth Munck's comments in J. Munck, *The Acts of the Apostles* (Anchor Bible; Garden City, N.Y.: Doubleday, 1967) vii-viii.

Apotheosis and Resurrection[1]

Adela Yarbro Collins

The thesis of this paper is that the understanding of resurrection expressed in the empty tomb story of the gospel of Mark is shaped by Greek and Roman traditions of the translation and apotheosis of human beings. In order to explicate the meaning of resurrection in Mark, it is necessary to place the empty tomb story in the context of the earliest understanding of resurrection in Christian tradition. The oldest Christian text that discusses the resurrection of Jesus in detail is 1 Corinthians 15.

The author has argued elsewhere that Paul's understanding of the resurrection of Jesus does not involve the revival of his corpse.[2] Paul's understanding of resurrection is like that of Daniel 12. Both Daniel 12 and 1 Corinthians 15 express the notion of resurrection in terms of astral immortality.[3] Neither the book of Daniel nor Paul shows any interest in what happens to the physical body. Presumably it decays and has no importance for the resurrected person. This interpretation of Daniel 12 is supported by the description of personal afterlife for the righteous in the book of *Jubilees*, "And their bones shall rest in the earth, and their spirits shall have much joy" (*Jub.* 23.22).

Appearances and Empty Tomb

Thus it is not surprising, although noteworthy, that the tradition cited by Paul in 1 Cor 15.3-7 does not mention the empty tomb. In his own elaboration and discussion of the theme, Paul also does not mention the empty tomb. The summaries of the gospel in the book of Acts, which some scholars believe are older than the book of Acts itself, also fail to mention the empty tomb.[4] The fact that

---

1. This article is a revised form of Chapter Five,"The Empty Tomb and Resurrection according to Mark," of the author's book, *The Beginning of the Gospel: Probings into Mark in Context* (Minneapolis, Minn.: Fortress Press, 1992). The philological aspect of the issue is treated in more detail in this article than in the book.
2. Yarbro Collins, *The Beginning of the Gospel*, 123-27.
3. On the notion of astral immortality in the ancient world, see Franz Cumont, *Lux Perpetua* (Paris: P. Geuthner, 1949).
4. Acts 2.22-24, 3.13-15, 4.10-12, 5.30-32. The book of Acts is of course considerably later than the gospel of Mark. Whether or not one can reconstruct sources used by the author of Acts is disputed. It is generally agreed that no continuous source was used in chapters 1-5 (Ernst Haenchen, *The Acts of the Apostles: A Commentary* [Philadelphia:

Paul, especially, does not mention it has led some scholars to argue that the tradition about the empty tomb was an apologetic invention intended to support the early Christian proclamation about the resurrection.[5] There are several problems with this theory. If such were the origin of the tradition, it is odd that it is not used apologetically in the book of Acts. Further, if the empty tomb story was invented to "prove" the resurrection of Jesus, it is odd that the only witnesses to the emptiness of the tomb, at least in Matthew and Mark, are women.[6] The status of women in the ancient world was such that a story fabricated as proof or apology would probably not be based on the testimony of women.

The issue is complicated by the textual problem regarding what the original ending of Mark was. Text-critical principles and linguistic studies indicate that the original ending was vs 8.[7] The list of women varies among the gospels; some argue that it varies even within Mark. The status of the stone varies among the gospels. Within Mark, why do the women go without having a plan for moving the stone? Whether Jesus was anointed before burial varies among the gospels. Within Mark, why do the women intend to anoint Jesus on the second day after his death? Assuming that Mark ended with 16.8, the women are told to tell but they do not. Why not? Was the empty tomb tradition new with Mark? Is their silence meant to explain why the tradition about the empty tomb was not known before Mark was written?

Another problem is who really buried Jesus. According to Acts 13.29, it was his enemies. According to the Synoptics, it was Joseph of Arimathea. It is quite credible that Acts 13.29 is as precise a historical report of the burial of Jesus as can be reconstructed. The Joseph story may be an apologetic legend; at least it seems to grow into one, as is evident from a comparison of the four canonical gospels.

Westminster, 1971] 81-90). The empty tomb is presupposed in Acts 2.25-31 and 13.34-37. These passages may be dependent on older tradition, but it is not clear that such tradition is as old as the gospel of Mark (ibid., 3-4, 409, 411). The passages in question may represent a strand of tradition unknown to Mark and Paul.

5. Rudolf Bultmann, *The History of the Synoptic Tradition* (rev. ed.; New York: Harper & Row, 1963) 290.

6. In Matthew, of course, the guards see the angel and know that the tomb is empty. It is generally agreed, however, that the story of the guards at the tomb and the lie that they spread about the disciples stealing the body is later than the empty tomb story and is definitely apologetic. One of the problems that this story addresses indirectly is the reliability of women as witnesses.

7. At least these studies indicate that the material that follows Mark 16.8 in many manuscripts is not original. Some scholars argue that the original ending of Mark has been lost or suppressed. See, for example, Bultmann, *History*, 285, n. 2. In this article, the assumption is made that the gospel ended with 16.8, since that is the earliest recoverable ending. Any attempt to reconstruct an earlier ending would be unduly speculative. An ending at vs 8 is also defensible.

Some argue that the very fact that the empty tomb tradition is only loosely related to the tradition of appearances of the risen Jesus is evidence that the empty tomb tradition is equally old.[8] Most New Testament scholars at present accept the argument that the Gospel of Mark is the oldest gospel. In the opinion of this majority, Mark 16.1-8 is, therefore, the oldest attestation of the tradition that the tomb was empty.[9] Many scholars who accept the Two Source Theory as the best explanation of the Synoptic problem consider Matthew to be at least ten years later than Mark and Luke to be even later. Like Mark, these two gospels are dependent ultimately on the early Christian resurrection and exaltation traditions.[10] But the detailed narratives of Matthew 28 and Luke 24 may be seen as redactional expansions of Mark 16.1-8. Some of the accounts of appearances may be pre-Matthean or pre-Lukan, but there is no evidence that they have independent tradition about the discovery of the empty tomb.

Therefore, one's judgment about the age of the empty tomb tradition will depend on the literary question regarding the origin of Mark 16.1-8. The options are: 1. it is based on a pre-Markan passion narrative; 2. it is based on another source, oral or written, adapted by the author of Mark; and 3. it was composed by the author of Mark.

The author has argued elsewhere that the evidence is insufficient to establish the use of a source in Mark 16.1-8.[11] The evangelist probably did make use of an older passion narrative, but this account ended with the death of Jesus. Mark 16.1-8 is best understood as a unified and effective composition by the evangelist that continues chapter 15 logically and appropriately.

The Ancient Notion of Translation

The idea that a human being could be removed from the sphere of ordinary

8. So, for example, Pheme Perkins, *Resurrection: New Testament Witness and Contemporary Reflection* (Garden City, N.Y.: Doubleday, 1984) 90.

9. P. Benoit has argued that John 20 contains an older form of the empty tomb tradition (cited by Joachim Jeremias, "Die älteste Schicht der Osterüberlieferungen," *Resurrexit: Actes du symposium international sur la résurrection de Jésus* [ed. E. Dhanis; Rome: Libreria Editrice Vaticana, 1974] 189-90; ET: J. Jeremias, *New Testament Theology: The Proclamation of Jesus* [New York: Scribner's, 1971] 304-305); but this hypothesis is unlikely; see John Dominic Crossan, "Empty Tomb and Absent Lord (Mark 16.1-8)," *The Passion in Mark: Studies in Mark 14-16* (ed. Werner H. Kelber; Philadelphia: Fortress, 1976) 138-45. As Crossan puts it, there may have been a presumption that the tomb was empty prior to the formulation of Mark 16.1-8 [or its source], but a presumption is not a tradition (ibid., 136).

10. On the exaltation tradition in the early church, see Gerhard Lohfink, *Die Himmelfahrt Jesu: Untersuchungen zu den Himmelfahrts- und Erhöhungstexten bei Lukas* (SANT 26; Munich: Kösel-Verlag, 1971) 80-146.

11. Yarbro Collins, *The Beginning of the Gospel*, 129-34.

humanity and made immortal is a very ancient one. The oldest narrative of such an event is found on a tablet excavated in Nippur that contains part of the Sumerian flood-story.[12] The hero of this story is the king Ziusudra. A deity informs him that there will be a flood and instructs him to build a huge boat. After the flood, Ziusudra offers sacrifice. Near the end of the passage that is preserved, it is said that the gods Anu and Enlil cherished Ziusudra. They give him life like a god. They give him breath eternal like (that of) a god. They cause him to dwell at the place where the sun rises. These honors are granted him apparently because he is the preserver of vegetation and the seed of humankind.

In the Akkadian Gilgamesh Epic, Gilgamesh journeys through a great mountain range and over the Waters of Death to reach the flood-hero, who in this epic is named Utnapishtim.[13] The purpose of the quest is to obtain the secret of immortality. In tablet XI of the epic, Utnapishtim recounts the story of the flood for Gilgamesh. At the end of the story he tells how the god Enlil announced, "Henceforth Utnapishtim and his wife shall be like unto us gods. Utnapishtim shall reside far away, at the mouth of the rivers!"[14] Earlier in the epic it was said that Utnapishtim had joined the Assembly [of the gods].[15] In the Atrahasis Epic, which includes a Babylonian version of the flood on tablet III, a similar story is told about the flood-hero Atrahasis and his wife.

In the Hebrew Bible it is not the flood-hero Noah who was translated, but the antediluvian patriarch, Enoch. His destiny is tersely related in chapter 5 of Genesis. It is said that "Enoch walked with God" (wayyithallēk hănôk et-hā 'ĕlōhîm) in vss 22 and 24 and that "he was no more, for God took him" (wĕ 'ênennû kî-lāqaḥ 'ōtô 'ĕlōhîm) in vs 24. The LXX of Gen 5.24 reads: καὶ εὐηρέστησεν Ενωχ τῷ θεῷ καὶ οὐχ ηὑρίσκετο, ὅτι μετέθηκεν αὐτὸν ὁ θεός ("And Enoch pleased God and he was not found, because God translated him"). It is not said that Moses was translated. In the book of Deuteronomy it is said that he died in the land of Moab (34.5). But it is implied that God buried him and that no one knows the place of his burial (vs 6). These latter remarks suggested to later readers that Moses had in fact been translated. The translation of Elijah is described in vivid detail in 2 Kings 2.11, "and Elijah ascended in a whirlwind to heaven" (wayya'al 'ēlîyāhû baśō'ārâ haššā-māyim). The LXX reads: καὶ ἀνελήμφθη Ηλιου ἐν συσσεισμῷ ὡς εἰς τὸν οὐρανόν ("And Elijah was taken up in a whirlwind into heaven"). The removal of Elijah, unlike that of Enoch, is explicitly said to have been witnessed (by

---

12. An English translation of this text by S.N. Kramer is given in *Ancient Near Eastern Texts Relating to the Old Testament* [hereafter, *ANET*] (ed. James B. Pritchard; 3rd ed.; Princeton, N.J.: Princeton University Press, 1969) 42-44.
13. An English translation by E.A. Speiser may be found in *ANET*, 72-99.
14. *ANET*, 95.
15. Ibid., 88.

Elisha): "And Elisha was watching ... and when he could no longer see him" (weʾĕlîšāʿ rōʾeh ... wĕlōʾ rāʾāhû ʿôd ...) (vs 12). The LXX reads: καὶ Ελισαιε ἑώρα ... καὶ οὐκ εἶδεν αὐτὸν ἔτι... ("And Elisha was watching ... and he did not see him any longer").[16]

The oldest surviving Greek texts that speak of translations of human beings are the *Iliad* and the *Odyssey*. According to the *Iliad*, Tros, the lord of the Trojans, had three sons. One of these, Ganymedes, because of his unsurpassed beauty, was caught up by the gods to themselves, made immortal and made the cupbearer of Zeus (20.230-35). The mortal Tithonos is mentioned in this context as the descendant of one of Ganymedes' brothers (20.237). Earlier in the epic, his translation by the goddess Dawn is mentioned (11.1). This allusion presupposes a tradition that Dawn had made Tithonos immortal to be her spouse and to dwell by the River Okeanos where Dawn rises (cf. *Iliad* 19.1-2).[17]

In book four of the *Odyssey*, Menelaos, the husband of Helen, tells Telemachos how he tricked the god Proteus into advising him how to make his way home and giving him news of his companions. Proteus' revelations include a prophecy that Menelaos will not die; rather the gods will cause him to dwell on the Elysian Plain at the (spatial) end of the world, where life is as pleasant as on Mount Olympos. The reason given for this great blessing is that he is, as husband of Helen, a son of Zeus (4.560-70).[18] Menelaos is to join Rhadamanthys who apparently was transported to the Elysian Plain earlier, according to tradition. The details of his story are lost, but it is interesting to note that he was also said to be a son of Zeus (*Il.* 14.321-22). The similarity between "son of Zeus" and "son of God" should be noted.

All of these traditions imply that the human beings translated became gods, i.e., immortal. They seem to assume that in these cases, the soul (ψυχή) was never separated from the body.[19] In some cases, however, the human being in question dies first and then is made immortal. The Aithiopis, a

---

16. Cf. 2 Kings 2.3, 5 LXX where λαμβάνω ("to take") is used to describe the event and 2 Kings 2.10 where ἀναλαμβάνω ("to take up") is used, as in vs 11 which is cited above.

17. The story of Kleitos, the mortal son of Manios, has similarities with both the stories of Ganymedes and Tithonos. Kleitos was carried off by Dawn to live among the gods because of his beauty (*Od.* 15.248-52).

18. Women, as well as men, were said to have been translated. There is a tradition that Helen herself was made immortal and made to dwell on the White Island or in the Islands of the Blest (Erwin Rohde, *Psyche: The Cult of Souls and Belief in Immortality among the Greeks* [New York: Harcourt Brace Jovanovich, 1925] 83, n. 21). The nereid Leukothea was once the mortal Ino (*Od.* 5.333-35). There was also a tradition that Iphigeneia, the daughter of Agamemnon, was not sacrificed, but was translated by Artemis and made immortal in the land of the Taurians (Rohde, *Psyche*, 64).

19. Rohde, *Psyche*, 57.

continuation of the *Iliad* that survives only in the form of references in other authors, tells how Memnon, the Ethiopian prince, brought help to the Trojans. He is slain by Achilles, whereupon Memnon's mother, Dawn, obtains permission from Zeus to carry his body to the end of the earth in the East and there to grant immortality to her son.[20] According to the same epic poem, when Achilles was slain and placed on his funeral pyre, his mother, the divine Thetis, carried his body from the pyre to White Island. The extract does not say so, but the story probably continued with an account of how she restored him to life there and made him immortal.[21]

All the traditions discussed so far involve immortal life in regions on the surface of the earth, most of which are normally not accessible to humanity. There is another type of translation-story that involves removal beneath the earth and subterranean immortality, often in a cave.[22] This type of immortality is analogous to that of the "heroes," who died, were buried, and from their graves gave proof of a higher existence and powerful influence.[23] It is noteworthy that the later belief in heroes required a grave at which the continued existence and potency of the hero was localized.[24]

Erwin Rohde's reconstruction of one of the traditions associated with the hero Hyakinthos is instructive. Originally a chthonic deity, he was later transformed into a hero, who died, was buried, and then was translated to heaven.[25]

The case of Asklepios as hero is likewise instructive. According to this tradition, he was a mortal who was transformed into an immortal by a flash of Zeus' lightning.[26] Part of this tradition is that Asclepios was buried.[27] Thus his story also is that of a hero who died, was buried and then translated.

The focus on the tomb in Mark may have been inspired by the importance of the graves of the heroes in the Greco-Roman world. Even if the location of the tomb of Jesus was unknown to the author of Mark, and even if there were no cultic observances at the site of the tomb, it would still be important as a *literary* motif in characterizing Jesus as hero-like.[28]

An example that does not involve the death of the hero, but is instructive for the role of the angel in Mark 16, is the case of Kleomedes of Astypalaia, related by Pausanias and several other writers. Kleomedes killed his opponent

---

20. Ibid., 64.
21. Ibid., 64-65.
22. Ibid., 89-92.
23. Ibid., 97.
24. Ibid., 98.
25. Ibid., 99-100.
26. Ibid., 100, 582.
27. Ibid., 101.
28. On the hypothesis that there were cultic observances performed at the tomb of Jesus from an early date, see Perkins, *Resurrection*, 93-94, 119.

in the boxing match at the seventy-first Olympic festival (486 BC) and was therefore disqualified. In his anger at this turn of events, he behaved destructively upon his return home. His behavior caused the death of some boys. He fled to the temple of Athena and hid in a chest. When the chest was forced open by his pursuers, Kleomedes was not inside. Envoys were sent to inquire of the oracle. They were told that he had become a hero and must be honored with sacrifice. The oracle is able to explain a supernatural occurrence to human inquirers because the oracle sees such events as one spirit sees another.[29] This perspective is instructive both for the role of the angel at the empty tomb and for the role of the demons or unclean spirits in Mark who know that Jesus is the son of God.

The case of Herakles is also interesting. In agony because of the poison on his garment, he made his own funeral pyre and mounted it. Apollodorus continues, "While the pyre was burning, it is said that a cloud passed under Herakles and with a peal of thunder wafted him up to heaven. Thereafter he obtained immortality, and being reconciled to Hera he married her daughter Hebe, by whom he had sons, Alexiares and Anicetus" (καιομένης δὲ τῆς πυρᾶς λέγεται νέφος ὑποστὰν μετὰ βροντῆς αὐτὸν εἰς οὐρανὸν ἀναπέμψαι. ἐκεῖθεν δὲ τυχὼν ἀθανασίας καὶ διαλλαγεὶς Ἥρᾳ τὴν ἐκείνης θυγατέρα Ἥβην ἐγημεν, ἐξ ἧς αὐτῷ παῖδες Ἀλεξιάρης καὶ Ἀνίκητος ἐγένοντο).[30] The traditional mythic view is obviously that immortal life is much like mortal life and that Heracles was embodied in his afterlife. Another interpretation is that the pyre burned away the mortal part of his nature, inherited from his mortal mother, so that the immortal part, inherited from his father Zeus, could ascend to the gods.[31] The Pythian priestess had promised Herakles immortality upon completion of the ten labors or tasks (Apollodorus, Library 2.4.12). Later writers interpreted this as an honor granted because of his great benefactions to humankind.

In the classical period of Greek culture, Sophokles seems to take the divine miracle of translation as a literal truth in his depiction of the disappearance of Oedipus in Oedipus in Colunus. As it once pleased the divine power to overwhelm the innocent victim with suffering, so it now pleases the same power to raise the sufferer to superhuman bliss.[32] The analogy between Oedipus and the Markan Jesus is striking and raises the question of the relation between Mark and tragedy.[33]

---

29. Rohde, Psyche, 129-30. See also the story of Aristeas, related by Herodotus and discussed by Arthur S. Pease, "Some Aspects of Invisibility," HSCP 53 (1942) 29.

30. Apollodorus The Library 2.7.7 (trans. James G. Frazer; LCL; Cambridge, Mass.: Harvard University Press, 1921) 1. 270-73.

31. So Lucian, Hermotimus 7, cited by Frazer, ibid., 271.

32. Rohde, Psyche, 430-31.

33. See Gilbert G. Bilezikian, The Liberated Gospel: A Comparison of the Gospel of Mark and Greek Tragedy (Grand Rapids: Baker House Books, 1977).

In the Hellenistic and early Roman periods these traditions of translation and deification were very widespread. The Hellenistic Babylonian historian Berossus, writing in Greek, retold the ancient flood-story. In his version the flood-hero is named Xisouthros. In recounting his translation, Berossus says that he "disappeared," using a term that had become almost technical in describing such occurrences (ἀφανὴς γίγνομαι).[34] A new element in the account is Berossus' explanation of the event: he was translated because of his piety. Josephus describes Enoch's translation with the words ἀνεχώρησε πρὸς τὸ θεῖον ("he returned to the divinity;" Ant. 1.85). His terminology is similar to that of Berossus in a later passage. He describes the translation of Elijah: Ἠλίας ἐξ ἀνθρώπων ἠφανίσθη ("Elijah disappeared from among human beings"). In the same passage, he says of both Enoch and Elijah that γεγόνασιν ἀφανεῖς, θάνατον δ' αὐτῶν οὐδεὶς οἶδεν ("they became invisible, and no one knows of their death;" Ant. 9.28).[35]

The terminology used by Josephus makes clear that he was presenting Enoch, Moses, and Elijah as Jewish forefathers who had not died, but had been translated alive and made immortal, like the forefathers of the Greeks and Romans.[36] Another Jewish writer who wrote in Greek shows that the idea of resurrection could be associated with the Greco-Roman ideas of translation and deification. Phocylides was a Greek poet from Miletus who lived in the sixth century BC. Around the turn of the era, a Jewish poet wrote a work under the name and in the style of Phocylides, possibly in Alexandria.[37] A section of this poem is devoted to death and after-life. The author advocates moderation in grief (lines 97-98) and the duty of burying the dead (99). He then advises against opening the graves of the deceased (100-3). The rejected practice may

34. For the text of Berossus, see Felix Jacoby, Die Fragmente der griechischen Historiker, Dritter Teil: Geschichte von Staedten und Voelkern, C: Autoren ueber einzelne Laender (Leiden: Brill, 1958) 380; for other examples of the use of this term, see Lohfink, Die Himmelfahrt Jesu, 41, n. 58.

35. On these passages, see Christopher Begg, "Josephus's Portrayal of the Disappearances of Enoch, Elijah and Moses: Some Observations," JBL, 109 (1990) 691-93. Begg's note is a response to an article by James D. Tabor, "'Returning to Divinity:' Josephus's Portrayal of the Disappearances of Enoch, Elijah, and Moses," JBL 108 (1989) 225-38. The text and translation of Ant. 1.85 cited above are from H. St. J. Thackeray, Josephus (9 vols.; LCL; Cambridge: Harvard University Press; London: Heinemann, 1978) 4.40-41; of Ant. 9.28 from Ralph Marcus, Josephus (9 vols.; LCL; Cambridge: Harvard University Press; London: Heinemann, 1978) 6. 16-17.

36. In spite of the statement in Deuteronomy that Moses died, Josephus did not believe that he did (see Begg, "Some Observations," 692).

37. P. W. van der Horst, The Sentences of Pseudo-Phocylides (Leiden: Brill, 1978) 81-83. Van der Horst dates the work between 30 BC and AD 40.

be secondary burial[38] or the removal of bodies from their graves in order to dissect the corpses.[39] The following statement is given as the reason, "For in fact we hope that the remains of the departed will soon come to the light again out of the earth. And afterwards they become gods" (καὶ τάχα δ' ἐκ γαίης ἐλπίζομεν ἐς φάος ἐλθεῖν λείψαν' ἀποιχομένων· ὀπίσω δὲ θεοὶ τελέθονται).[40] The coming to light of the remains of the departed out of the earth is a clear expression of hope in the bodily type of resurrection, which will be discussed below. The statement that the dead become gods after being raised is an expression of the idea of resurrection in Greco-Roman terms. The word "god" in Greek is synonymous with the word "immortal." So Pseudo-Phocylides is using typical Greek language of the blessed dead to express the idea that the resurrected faithful are exalted to the angelic state. We should recall at this point that the community at Qumran referred to angelic beings as "gods" ('ēlîm).

The Resurrection of Jesus in Mark

At the time the gospel of Mark was written, there were two basic notions of resurrection current, one that emphasized its heavenly character and one that emphasized its bodily character. The heavenly type was expressed in Daniel 12, as was pointed out earlier.[41] The bodily or physical type is attested by the second book of Maccabees.[42] This work contains the story of seven brothers and their mother who were tortured and killed during the persecution of Antiochus IV Epiphanes. Among the tortures were the cutting out of the tongue and the cutting off of hands and feet. Regarding the torture of the third son, the text reads,"When it was demanded, he quickly put out his tongue and courageously stretched forth his hands, and said nobly, 'I got these from

---

38. The placement of bones in an ossuary was a common form of secondary burial in the ancient world (Jack Finegan, *The Archaeology of the New Testament* [Princeton, NJ: Princeton University Press, 1969] 216-18).

39. Van der Horst, *Pseudo-Phocylides*, 82, 183-84.

40. Text and translation from van der Horst, ibid., 94-95; see also the discussion on pp. 186-88.

41. The heavenly notion of resurrection is also expressed in The Epistle of Enoch (chaps. 91-104 of *1 Enoch*). The righteous "will shine like the lights of heaven" and the gate of heaven will be opened to them. They will "have great joy like the angels of heaven" and will "be associates of the host of heaven" (*1 Enoch* 104.2, 4, 6; the translation cited is by M.A. Knibb in [ed. H.F.D. Sparks; *The Apocryphal Old Testament* Oxford: Clarendon, 1984] 312). See also the Similitudes of Enoch, in which it is said that the resurrected righteous "will become angels in heaven" (*1 Enoch* 51.4; Sparks, *The Apocryphal Old Testament*, 231).

42. The rabbinic notion of resurrection, which emphasizes the similarity of the resurrected body to the earthly, physical body, is a later development of the kind of understanding of resurrection attested by 2 Maccabees.

Heaven, and because of his laws I disdain them, and from him I hope to get them back again'" (2 Macc 7.10-11).[43] There is no sign in the book of Daniel of a belief in bodily resurrection of the type present in 2 Maccabees. In the later period, however, the two types could be combined as the example of Pseudo-Phocylides shows.[44]

Two elements are constant, however, in Jewish literature of the time, namely, that resurrection is a collective event and that it is an event of the future.[45] The notion of resurrection did not necessarily imply its universality.[46] The picture of Daniel 12 is collective, but not universal: "many ... shall awake" (vs 2). In 2 Maccabees, the emphasis is on the restoration of individuals, because of the narrative context. Nevertheless, the implicit context of the resurrection is the apocalyptic notion of the renewal of all creation.[47] Thus, one of the innovations of the Christian movement was the claim that God had raised a single individual, Jesus. Paul explained the resurrection of Jesus as the beginning of the renewal that would be followed soon by the resurrection of those who belong to him (1 Cor 15.20-23, 51-52).

The author of Mark was heir to the shocking but simple Christian proclamation that God had raised Jesus from the dead and to the tradition that the risen Jesus had appeared at least to Peter and the Twelve. In writing an extended narrative that expressed the "message" (εὐαγγέλιον) (1.1) of God's activity through Jesus, this author was faced with the challenge of narrating the resurrection. The author has argued elsewhere that the genre of Mark is history in the apocalyptic mode.[48] The working hypothesis in this essay is that Mark 16.1-8 is fiction. In composing the story of the empty tomb, the author of Mark interpreted the proclamation that Jesus had been raised.

I am aware that objections have been raised to the notion that evangelists

---

43. See also 2 Macc 14.37-46.
44. Pseudo-Phocylides incorporates several different understandings of afterlife with little concern for systematic coherence (see van der Horst, *Pseudo-Phocylides*, 188-89).
45. The idea that individual humans who had been translated would return to the earth at the end was widespread in Jewish literature of the second temple period, but these were men who had not died and thus did not need to be resurrected (e.g., Malachi 4.5 [3.23 MT], *1 Enoch* 90.31).
46. Many texts speak only of a resurrection of the just, e.g., *Psalms of Solomon* 3.10-12 [3.13-16].
47. On the apocalyptic background of the resurrection in 2 Maccabees and the reasons for its muted character, see George W. E. Nickelsburg, Jr., *Resurrection, Immortality, and Eternal Life in Intertestamental Judaism* (HTS 26; Cambridge, Mass.: Harvard University Press, 1972) 93-109.
48. Yarbro Collins, "Narrative, History, and Gospel: A General Response," in Mary Gerhart and James G. Williams, ed., *Genre, Narrativity, and Theology, Semeia* 43 (1988) 145-53; see also *The Beginning of the Gospel*, 1-38.

made up episodes and speeches.[49] With regard to speeches, it is widely known that Thucydides, the ancient historian with the most rigorous standards of evidence, stated explicitly that he constructed the speeches in his history of the Peloponnesian War by giving "whatever seemed most appropriate to me for each speaker to say in the particular circumstances, keeping as closely as possible to the general sense of what was actually said" (1.22).[50] I submit that the author of Mark did something analogous. He was convinced that what actually had happened was that Jesus had been raised from the dead. In composing 16.1-8, he described that event in what seemed to him the most appropriate way. So I am not arguing that the author of Mark made up this episode out of whole cloth. He regarded the resurrection of Jesus as an event attested by those to whom the risen Jesus had appeared. Since he did not have evidence for the details regarding how Jesus was raised, he supplied those details in accordance with his sense of what must have happened. Since the male disciples had fled from the scene of the arrest, presumably because their lives were in danger, and since the author apparently assumed that they were in hiding at the time of the crucifixion and burial, it seemed most appropriate to have female disciples discover the empty tomb.

The creation of the empty tomb story shows that the author of Mark had a notion of resurrection closer to that of 2 Maccabees than to that of Daniel 12. Resurrection for Mark is not the giving of a new, spiritual body to the inner person in a way that the former body does not matter. For Mark it is either a revival or transformation of the earthly body. If the text implies that Jesus pushed the stone away from the tomb and walked out, the resurrection is understood as the revival of the body.[51] But such is not a necessary implication. The stone had to be rolled aside so that the women could enter the tomb and see that Jesus was not there. The stone could just as well have been moved by the angel. At least this is how the author of Matthew seems to have understood Mark (Matt 28.2).[52] If the text does not imply that Jesus walked out of the tomb, his resurrection, according to Mark, is best understood as a transformation of his earthly body.

If the risen Jesus is not pictured as walking out of the tomb, the alternative

---

49. Eleonore Stump, "Visits to the Sepulcher and Biblical Exegesis," *Faith and Philosophy* 6 (1989) 367-68.

50. Cited by Oswyn Murray, "Greek Historians," *The Oxford History of the Classical World* (ed. John Boardman et al.; New York: Oxford University Press, 1986) 193-94.

51. Bultmann implies that the position of the stone when the women come to the tomb indicates that Jesus pushed it aside (*History*, 290, n. 3).

52. Compare the *Gospel of Peter* in which the stone rolls away by itself, presumably by divine power (*Gospel of Peter* 37; an English translation is given in *Documents for the Study of the Gospels* [eds. David R. Cartlidge and David L. Dungan; Philadelphia: Fortress, 1980] 85).

is that he ascended to heaven immediately.[53] It has been pointed out that the ascension of Jesus, as narrated in Luke 24.51 and Acts 1.9, is similar to the Greco-Roman narratives of translation.[54] Luke 24.51b reads καὶ ἀνεφέρετο εἰς τὸν οὐρανόν ("and he was carried up into heaven").[55] Acts 1.9 reads καὶ ταῦτα εἰπὼν βλεπόντων αὐτῶν ἐπήρθη καὶ νεφέλη ὑπέλαβεν αὐτὸν ἀπὸ τῶν ὀφθαλμῶν αὐτῶν ("and having said these things, while they were watching, he was lifted up and a cloud took him from their eyes"). The LXX account of the translation of Elijah may have influenced the wording of the account in Acts (the root λαμβάνω ["to take"] is used in both). In spite of the lack of the typical terminology found in Berossus and Josephus, the influence of the Greek and Roman notions of translation and apotheosis is evident. But it is unlikely that the author of Luke-Acts was the first to make this connection.[56] I am suggesting that this tradition also influenced how Mark narrated the resurrection.[57] Mark's statement οὐκ ἔστιν ὧδε ("he is not here" in 16.6) is analogous to Josephus' ἠφανίσθη ("he disappeared") and γεγόνασιν ἀφανεῖς ("they became invisible"). The Christian affirmation was that a single individual, Jesus, had been raised from the dead. Apart from the usual collective context of the Jewish notion of resurrection, this affirmation seemed quite similar to the claim made by Jews like Josephus that Enoch had been taken up to heaven and to the claims made in Greco-Roman circles regarding the translation or apotheosis of heroes, rulers, and emperors.[58] I am not claiming that the empty tomb story was created with an apologetic purpose in the narrow sense. It was not meant to *prove* to outsiders that Jesus really was raised. Rather, the narrative pattern according to which Jesus died, was buried, and then translated to heaven was a culturally defined way for an author living in the first century to narrate the resurrection of Jesus.

It could be objected that it is hard to find much influence of Greco-Roman literature in Mark. The first response that must be made to such an objection is to remind the objector that the gospel of Mark was composed in Greek. This simple fact speaks volumes about the cultural milieu in which the text was

---

53. Bultmann, *History*, 290, n. 3.
54. Lohfink, *Die Himmelfahrt Jesu*, 32-79; Hans Conzelmann, *Acts of the Apostles* (Hermeneia; Philadelphia: Fortress, 1987) 7, n. 26; Haenchen, *The Acts of the Apostles*, 149, n. 5.
55. Codex Sinaiticus, Codex Bezae, the Old Latin version, and the Sinaitic Syriac version lack these words.
56. See the review of Lohfink, *Die Himmelfahrt Jesu*, by Fred O. Francis (*JBL* 91 [1972] 424-25).
57. Pease, citing a brief suggestion by F. Pfister, notes that there are certain likenesses between the disappearance of the body of Jesus from the tomb and certain pagan traditions, but he does not attempt to explain them or to reconstruct the process by which they arose ("Invisibility," 29).
58. On the translation of rulers and emperors, see ibid., 16-17.

NYACK COLLEGE MANHATTAN

written. One does not learn and use a language without being influenced by the culture of which it is part. Similarly, one does not address people competent in a certain language without drawing upon the thought-world for which that language is a vehicle. Recent studies have supported older suggestions that there are significant similarities between Mark and Greco-Roman literature in form, content and style.[59]

If, according to Mark, Jesus was translated from the grave to heaven, then there was no period of time during which the risen Jesus walked the earth and met with his disciples. The book of Acts states that he did so for forty days. The gospels of John and Luke also imply that he did so, but, in the case of John at least, for a shorter period. Even Matthew recounts a scene in which the women meet the risen Jesus and take hold of his feet (28.9). If, as was concluded above, the author of Mark accepted the tradition that the risen Jesus had appeared to Peter and the Twelve, this appearance (or appearances) was probably of a more heavenly type, like the apocalyptic visions of heavenly beings. Jesus' body, according to Mark, was not simply revived; it was transformed. He had been exalted from an earthly status to a heavenly status, body and soul. The appearance to the Eleven in Galilee in Matthew (28.16-20) may be understood as a heavenly type of resurrection appearance. The appearance to Paul as it is narrated in Acts is definitely of this type.

The effect of this understanding of the resurrection of Jesus is to place the accent on the absence of Jesus more than on the presence of Jesus during the time of the readers. As noted earlier, this accent is related to apocalyptic expectation. The disciples have a mission in this world (13.9-13, 8.34-37) and they will be judged on the basis of their fulfillment or non-fulfillment of that mission (8.38). The interpretation of the resurrection of Jesus as a type of translation has an effect on one's reading of the apocalyptic discourse of chapter 13. That discourse has its climax in the prediction of the coming of the Son of Man in clouds with great power and glory. The result of his appearance is his sending out the angels to gather the faithful "from the four winds, from the end of the earth to the end of heaven" (13.27). It is likely that this prediction refers to the same event that Paul describes in 1 Thess 4.17 and 1 Cor 15.52. As their master was translated, so will his faithful disciples be.

59. Hubert Cancik, "Die Gattung Evangelium. Markus im Rahmen der antiken Historiographie," *Markus-Philologie: Historische, literargeschichtliche und stilistische Untersuchungen zum zweiten Evangelium* (ed. Hubert Caneik; WUNT 33; Tübingen: Mohr [Siebeck], 1984) 85-113; idem, "Bios und Logos. Formengeschichtliche Untersuchungen zu Lukians 'Leben des Demonax,'" *Markus-Philologie*, 115-30; Marius Reiser, "Der Alexanderroman und das Markusevangelium," *Markus-Philologie*, 131-63; Gert Lüderitz, "Rhetorik, Poetik, Kompositionstechnik im Markusevangelium," *Markus-Philologie*, 165-203; David E. Aune, *The New Testament in Its Literary Environment* (Philadelphia: Westminster, 1987); Vernon K. Robbins, *Jesus the Teacher: A Socio-Rhetorical Interpretation of Mark* (Philadelphia: Fortress, 1984).

The Hellenistic *Theios Aner* —
A Model for Early Christian Christology?

Aage Pilgaard

I. Introduction

In 1961 the first professor of the theological faculty in Århus, the late Johannes Munck, wrote concerning the problem of gnosticism: "One cannot therefore be too careful as to scientific vocabulary if one really wishes to carry on research and achieve lasting results."[1] I think the same can be said concerning the term *theios aner*. The term became a favourite term in New Testament scholarship from the sixties onwards especially in the redaction-critical school. It attained the role as the key to solve problems concerning the formation, function, and christology of the miracle traditions in the gospels, and especially concerning Mark's handling of this tradition when shaping his gospel.[2]

In fact, the linkage of the miracle tradition to *theios aner* had been done already by the masters of the form-critical school, R. Bultmann and M. Dibelius, who in this respect were dependent on the history-of-religions school, where the term as scientific term originated.[3] Although the redaction-critical school seems to be losing ground, the debate concerning *theios aner* is still going on as the appearance of two monographs on the subject in 1986 and 1991

---

1. "The New Testament and Gnosticism", *ST* 15 (1961) 181-95, esp. 192.
2. For a survey of history, see M. Smith, "Prolegomena to a Discussion of Aretalogies, Divine Men, the Gospels, and Jesus", *JBL* 90 (1971) 174-99; C. Holladay, *Theios Aner in Hellenistic Judaism* (SBLDS 40; Missoula: Scholars, 1977) 1-47; G.P. Corrington, *The "Divine Man"* (American University Studies VII.17; New York: Peter Lang, 1986) 1-58; H. Blackburn, *Theios Anēr and the Markan Miracle Traditions* (WUNT 40; Tübingen: Mohr [Siebeck], 1991) 1-10.
3. R. Bultmann, *Die Geschichte der synoptischen Tradition* (FRLANT 12; Göttingen: Vandenhoeck & Ruprecht, 1921. Reprinted, Göttingen: Vandenhoeck & Ruprecht, 1970) 256; R. Bultmann, *Theologie des Neuen Testaments* (Tübingen: Mohr-Siebeck, 1958. Reprinted, Tübingen: Mohr [Siebeck], 1965) 132; M. Dibelius, *Die Formgeschichte des Evangeliums* (Tübingen: Mohr [Siebeck], 1919. Reprinted, Tübingen, 1966) 90-100; R. Reitzenstein, *Die Hellenistischen Mysterienreligionen* (Leipzig: Teubner, 1910) used the term "theios anthropos", so also O. Weinreich, "Antikes Gottmenschentum", *Neue Jahrb. für Wissenschaft und Jugendbildung* 2 (1926) 633-51. With L. Bieler's book entitled *Theios aner*, this term became common.

clearly demonstrates, but critical voices, as is Blackburn's, are getting stronger.[4] Should J.C. Kingsbury's question: "The "Divine Man" as the Key to Mark's Christology — The End of an Era?" prove to be answered in the affirmative I find it useful to take up the question in light of recent research on the question.[5] And the more so as the employment of the term in Biblical scholarship clearly demonstrates that the term has been seen as a focal point for problems concerning the relationship between Judaism and Hellenism (Hellenistic Judaism/Palestinian Judaism) and between Judaism and Early Christianity (Palestinian Jewish Christianity/Hellenistic Jewish Christianity).[6] So the term is relevant as regards the theme of this conference. In this paper I will confine myself to the question as far as it regards the miracles and with special reference to the Gospel of Mark.

II. The Thesis

The thesis can be sketched briefly in the following way: The term *theios aner* designates a rather clear concept personified in several historical figures in the Hellenistic-Roman period. The substantial element in the concept is that men can participate in divinity, and that this divine quality is demonstrated primarily through miraculous power and extraordinary wisdom.

Sociologically, men, classified under the concept, were itinerant preachers of salvation, or they were by their adherents preached as divine saviours, a status which was emphasized by appeal (primarily) to their miraculous power. The miraculous deeds of the divine men were communicated through a specific genre, the aretalogy.

The concept as well as the missionary activity were taken over by Hellenistic Judaism in the Diaspora to defend and promote the Jewish religion. Hellenistic Judaism so functioned as medium for the transfer of the concept to early Hellenistic Jewish Christianity.

By means of this concept a specific christology developed, a *theios aner* christology. This explains the origin of collections of miracle stories (= aretalogies) functioning as handbooks for the missionaries.

Theologically, this christology is classified as a *theologia gloriae* in opposition to a *theologia crucis*. It was in order to combat or modify this *theologia gloriae* in favour of a *theologia crucis* that Mark wrote his gospel. To achieve this goal he used the *Messianic secret*. Against this hypothesis the question can be

---

4. G.P. Corrington, H. Blackburn, see note 2. See also R. Glöckner, *Neutestamentliche Wundergeschichten und das Lob der Wundertaten Gottes in den Psalmen* (Walberger Studien 13; Mainz: Matthias-Grünewald, 1983); E.V. Gallagher, *Divine Man or Magician? Celsus and Origin on Jesus* (SBLDS 64; Chico: Scholars, 1980); J.R. Brady, *Jesus Christ. Divine Man or Son of God?* (Lanham: University Press of America, 1992).
5. *Interpretation* 35 (1981) 243-57. See Corrington, *"Divine Man"*, 1-4.
6. Cf. Holladay, *Theios Aner*, 7.

raised: is there another setting for understanding the christology of Mark?

III. The Problem of Defining the Term

In the debate concerning *theios aner* critics have focused upon the relation between the term *theios aner* and the concept *theios aner*, a debate which demonstrates that the definition of the concept needs to be considered.

It has been argued that the term *theios aner* never occurs in the Septuagint and the New Testament, and as regards the Greek-Hellenistic world, W. von Martitz has shown that in pre-Christian sources the term *theios aner* is not used as a title, and also that there is no close connection between *theios* and the charismatic until New-Platonic and New-Pythagorean literature.[7] But H.D. Betz rightly claims that the occurrence of the term can not be decisive for the question of the existence of the concept.[8] The concept can be expressed through a variety of terms. So it is clear that the term *theios aner* is a scientific term which is used to explain and to classify certain figures in the ancient world. But one still has to ask if the term would not have occurred more often if it expressed a well-known category. More important, however, is the question whether a specific semantic content (the concept of a *theios aner*), assumed to be contained in the syntagm *theios aner*, has determined the definition of the scientific term *theios aner* in an inappropriate way.

1. H.D. Betz
According to H.D. Betz the background to this concept *is a specific anthropology:*

This concept must be seen within the framework of Hellenistic anthropology for which man was not simply a given species of being. Man in this concept is not simply what he is, but he is a being hovering between his two possibilities, the divine (*theion*) and the animal (*theriodes*). Only the Divine Man is man in the full sense.[9]

So, for H. D. Betz it is the anthropology which constitutes the concept. But this is a too narrow definition, if the concept shall be used for a typological classification of *theios aner* figures. This becomes clear when, on the next page

---

7. O. Betz, "The Concept of the So-Called 'Divine Man' in Mark's Christology", *Studies in New Testament and Early Christian Literature* (NovTSup 33, ed. D. Aune; Leiden: Brill, 1972) 229-40. "υἱός", *TWNT* 8.335-340, esp. 338. Idem, 338. Against von Martitz: H.D. Betz, "Gottmensch", *RAC* XII, 234-312, esp. 248.
8. *Lucian von Samosata und das Neue Testament* (TU 76; Berlin: Akademie-Verlag, 1961) 102. "Gottmensch", 235. See also H.-W. Kuhn, *Ältere Sammlungen im Markusevangelium* (SUNT 8; Göttingen: Vandenhoeck & Ruprecht, 1971) 195.
9. "Jesus as Divine Man", *Jesus and the Historian* (ed. F.T. Trotter; Philadelphia: Westminster, 1968) 114-33, esp. 116.

(p. 117) Betz writes about the variations of the *theios aner*, within the New Testament: "Although they presuppose his [Jesus'] *full* [my italics] humanity,..." Without mentioning the problem concerning the anthropological concept which in the basic definition is semantic constitutive: "Only the Divine Man is man in the *full* [my italics] sense", the anthropological concept has now been changed ("although"). He is presupposed in the New Testament variations to have "full humanity", but at the same time "Jesus is not merely a *human being* [my italics], but a *higher being* in human *form*", and yet "he is presented quite undualistically."

The distinction between *being* and *form* then seems to be at the center of this anthropology; to be "hovering between the divine and the animal" then seems to be belonging to "the animal" in regard to *form* and to "the divine" in regard to *being*. Such an anthropology I would classify as dualistic, but Jesus is presented quite undualistically. It seems strange to me that a christology that has as its central goal to present Jesus as divine being in human form can at the same time presuppose his *"full humanity."*

Yet, H.D. Betz refers to a Hellenistic *variant* of the concept behind the New Testament.[10] Obviously it is this variant which shall explain the change from an anthropology according to which "only the Divine Man is man in the full sense" to an anthropology according to which a man can be Divine Man, although he shares in "full humanity" and "in contrast to comparable figures in Hellenistic texts ... is presented quite undualistically." But if the constitutive content of the concept is a specific anthropology, how then is it possible to talk about a *theios aner* concept which seems to presuppose a fundamentally different anthropology as just a *variation*?

What has happened is a shift from the basic definition of the concept which is based on a specific anthropology, to a tacit definition which pre-supposes an anthropology according to which a man can have "full humanity" and at the same time be divinely gifted. But this is an anthropology which is well-known in Old Testament-Jewish thinking. So, H.D. Betz' definition of the New Testament variants raises the question, whether this concept in the New Testament cannot be better explained within Old Testament-Jewish con-ceptuality, and it also seems that the critics' pointing to the absence or rare use of the term in the sources is not quite unjustified.[11]

I think that the term, as scientific term, must be defined so broadly that it

10. "Jesus", 117.
11. See also Gallagher's critique. (*Divine Man*, 15): "His interpretative strategy echoes those of his predecessors in a disturbing way". Gallagher rehabilitates L. Bieler whose typological method, he claims, has been misunderstood. According to Gallagher scholars have misunderstood Bieler's method: "By misapprehending Bieler's use of the ideal type and by appealing to his work as support for the existence of a Hellenistic type of the divine man, scholars like Koester and Betz have perpetrated a historical anachronism." (*Divine Man*, 16).

allows for different anthropologies to be classified as "subtypes" under a basic type. And then it is very important that the scientific term and the empirical phenomena, classified by means of this term are kept apart. H.D. Betz' procedure implies that when the basic definition has been given, then in the analysis of the texts all traits which have some similarity with traits ascribed to *theioi andres* of the Hellenistic anthropological type are qualified as evidence of a *theios aner* christology, and the basic difference is forgotten.

That is to say that the basic anthropology functions as a creative force, translating or producing similar traits which remove Jesus from an eschatological type and places him under the *theios aner* type. Such a transformation certainly is a possibility and maybe also what actually happened. But H.D. Betz' argumentation moves in a circle, resting on the assumption that similarities between A and B have to be explained by assuming dependency (B dependent on A or vice versa). So similarities between the Hellenistic *theios aner* type and the Jesus of the gospels prove dependency on a specific anthropology, and then this dependency is proved by the similarities, although H.D. Betz admits (indirectly) that the basic anthropology which functions as the creative force in the proces of translation is not to be found in the material.

When similarities (and differences) are explained solely on a diacronic level without considering the synchronic level (as is the case with H.D. Betz) the possibility that different anthropologies (and theologies) can produce similar traits is excluded beforehand. So I do not think a definition of *theios aner* as scientific term to be used in comparative studies of religions, based on a specific anthropology, is very helpful.

The question concerning a definition focusing upon the anthropology raises another question: what is the implied theo-logy? The concept behind the term *theios aner* involves not only man's relation to the divine, but also the relation of the divine to man. In the concept *theios aner* the anthropology is the one pole on an axis on which the divine is the other pole, and the relations between these two poles in both directions are decisive for both poles. So I have to ask: should it be the implied theology that motivates this "variant" which in fact is not just a variant but a basic shift? What does it mean for the anthropology, whether the implied theology is e.g. polytheistic, pantheistic-cosmological or monotheistic dynamic?

2. E.V. Gallagher

The problem of defining the concept of *theios aner* also has an ethical aspect which points to the ambiguity of *theios aner* figures. A *theios aner* needs "veridiction": he can be accepted or unmasked as, e.g., a magician. This ethical aspect has been stressed by E.V. Gallagher in an important methodological study of the *theios aner* figure.[12]

---

12. See note 4.

His investigation leads him to the conclusion that:

there was no native Hellenistic conception of the divine man — at least in the sense
in which that term has been recently used. There is no pre-existent device or
pattern, but rather the attempt to situate, for whatever purposes, a specific candidate
within a spectrum of possible evaluations.[13]

The reason is "that there was no unanimous assent to a single "Image" of
society, human activity, and *the nature* [underlining mine] of divinity."[14]
Gallagher also emphasizes that there is no necessary connection between
"divine men, aretalogies, and religious propaganda." It is not possible to isolate
religious propaganda from apologetic, as "the missionary scenario in Late
Antiquity was a very complex scenario."[15] *Theioi andres* can be found "in a
wide range of texts not specifically biographical in form."[16] According to
Gallagher the decisive criterion for classification of a theios aner is to be found
— not on the anthropological but on the ethical level: for a man to be a *theios
aner* he must be a good man and communicate good things to men. But the
criteria for what is good can vary heavily.[17]

In my opinion, Gallagher through his investigation has demonstrated that
the traditional use of the *theios aner* concept is too narrow.

13. *Divine Man*, 174. Gallagher seeks "native systems of classification" following M.
    Douglas and R. Bulmer who have studied "primitive" systems of classification (R.
    Bulmer, "Why the Cassowary is not a bird", *Rules and Meanings* [ed. M. Douglas;
    Harmondsworth: Pinguin Books, 1973] 167-93; M. Douglas, "Animals in Lele
    Religious Symbolism", *Essays in Anthropology* [London: Routledge & Kegan, 1975]
    27-46). He seeks the native arguments for placing a figure in the position of a *theios
    aner*, and counterarguments. They can be brought on the following formula: X (subj.)
    should be considered Y (quality). Y shows the implicit principles of classification:
    because Z (*Divine Man*, 35).
14. *Divine Man*, 178. As regards the rise of *theioi andres* R.P. Brown ("The Rise and
    Function of the Holy Man in Late Antiquity", *JRS* 61 (1971) 80-101), has argued that
    the interest in these figures' spectacular thaumaturgical performances has had the
    consequence that the social background has been neglected. They gained their power
    through hard work for their locality. For Brown they constitute a particular type to
    be differentiated from earlier Hellenistic *theioi andres* whose source of power was
    occult wisdom. Another difference is, according to Brown, that the first type came
    from outside (patronage — institution), while the *theioi andres* were located within
    the society. Against this latter view see D. Georgi, "Socioeconomic Reasons for the
    "Divine Man" as a Propagandistic Pattern", *Aspects of Religious Propaganda in Judaism
    and Early Christianity* (ed. E. Schüssler-Fiorenza; Notre Dame: University of Notre
    Dame Press, 1976) 27-42, who maintains that the concept of the divine man has its
    origin from the polis.
15. *Divine Man*, 173.
16. *Divine Man*, 174.
17. *Divine Man*, 175.

3. Different Types of Theios Aner

Attempts to distinguish different types of *theios aner* have been made by D.L. Tiede and C. Talbert.[18] Tiede classifies according to the criteria for authenticating divine status. By means of a diachronic analysis he thinks it is possible to demonstrate the existence of two classes of criteria, one being wisdom/moral virtue, the other miraculous deeds or events, so that two types of *theios aner* must be kept apart: the philosophical type which he traces back to Sokrates, and the divine miracle worker. But he does not mention a prototype for the miracle worker type, so his typology seems to need further clarification.[19]

For Talbert the criterion is the position in regard to mortality — eternity, so he distinguishes between two types of *theios aner*: a type displaying divine presence in their historical life and a more selected group attaining immortality, a group which must be distinguished from the eternals.

H. Blackburn has examined sources from Homer to Philostratus about *theioi andres*, to whom miracles are ascribed. He comes to the result that several parallels can be found on several levels as regards their *status* (divine beings) and *types* of miraculous actions (exorcism, healing, raising the dead, mastery

---

18. D.L. Tiede, *The Charismatic Figure as Miracle Worker* (Missoula, Montana: Scholars Press, 1972). C. Talbert "The Concept of Immortals in Mediterranean Antiquity", *JBL* 94 (1975), 419-436.

19. Cf. Gallagher, *Divine Man*, 19-20. The need for further clarification as regards the use of the concept as criterion for selecting sources containing a *theios aner* christology becomes clear when the attempts of H.-W. Kuhn (*Sammlungen*, 191-213); L.E. Keck ("Mark 3,7-12 and Mark's Christology", *JBL* 84 (1965) 341-58); P.J. Achtemeier ("Towards the Isolation of Pre-Markan Miracle Catenae", *JBL* 89 (1970) 265-91); U. Luz ("Das Geheimnismotiv und die markinische Christologie",*ZNW* 56 (1965) 9-30); and H.D. Betz are compared. For Kuhn the decisive criterion is the degree of the miraculous, for L.E. Keck it is important that there is no conflict with the Jews and only peripherical connection with Jesus' message in its original setting. According to H.D. Betz the *theios aner* christology can be seen, not only in the miracle stories (incl. controversy dialogues) and the legends but also in the passion — and resurrection narratives. Also Jesus' authority as teacher, the atoning power of his death and his calling of disciples are for H.D. Betz characterized by a *theios aner* christology. As regards the role of faith, it is important for Keck that this motif plays a minor role in his collection — this being typical for the *theios aner* christology, while this motif for H.-W. Kuhn and H.D. Betz should be classified as *theios aner* christology. But for U. Luz this motif shows that the *theios aner* christology has been overcome. The question concerning two types: Wise man/teacher and miracle worker or one type combining boths qualities is relevant for passages where Jesus is presented as both miracle-worker and teacher. Some scholars think that e.g. Mark by means of the teaching motif minimizes the miracle motif (*theios aner*), see e.g. L. Schenke, *Die Wundererzählungen des Markusevangeliums* (SBB; Stuttgart: Katolisches Bibelerk, 1974) 105. See also W.A. Meeks, "The Divine Agent and his Counterfeit in Philo and the Fourth Gospel", *Aspects* (cf. note 14), 43-67: "The expression ["Divine Man"] is not a completely satisfactory one..." (43).

over elements, miraculous provision of food, prediction, supernatural knowledge of present but hidden reality, and postmortem activity).[20]

As regards the *genre* of the material there are a few pre-Christian and several post-Christian narratives which have a narrative structure similar to that of the Gospel miracle narratives.[21] But the position and the miraculous activity of these figures vary, so they can not be seen as one group. So it seems that not even the miracle working *theioi andres* can be taken as just one group but have to be divided into subtypes according to relevant criteria.

Blackburn does not develop a typology for a closer classification, however, but states: "In view of this situation it is misleading to ask: "Does the Markan miracle tradition assimilate Jesus to the typical miracle-working *theios aner*?".[22]

Blackburn does not either investigate the question concerning characteristic changes in the portraits of these figures on a diacronic line. I think this would have been very useful.

IV. Social Setting and Literary Genre

That itinerant preachers preaching salvation and authenticating their message by means of miraculous power were known in the first century AD is beyond doubt.[23] I need only mention Apollonius of Tyana, who certainly was not the only one. The main problem, however, is the sources available to us in order to get a clear picture of such figures[24] Not only is much of the source material of much later date, but the position which the authors take to these figures is also very different, e.g. that of Philostratus and that of Lucian.

The problems concerning the source material become very obvious, when one asks the question regarding the *genre* of the stories about such figures and their activity. According to some scholars it is possible to reconstruct a specific literary genre. So M. Hadas and M. Smith have tried to reconstruct an aretalogical genre, although they recognize that the material is sparse.[25] They define it as a type of biographical writing:

---

20. *Theios Anēr*, 92-96.
21. *Theios Anēr*, 92.
22. *Theios Anēr*, 96.
23. See Corrington, *"Divine Man"*, 159-81.
24. See H.C. Kee, *Medicine, Miracle and Magic in New Testament Times* (SNTSMS 55; Cambridge: Cambridge University Press, 1986) 78. "The evidence adduced for comparison with the gospel narratives dates from a century to a century and a half — or more — after the gospels were written: Lucian, Philostratus, Greek magical papyri. This material.... embodies basic shifts in the worldviews prevalent from the first part of the first century A.D. down into the second and third centuries. Evident as those changes are, they are ignored by the interpreters who stand in this older history-of-religions tradition".
25. *Heroes and Gods*, (New York: Harper & Row, 1963).

... a formal account of the remarkable career of an impressive teacher that was used as the basis for moral instruction. The preternatural gifts of the teacher often included power to work wonders; often his teaching brought him the hostility of a tyrant, whom he confronted with courage and at whose hands he suffered martyrdom. Often the circumstances of his birth or death involve elements of the miraculous.[26]

According to Hadas, it is "the aretalogy of Sokrates implied, or even premised, in Plato that doubtless became the model for an independent literary genre", but the pattern is fully developed in Philostratus' Life of Apollonios.[27]

H.C. Kee has pointed out the discrepancies between this definition and the material adduced to support it.[28] Kee is willing, however, to accept a formal definition of the aretalogy if it is limited to designate: "a collection of miracle stories and that the primary use of such a collection was praise or propaganda for the deity supposed to have done such deeds", which was Smith's initial definition.[29] But Kee is not willing to accept the implication that this definition, when applied to the gospel miracle narratives, also determines their christology (*theios aner*). But I think that Smith is quite logical when he draws that conclusion from his initial definition.

Kee's point, however, seems to be that although this implication holds true for the aretalogical material in writings such as those of Lucian and Philostratus, this need not be the case for the miracles in the gospels:

On the contrary, what must be recognized is that critic cannot draw general conclusions about the cultural context or theological intention of the miracle tradition or of the "aretalogies" in which they are loosely grouped. The aim of a miracle story is a function of the use to which the story is put rather than something that inheres in the miracle story as such.[30]

I agree that the "pragmatic" level is important for the understanding of the intention which the narrator pursued with his narrative. But then Kee should not have accepted even Smith's first definition of an aretalogy as a general definition, for as a general definition it is also a basic definition, and then we are confronted with the same problem as before concerning the term *theios aner*. It is not a question concerning what is inherent or not inherent in the miracle narratives, but it is a question concerning the definition of these narratives. If the term "aretalogy" is defined as Smith did in his first definition ("a collection of miracle stories", primarily for "praise or propaganda for the deity supposed

---

26. *Heroes*, 3.
27. *Heroes*, 58.
28. "Aretalogy and Gospel", *JBL* 92 (1973) 401-422, esp. 204-8.
29. "Aretalogy", 408-409. *JBL* (1971) 176-77.
30. "Aretalogy", 112.

to have done such deeds") then it seems confusing to use the term to designate a genre, the main character of which is not in some sense divine.

Such a definition of the form is quite natural, as the difinition is the result of diacronic analysis, and by diacronic analysis it can be proved that the term was connected with cult gods and used as designation for the recital of the benefactions of the god, although not for the form but the content of the recital, as I think D. Esser has convincingly shown.[31] The transfer of the term to narratives of *theioi andres* is then quite naturally seen as an expression of the conviction that these men were in some kind divine. This means that if one wants to use the term *aretalogy* as designation for a collection of narratives, the main character of which is not seen as divine, one has to give up a definition by means of diacronic criteria and make it so broad that it can encompass a wide scale of main characters.

But this problem is not the only one which Smith's definition raises. The definition considers in fact also the pragmatic level, in so far as it defines the *function* of the form to be "praise or propaganda", but I am not sure that this is the sole purpose of the gospel miracle narratives, although it is an important one. So the definition must also allow a range of possibilities as regards the function of the form.

V. Theios Aner and Hellenistic Judaism

C. Holladay has emphasized that the very term Hellenization presupposes "a one-way movement in the direction of influence" between Judaism and Hellenism, i.e.: from Hellenism to Judaism.[32]

As regards the concept of *theios aner* this means that two different worlds: the Hellenistic (expressed by the term *theios aner*) and the Old Testament-Jewish world (expressed by the term *man of God*) were fused by a Hellenistic transformation of the Old Testament-Jewish world into a Hellenistic-Jewish world (Moses = *theios aner*), a fusion that in particular took place in the Diaspora. So the way was opened for a similar transformation of Jesus.[33] The *theios aner* hypothesis so presupposes the classic history-of-religions division of the Jewish world into a Palestinian and a Hellenistic world.

Jesus and the Primitive Church in Palestine lived in a world unaffected by Hellenistic conceptuality. It was the meeting with the Hellenistic (Jewish and pagan) world outside Palestine which caused the translation of parts of the Jesus tradition into the *theios aner* concept.

---

31. *Formgeschichtliche Studien zur hellenistischen und frühchristlichen Literatur unter besonderer Berücksichtigung der vita Apollonii des Philostrat und der Evangelien* (Bonn; Masch. Diss., 1969), esp. 101.
32. *Theios Aner*, 6.
33. *Theios Aner*, 15-17.

This separation between Hellenistic and Palestinian Judaism seems now to have been left. In a paper, read on the seminar, "Paul and his Hellenistic Background" (Copenhagen 1991), P. Borgen characterizes the present state of research in this way: "The prevailing trend within research on Judaism is moving away from the distinction traditionally drawn between Palestinian (normative) Judaism and Hellenistic Judaism." And he continues: "Similarly the distinction between the Palestinian Jewish church and the Hellenistic church is also largely abandoned, at least in principle."

This "in principle" is important, for it raises the question, whether New Testament research as regards the term *theios aner* while acknowledging the "in principle" — still has to draw the consequences of this "in principle".

In this connection it is also important that Borgen emphasizes the "complexity of Judaism both in Palestine and in the Diaspora and the variety of tendencies which existed within Christianity as it emerged within Judaism and moved out into the nations."

As regards Jewish Messianism this complexity is clearly indicated by the following book title: *Judaisms and Their Messiahs*.[34] How then are we to define Judaism? What is the central criterion for the classification of Judaism?[35] And how to define Hellenistic Judaism? I would prefer a broad but then also rather vague definition: Hellenistic Judaism is the Judaism of the Hellenistic period.[36]

Keeping this complexity in mind the search for Jewish parallels to figures, classified as *theioi andres*, can not be limited to the Jewish diaspora.[37] Traditionally, sources for detecting influence from the alleged Hellenistic *theios aner* type have been found mainly in the writings of Philo and Josephus. Most important for the hypothesis that Hellenistic Jews were engaged in missionary propaganda and for that end clothed the Jewish heroes of the past in the dress

---

34. Ed. J. Neusner, W. Scott Green, E.S. Frerichs; Cambridge: Cambridge University Press, 1987.
35. Cf. Tiede, *Charismatic Figure*, 107, Holladay, *Theios Aner*, 13.
36. The question is discussed by M. Hengel, see *The Hellenization of Judea in the First Century after Christ*, (London: SCM Press, 1989).
37. The question of Jewish and rabbinic miracle workers was taken up by Fiebig, see: *Jüdische Wundergeschichten* (Tübingen: Mohr-Siebeck, 1911). Fiebig was criticized by A. Schlatter, *Das Wunder in der Synagoge* (BFCT 16,5; Gütersloh: Bertelsmann, 1912). Critical to Fiebig also M. Smith, cf. note 2. G. Vermes, *Jesus the Jew* (London: Collins, 1973) has emphasized the Jewish setting for Jesus' miraculous activity, but the reliability of much of the source material as witness to the 1st century is questionable. Well-known miracle workers were Hanina ben Dosa and Eliezer ben Hyrkanos. Josephus tells about revolutionary rebels who promised that the great miracles of the past would be repeated, J.W. 2.258-64; cf. U. Mauser, *Christ in the Wilderness* (SBT 39; London: SCM, 1963) 56-58.

of Hellenistic *theioi andres* has been D. Georgi's analysis of 2 Corinthians.[38] Although Georgi also draws on other sources than Philo and Josephus, I can not let me convince that the source material adduced by Georgi can legitimize his conclusions.[39] The primary setting for those sources was not mission but apology.[40] To how far a degree Philo and Josephus give their Old Testament heroes divine qualifications is difficult to decide, but it seems clear to me that it is not miraculous power which constitues their exalted status but wisdom.[41]

When valuing the importance of the miraculous element one also has to remember the role which this element played in the Old Testament's traditions about, in particular, Moses.[42]

Holladay is reluctant to use the term *theios aner* about Philo's and Josephus' Moses because of the ambiquity of this term, and he even thinks that an effect of the Hellenization was a tendency rather to widen the gap than to bridge it, while Blackburn recognizes a tendency to qualify Moses as divine although not in the strict sense.[43]

Against Tiede and Holladay, G.P. Corrington is right to argue that parallels to the New Testament miracles and their christology must be sought from sources evidencing more popular beliefs than those found in Philo and Josephus. And she thinks that we in Artapanus' portrait of Moses "find the popularized picture of a Jewish national hero who combines philosophic virtue with wonderworking power: in short, a *theios aner*".[44]

Corrington also includes the Hermetic literature and the magical papyri.[45] Quite apart from the question concerning the dating of this material I think

---

38. *Die Gegner des Paulus im 2. Korintherbrief* (WMANT 11; Neukirchen: Neukirchener Verlag, 1964).
39. See also Glöckner, *Wundergeschichten*, 14-15. E. Schweizer, "Towards a Christology of Mark?", *God's Christ and his People: Studies in Honour of Niels Alstrup Dahl* (ed. J. Jervell, W.A. Meeks; Oslo, Bergen, Tromsö: Universitetsforlaget, 1977) 29-42, who remarks: "A link between these miracle stories [Mark's] and the opponents of Paul in Corinth remains very uncertain" (30).
40. Cf. Meeks, "Divine Agent" (note 19).
41. So Tiede and Holladay, cf. Schweizer, "Christology", 30-31.
42. G. Theissen, *Urchristliche Wundergeschichten* (SNT 8; Gütersloh, 1974) 269, emphasizes that the reason why Jewish apologists portrait the Old Testament heroes as miracle workers was the traditions about them in the Old Testament, not that this activity was constituent for a *theios aner*. W.A. Meeks, "Divine Agent", 53-54: Philo has combined the Hellenistic theory of kingship with the scriptural tradition of the apostolic prophet in order to emphasize the uniquely divine quality of Moses' *politeia*. Meeks sees a connection between Philo's stress on the politeia and the situation of the Jews in Alexandria (they were not citizens, but *metoikoi*).
43. *Theios Aner*, 237-38; *Theios Anēr*, 72.
44. "*Divine Man*", 143.
45. "*Divine Man*", 110-130.

there are great differences between this material and the New Testament miracle narratives. The concept which makes it possible for Corrington to unify very different material under the *theios aner* type is not — as with H.D. Betz — the anthropology but the concept of power. This concept was introduced into research on the *theios aner* by G.P. Wetter under the term *mana*, borrowed from the comparative history of religions.[46] For Wetter it was this concept which made it possible for him to assimilate different figures from different times (e.g. Saul, Muhammed, Melanesian chiefs, and Jesus). In fact it is the same concept of power which justifies Corrington's neglect of differences as regards the understanding of power. Such differences must be taken in consideration in order to decide, if there was a general trend in Hellenistic Judaism to transform their Old Testament heroes into *theioi andres* for whom miracles were the decisive qualification. In fact, Corrington has to admit that the best witnesses to the transfer of this alleged type from Hellenistic Judaism to Early Christianity is "the Gospels themselves".[47] But then the conclusion rests on what indeed had to be proved.

VI. The Development of a Theios Aner Christology

According to H. Köster the *theios aner* concept was taken over in the Syriac area by Jewish-Christian missionaries, "die einen neuen Bund verkündeten und ihre Predigt durch Krafttaten und Wunder unterstrichen."[48] As support for their propaganda they collected miracle narratives which were used as "Handbücher". In those "Handbücher" Jesus was presented as "der göttliche Mensch *schlechthin*." [underlining mine]. From this christology Köster separates other distinct christologies: a christology centered around cross and resurrection, a christology qualifying Jesus as "Ruf der himmlischen Weisheit", and a christology which saw Jesus as the apocalyptic Son of Man.[49]

I think that Köster's analytical strategy is very useful to discover basic concepts in the material. The procedure makes it possible to classify the material in different subtypes of christology. The problem, however, is that the analytical classification is identified with empirical classification. This identification presupposes that the differences between various christologies were also clearly recognized by those who transmitted the material. This may be the case, but it is not in itself necessary. What we must keep apart on the analytical level, can cohere on the empirical level. Taking in consideration the

---

46. *Der Sohn Gottes*, (FRLANT 26; Göttingen: Vandenhoeck & Ruprecht, 1916).
47. *"Divine Man"*, 35.
48. *Einführung in das Neue Testament* (Berlin, New York: de Gruyter, 1980) 601.
49. *Einführung*, 601; "Ein Jesus und vier ursprüngliche Evangeliengattungen", *Entwicklungslinien durch die Welt des frühen Christentums* (ed. H. Köster, J. Robinson; Tübingen: Mohr [Siebeck], 1971) 147-90. Critical Gallagher, *Divine Man*, 16.

complexity of ideas which was characteristic for this period it is only natural that different concepts and ideas were fused, if people thought that this fusion could serve to emphasize their message.

In this respect I think that M. Hengel is *quite right* when he remarks:

The remarkable number of names applied to wisdom and the various ways of conceiving of it, and even more the similar variety in the case of Philo's Logos, show us that it is misleading to unravel the web of christological titles into a number of independent and indeed conflicting christologies with different communities standing behind each. To adopt this approach brings one as near to historical reality as if one were to suppose that there was an independent 'Logos doctrine' behind each of the names given to Philo's Logos. Such a method only opens up a wide range of historical absurdities.[50]

The assumption behind Köster's procedure is that there exists a one-to-one relationship between genre/form and *Sitz im Leben*, and that a specific Sitz im Leben can be taken as expression of the whole or dominant life of a community. But this can not be presupposed, it has to be *proved*.[51]

There is still another matter to be considered: Köster does not only classify the christology of the assumed aretalogies as a *theios aner* christology, but he also brings this christology in connection with the christology represented by Paul's opponents in 2. Corinthians., thus following Georgi. This linkage of the christology of the miracle narratives with the christology of Paul's opponents has dominated a good deal of redaction-critical research on the gospel of Mark.[52]

The importance of this linkage is that a history-of-religions problem: the problem concerning the influence of a Hellenistic concept of the charismatic figure upon the early Christian tradition has been translated into the heavily loaded theological concept of a *theologia gloriae* in opposition to a *theologia crucis*. The consequence is that the miracle tradition and the passion tradition per se must be mutually exclusive. So the history-of-religions problem concerning the influence of Hellenistic Judaism upon early Christianity has become a theological-dogmatic problem concerning the christology of (a group of) Hellenistic-Jewish Christians representing a *theologia gloriae* and the opposition between this group and other groups, especially the one representing a *theologia crucis*.

T.J. Weeden's analysis of the origin of Mark is a clear example of that.[53]

---

50. *The Son of God* (Philadelphia: Fortress, 1976) 57.
51. Cf. Glöckner, *Wundergeschichten*, 13.
52. Cf. note 19.
53. "The Heresy that Necessitated Mark's Gospel", ZNW 59 (1968) 145-58; idem, *Mark: Traditions in Conflict* (Philadelphia: Fortress, 1971). Against Weeden: W.L. Lane, "THEIOS ANER" Christology and the Gospel of Mark", *New Dimensions in New*

According to Weeden Mark tries by means of his redaction of the miracle traditions to overcome the *theologia gloriae* by means of his *theologia crucis*.

I think there is another solution to the christology of Mark, and I think we can find it in another movement, which was very important in Judaism of the Hellenistic Era: Apocalypticism.

VII. Jesus and Early Christianity within an Apocalyptic Setting

In his book about Ancient Judaism, B. Otzen writes concerning Jewish apocalypticism:

Like the Qumran community, the earliest Christianity was an apocalyptic — eschatological phenomenon. And Christianity would not have become a world religion, had it not been borne along by Jewish apocalyptic.[54]

When Otzen emphasizes the importance of apocalypticism for early Christianity it is natural to ask how the historical Jesus can be characterized in relation to apocalypticism.

H.D. Betz remarks that we can find some *theios aner* traits in Jesus' understanding of himself as God's eschatological messenger and as the one who was God's representative and inspired by the Spirit of God, and in this connection he mentions his exorcisms and healings.[55]

The relationship between Jesus' message and his miracles has been examined by my colleague, Helge Kjær Nielsen, who has shown how important the healing miracles are in Jesus' eschatological message:

Sowohl durch Heilung als auch durch Sündenvergebung, sowohl in der Tat als auch im Wort wird das Reich Gottes *proleptisch* verwirklicht, und diese *vorausgreifende* Verwirklichung wird als Güte und Liebe erlebt [my italics].[56]

According to Otzen, the concept underlying the complex phenomenon of apocalypticism is the concept of dualism which he finds on three levels: the cosmic, the anthropological-ethical, and the eschatological.[57] In this connection I confine myself to the cosmic and the eschatological level. It is a dualism between the world of God and the world of man and between the present and the future world order. The dualism on these levels cohere in so far as the cosmic dualism lasts until the eschatological dualism has been overcome.

Testament Study (ed. R.N. Longenecker, M.C. Tenney; Grand Rapids: Zondervan, 1974) 144-61.

54. B. Otzen, *Judaism in Antiquity* (Sheffield: JSOT Press, 1990) 221.
55. "Divine Man", 128.
56. *Heilung und Verkündigung* (ATDan 22; Leiden: Brill, 1986) 106.
57. *Judaism*, 170-71.

The proleptic realization of the Kingdom of God can thus be understood as Jesus' way to overcome the apocalyptic dualism on the cosmic and eschatological level.

The apocalyptic, universal dimension in Jesus' understanding of his miracles as proleptic, partial realizations of the Kingdom has been emphasized by G. Theissen:

Er verbindet zwei geistige Welten, die vorher nie in dieser Weise verbunden worden sind: die apokalyptische Erwartung universaler Heilszukunft und die episodale Verwirklichung gegenwärtigen Wunderheils."[58]

According to Theissen, this connection distinguishes Jesus from other Jewish movements: Jewish apocalyptic knew the importance of miracles but they never functioned as they did in Jesus' appearance, whether performed by God (cf. the Book of Daniel), by exorcistic tradition (cf. Qumran) or as promised but unrealized miracles (cf. Jewish rebels).

This understanding of Jesus' miracles as partial realization of future salvation is according to Theissen only to be found in Q.[59] The miracle narratives in the Gospels are characterized by the complete disappearance of an eschatological interpretation of the miracles. Similarly, U. Luz will perceive a tendency to "Enteschatologisierung" in Mark, when compared with Q.[60] A quite different estimation is held by H.C. Kee, who situates Mark in an apocalyptic setting in which the ministry of Jesus, which is carried further by the community, is seen as anticipation of the soon-awaited consummation of the kingdom of God and the revelation of Jesus as the heavenly Son of Man.[61]

VIII. Mark's Christology within an Apocalyptic Setting

When considering the eschatology of the Markan miracle narratives and the eschatology in Jesus' ministry one has to remember that while Jesus' way of overcoming the eschatological dualism involved an implicit christology, the eschatological dualism in Mark is overcome by an explicit christology.[62] This

---

58. *Wundergeschichten*, 275-276.
59. *Wundergeschichten*, 276.
60. "Das Jesusbild der vormarkinischen Tradition", *Jesus Christus in Historie und Theologie* (Nt. Festschr. H. Conzelmann, ed. G. Strecker; Tübingen: Mohr [Siebeck], 1975) 347-374.
61. *Community of the New Age* (London: SCM, 1977).
62. The fundamental role of the christology in relation to eschatology is evidenced by the title of Mark's Jesus-story: "The beginning of the gospel of Jesus Christ (the Son of God)" and by the introduction where Jesus at the baptism is appointed the beloved Son of God. To the traditio-historical problems see S. Pedersen, "Dåbsteologien i Markusevangeliet", *Dåben i Ny Testamente*, (ed. S. Pedersen; Århus: Aros,

means that in Mark the eschatology is founded in the christology. In Jesus' ministry the miracles as partial manifestations of the Kingdom of God pointed to the universal, transcendent realization of the Kingdom, while in Mark Jesus' earthly ministry pointed to his revelation as the heavenly Son of Man (13.26; 14.62).[63] It must not be forgotten that this revelation for Mark is the final goal which he probably expects to be accomplished. So, for Mark it is the partial revelation of Jesus as God's eschatological agent in Jesus' earthly ministry, with its climax in his death and resurrection, that confirmed his universal revelation as the heavenly Son of Man.

Mark's understanding of Jesus' resurrection as his way to the enthronement at God's right hand (12.36; 14.62) clearly belongs to an apocalyptic conceptuality. So his enthronement implies a dualism on the spatial level: Jesus is in Heaven while the community is on the earth. This dualism on the spatial level will be overcome when Jesus appears as the heavenly Son of Man on the chronological level. In the meantime the dualism on the spatial and chronological level must be mediated through the experience of the presence of the exalted Jesus in the community. It is this kind of presence which confirms the community of the final solution of the apocalyptic dualism when Jesus appears as the heavenly Son of Man. But this presence is experienced through Mark's story about Jesus.[64] As a story about Jesus' partial realization of the Kingdom of God in the past — confirmed by his death, resurrection, and enthronement at God's right hand — the community experiences his presence as the exalted Son of Man and so is confirmed of his future revelation.

This means that the fundamental role of the miracle narratives in Mark is to strengthen the belief in his final — and soon awaited — revelation as the heavenly Son of Man. This explains why in Mark it is the christology that confirms the eschatology.

I think this can be illustrated by looking at the relationship between the two terms *the Kingdom of God* and *the Son of Man* in Mark.

1982) 49-72.That the story is understandable within Aramaic Jewish framework has been shown by Blackburn, *Theios Anēr*, 98-109, Blackburn thus refutes Bultmann and Hahn.

63. To the problems of 14.62 see J. Schaberg, "Mark 14.62. Early Christian Merkabah Imagery?", *Apocalyptic and the New Testament: Essays in Honour of J. Louis Martin* (JSNTSup 24, ed. J. Marcus and M.L. Soards; Sheffield: SJOT, 1989) 69-94, who ventures the hypothesis that it's the chariot imagery which lies behind the verse.

64. To the question of the "narrative Jesus" of Mark see O. Davidsen, "Narrativitet og eksistens", *DTT* 49 (1986) 241-267 (also in *Semiotique et Bible* 48 (1987) 18-41); idem, *The Narrative Jesus* (Århus: Aarhus University Press, 1993). For the evaluation of Mark as an "apocalyptic historical monograph" see A.Y. Collins, *Is Mark's Gospel a Life of Jesus?* (Milwaukee, Wisconsin: Marquette University Press, 1990) 46-66.

IX. The Kingdom of God and the Son of Man in Mark

In the first section of Mark (1.14-8.26) after the introduction (1.2-13) Jesus' proclamation of the Kingdom of God (1.14-15) marks the theme of his ministry. I think there is here an allusion to Dan 7.14 (the surrender of the kingdom to the Son of Man). Jesus announces that this kingdom is now being realized.[65] And his message is evidenced by first and foremost his exorcisms (1.23-28,39; 3.11-12,22-30).[66] The apocalyptic-eschatological perspective of the exorcisms is clearly demonstrated: The unclean spirit represents the *basileia* of the demons which Jesus has come to destroy (1.24a). On the opposite side the scribes claim that Jesus represents the *basileia* of Beelzebul (3.22), while Jesus confirms the viewpoint of the unclean spirit: with Jesus' exorcisms the eschatological struggle has begun (3.23-27).[67]

In the collection of controversy stories we for the first time meet the term the *Son of Man* (2.10,28). Jesus' claim that he as the Son of Man has *exusia* to forgive sins on earth is evidenced by his healing of the paralytic.[68] The use of the term the *Son of Man* as well as the terms *exusia* and *kyrios* has allusion to Dan 7.13-14 as was the case with 1,15, but here the *Son of Man* from the Book of Daniel is explicitly mentioned.

After the basic conflict between Jesus and the scribes regarding the two kingdoms and which of them Jesus represents, the theme of *the mystery of the kingdom* is introduced in connection with Jesus' teaching in parables (4.1-34). I think it is important that the parable motif is introduced already in the conflict with the scribes (3.23). The motif emphasizes that the partial realization of the Kingdom of God as evidence of its future universal realization can only

---

65. To Mark 1.15 see the interesting analysis by J. Marcus, "'The time has been fulfilled!' (Mark 1.15)", in *Apocalyptic* (cf. note 63), 49-68. Marcus paraphrases the verse in the following way: "The time of the dominion of Satan has been fulfilled, and the kingly power of God has drawn near. Turn away, therefore, from the dominion of Satan, and turn to the coming manifestation of the power of God". (56).

66. Marcus' interpretation of v. 15 emphasizes the apocalyptic aspect of the kingdom: The antagonist is not the Roman dominion but the dominion of a trancendent power. With Marcus' analysis of v. 15 in mind the apocalyptic-transcendent aspect of the exorcisms become clear. Cf. H.C. Kee, "The terminology of Mark's exorcism Stories", *NTS* 14 (1967/68) 232-246. It is also to be noted that this apocalyptic-transcendent dimension in Jesus' proclamation of the Kingdom of God according to Mark also implies that the antagonist is not the Roman power as was the case with the political messianism, described by Josephus (cf. note 37).

67. It's worth noting that it is the Spirit which came upon Jesus that leads him into the temptation from Satan as well as into the victory over the demons. So, the charge against Jesus is a charge against the Spirit of God. It is the same Spirit that will speak for the community, when brought to trial (Mark 13.11).

68. Concerning the unity of Mark 2.1-12, see H. Simonsen, *Traditionssammenhæng og forkyndelsessigte* (København: Gad, 1966) 46-48.

be expressed metaphorically. So already 3.23 looks forward to the final vindication of the evil powers, and the same must be the case in 4.10-12. The secrecy regards not only Jesus' death as his way to the final vindication but also the time between his enthronement and final revelation.[69]

It is also worth noting that many of the miracle stories in the section 4.35-8.26 deal with the situation of the disciples in relation to Jesus (4.35-41; 6.45-52) and the importance of this as regards their relation to the crowds (6.30-44; 8.1-9) and Jesus' opponents (8.14-21). Especially in 4.35-41 and 6.45-52 the problem of Jesus' absence in the time between his exaltation and his final revelation is reflected. The experience of his intervening confirms the belief in his final revelation.[70]

In the second section (8.27-10.52) the connection between *the Son of Man* and *the Kingdom of God* is still closer than in the first section. Jesus here introduces the theme of the suffering Son of Man who will be resurrected and appear as the heavenly Son of Man (8.31,38), and then he promises the coming of the Kingdom of God with power (9.1). So the coming of the heavenly Son of Man and of the Kingdom of God in power coincides. Here the allusion to Dan 7.13-14 is still closer than in the first section of the gospel. The Markan Jesus looks forward to the final realization of the Danielic vision which he proleptically realized in his earthly ministry.

The following transfiguration story (9.2-8) is thus best understood as a prolepsis of the final revelation. This means that it must be explained within an apocalyptic framework. The secrecy motif (9.9) emphasizes that the Son of Man's way to the final revelation goes through suffering and death (cf. 8.31). The story about the epileptic boy (9.14-29) reflects the disciples' situation between Jesus' exaltation and final revelation (cf. 4.35-41; 6.45-52). The stress on prayer is characteristic in that connection: through prayer the community can experience the presence of the exalted Jesus and so be strengthened in their hope for his final revelation.

In 10.45 the atoning power of the Son of Man's death is implied. So there is a correspondence between the Son of Man's *exusia* to forgive sins (and to heal) and the atoning power of his death.[71] For Mark the miracle working Jesus and the crucified Jesus are not mutually exclusive. It is only to men that such an exclusiveness exists, from God's and Jesus' perspective they belong together. The ministry of forgiving and healing is condensed in his death and resurrection. Forgiveness and healing as well as death and resurrection function

---

69. To the problems concerning Mark 4 and its apocalyptic aspects see J. Marcus, *The Mystery of the Kingdom of God* (SBLDS 90; Atlanta, Georgia: Scholars, 1986).
70. The importance of the resurrection for the understanding of Mark's miracle stories has been stressed by Blackburn, *Theios Anēr*, 234-238. Regarding Divine Agency in Jewish tradition see also L.W. Hurtado, *One God, One Lord* (London: SCM, 1988).
71. Cf. M. Hengel, *Studies in the Gospel of Mark* (London: SCM, 1985) 37-38.

as partial realization of the final universal realization of the Kingdom of God.

In the trial scene (14.55-64) Jesus answers the question if he is the Son of the Blessed by pointing to his status as the exalted Son of Man who will come in glory (14.62).[72] Jesus' announcement of his exaltation coincides with his announcement of his sitting at table in the Kingdom of God (14.26).

The problem concerning the time between Jesus' exaltation and his final revelation is the theme of chap. 13.[73] In a situation of persecution and suffering the community has to proclaim the gospel to all the peoples (13.10) and at the same time be ready to receive Jesus at whatever time (13.33-37) as the heavenly Son of Man (13.26).

The clear connection between world mission and the parousia of the Son of Man in Mark is to me a clear evidence of the apocalyptical eschatological perspective in Mark. It is a consequence of the way in which the apocalyptic dualism is overcome. In Dan 7.13-14 the revelation of the heavenly Son of Man and the Kingdom follows after the four world powers. In Mark the beginning realization of the Danielic vision begins in and during the reign of the Roman worldpower with Jesus' earthly ministry. The central event in this realization was his — in an apocalyptic framework understood — death, resurrection and exaltation. After this central event the Kingdom's realization went on through the community — still in the Roman Empire.[74] Mark was convinced that this realization would end with an apocalyptic new creation (13.31) and the appearance of Jesus as the heavenly Son of Man who would gather his elected people from all the world (13.26).

When looking at the relationship between the terms *the Kingdom of God* and *the Son of Man* on a syntagmatic level, one can observe that they come closer to each other: in the first section *the Kingdom of God* (1.15) was followed by *the Son of Man* in 2.10,28. In the second section (8.27-10.52) they are directly connected (8.38; 9.1), and in 13.26 (cf. 14.62) *the Kingdom of God* is not mentioned. That does not mean that the motif is lacking; it has been integrated into *the Son of Man*. If we compare with the syntagmatic structure in Dan 7.13-

---

72. Regarding the relationship between temple charge and Messianic status see D. Juel, *Messiah and Temple* (SBLDS 31; Missoula, Montana: Scholars, 1973).

73. Regarding the problems of Mark 13 see E. Brandenburger, *Markus 13 und die Apokalyptik* (FRLANT 134; Göttingen: Vandenhoeck & Ruprecht, 1984).

74. There is thus a parallel between Jesus' message about the Kingdom of God and the community's proclamation of the Gospel: The real antagonists are not political authorities but the transcendent demonic powers. Political (and religious) authorities become antagonists in so far as they become tools for the transcendent evil powers. But it is characteristic that the only weapon in this situation is the Spirit and perseverance. (Mark 13.11, 33-37). We have the same attitude in the Revelation of John as regards the appeal to perseverance (Rev 1.9; 2.2-3; 13.10; 14.1-2). It is a clear evidence that the final struggle and salvation is seen in an apocalyptic transcendent perspective.

14 we can se that the Son of Man is seen first and then the surrender of the kingdom is mentioned. When in Mark 13.26 the kingdom motif need not be mentioned explicitly it is a consequence of a change in the apocalyptic structure: Jesus' resurrection is understood as the occasion when he received the kingdom. So the revelation of the kingdom coheres with the revelation of Jesus as the heavenly *Son of Man*.

It is still much discussed whether the term *the Son of Man* is a title or not.[75] In Mark I do not think that it functions as a title but as a symbol. E. Schüssler-Fiorenza has in an article about early Christian apocalyptic stressed the importance of symbols in apocalyptic literature.[76] She refers to Wheelwright's distinction between "steno symbols" and "tensive symbols". While a "steno symbol" bears a one-to-one relationship, the "tensive symbol" can evoke a whole range of meanings and can never be exhausted or adequately expressed by one referent.

I think this distinction is useful for the understanding of the term *the Son of Man* in Mark. If the term is understood as a "tensive symbol", the different predicates, ascribed to it, can not be completely understood by a history-of-religions and a tradition-historical analysis. The predicates are not only *ascribed to the Son of Man*, they are first of all *unfoldings* of the meaning potential of the symbol *the Son of Man*.

The symbol *the Son of Man* is rooted in Jewish apocalyptic and with this is shares the dialectic between revealing and concealing. So one can not just say that the predicates about *the Son of Man* reveal its meaning, for at the same time it keeps, by the very symbol *the Son of Man*, an element of concealing. So the symbol *the Son of Man* in Mark signals how the apocalyptic dualism is overcome: by a revelation which at the same time keeps an element of secrecy until he who used the symbol of himself is revealed. So, Mark's gospel can be characterized as the unfolding of the meaning potential in the symbol *the Son of Man*. When Jesus, according to Mark, uses this symbol of himself, Mark's story at the same time overcomes and maintains the apocalyptic dualism by unfolding it through narration and by keeping the story open until the final solution of the apocalyptic dualistic tension. This might explain the lack of a *narrated* appearence story in Mark.

So, although the term *the Son of Man* occurs only once in a Markan miracle narrative (2.10) I think Mark's redaction of the miracle traditions is marked by his understanding of Jesus as *the Son of Man*, not as a title, but as a symbol which signals how the apocalyptic dualism is overcome in the story about

---

75. See Mogens Müller, *Der Ausdruck "Menschensohn" in den Evangelien* (ATDan 18; Leiden: Brill, 1984).

76. "The Phenomenon of Early Christian Apocalyptic", *Apocalypticism in the Mediterranean World and the Near East* (ed. D. Hellholm; Tübingen: Mohr [Siebeck], 1983) 295-316.

Jesus, and how it is to overcome in the life of the community through this story. It is not overcome through national Jewish, political rebellion (13.6, 21-22), not through imitation of the rulers (10.42), but through the one who inaugurated God's eschatological world and who's transcendent revelation will end the present world order and comsummate the new order.

In their meeting with the pagan world and their traditions Mark and the community to which he belonged could adopt traits from traditions about pagan charismatic types, but a *theios aner* based on a specific pagan anthropology they did not adopt. Their basic patterns did they get from Old Testament-Jewish traditions, including Jewish apocalypticism.

With apocalypticism Mark shares the interest in the notion of creation/new creation which can be seen both in the introductional section of his gospel (1.12-13. Adam-Christ typology) and in 13.24-26,30-31.

In an article on the anthropology in the Gospels my adviser, the late Hejne Simonsen, pointed to the importance of this notion to the creation in some of the miracle narratives.[77] He saw this as an obstacle for an anthropology which erases the limit between God and man sent by God. I think the two terms *theios aner* and *ho hyios tou anthropou* clearly signal two very different conceptions of man: only the divine man is man in the full sense (= *theios aner*), and: only the created man is man in full sense (= *the Son of Man*). The last conception is a consequence of the Old Testament-Jewish understanding of creation, still active in Jewish apocalypticism. So the question concerning the relation between the New Testament and Hellenistic Judaism exemplified on the relationship between *theios aner* and *ho hyios tou anthropou* clearly shows that in the end this question is a question of how Judaism and early Christianity succeeded in maintaining the close relationship between monotheism and creation in their common Old Testament heritage. In my opinion the use of Hellenistic concepts of *theioi andres* as a model for the early Christian christology without further qualification rather confuses than clarifies this question.

---

77. "Menneskeopfattelsen i evangelierne" [The concept of man in the Gospels], *Menneskesynet* [The concept of Man] (ed. S. Pedersen; Copenhagen: Gad, 1989) 99-116, esp. 104.

The Distinctive Character of the New Testament Love Command in Relation to Hellenistic Judaism

Historical and Hermeneutical Reflections

Johannes Nissen

Introduction

In this article, two different ways of reading the New Testament are combined. The first is characterized by the pure history-of-religion stance where attention is devoted exclusively to the critical and historical study of early Christianity. The second is the hermeneutical approach where the results of the descriptive study are held in some way normative for modern Christianity.

By combining these two approaches I shall attempt to discuss questions like these: What was unique about the morality of the first Christians? Are there any distinctive or characteristic features of the New Testament love command as compared to its surroundings, especially Hellenistic Judaism? The reasons for asking these questions are several. Today a major trend within moral theology is marked by an ethic which owes more to a general moral consensus than to any distinctively Christian principle. Many Christians are engaged in public discussions on various issues, but they do not attempt to start from specifically Christian principles. As a result they seldom appeal to a distinctive "ethic of Jesus".[1] Instead they argue in favour of a theology of creation or "autonomous ethics".[2]

This reluctance to invoke the special authority of Jesus in moral questions seems to be supported by the results of biblical scholarship which call into question the very notion that we can confidently attribute any distinctive ethic

---

1. Cf. the discussion among Roman Catholic theologians on the "Proprium" of Christian ethics. For a review of this discussion in relation to the NT see R. Schnackenburg, *Die sittliche Botschaft des Neuen Testaments,* 1 (Freiburg: Herder, 1986), 17-27.
2. The term "autonomous ethics" has been introduced by the Roman Catholic moral theologian A. Auer in his book: *Autonome Moral und christlicher Glaube* (Düsseldorf: Patmos, 1971). In Protestant circles the Danish theologian K.E. Løgstrup is an outstanding example of a theology of creation or an ontological ethic which dissociates itself from specifically Christian ethics. See, among others, his work: *Den etiske fordring* (Copenhagen: Gyldendal, 1957).

to Jesus at all.[3] In addition, it has been argued that within the New Testament itself we see that both Jesus and the New Testament authors draw heavily on the ethical traditions of the Old Testament, of common wisdom traditions, and of the Hellenistic ethical codes generally to address concrete situations. They do not attempt to elaborate a special system of Christian ethics.

This, however, is only one side of the coin. Readers of the New Testament cannot avoid noticing the centrality of the love command. This centrality is attested also in the second century, not only by Christian writers who consistently stress the love imperative, but also by ancient pagan testimony to the actual life of love observed to be characteristic of the early Christian congregations.[4] Even today we see the same phenomenon. If we want to know what is distinctive about Christian ethics, we do well to attend to what is usually meant when people describe an act or an attitude as "Christian"; they think of unselfishness and concern for others regardless of sex, race or social status.

This means that we are facing a dilemma. On the one hand is an ethic which has been widely recognized as distinctive and which has given the word "Christian" to our moral vocabulary. On the other hand, this distinctive ethic has often been relegated to a footnote. As a result, the Sermon on the Mount and the loving of enemies, instead of being an inspiration for Christian moral thinking, became a problem for systematic theology by reason of its alleged impracticability.[5]

It could be argued against this search for the distinctiveness of the New Testament love command, that to obtain the essence of something, we have to boil it down, distill and filter out; what is left is not a living thing, but an abstraction. Hence, if we are looking for some "pure" Christian values and beliefs, unmixed with the surrounding culture, we are certainly on the wrong track. In order to understand the first Christians, it is not enough to abstract their novelties or add up the "parallels" or "influences" from their environment. Instead we must try to discern the pattern of the whole. "What was Christian about the ethos and ethics of those early communities we will discover not by abstraction, but by confronting their involvement in the culture of their time and place, and seeking to trace the new patterns they made of old forms, to hear the new songs they composed from old melodies."[6]

---

3. For a criticism of this neglect in biblical scholarship see A.E. Harvey, *Strenuous Commands: The Ethic of Jesus* (London: SCM, 1990) 3.
4. Cf. V.P. Furnish, *The Love Command in the New Testament* (London: SCM, 1973) 17. For a discussion of the second and third century see also the evidence in: J. Whittaker, "Christianity and Morality in the Roman Empire", *VC* 33 (1979) 209-225.
5. E.A. Harvey, *Strenuous Commands*, 10, points out that from the very beginning sociological pressures were at work to shift attention from the challenging ethic of Jesus to moral rules and principles of more general application.
6. W. Meeks, *The Moral World of the First Christians* (London: SPCK, 1987) 97.

This is an important caution against abstracting some Christian ideas, but it cannot invalidate the search for the distinctive character of the New Testament ethics. Instead it can help us to broaden the ground for this search. When looking for a New Testament love ethic, one should not only see what Jesus and the first Christians taught. One should also see how they taught, and ask what was the symbolic and social world within which that teaching made sense.[7]

One further introductory remark is appropriate. It applies to the use of terms in the title of this article. The two phrases "the New Testament love command" and "Hellenistic Judaism" need to be clarified. I take them in reverse order.

The phrase "Hellenistic Judaism" is used in a broad sense, since it is often difficult to say whether a particular injunction comes from a Jewish or a Greco-Roman source. There is a great quantity of comparative material from Hellenistic Judaism, and in this article I must limit myself to mentioning a few representative texts. As can be seen from the following paragraphs, some of the most interesting parallels to the New Testament are found in *The Testaments of the Twelve Patriarchs*[8], the *Epistle of Aristeas* and in the writings of *Philo*.

As to the first phrase "the New Testament love command", it should be considered in which way one can speak of *the* New Testament love ethic. According to many scholars, such a terminology presupposes a unity which is questionable. To take just one example,[9] it is argued that "not all early christian circles were as single-mindedly dedicated to a 'love morality' (whatever precisely that may mean) as is often supposed, and that even those which might be thus described meant by it many different things, ranging from

---

7. Cf. W. Meeks, *The Moral World*, 17. I disagree, however, with Meeks that one has to choose between a historical description of early Christian ethics and proposals about using early Christian writings normatively in ethical discourse of later times. "Both are valid and important fields of inquiry; the essential thing is that we not mix them up" (W. Meeks, "Understanding Early Christian Ethics", *JBL* 105 [1986], 3-11, 3).

8. It should be noticed that there is no consensus among scholars concerning the question as to what extent the Testaments have been christianized. It is quite possible that the origin of these texts occurred in three stages: (1) a Hellenistic Jewish "Grundstock", (2) later Hellenistic Jewish expansions, and finally (3) a Christian redaction. Cf. J. Becker, *Untersuchungen zur Entstehungsgeschichte der Testamente der Zwölf Patriarchen* (Leiden: E.J. Brill, 1979). M. de Jonge, in his first book from 1953 (*The Testaments of the Twelve Patriarchs: A Study of their Text, Composition and Origin* [Assen: Van Corcum's Theologische Bibliotheek Nr. 25, 1953]), classified the Testaments among the literary products of the early Christian church. In a later book from 1975 (*Studies on the Testaments of the Twelve Patriarchs* [Leiden: E.J. Brill, 1975]) he expresses himself more cautiously, but he thinks that the Testaments "underwent at any rate a thoroughgoing redaction" (209-210).

9. J.L. Houlden, *Ethics and the New Testament* (Harmondsworth: Penguin Books, 1973) 73.

the intra-community love of the Fourth Gospel to the devotion to the Torah in Matthew."

It is true that one should avoid an unjustified homogenization of the different perspectives and emphases within the New Testament itself. The love command must be studied as to the various ways in which the command has been received, interpreted and applied by the first Christians. There is a variety of expressions as well as a variety of settings. But at the same time it is obvious that the love ethic is a crucial aspect of both the literature and the life of the earliest Christianity.

To speak of *the* New Testament love command is to search for a unity within the diversity.[10] It is to ask questions like these: Does the New Testament provide us with some basic perspectives, patterns and priorities in ethics?[11] Was there one single, normative expression of the love ethic in the earliest days of Christianity?

This article does not deal with all New Testament texts which might be of relevant to our discussion.[12] The main focus is on the gospels, especially the Synoptic gospels since they most clearly reflect the basic patterns of the love command ("the ethic of Jesus").[13] However, the attention is also drawn to the Fourth Gospel since this gospel provides us with some additional perspectives. Yet if we make a comparison between the Synoptic gospels and John we must note a certain tension or even contradiction.[14] The crucial question is: Could

---

10. Among those who have addressed this issue are W. Schrage, "Zur Frage nach der Einheit und Mitte neutestamentlicher Ethik", *Die Mitte des Neuen Testaments: Einheit und Vielfalt neutestamentlicher Theologie. FS. E. Schweizer* (ed. U. Luz and H. Weder; Göttingen: Vandenhoek & Ruprecht, 1983) 238-53. Schrage states that "zumindest in den Hauptschriften des Neuen Testaments besteht eine inhaltliche Einheit der Paränese darin, dass sie das Liebesgebot als oberstes Gebot christlicher Ethik ansehen" (p.249).

11. For the use of the terms "perspectives, patterns and priorities" see E. Osborn, *Ethical Patterns in Early Christian Thought* (Cambridge: Univ. Press, 1976). See also the methodological reflections on "ethical perspectives" in P. Hoffmann and V. Eid, *Jesus von Nazareth und eine christliche Moral: Sittliche Perspektiven der Verkündigung Jesu* (Freiburg: Herder, 1975), especially 17-25.

12. This limitation is for reasons of space. There are, however, a few references to the Pauline literature, see the paragraph on enemy love and my concluding remarks (cf. note 114).

13. Many scholars are sceptical to the possibility of analyzing Jesus' own teaching. As a result we know more about the ethic of Mark, Matthew and Luke than about the ethic of Jesus. I do not share this scepticism. On the various criteria for critical identification of the historical Jesus see, for instance, E. Schillebeeckx, *Jesus: An Experiment in Christology* (London: SCM, 1983), 83-100.

14. According to J. Becker the development in early Christianity is marked by a significant shift from the the love of enemies in Jesus' own teaching to the love of other Christians in the Johannine communities: "Von einer grenzüberschreitenden Offenheit im Ansatz bis zu einer bewussten nur noch gruppenspezifischen

we speak of any common features despite this diversity of expressions? Are there any characteristic or constitutive elements in Jesus' love command which can be found in both traditions?

Here it should be added that in this article the word "love command" is taken to include four different sayings in the gospels: the double commandment, the golden rule, the commandment to love one's enemies (the Synoptic gospels) and the commandment to "love one another" (the Gospel of John).

Many earlier works on the specific character of the love command in the New Testament have an almost exclusive philological orientation. They claim that the noun ἀγάπη carries a particular freight of meaning and of theological significance.[15] However, the study of the love motif in early Christianity cannot proceed very far on an exclusively lexical basis. The meaning of love in the earliest Christian literature is not tied to semantics, but to the whole range of Christian beliefs about God, man and the world.[16]

In what follows, four other suggestions for identifying the distinctiveness and newness of the love command are reviewed and discussed.[17] These suggestions are:

— the combination of the two commandments
— the positive form of the golden rule
— the command to love one's enemies
— Christ as the motivating power.

The double commandment

The first suggestion is that the distinctive element can be found in the way in which Jesus has *combined* the two commandments.

This claim is supported by the fact that the combination of Deut 6.5 and Lev 19.18 is without parallels in the Jewish sources.[18] Against this it is argued

Begrenzung". J. Becker,"Feindesliebe – Nächstenliebe – Bruderliebe," *ZEE* 25 (1981), 5-17, 17.

15. So, for instance, V. Warnach, *Agape: Die Liebe als Grundmotiv* (Düsseldorf: Patmos, 1951) 18. Warnack speaks of the specifically Christian character of the word and describes it as an authentic revelation-word. Also C. Spicq, in his great volumes *Agapè dans le Nouveau Testament: Analyse des Textes* (3. vols., Paris: Lecoffre, 1958-9), focuses on the word "love".

16. Cf. V.P. Furnish, *The Love Command*, 222.

17. See also the helpful article by G. Schneider, "Die Neuheit der christlichen Nächstenliebe", *TTZ* 83 (1973) 257-75, with five suggestions.

18. A. Nissen, *Gott und der Nächste im antiken Judentum: Untersuchungen zum Doppelgebot der Liebe* (Tübingen: Mohr [Siebeck], 1974), p. 241: "Eine Verknüpfung von Dt 6,5 und Lev 19,18 ist übrigens in der gesamten antik-jüdischen Literatur zumindest bis ins Mittelalter nirgendwo belegt!"

that the substance and the function of the double command has already been found in Hellenistic Jewish sources.[19] Thus, *The Testaments of the Twelve Patriarchs* use formulations which remind us of Mark 12.30-31. This applies particularly to T. Iss. 5.2. "But, love the Lord and your neighbour; have compassion on the poor and the weak"; and T. Dan. 5.3. "Love the Lord all your life and one another with a true heart". But in these cases the commandments are not called "first" or "second", and they do not provide a sum of all the other commandments.

Another example from the Hellenistic Jewish literature is *Philo* who in *Spec.* 2.63 speaks of the two major points which sum up all the numerous single laws. One is identified — in accordance with Hellenistic ethics — as "adoration and piety" (εὐσέβεια καὶ ὁσιότης); the other as "philantrophy and righteousness"(φιλανθρωπία καὶ δικαιοσύνη). Here we have, then, something like a summary of the law; but the summary is not expressed directly in terms of commandments, nor is there any (direct) reference to love of God or neighbour.

As a consequence it is relevant to ask: Can these parallels be seen as more than formal similarities? Is the substantial meaning of the double commandment in these Hellenistic Jewish sources the same as in early Christianity? Can the double love command be characterized as the "common possession" of Jews and Christians?[20] In order to answer these questions we must look at the understanding of this commandment in each of the Synoptic gospels, because the gospels "do not just *exhibit* Jesus' teaching but rather receive, transmit, and apply it in specific ways relevant to the needs of the church in the writer's own time."[21]

Most scholars agree that the *Gospel of Mark* (12.28-34) has presented the love command as part of the early church's missionary preaching in Hellenistic society — in order to demonstrate the oneness of God against the many gods of Hellenism. The overall point is this: What is important for true religion is

19. So, for instance, C. Burchard, "Das doppelte Liebesgebot in der frühen christlichen Überlieferung", *Der Ruf Jesu und die Antwort der Gemeinde. FS J. Jeremias* (ed. E. Lohse, C. Burchard and B. Schaller; Göttingen: Vandenhoek & Ruprecht, 1970) 39-62.
20. C. Burchard, "Das doppelte Liebesgebot", claims that the substance of the double command is "jüdisch vorgebildet". J. Piper, '*Love Your Enemies': Jesus' Love Command in the Synoptic Gospels and the Early Christian Paraenesis* (Cambridge: University Press, 1979) 93, considers this approach to be exclusively formalistic. G. Schneider, "Die Neuheit der christlichen Nächstenliebe", 260, points out: "Man wird betonen müssen, dass weder Dt 6,4 noch Lev 19,18 anklingt, sondern der Versuch vorliegt, die Vielfalt der Toravorschriften auf eine Grundlage, auf Hauptstücke...zurückzuführen".
21. V.P. Furnish, *The Love Command*, 23. Cf. also G.M. Soares-Prabhu, "The Synoptic Love-Commandment: The Dimensions of Love in the Teaching of Jesus", *Jeevadhara* No. 74 (March-April 1983), 85-103, 85.

belief in and worship of the one God and obedience to the moral law, not religious ceremony of cultic performance.[22]

It has been suggested that the story as it was used by Mark represented the scribe as a seeker after wisdom (as in Wis 6.17-20). He comes to Jesus, the mediator of wisdom, and leaves with a new understanding of the law gained from that wisdom. In this way the story explains how Christians can worship the true God and stand in the Old Testament tradition without continuing to follow the ritual and cultic obligations of the law.[23]

One remarkable aspect of the story in Mark's gospel is its irenic tone. The questions and answers are neither specifically Christian nor peculiarly "Jesuanic", as is in fact admitted by the scribe (12.32). Jesus approves of the scribe's response (12.34), but he does not stop at that. By adding "you are not far from the Kingdom of God" (12.34), he indicates that there is *something more* besides the two commandments, and this "more" is what Christianity is about, the Kingdom of God.[24]

Thus, in Mark's presentation the loving relationship to God and neighbour is shown to be integral to an understanding of the Kingdom of God.[25] It is precisely this coherence of the twin commandments with the dynamics of the Kingdom, which constitutes the difference between the love command in the gospels and the Hellenistic Jewish tradition.

---

22. Cf. G. Bornkamm, "Das Doppelgebot der Liebe", in: *Geschichte und Glaube*, Teil 1 (*Gesammelte Aufsätze*, III, München: Kaiser, 1968) 27-45.

23. Cf. K. Berger, *Das Gesetzauslegung Jesu. Teil I: Markus und Parallellen* (Neukirchen-Vluyn: Neukirchener, 1972).

24. So, correctly, J. Becker, "Feindesliebe - Nächstenliebe - Bruderliebe, 15: "...dass für Mk. durch das Doppelgebot nicht einfach das Christentum beschrieben wird...Also kann *das Doppelgebot das Juden und Christen Einende* bezeichnen; aber Christentum ist mehr als die Frage nach den Gesetz. Das alles Entscheidende ist erst mit der Gottesherrschaft benannt" (his italics). F. Prast argues convincingly that Mark 12.28-34 presupposes Christian circles in vivid contact with Hellenistic Jewish groups. These groups are considered to be partners of communication and not just preparatory for Christianity. Prast, however, is too vague on the importance of the Kingdom of God. See F. Prast, "Ein Appell zur Besinnung auf das Juden wie Christen gemeinsam verpflichtende Erbe im Munde Jesu", *Gottesverächter und Menschenfeinde* (ed. H. Goldstein; Düsseldorf: Patmos, 1979) 79-98, esp. 98.

25. Instead of this R. Fuller suggests that the relating of the love command to the eschatological proclamation is due to the post-Easter community. Fuller underlines the affinity of Jesus' teaching with the wisdom tradition, as in *The Testaments of the Twelve Patriarchs*. See his article "Das Doppelgebot der Liebe. Ein Testfall für die Echtheitskriterien der Worte Jesu", *Jesus Christus im Historie und Theologie. FS. H. Conzelmann* (ed. G. Strecker; Tübingen: Mohr [Siebeck], 1975) 317-329, esp. 329. For a critique of this position see B. Chilton and J.I.H. McDonald, *Jesus and the Ethics of the Kingdom* (London: SPCK, 1987) 108-9, note 137: "In short, to adopt Fuller's solution is to resort to a scarcely conceivable separation of ethics and eschatology in the teaching of Jesus".

The *Gospel of Matthew* (22.34-40) omits the agreement of the scribe, probably because it is his intention to contrast Jesus and the scribes as interpreters of the law. More importantly, he sees the whole law and the prophets hanging on the twin commandment (22.40). The meaning is that the whole law can be deduced from these commandments. This can be compared with Hillel's famous response to a proselyte (see below).

In addition, there is another aspect of the love command which is important. In Matt 5.43-47 Jesus expresses a strong critique of mere neighbourly love. It has to be replaced by loving one's enemies. In light of this it is relevant to ask whether Jesus and the scribe in the Matthean understanding really meant the same thing when speaking of love for our neighbours.

In the *Gospel of Luke* (10.25-37) it is the lawyer and not Jesus himself who formulates the great commandment to love God and the neighbour (10.27). In approving the lawyer's response to his challenge, Jesus says "You have answered rightly" (10.28). It seems as if the two persons agree on the double commandment. Evidently, "for Luke the "punch line" in the dialogue comes not in the formulation of the Commandment as such (as in Matthew), but in Jesus' urging the lawyer to *do* what he himself acknowledges to be the essence of the law."[26] Does this mean that the double command is the common possession of Jews and Christians, while the difference is that Jews do not keep it, as the parable of the Samaritan shows?[27]

This is only part of the explanation. The meaning of the parable of the good Samaritan is not merely that Christians do obey the double commandment and the Jews do not. In v. 29 the lawyer had asked the question "Who is my neighbour?" and the implication of the parable is that the whole question of "who" is neighbour and "how far" do I have to go, misses the point. One does not calculate, not even friend and enemy. Therefore, it is only on the surface that the lawyer and Jesus come to an agreement. On a more fundamental level, the lawyer's understanding of the commandment and Jesus' understanding are *not* identical.[28]

Although the context of the parable may not be original, the parable itself nevertheless renders the essence of Jesus' understanding of neighbourly love. "What is distinctive of Jesus in the parable does not lie in the doctrine of the two great commandments. Luke intimates that without Jesus we can perfectly well read the one twofold great commandment in the Bible, but now, cutting across that, comes Jesus' teaching: The Good Samaritan, as making concrete that great commandment. Luke turns the idea of "neighbour" right around (from Lev 19.18 LXX): the neighbour is not so much an object of activity, but

---

26. V.P. Furnish, *The Love Command*, 38.
27. So, for instance, C. Burchard, "Das doppelte Liebesgebot", 59.
28. Cf. J. Piper, *'Love Your Enemies'*, 93-94.

the active subject himself makes himself neighbour and helper of the other."[29]

By way of summary, we may say that Hellenistic Judaism by this time had provided an atmosphere in which the combination of the two commandments would have been natural. However, there is no evidence of the specific coupling of the two texts from Deut 6.5 and Lev 19.18. In the Synoptic gospels we have the coupling, although we cannot with certainty ascribe it to Jesus himself. On the other hand there is no compelling reason for doubting that such summary was formulated by him.[30] Yet, the main point in Jesus' teaching is not the combination of the two commandments, but rather its radicalization due to the Kingdom of God and the love of one's enemies.

The golden rule

The second suggestion for identifying the newness of the New Testament love command has focused on the golden rule. The point of discussion has been whether the positive form coined by Jesus adds anything to the various negative forms that were in circulation, or whether it simply amounts to the same thing. Some interpreters have been keen to prove that Jesus was being original and innovative, and the *positive form* is morally superior to the negative.[31] But others have regarded Jesus' positive form as simply a stylistic variation on a familiar theme, involving no difference in meaning.

Some scholars have also been critical of the *maxim itself*, regardless of its positive or negative form. According to R. Bultmann it represents the moral of negative egotism.[32] And according to A. Dihle it is an elaboration of the ancient idea of reciprocity.[33] This means that we are facing at least two questions. How are we to evaluate the rule itself? And how are we to evaluate its positive form in the gospels?

The golden rule seems to be universal in character. It belongs to the heritage of the human mind which is seen from the fact that it appears in both Indian and Chinese cultures. It is also well-known in Greek tradition where the

---

29. E. Schillebeeckx, *Jesus*, 255.

30. Cf. V.P. Furnish, *The Love Cammand*, 62.

31. So, for instance, J. Jeremias, in his article "Goldene Regel", *Die Religion in Geschichte und Gegenwart*, 3rd ed., Vol II (Tübingen: Mohr [Siebeck], 1958), cols. 1687-89; I.H. Marshall, *The Gospel of Luke* (Exeter: Paternoster, 1978) 262.

32. R. Bultmann, *Die Geschichte der synoptischen Tradition* (Göttingen: Vandenhoek & Ruprecht, 1961²) 107: "denn ob positiv oder negativ enthält das Wort, als Einzelwort genommen, die Moral eines naiven Egoismus".

33. A. Dihle, *Die Goldene Regel* (Göttingen: Vandenhoek & Ruprecht, 1962), esp. 11-12; 80-82. According to Dihle, the golden rule has become a general code for appraisal of one's actions according to the principle of balance. This means that one's own actions are determined by the actions expected or hoped for from others.

rule is found both in its negative and positive formulation.[34] The same applies to the Jewish writings.

In *Palestinian Judaism* the rule is only known in a negative form. One example of this is the Mishnah tractate *b.· Šabb.* 31a: A pagan addresses a famous teacher of the law with a question: 'Make me a proselyte on condition that you teach me the whole of the Torah while I am standing on one foot'. The teacher, Schammai, throws him out of the house. However, another teacher Hillel, makes him a proselyte by saying: 'That which you hate, do not do it to your neighbour. That is the whole of the Torah; everything else is just explanation. So go and learn!' Here, the rule (in its negative form) becomes the didactic principle that is to guide the student of the law in the process of learning. This is a function quite similar to that of Matthew's version (in its positive form).

In Hellenistic Judaism we meet the rule in its positive as well as its negative form. Sometimes the two forms are mingled in such a way that the outcome becomes strangely "neutral".[35] The most famous examples from Hellenistic Judaism are from the writings of *Aristeas, Tobit, Sirach* (LXX), the *Testaments of the Twelve Patriarchs* and *Philo*. A few examples must suffice. In Tob 4.15 we read: "That, which you detest, do not do to another person". The context does not put a particular accent on the sentence, it is just a rule of education such as any other. But it is notable that the negative form of 4.15 is preceded by a positive commandment in 4.13 to love one's brother.[36]

The *Epistle of Aristeas* contains a banquet conversation (187-294) by which the author intends to show the superiority of the virtue and knowledge of the Jewish envoys over that of the "philosophers". But a close examination of the content of the Jewish responses at the banquet conversation shows that the wisdom of the Jews is not essentially different from that of the "philosophers" and shows distinct Stoic influence.[37]

In *Ep. Arist.* 207 we find a form of the golden rule where the negative and positive form are somehow combined:

The King...said: 'What is the teaching of wisdom?' And the other replied: 'As you wish that no evil should befall you, but to be a partaker of all good things, so you

---

34. For further references see among others M. Behnisch, "The Golden Rule as an Expression of Jesus' Preaching", *Bangalore Theological Forum*, vol xvii, no.1 (January-March 1985) 83-97, esp. 85-87.

35. Cf. the following comments on Sir 34.15 LXX and *Ep. Arist.* : "Sowohl der griechische Sirach-Text als auch der Aristeasbrief bleiben bezüglich der Fassung der Regel merkwürdig 'neutral'" (G. Schneider, "Die Neuheit der christlichen Nächsten-liebe", 269).

36. Cf. B. Chilton and J.I.H. McDonald, *Jesus and the Ethics of the Kingdom*, 8.

37. For more detailed references to the *Epistle of Aristeas* see J. Piper, *'Love Your Enemies*, 35-36.

should act on the same principle towards your subjects and offenders, and you should mildly admonish the noble and the good. For God draws all men to Himself by his benignity.'

From the fact that both the positive and the negative form are found in Greek as well as Jewish sources, the conclusion can be drawn that the negative form cannot only be interpreted in a negative way in the sense of "not harm". It must rather be understood as a restraint on unwanted action as a necessity for vital and positive action.[38] It has also been argued that the negative and positive formulations are expressions of the same basic aphorism, and that *Ep. Arist.* 207 should rule out any claim to the effect that Jesus was absolutely unique among Jews in positively stating the same basic principle.[39]

This leads us to the question: Is Jesus' maxim simply an alternative version of all these formulations? Or does the rule receive a new tone when Jesus says it? What occurs with the rule when it is made part of the Sermon on the Mount (Matt 7.12), and when it is combined with the command to love enemies (Luke 6.31)?

The golden rule and the Sermon on the Mount

The golden rule plays an important role in the Sermon on the Mount. The word οὖν in Matt 7.12 gives the rule its function of being a conclusion of the main body of the sermon (5.17-7.12), and likewise, its conclusive character appears from the correlation between 5.17-20 and 7.12.[40]

Matt 7.12 also points forward to Matt 22.40. The same formula occurs in the two passages. Therefore it is natural to conclude that Matthew understands the rule in 7.12 in the sense of the commandment of love. However, there is one noticeable difference between the two passages. The golden rule speaks about something which is merely "human" or "social", while Matt 22.40 has two dimensions: a human one and a divine one, cf. "on these *two* commandments hang all the law and the prophets".

This does not necessarily mean that the golden rule only operates on the

---

38. Cf. P. Borgen, "The Golden Rule. With Emphasis on Its Usage in the Gospels", *Paul Preaches Circumcision and Pleases Men and Other Essays on Christian Origins* (Trondheim: Tapir, 1983) 99-114, 103.

39. Cf. B. Chilton and J.I.H. McDonald, *Jesus and the Ethics of the Kingdom*, 8.

40. Cf. P. Borgen, "The Golden Rule", 106; V. P. Furnish, *The Love Command*, 57. J. Piper, *'Love Your Enemies'*, 227-8, note 73, interprets differently: It is probably no accident that Matthew connected the rule to the preceding sayings on the Father's generosity with οὖν. This accords with Matthew's conception of God's fatherhood and ethics. We are called to fulfill the love command precisely because the Father is generous and will give us necessary resources.

level of human interaction. M. Behnisch[41] has pointed to a similarity between 7.12 and 5.48. The rule in 7.12 says *as — so*: 'as you wish...do so...'. This reminds us of 'as' in 5.48: "You, therefore, must be perfect, as your heavenly Father is perfect". In the last passage the substance and mode of God becomes the criterion of human action.

Apparently the rule in 7.12 operates on the human level, but once the egotism is destroyed and the needs of the neighbour become visible, the possibility is that our eyes are opened up for this other divine dimension. At this point it is interesting to read Matt 25.40: "Verily I say onto you. Inasmuch as you have done it unto one of the least of these my brethren, you have done it unto me". These observations lead to the possible conclusion that the golden rule has as its implicit (but necessary) background the criterion 'such as God'. This way of reading seems to be supported by another saying of Jesus, Matt 7.1-2 which can clarify the meaning of the golden rule: The measure with which I judge my own person and with which I want to be judged by others is understanding, magnanimity and forgiveness.

If this interpretation is valid, then the criterion for our behaviour towards our neighbour is found in the Father who is above us. This merger between the horizontal and vertical perspectives brings us to the heart of Jesus' preaching. We are in a better position to understand how the golden rule is transformed in the light of the message of Jesus.

As mentioned above, the golden rule has been understood as a further evolution of the idea of reciprocity.[42] In this sense it corresponds to a basic principle of behaviour which dominates the relationship between people: What people do to you, do the same thing to them. Be a friend to a friend and an enemy to an enemy, cf. the *jus talionis* which is presupposed in Matt 5.38a.
If this is the meaning of the rule, it is based on facts, on experiences. And then it is nothing more than re-action. In a positive sense the rule would add more good to what one receives. But in a negative sense it would just create more evil in a vicious circle.

However, the golden rule receives a new tone when Jesus says it. It does not mean: 'Do to people what they *have done* to you — or what they *do* to you'. Neither does it mean: 'Do to people what one *is used to doing* — according to the custom'. Neither does it mean: 'Do to people what you *want* them to do - provided they do it to you'. Instead it means: 'Take what you *naturally wish* others to do for you as the criterion for your actual behaviour towards other people *no matter* how they behave towards you'.

In other words, the golden rule has to be understood as an injunction to do for others the good thing we wish for ourselves, quite apart from the be-

---

41. I owe the following observations to M. Behnisch, "The Golden Rule as an Expression of Jesus' Preaching", esp. 91-97.
42. See also note 33.

haviour we experience or expect from them. In this way the rule corresponds to the behaviour which is characteristic of the heavenly Father[43]. He grants in advance and he grants contrary to what we would expect: "He makes His sun rise on the evil and on the good" (Matt 5.45, cf. Luke 6.35). This, however, means: *"Following the Golden Rule opens up in practical life the perspective of the merciful Father* in a world marked by the principle of retaliation."[44] Here — in the context of the Sermon on the Mount — is presupposed a surplus, a confidence which the rule itself cannot create. It is out of this confidence the person can act according to the rule.[45]

A note must be added on the *positive* form of the golden rule as compared to the non-Christian environments. Those relatively few parallels to Jesus' positive form of the rule almost all limit its application to situations where some reciprocity can be reasonably expected — between neighbours, or between a king and his subjects.[46] Or as E.A. Harvey observes[47]:

Stated quite generally, as Jesus states it, the maxim (unlike its negative counterpart) goes beyond even the most enlightened common sense. That is to say, like "love your enemies", or "divorce is equivalent to adultery", it takes up a theme already rehearsed in the tradition of moral teaching, but expresses it in an extreme and unconditional formulation (due this time to its positive, instead of negative form) that goes beyond the maxims of other moralists.

To sum up, then, three things can be said about the positive form of the

---

43. *Imitatio Dei* is an important ethical motif in Hellenistic Judaism. See for instance *Philo* (*De virtutibus* 165; 168-69) and *Ep. Arist.* (187f. 190; 192; 205; 207; 210; 281). Cf. also G. Schneiders remarks on Philo: "Die Nachahmung Gottes im menschlichen Wohltun ist für Philon – wie für Griechen und Juden seiner Zeit – ein besonderes Anliegen" ("Imitatio Dei als Motiv der 'Ethik Jesu'", *Neues Testament und Ethik. FS.R. Schnackenburg* [ed. H. Merklein; Freiburg: Herder, 1989] 71-83, 77). On the use of this motif in the teaching of Jesus, Schneider states: "Wie die Goldene Regel...kann auch die Forderung nach Imitatio der göttlichen Barmherzigkeit nur mit einigem Vorbehalt als jesuanisch angesehen werden, wenngleich sie sich seiner Verkündigung gut einfügen" (83). See also P. Hoffmann, "Tradition und Situation. Zur 'Verbindlichkeit' des Gebotes der Feindesliebe in der synoptischen Überlieferung und in der gegenwärtigen Friedensdiskussion", *Ethik im Neuen Testament* (ed. K. Kertelge; Freiburg: Herder, 1984) 50-118, 72.
44. M. Behnisch, "The Golden Rule", 94 (his italics).
45. Cf. M. Behnisch, "The Golden Rule", 96. See also H.-R. Reuter, "Bergpredigt und politische Vernunft", *Die Bergpredigt: Utopische Vision oder Handlungsweisung?* (ed. R. Schnackenburg; Düsseldorf: Patmos, 1982) 60-80. Reuter points out that the Lord's Prayer — the centre of the Sermon on the Mount — makes us better understand the meaning of the golden rule in the light of the gospel.
46. Yet, in some cases the golden rule is used in conflict with existing circumstances of rank and position, cf. P. Borgen, "The Golden Rule", 104-05.
47. A. E. Harvey, *Strenuous Commands*, 107.

rule.[48] First, it is not unique for the Christian tradition. It has parallels both in Greek and Jewish writings. Secondly, the positive form is nevertheless of importance, since it underlines the responsibility to take the first step.[49] Thirdly, this point has often been missed by later Christian generations. In many cases the negative form was "re-adopted"; see for instance *Did*. 1.2 and the Western text of Acts 15.20 and 29.

The golden rule and the love of enemies

While the golden rule in Matthew is used as a concluding *general* maxim, its function in Luke is less clear. It seems as if Luke uses it to apply to a *particular* situation, the one relating to the enemies. The relevant question then is: What is the relationship between these two motives? Is the golden rule consistent with the idea of loving one's enemies, or is it instead a contradiction of this idea?

The golden rule (Luke 6.31) is found in the passage about love towards enemies (vv. 27-35). This passage can naturally be divided into two parts, vv. 27-31 in the imperative form, and vv. 32-34 in the indicative form, with a concluding word in imperative (v. 35). The rule is separated from the preceding verses (vv. 29-31) by virtue of its return (cf. v. 27-28) to the second personal plural, and from the following verses (vv. 32-34) by virtue of what it says. Indeed, the commandment to "treat others as you would like them to treat you" seems to presuppose the kind of eagerness of *reciprocity* in moral conduct, which vv. 32-34 go on to condemn.[50]

A. Dihle attempts to solve the tension between v. 31 and the following verses by reading v. 31 as an indicative rather than imperative sentence. According to this understanding v. 31 does not belong to the preceding passage but to the ones immediately following. This would mean that the rule invites reciprocity. This suggestion, however, is not convincing.[51] The context calls for love of enemies, not reciprocal love. If we read the passage as a whole (vv. 27-35), we see that to love one's enemies is directly supported by means of a *criticism* of the commonly practiced "reciprocity ethics". The point is that one's

---

48. Cf. U. Luz, *Das Evangelium nach Matthäus*. Mt 1-7 (EKKNT; Zürich: Benzinger,1985) 392, note 36.

49. Cf. P. Hoffmann and V. Eid, *Jesus von Nazareth und eine christliche Moral*, p.150. "Da die Regel auf eine *Veränderung des Verhaltens* abzielt und nicht nur allgemein sittliche Maximen darbietet, ist es durchaus von Belang, ob sie negativ oder, wie es auch in der Jesustradition geschieht, positiv formuliert wird" [italics of the authors]. See also C. Frey, *Theologische Ethik* (Neukirchen-Vluyn: Neukirchener, 1990) 145.

50. Cf. V.P. Furnish, *The Love Command*, 57.

51. See, among others, P. Borgen, "The Golden Rule", 109; V.P. Furnish, *The Love Command*, 57, note 107.

action toward others should *not* be shaped by what he has received or can expect or hope from them.[52]

It has been argued persuasively (by W.C. van Unnik) that Luke is writing for a society that was significantly different from that in which Jesus lived.[53] The Jewish culture took for granted an obligation on the part of the well-to-do to relieve the need of the poor through almsgiving. By definition, the objects of such charity could never repay it; any recompense must be paid by God. The pagan world, on the other hand, knew little of this "social conscience". Acts of generosity would usually be directed toward one's social equals or superiors. Through one's acts of kindness one hoped to gain credits (χάρις): there was no point in doing them to someone so low down in the social scale that he had no credit out of which to return it.

It was to a society with conventions such as these that Luke had to give some plausibility to Jesus' command to love one's enemies. "The example he gives is 'doing good', which would normally be a reciprocal undertaking between social equals. But look at God! He shows kindness to those altogether without credit (cf. v. 35). 'Loving your enemies' means deliberately breaking with the social conventions that govern 'doing good', and showing your generosity..., as godly Jewish people do, to those who are really in need."[54]

We may sum up briefly that Luke's understanding of the golden rule cannot be fully captured without taking the *context* into consideration. This context spares the rule from possible misuse as a justification of egotistical calculation of reciprocal benefits.[55] But the context also gives the positive framework within which the golden rule is to be interpreted. The emphasis is on the mercy of God towards the ungrateful and evil doers, Luke 6.35-36. One of the main characteristics of God's action in Luke's gospel is that he practices redistribution through reversal (1.51-53; 6.20-26). Therefore, to give without expecting a return is to act like God, to be merciful and to show compassion.[56]

---

52. Cf. V.P. Furnish, *The Love Command*, 58.
53. W.C. van Unnik, "Die Motivierung der Feindesliebe in Lukas vi,32-35", *NovT* 8 (1966) 284-300. See also S.C. Mott, *Biblical Ethics and Social Change* (New York/ Oxford: Oxford Univ. Press, 1982), 57: "Christian love is different from Hellenistic benevolence, which was based on the institution of reciprocity"; and S.C. Mott, "The Power of Giving and Receiving. Reciprocity in Hellenistic Benevolence, *Current Issues in Biblical and Patristic Interpretation. FS. M. Tenney* (ed. G. Hawthorne; Grand Rapids: Eerdmans, 1975) 60-72.
54. A. E. Harvey, *Strenuous Commands*, 104.
55. Cf. A. Verhey, *The Great Reversal: Ethics and the New Testament* (Grand Rapid: Eerdmans, 1984) 57.
56. Cf. H. Moxnes, *The Economy of the Kingdom: Social Conflict and Economic Relations in Luke's Gospel* (Philadelphia: Fortress, 1988) 138. The author makes a helpful distinction between balanced reciprocity and redistribution.

When disciples are influenced by this goodness and mercy of God, a submission to the golden rule leads to love of enemies. There need not be any contradiction between the two issues, neither in Luke nor in Matthew. In both cases belief in the heavenly and merciful Father is the basis on which to understand the rule. It is particularly the Lucan version which makes clear that the rule *in itself* is a *formal* principle, close to the principle of reciprocity. But its positive form and its connection to the love of enemies keep it from any egoistical calculation and fill it with the contents of boundless and uncalculating neighbour-love.[57]

Love of enemies

A third way of describing the distinctive charcter of the New Testament love command is to focus on the admonition to love our enemies.[58] Since I have already referred to this item in the previous paragraphs, I shall confine myself to a few additional remarks. This includes some remarks on enmity love in Greek and Jewish sources.

The idea of loving one's enemies is not unknown to Hellenistic philosophy, but it is motivated in a way different from that of the New Testament paraenesis. Thus, non-retaliation and love of enemy are viewed as a sign of the philosopher's freedom from and superiority to the passions and illusions of the masses. A person not caught up in these passions cannot be judged[59]. For instance, "in Seneca every description of the wise man's conduct towards those who abuse, insult or do him an injustice only serves to magnify the inviolate wise man who is raised far above common mortals."[60] In the New Testament love is not motivated by a concern for one' s own greatness and nobility. It is motivated by the freeing mercies of God and the concern is for the other person's God.[61]

Hellenistic Jewish writings also make use of the Stoic vision of superior tranquility as the basis of non-retaliation. The *Epistle of Aristeas* states that Judaism is superior to pagan philosophy because it combines philosophical freedom from passion with devotion to God (235) and that God assists people in achieving this philosophical ideal (256).

57. Cf. A. Verhey, *The Great Reversal*, 25.
58. See, e.g. V.P. Furnish, *The Love Command*, 66: "It is Jesus' commandment to love the enemy which most of all sets his ethics of love apart from other "love ethics" of antiquity, and which best shows what kind of love is commanded by him". J. Jeremias, *Neutestamentlicher Theologie, I* (Gütersloh: Gütersloher, 1971) 206. Even Jewish authors emphasize this aspect: D. Flusser, *Jesus in Selbstzeugnissen und Bilddokumenten* (Hamburg: Rowohlt, 1968) 68-69.72. See also note 69.
59. Cf. Ph. Perkins, *Love Commands in the New Testament* (New York: Paulist, 1982) 31.
60. J.N. Sevenster, *Paul and Seneca* (Leiden: Brill, 1961) 183.
61. Cf. J. Piper, *'Love Your Enemies'*, 24.

In *Joseph and Asenath*,[62] various commands are issued not to repay evil. As noted by several scholars, these are striking parallels to Rom 12.17; 1 Thess 5.15 and 1 Pet 3.9.[63] But in spite of these parallels we cannot conclude that the same ethic is present in both. This Hellenistic Jewish element was not merely taken over by the early church; it was put into the context of the gospel by which a man is made new (cf. e.g. Rom 12.2) and it was expanded so that "it became only the negative counterpart to the positive love command. In *Joseph and Asenath* the commands relating to neighbour (Joseph's brothers) and enemy (Pharaoh's son) are all prohibitions."[64]

In *The Testaments of the Twelve Patriarchs* several sayings give expression to the notion of enemy love. The most important texts are *T. Benj.* 4.2-3; *T. Jos.* 18.2; *T. Gad.* 6.7; *T. Iss.* 7.6 and *T. Zeb.* 7.2-4. However, the situation is complicated since it is not clear to what extent the texts have been christianized.[65]

Furthermore, we cannot presume that the Testaments present a unified view on neighbour love — in *T. Reub.* 6.9 the neighbour is a brother, whereas in *T. Zeb.* 6.6 and 8.3 the word neighbour refers to "all men". It is probable that the universal expressions are expansions under the influence of Stoicism.[66] On the other hand, the admonitions to have mercy upon, forgive and pray for one's enemies (*T. Gad.* 6.7 and *T. Jos.* 18.2) are singular in this literature. If the "enemy" here is not intended to be restricted to fellow Jews, then these admonitions come quite near to the New Testament paraenetic commands of enemy love. However, in view of the arguments for a Christian redaction of the Testaments, it is not possible to make any assertions about the direction the influence may have taken between the early Christian paraenetic tradition and *The Testaments of the Twelve Patriarchs*.[67]

There are more examples of enemy love in Hellenistic Judaism as well as in the Old Testament and Greek writings.[68] Seen from this perspective, *Jesus'* command to love one's enemy is part of a widespread moral attitude, but it is

---

62. There is no agreement on the dating of the book, the range being from 100 BC to about 200 CE with a consensus emerging that it is pre-Christian. No serious argument has been made that the ethics of the book are non-Jewish. See W. Klassen, *Love of Enemies: The Way to Peace* (Philadelphia: Fortress, 1984) 53.

63. Nowhere in the New Testament outside the Synoptics do we find Jesus' command; 'Love your enemies!' in this form. However, in texts like Rom 12.14.17-20; 1 Thess 5.15 and 1 Pet 3.9 there are clear indications of a reception and application of the command of enemy love. For an analysis of the parallels between these texts and *Joseph and Asenath* see J. Piper, *'Love Your Enemies'*, 37-39.

64. J. Piper, *'Love Your Enemies'*, 39

65. On this problem see note 8.

66. Cf. J. Piper, *'Love Your Enemies'*, 45.

67. So J. Piper, *'Love Your Enemies'*, 45 (with references to J. Becker and M. de Jonge).

68. See, e.g., W. Klassen, *Love of Enemies*, 27-42.

expressed in a characteristically trenchant manner. His love command is radically comprehensive. Even those Jewish commentators who are most anxious to claim Jesus as an exponent of the best in Jewish moral teaching are agreed that there is no real parallel to such an uncompromising and unconditional message: to be told to love your enemy *as* such, without qualification, goes beyond any known Jewish maxim — even if there are noble examples in Jewish as well as Christian history of individuals having achieved it.[69]

Two passages in particular give expression to this radicalism. The first one is the parable of the good Samaritan (Luke 10.30-37) where the point is that the enemy becomes the loving neighbour. The second one is Matt 5.43-47. Jesus' command to love enemies must have appeared shocking in a society where love was largely restricted to the confines of a tighty-knit ethnic or religious group, and where hatred of the foreign oppressor was preached with religious fervour.[70] Clan solidarity is a phenomenon common to many cultures. The group dynamics of the kingdom are very different: characterized — not by exclusiveness or defensiveness but by openness to others that, indeed, reflects the openness of God to his children. The community must reach out to those who oppose it, and always seek to "overcome evil with good" (Rom 12.21).[71]

The centrality of the enemy love in the Synoptic gospels is beyond question.[72] It is also beyond question that Jesus' command to love one's enemy must be seen in the light of his announcement of *the inbreaking Kingdom of God*.[73] The power of the conventional pattern of reciprocity is only broken by trust in the coming rule of God.[74] Enemy love is a surprising, radical inversion of common folk morality which is a distinctive mark not only of the

---

69. Cf. A.E. Harvey, *Strenuous Commands*, 99. See also the Jewish commentator P. Lapide, *Die Bergpredigt: Utopie oder Programm* (Mainz: Matthias-Grünewald, 1982) 99 (cf. note 58). It is interesting to discuss the implication of this for the relation between Judaism and Christianity. J. Piper, *'Love Your Enemies*, 91-92, claims that "the perspective Jew must have viewed Jesus' love command as an attack on the Torah, first because it contradicted his understanding of Lev 19.18, and second, because it seemed in general to devaluate the distinction between Jew and Gentile — a distinction grounded in the Torah. Jesus' command to love the enemy as well as the friend contained the seed for dissolution of the Jewish distinctive". In opposition to this, W. Klassen, *Love of Enemies,* argues that "Jesus' teaching to love the enemy contained the seed, not for the dissolution of the Jewish distinction, but for its survival after the year 70 C.E." (43), and that "there is no conflict between the teaching of Judaism on this matter, and what Jesus himself as a first-century Jew taught" (66). Both Piper and Klassen are Christian theologians.

70. Cf. G.M. Soares-Prabhu, "The Synoptic Love-Commandment", 93.

71. Cf. B. Chilton and J.I.H. McDonald, *Jesus and the Ethics of the Kingdom*, 102.

72. Cf. the thorough examination of P. Hoffmann, "Tradition und Situation" (with further literature).

73. For further evidence see, among others, J. Piper, *'Love Your Enemies'*, 69-88.

74. Cf. A. Verhey, *The Great Reversal*, 25.

earliest traditions in the New Testament, but also of the succeeding development in the second and third century.[75]

Christ as the motivating power and as the pattern

Until now, the focus has been on the Synoptic gospels. But if we turn our attention to the Fourth Gospel and to other parts of the New Testament, a fourth suggestion for identifying the distinctiveness of the love command becomes relevant. The suggestion is that we should look for the motivation of the love command by asking: What did the New Testament authors conceive to be the motivating power behind the obedience to the love command? Insofar as the motivation is christologically founded, we should expect no parallels in the Hellenistic Judaism.[76]

The christological motivation of the love ethics is apparently absent in the Synoptic gospels. Yet, there are a few hints which seem to point in that direction. Jesus not only taught the double love commandment and gave the sayings of the Sermon on the Mount, but he also lived them out in his own life?[77] There is *a consistency between what he taught and what he lived*[78] He is a living parable of non-resistance to evil and love of enemies. This is seen most clearly in the Gospel of Luke where Jesus is presented as one who is practising enemy love immediately before his death (Luke 23.34).[79] One should ask if not the command to love one's enemies is grounded more in Jesus' own attitude and action than in an explicit word of his.

The intimate relationship between Jesus' teaching and his existence is basic to the Gospel of John. Furthermore, this gospel provides a new theistic and christological founding for the love command: it is rooted in God's love for the

75. Tertullian, for instance, considered the love of enemies to be the "proprium" of Christian morality (*Ad Scapulam* 1). See also the introduction to this article.

76. Another possibility would be a theistic motivation, cf. the motif of *imitatio Dei* which is often found in Hellenistic Judaism. Cf. note 43.

77. In an interesting article entitled "Jesus und das Hauptgebot" (in: *Neues Testament und Ethik. FS. R. Schnackenburg* [ed. H. Merklein; Freiburg: Herder, 1989] 99-109, R. Pesch has pointed out how Jesus' own existence and his teaching is strongly marked by the Sch^{e}ma. "...das Hauptgebot mutet dem Umkehrenden — im hörenden Gehorsam - die ungeteilte, ganze Existenz des Glaubenden zu, die Jesus vorlebt und die er fordert:'Ihr sollt ganz sein, wie auch...(Mt 5,48)'" (99). "Neutestamentliche Ethik als Ethik der Nachfolge Jesu ist durch das Hauptgebot geprägt, wie es Jesus in seiner Existenz, in seinem Wirken und in seinem Wort ausgelegt hat" (100). Cf. also several contributions from B. Gerhardsson, e.g. "Enhetsskapande element i Bibelns etiska mångfald", SEÅ 62 (1986) 49-58.

78. See also J.M. Gustafson, *Christ and the Moral Life* (Chicago and London: Chicago Univ. Press, 1968), especially the paragraph "Jesus Christ, the Pattern" (150-187).

79. On this passage see J.M. Ford, *My Enemy Is My Guest: Jesus and Violence in Luke* (New York: Orbis, 1984), esp. 131-33.

world which is manifested in the mission of Jesus (e.g. 3.16-21). The christological motivation becomes particularly clear in 13.34-35. "A *new* commandment I give to you that you love one another; even *as I have loved* you, you
must love one another..." When the Johannine Jesus speaks of a "new"
commandment, this "newness" must be rightly understood. The commandment, of course, is hardly novel, but it is "new" precisely because of the *new
situation* Jesus had inaugurated. This distinctive character of the Jesuanic love
command is also expressed in 15.13. "There is no greater love than this that a
man should lay down his life for his friends".[80]

Yet, it is a vexed question how these texts should be interpreted when
compared with the Synoptic evidence. The fact that John always refers to love
for "one another", never love for the neighbour or the enemy, is taken by
many scholars to be a narrowing of the scope of love. Thus, E. Käsemann finds
that according to John, the love of God cannot be connected with the love of
the world. The Son's mission of love is to the world only in the sense that it is
to gather the scattered elect of God together, out of the world.[81] A more
moderate view is held by J. Knox. He finds an implicit universalism in John.
But at the same time he suggests that the evangelist departs from the "ethical
universalism" of the Synoptic writers and the prophets and returns to the
teaching of Leviticus where "love your neighbour" had meant "love those
within your own group".[82]

Could Johannine Christianity include a love of enemies? That is a question
we cannot answer. The gospel and the epistle simply do not speak of such
love, and we can hardly go behind them to ask what their author (or authors)
might have spoken of.[83] If this question remains unsolved what then can we
say of these texts? Here I shall make two points, one concerning their literary
genre, the other concerning their *Sitz im Leben*.

First, we should acknowledge that the Johannine love commandments are

80. Hellenistic Jewish traditions probably played an important role in the development
of Johannine thought. They enabled the Johannine Christians to picture Jesus as the
divine Word. They also influenced the Johannine interpretation of the love
command; see K. Berger, *Die Gesetzauslegung Jesu*, 173.

81. "The object of Christian love for John is only what belongs to the community under
the Word, or what is elected to belong to it, that is the brotherhood of Jesus". E.
Käsemann, *The Testament of Jesus: A Study of John in Light of Chapter 17*, trans. G.
Krodel (Philadelphia: Fortress, 1968) 65. See also J. Becker, "Feindesliebe –
Nächstenliebe – Bruderliebe" (compare note 14).

82. J. Knox, *The Ethic of Jesus in the Teaching of the Church: Its Authority and Relevance*
(Nashville: Abingdon, 1961) 95-96. See also A. Nygren's discussion of the Johannine
view in his famous book, *Agape and Eros*, trans. P.S. Watson (Philadelphia:
Westminster, 1958), esp. 153-55.

83. Cf. D. Rensberger, *Overcoming the World: Politics and Community in the Gospel of John*
(London: SPCK, 1989) 129.

all to be found in the "Farewell discourses" (chaps. 13-17) which is a literary genre with many parallels to other biblical and post biblical speeches ascribed to famous men who anticipate their own death. A well-known example of this is *The Testaments of the Twelve Patriarchs*. Here, as in the Gospel of John, the unity of the brethren is underlined (*T. Zeb.* 8.5-6; *T. Jos.* 17.3). In John's gospel Jesus, like the patriarchs of old, is described as preparing his own people (his "friends") for his imminent departure. The love command is seen as the testament of Jesus which is to help maintain their corporate identity as *his* people even under difficult circumstances.[84]

This brings us to the second point. The injunction to love one another reflects the condition of the Johannine community drawn together into communal solidarity in the face of the hostility of the believing world.[85] It is a much debated question in which sense the community can be characterized as a "sect". Some scholars find the term "sectarian" appropriate for John; others do not.[86] No matter what the answer is, we must try to understand the basic characteristics of the Johannine community.

The Johannine community is a community of love. In and through the love for each other the disciples are called to give public witness to the life-giving power of God's love revealed in Jesus. By this *praxis of agape* all people will know that they are Jesus' disciples (13.34-35).[87] The existence of the community of love itself is a significant factor in understanding John. In this community love and action for the sake of others are to replace the world's persecution, oppression and self-interest. Within the community, relationships are established not on the basis of rank or class, but on the basis of the love

---

84. Cf. R. Brown's excursus on the literary genre or the "Farewell Discourses", *The Gospel According to John I-II*, 2.vols (Garden City, New York: Doubleday, 1966, 1970) 597-600, 611.

85. Cf. D. Rensberger, *Overcoming the World*, 79. The connection between persecution and communal solidarity, i.e. love of one another, is also drawn by K. Wengst, *Bedrängte Gemeinde und verherrlichter Christus: Der historische Ort des Johannes-evangeliums als Schlüssel zu seiner Interpretation* (Neukirchen-Vluyn: Neukirchener, 1983) 123-24.

86. Examples of those who find the term appropriate are E. Käsemann, *The Testament of Jesus*, 38-40. 65-66; W. Meeks, "The Man from Heaven in Johannine Sectarianism," *JBL* 91 (1972) 44-72; and F. Segovia: "The Love and Hatred of Jesus and Johannine Sectarianism" *CBQ* 43 (1981) 258-72. R.E. Brown, on the other hand, is hesitant in using this terminology. See his discussion in: *The Community of the Beloved Disciple: The Life, Loves and Hates of an Individual Church in New Testament Times* (New York: Paulist, 1979) 14-17. 88-91. To a considerable extent it is a matter of definition. Thus Brown confines the discussion of sectarianism to the breaking of the communion with other Christians. For futher analysis of the whole issue see D. Rensberger, *Overcoming the World*.

87. Cf. E. Schüssler Fiorenza, *In Memory of Her: A Feminist Theological Reconstruction of Christian Origins* (London: SCM, 1983) 323.

that obtains among those who are, all alike, the children of God through their faith in God's Son. "Thus, the absence of oppression among them is what indicates that *here* God's eschatological act has been recognized and affirmed".[88]

Two comparisons might help us to understand the specific character of the Johannine community. According to 15.13 the highest example and foundation of love is Jesus' death for his friends, for the Johannine disciples are now friends, not slaves. John's use of the concept of friendship seems to be influenced by the Hellenistic friendship tradition. True friendship was commonly said to be between those equal in virtue. In Jewish writings this ideal is applied to Moses, the friend of God.[89] One of the privileges of such a friendship with God was that this person could speak boldly (in prayer) to God. In the Gospel of John the disciples have a similar privilege, but now it is made clear that this new status does not derive from the particular progress toward philosophical virtue which Jewish traditions attributed to Moses. "Christians are 'friends of God' because they are 'friends of Jesus'. That friendship is grounded, not in equality of virtue, but in the Christian community's obedience to his command of love".[90]

Another comparison refers to the Qumran community. As in the writings from Qumran, the focus in John is on love within the chosen community. But there are important differences as well. In contrast with the Oumran ideas, there is no mention in this gospel to the hating of the enemy or avenging the wrongs which others may have perpetuated. Moreover (contrary to Käsemann) the Son's mission of love is conceived of as a mission to the whole world, and thus "the world" itself is conceived of in a very non-Gnostic way.[91] As R.E. Brown notices, in Qumran "love is a duty consequent upon one's belonging to the community", but in John "Jesus' love for men is constitutive for the community".[92]

However, the understanding of community in the Johannine Epistles seems closer to that of the Qumran literature. A reading of 1 John reveals a great anomaly. No more eloquent voice is raised in the New Testament for love within the Christian brotherhood and sisterhood (see for instance 1 John 4.19). Yet, that same voice is extremely bitter in condemning opponents who had

---

88. D. Rensberger, *Overcoming the World*, 129.
89. The wisdom tradition also held that the righteous are "friends of God" (Wis 7.27).
90. Ph. Perkins, *Love Commands*, 110.
91. Cf. V.P. Furnish, *The Love Commandment*, 147.
92. R.E. Brown, *The Gospel According to John*, 613. S. Legasse asks the question if John condemns non-Christian humanity, on its way to perdition. The answer is negative: "a call to hate the world would be a contradiction, for hatred belongs to the world (7.7; 15.18f.) .... The Johannine ideal cannot be reduced to a community loving itself and hostile to the world..." S. Legasse, "Interhuman love: New Testament limits and promise", *TD* 27,1 (Spring 1979) 9-13.10.

been members of his community and were so no longer (e.g. 1 John 3.8-13). We see in I John a dualistic articulation which from a theological point of view can become dangerous. In fact it encouraged Christians of later generations to see a dualistic division of humankind into believers (Christians) and non-believers, into an "us" who are saved and a "them" who are not.[93]

In the Johannine tradition, then, we find a tension which is clearest in I John. The use of a dualistic language could easily undermine the fabric of love, which the Johannine tradition sees as the essence of the Christian vision. The vision is a community of love which is a sign for non-believers (John 13.35). The foundation of its fellowship in the divine commission to continue witness to his Son must keep the community oriented toward the world. In fact, the main point for John is that "the transcended reality of God, the love between Father and Son, is revealed in and through the life of the Christian community and its expressions of love".[94]

One additional note should be made. It is interesting to notice that all the references outside the Synoptic gospels refer to love of other human beings (neighbour or brother),but not to the love of God. Only in 1 John 4.21 is the conjunction made with specific reference to the teaching of Jesus: "And this commandment we have from him, that he who loves God should love his brother also".

Why is the law of love in almost all extra-Synoptic passages without reference to the love of God? The context of 1 John 4 gives the answer. Here the love of God had been defined in terms of the life of Jesus. The act whereby God sent his Son into the world to die for sinners has become the *pattern* and the *paradigm* of his love. "For the early Church in general, since the death of Jesus, the connotation of the phrase "the love of God" had been historically₎ conditioned and illumined. The nature of God's love was seen in Jesus' self-giving and the nature of our love to him came to be understood in the same terms — in the love of the brother."[95]

Commentators differ as to the question whether "brother" in 1 John 4.21

93. Cf. R.E. Brown, *The Community of the Beloved Disciple*, 132-35. G. Strecker ("Gottes- und Menschenliebe in Neuen Testament," *Tradition and Interpretation in the New Testament. Essays in Honor of E.E. Ellis* [ed. G.F. Hawthorne and O. Betz; Grand Rapids: Wm. Eerdmans, 1987] 53-63, argues that the Johannine community cannot be a closed sect since it subscribes to the sentence "God is love" (1 John 4.8.16). "Ist Gott der unumschränkt Liebende, so ist seine Agape nicht auf den Kreis der Christen zu begrenzen, sondern schliesst Christen und Nichtchristen ein" (62).

94. Ph. Perkins, *Love Commands*, 105.

95. W.D. Davies, *The Sermon on the Mount* (Cambridge: Cambr. Univ. Press, 1969) 118. Davies points out that the same orientation is found in Paul. He seldom speaks of the love of God or of loving God. He speaks of loving the neighbour in terms of God's action in Christ (118-19).

means "a Christian brother" or "any person in need" (= "neighbour")[96] It is beyond question, however, that in the Johannine tradition Christ is seen as pattern and paradigm; as "life model" (cf. also John 13.15). Christ as pattern or paradigm means that God's work in Christ shapes our deeds; our deeds are to be shaped according to the pattern of divine activity in Jesus Christ.[97]

Moral consensus and moral distinctiveness

In two concluding paragraphs I shall return to the questions raised in the introduction to this article. First I shall try to summarize the findings as to the four suggestions for identifying the distinctive element of the love commandment in the gospels. And I shall do so with a special view to the hermeneutical implications.

The first three suggestions have been discussed in relation to the Synoptic gospels, the fourth one in relation to the Gospel of John. We have seen that the surrounding culture provides us with many parallels, especially to the first three. However, we should also be open to the possibility that the different proposals need not be exclusive of each other. It is conceivable that the various aspects of the commandment merge and form altogether the "new constellation" of the distinctive Christian element.[98] Yet, two of the four proposals are of particular interest: the command to love one's enemy and Christ as the motivating power. The question is: In what way are they "new" in relation to the environment?

It has been argued that the early Church did not attempt to formulate a new ethical system; rather it took over all that it found best in contemporary moral teaching, with only occasional reference to a new conception that could be traced back to Jesus.[99] Today the situation is the same. Christians are asked to formulate moral norms and standards which can be seen to be reasonable and just and to encourage a pattern of social and personal morality which can be stimulated by the power and resources of Christian love. The ethic of Jesus must be in the background of this activity, as has often been the case.

At first sight the same appears to be true of Jesus' own moral teaching. He seems to have used methods and forms inherited from generations of moral teachers. His use of the golden rule, the love commandment and various sayings related to the wisdom tradition shows that his project was not

---

96. See the different commentaries on I John.
97. Cf. J.M. Gustafson, *Christ and the Moral of Life*, 172. See also Eph 5.2. "And walk in love, as Christ loved us and gave himself up for us".
98. Cf. G. Schneider, "Die Neuheit der christlichen Nächstenliebe", 259.
99. An instructive example of this is the so-called "household codes". The many parallels to similar household codes in Jewish and Hellenistic morality raise the question whether the Christian authors simply borrowed conventional morality or transformed it substantially in the light of the gospel.

fundamentally dissimilar to the environment. On the other hand, the ethic of Jesus is not exhausted with these parallels. He offered *something more* over and above the generally accepted principles of morality.[100] He was more radical in his words on enemy love and in his words on self-denying discipleship.

How is this "something more" to be defined? What are the consequences of this for our moral life? These questions can be answered in various ways. One way is to argue — as R. Bultmann did — by saying that the significance of Christ for moral life is to be located in the new dispositions; the new stance towards the world is made real in faith. This is a *"Gesinnungsethik"*, an ethic of disposition, rather than an *"Objektethik"*, an ethic which provides norms and patterns of moral behaviour. According to Bultmann, there are no Christian ethics in the sense of a specific pattern of life to be actualized in Christians.[101]

However, the ethic of Jesus is not just an "ethic of intention". There is "something more" in his moral teaching. Jesus' love command has an *eschatological basis* which cannot be reduced to a "new disposition". Although Jesus made use of wisdom-type maxims, there was a fundamental presupposition of the wisdom tradition that Jesus did not share. This was the expectation that the future would be like the present, that tomorrow's decisions could be determined by yesterday's experience, that human nature is the same.

Contrary to this, Jesus taught that the Kingdom of God is at hand. The ideal of that kingdom is not beyond the horizon of the experienced possibilities. It is something received by faith and it challenges us *to live "as if"* the kingdom were already a reality.[102] In the teaching of Jesus eschatology and ethics go close together, the proclamation of God's imminent Rule is coordinate with the promulgation of the commandment to love.

This can be illustrated by the way in which the golden rule is transformed in the light of the gospel.[103] Interpreted literally, the rule can be taken as a sheer refinement of the law of retaliation. Its formulation would be 'I give *in order that* you give'. The doer takes the initiative, but does it for the sake of receiving a reward in return. This is what P. Ricoeur designates the *logic of equivalence*. Contrary to this is the *logic of superabundance*, which is a reading of the rule in the light of the gospel. The gospel means the irruption of the economy of gift and its logic of superabundance in the midst of the merchant's economy of exchange and its logic of equivalence. The economy of

100. Cf. A.E. Harvey, *Strenuous Commands*, 200-1.
101. See, for instance, R. Bultmann, *Jesus and the Word* (New York, 1934) 110. K.E. Løgstrup, *Den etiske fordring*, 122-32, also denies the existence of a special Christian ethic.
102. See A.E. Harvey, *Strenuous Commands*, 207-10.
103. For this transformation see the former paragraphs on the use of the golden rule in the Gospel of Matthew and the Gospel of Luke. H.-R. Reuter is correct in noticing, "dass das Evangelium die Goldene Regel erst richtig vergoldet" (H.-R. Reuter, "Die Bergpredigt als Orientierung unseres Menschseins", *ZEE* 23 [1979] 84-110, 102).

gifts is construed around a because: *'because* it is given to you, go and do alike'.[104]

The love command as a call to community

A final remark relates to the use of the term "distinctive" in this article. Several times we have asked the question: What is distinctive about the New Testament love command?

Strictly speaking, we may admit that it is difficult to give an answer. Teaching can properly be called "distinctive", only if people are not saying the same thing.[105] As we have seen, this claim is not without problems when we relate the New Testament to the Hellenistic Judaism. Moreover, if we by "distinctive" also mean modes of conduct completely *unique* to Christians, then the answer similarly must be negative.

If, however, we by "distinctive" mean some sort of *characteristic* Christian style of life, then the answer can be clearly affirmative, for love is without question the hallmark and urgent imperative of Christian existence.[106] In fact, it is precisely the New Testament love ethic as *embodied* in the life of the community which characterizes Christianity.

By the love command a community of love is called into being and summoned to responsible action.[107] The word community here has two levels of meaning. The first level relates to the way in which community functioned in the life of Jesus. The second level relates to the way in which love formed the life of the first Christians in the time after Easter.

As to the first level of meaning, it is noticeable that the command to love one's enemies was intimately connected with the community of Jesus. In this community group solidarity was transcended. This becomes clear if we compare the Jesus fellowship or movement with other movements of his time.[108] It is characteristic that they cared for their own groups and usually divided people into two categories: the righteous and the sinners (the Pharisees) or the

---

104. P. Ricoeur, "The Golden Rule: Exegetical and Theological Perplexities," *NTS* 36 (1990) 392-97, esp. 395-97.
105. Cf. A.E. Harvey, *Strenuous Commands*, 190.
106. See the conclusion in V.P. Furnish, *Theology and Ethics in Paul* (Nashville and New York: Abingdon, 1968) 241.
107. Cf. V.P. Furnish, *The Love Command*, 210.
108. Sociological approaches to the New Testament often use the term Jesus movement. This movement is understood as a renewal movement within Judaism. So, for instance G. Theissen, *Soziologie der Jesusbewegung: Ein Beitrag zur* Entstehungsgeschichte des Urchristentums (München: Kaiser, 1977). Theissen underlines the vision of love and reconciliation in the Jesus movement.

sons of light and the sons of darkness (the community at Qumran).[109] The Jesus movement was different. Here a new ethos took shape. The traditional interpretation of the command to love was criticized and a stress was placed on reconciliation between former enemies and friends (cf. Matt 5.38-48 par.).[110]

In the Jesus movement, people were challenged to live "as if" the Kingdom of God were already a reality. Since the Kingdom was characterized by grace, the Jesus fellowship came to be marked by grace, openness, willingness to receive and forgive.[111] This group was different from most other groups of that time by showing that it is possible to love one another without giving up the universal scope of love.[112] If it occurs that enemy love is replaced by a group solidarity (i.e. loving those who love you), then an open fellowship has turned into an introverted sect. This is the risk which the Johannine Christians were facing.[113]

The crucial question is how to combine the two forms of the love command: love toward members of the community and love toward outsiders. Examples from the early Christian ethical preaching indicate that the two forms can be combined without narrowing the scope of love (e.g. Rom 12.9-21 and 1 Pet 3.8-12).[114] On the other side, it is also clear that the main focus in the New Testament letters is on loving one another within the community of

---

109. J.D.G. Dunn states: "It was the *openness* of the circle round Jesus which distinguished the following of Jesus so sharply from the community at Qumran. Jesus founds no new Church; for there is no salvation even by entering a religious society, however radically transformed" (his italics). J.D.G. Dunn, *Unity and Diversity in the New Testament: An Inquiry into the Character of Earliest Christianity* (London: SCM, 1977) 105.

110. The nature of the Jesus fellowship has been described by H.-R. Weber as follows: "Gathering together poor Galileans with a former tax collector, some who were probably formerly Jewish rebels, and including women as part of the community, a sociologically and politically impossible group had come into being" (H.-R. Weber, "Kingdom = Glory = Service. Notes to 'The Crucified Christ Challenges Human Power'", *Your Kingdom Come: Ten Bible Studies* [Sydney: Austr. Council of Churches, 1979] 24). See also J. Nissen: *Poverty and Mission: New Testament Perspectives on a Contemporary Theme* (Leiden: Interuniversitair Instituut voor Missiologie en Oecumenica, 1984) 173, 20-23.

111. Cf. G. Forkman, *The Limits of the Religious Community* (Lund: Gleerup, 1972) 189.

112. The Jesus fellowship was based on the fact that Jesus himself in his life and teaching went beyond neighbour ethic to universal ethic. (By neighbour ethic is meant an in-group which teaches a higher ethical responsibility toward those belonging to one's own group). Cf. S.C. Mott, *Biblical Ethics and Social Change*, 43.

113. This applies especially to I John; see also note 86.

114. Cf. Ph. Perkins, *Love Commands*, 90. On love of brothers and love of neighbours in the Pauline literature see the penetrating study of K. Schäfer, *Gemeinde als "Bruderschaft": Ein Beitrag zum Kirchenverständnis des Paulus* (Frankfurt a. M.: Peter Lang, 1989), esp. 174-88.

believers. This is not be interpreted as a neglect of those outside of the community. Rather, it means that the *communities are in themselves a sign of reconciliation*, Here enemy love is realized.[115]

The love command is not unique in the history of ideas; what is new is its relationship to Jesus Christ who calls forth a new world, a new community which makes love possible.[116] The New Testament love ethic is a call to community. That is why the ethics of Jesus cannot be separated from the ethos of the community. The Christian vision is a vision of a community in which all are "friends of God".[117] It is a community free from social hierarchy and partiality, but also a community in which love of enemies has the highest priority.

---

115. Cf. the following remarks on 1 Thess 5.15 by K. Wengst, *Pax Romana. Anspruch und Wirklichkeit: Erfahrungen und Wahrnehmungen des Friedens bei Jesus und im Urchristentum* (München: Kaiser, 1986) 110. "An erster Stelle kommt hier zunächst die Gemeinde in den Blick; sie ist selbst ein Raum unterbrochener Gewalt, der nächstliegende Ort christlicher Friedenspraxis". See also U. Luz, "Eschatologie und Friedenshandeln bei Paulus", *Eschatologie und Friedenshandeln: Exegetische Beiträge zur Frage christlicher Friedensverantwortung* (ed. U. Luz e.a.; Stuttgart: Katholisches Bibelwerk, 1981) 155-93. Life of love *interior* to the Christian community has at the same time an *exterior* visibility and effect (cf. also John 13.34-35).

116. As has been noticed in the introduction to this article, the teaching of Jesus and the first Christians must be seen in relation to their symbolic and social world. Cf. note 7.

117. Cf. Ph. Perkins, *Love Commands*, 124-25. It is interesting to see that J. Moltmann under the headline "Offene Freundschaft" has developed the concept of friendship in his ecclesiology: *Kirche in Kraft des Geistes: Ein Beitrag zur messianischen Ekklesiologie* (München: Kaiser, 1975) 134-41. Cf. the following statement: "Wegen des Grundsatzes der Gleichheit und Gleichrangigkeit neigte das griechische Freundschaftsideal zu einem exklusiven Begriff der Freundschaft. Dieser geschlossene Kreis der Freundschaft wird durch Jesus sowohl im Blick auf Gott, wie auf die Jünger, wie auf die Sünder und Zöllner durchgebrochen" (139).

Some Hebrew and Pagan Features in Philo's and Paul's Interpretation of Hagar and Ishmael

Peder Borgen

The Research Situation

A central problem in Paul's Letter to the Galatians is whether Gentiles who confess Christ must become Jewish proselytes, undergo circumcision and join the Jewish community under the Law of Moses. In this situation, how could Paul in Gal 4.21-5.1 use the story of Abraham, Hagar/Ishmael and Sarah/Isaac as a relevant argument?

Scholars have had difficulties both in explaining why Paul has included the passage and with several details in it. In his commentary, E. de W. Burton introduces his exegesis of the passage in this way:

A supplementary argument based on an allegorical use of the story of the two sons of Abraham, and intended to induce the Galatians to see that they are joining the wrong branch of the family (4.21-31). Before leaving the subject of the seed of Abraham it occurs to the apostle, apparently as an after-thought, that he might make this thought clearer and more persuasive by an allegorical interpretation of the story of Abraham and his two sons, Ishmael and Isaac, the one born in course of nature only, the other in fulfillment of divine promise.[1]

A. Oepke and H. Schlier also regard the section as an afterthought. Oepke writes: "Der folgende mühsam wieder von vorn anfangende Schriftbeweis hätte seinen gegebenen Platz in Kap. 3 gehabt. Er ist dem Apostel wohl erst nachträglich eingefallen."[2] H. Schlier agrees with Burton and Oepke that the section seems to be an afterthought, but gives it more weight: "Gerade das Bewusstsein von der schwierigen Situation in den galatische Gemeinden veranlasst den Apostel, noch einmal etwas zur Sache zu sagen."[3] F. Mussner admits that the paragraph may give the impression of being an afterthought, but he himself thinks that this after-thought was caused by the perplexity

---

1. E. de Witt Burton, *A Critical and Exegetical Commentary on the Epistle to the Galatians*, (Edinburgh: Clark repr. 1977) 251.
2. A. Oepke and J. Rohde, *Der Brief an die Galater* (Berlin: Evangelische Verlagsanstalt, 1973) 3rd ed. 147.
3. H. Schlier, *Der Brief an die Galater* (Göttingen: Vandenhoek & Ruprecht, 1971) 5. ed. 216.

which Paul expresses in 4.20.[4] H.D. Betz also raises the question of the place of the section and of its argumentative force. In the light of rhetorical considerations he finds that the place and function of the allegory 4.21-31 become explicable: "Paul had concluded the previous section in 4.20 with a confession of perplexity. Such a confession was a rhetorical device, seemingly admitting that all previous arguments have failed to convince. Then, in 4.21, he starts again by asking the Galatians to give the answer themselves."[5]

In his essay "The Allegory of Abraham, Sarah and Isaac in the Argument of Galatians," C.K. Barrett gives an extensive discussion of Gal 4.21-31.[6] He sees the main importance of the passage in the situation of conflict in which Paul finds himself. The Judaizers championed a certain exegesis of the Old testament story about Abraham, Sarah, Hagar, Isaac and Ishmael, and Paul rebuts their views. Thus, Barrett looks into Jewish expository traditions which might throw light upon the dispute. Paul's opponents, according to Barrett, followed the view expressed in Jewish writings such as Jubilees 16.17ff. and the Targum of Pseudo-Jonathan. In Jubilees 16.17ff. it is said to Abraham that "all the seeds of his sons should be Gentiles, and be reckoned with the Gentiles; but from the sons of Isaac one should become a holy seed, and should not be reckoned among the Gentiles. For he should become the portion of the Most High, and all his seed had fallen into the possession of God, that it should be unto the Lord a people for (his) possession above all nations and that it should become a kingdom and priests and a holy nation." According to the Targum of Pseudo-Jonathan it was a fact "that Sarah's descendants were the Jews, and elect by God, and Hagar's descendants were Gentiles and stood outside the promise." Barrett concludes: "The Judaizing argument is clear. The true descendants of Abraham are the Jews, who inhabit Jerusalem. Here are the true people of God, now called the church. Those who are not prepared to attach themselves to this community by the approved means (circumcision) must be cast out; they cannot hope to inherit promises made to Abraham and his seed."[7]

Against such an interpretation, which was championed by the Judaizers, Paul develops an alternative interpretation. C.K. Barrett suggests that Paul, by using Jewish methods of exegesis, here gives a fresh interpretation of the story of Abraham, Hagar and Ishmael. Paul in this way identifies the woman Hagar with the mountain of Sinai where the law was given. "Hagar stands for the

---

4. F. Mussner, *Der Galaterbrief* (Freiburg: Herder, 1974) 316-17.
5. H.D. Betz, *Galatians* (Philadelphia: Fortress, 1979) 239-40.
6. C.K. Barett, "The Allegory of Abraham, Sarah and Isaac in the Argument of Galatians," *Rechtfertigung. FS E. Käsemann* (ed. J. Friedrich, W. Pöhlmann, P. Stahlmacher; Tübingen: Mohr [Siebeck] and Göttingen: Vandenhoeck & Ruprecht, 1976) 1-16.
7. ibid., 10.

covenant of Sinai, that is, the covenant of the law; she is a slave, and her children are slaves. Those therefore who adhere to the law are slaves and do not inherit the freedom of Abraham and Sarah." Paul "agrees that the children of Sarah are to be distinguished from the children of Hagar; but the Jews (and Judaizers), the children of the legal, Sinaitic, covenant, are the children of Hagar — and therefore slaves."[8]

An objection must be raised with regard to Barrett's interpretation: it seems improbable that Paul, by a fresh interpretation of his own making, could identify the gentile Hagar with the Jewish covenant of the law. Paul's way of arguing would then hardly stand up against the view of his opponents.

Nevertheless, Barrett's search into the Jewish expository traditions might be explored further. Such an approach is of importance because the modern authors of the exegetical commentaries do not have any broad presentation of the material, but mainly draw on it piecemeal at points in the running exegesis. According to Barrett, Philo's very extensive allegories of Abraham, Sarah, and Hagar contribute little, in form or substance, to the discussion of Gal 4.21-31.[9] Nevertheless, since the exegetes are still searching for clues, it may be of importance to look at this material afresh to see if it may be of some help. A main question for the present study then is the question: How can Paul's exegesis serve as a forceful argument against the Judaizers? At the end the question will be raised why it was important for Paul to include this section in his letter.

Hagar: Egyptian by birth, Hebrew by choice and way of life

Most of the material on Abraham, Hagar and Ishmael is found in the commentary series called "The Allegory of the Laws": *Leg. all.* 3.245; *Cher.* 3, 6 and 8; *Sacr.* 43; *Post.* 130-37; *Sobr.* 8f.; *Congr.* 1, 11f., 20-24, 71f., 81, 88, 121ff., 127-29, 139, 153-58, 180; *Fug.* 1, 5f., 202-04, 208-12; *Mut.* 201-63; *Somn.* 1.240.

In Philo's commentary "Questions and answers" there is also much material on Hagar and Ishmael, *QG* 3.19-38, 57, 59,61; 4.147,245. In the comprehensive collections of books called "The Exposition", which are a rewriting of the Pentateuch, Hagar and Ishmael are referred to in *Abr.* 247-54.

As seen from the survey, Philo has extensive interpretations of Hagar and Ishmael in the treatise "On the Mating with Preliminary Studies" (*De congressu quaerendae eruditionis gratia*). The reason is that the story about Abraham's family situation is applied by him to the role which encyclical education should play for Jews. For the present study the most important observations are to be made on aspects of the rawmaterial which he has utilized when developing such a philosophy of education. Throughout Philo's writings it is stressed that

8. ibid., 11-12.
9. ibid., 11, footnote 24.

Hagar was an Egyptian. Her relationship with Abraham and Sarah — even having a son with Abraham — connects her closely with the Hebrew nation, of which Abraham is the founder. Thus, Hagar is a figure 'on the borderline'.

In *Congr.* 22-23 Hagar's place on the borderline is formulated in a principal way, by means of etymological interpretation of her name: The name Hagar is understood to be derived from *gwr*, to be a stranger, sojourn, dwell.[10] Philo renders the etymological interpretation by the Greek word παροίκησις, sojourning.Thus Hagar means a person on the borderline between foreigners and citizens (μεθόροι ξένων καὶ ἀστῶν, *Congr.* 22). At times Philo understands the word to mean an alien (*Sacr.* 44, etc.), but he can also use the word to mean the integration of a sojourner into the society: "The sojourner in so far as he is staying in the city is on par with the citizens, in so far as it is not his home, on par with foreigners" (*Congr.* 23). The borderline place of Hagar is also illustrated from the situation of a person who is adopted into a family: "In the same way, I should say, adopted children, in so far as they inherit from their adopters, rank with the family; in so far as they are not their actual children, with outsiders" (*Congr.* 23).

In "The Exposition", Philo retells the story of Hagar in *Abr.* 247-54. The book *On Abraham* praises Abraham for his piety and his virtues shown in his dealings with men (*Abr.* 208). Then in *Abr.* 245-54 Sarah receives the praise. After a general characterization in #245-46, the story about Sarah, Abraham and Hagar is introduced in #247: "Many a story I could relate in praise of this woman, but one I will mention which will be the clearest proof that the others are true. Being childless and barren and fearing lest the house beloved of God should be left entirely desolate, she came to her husband and said:...."

Then a free elaboration of parts of Gen 16 follows, drawing in particular on Gen 16.1ff.

The scriptural basis in Gen 16.1-2 reads in LXX as translated into English:[11]

1 And Sarah the wife of Abram bore him no children; and she had an Egyptian maid, whose name was Agar. 2 And Sarah said to Abram: 'Behold the Lord has restrained me from bearing, go therefore in to my maid, that I may get children for myself through her.'

---

10. In Hebrew the verb in piel means to make a proselyte, in hithpael to become a proselyte Se M. Jastrow, *A Dictionary of the Targumim, the Talmud Babli and Yerushalmi, and the Midrashic Literature* (reprinted in Israel, no date) 1,226.

11. The translation is taken from *The Septuagint Version of the Old Testament with an English Translation* (London: Bagster, no date). The Greek text and English translation of Philonic Texts are (with some modifications) taken from *Philo with an English Translation*, 1-10 (trans. F.H. Colson and G.H. Whitaker; LCL, Cambridge, Mass: Harvard University Press, 1929-62 with several reprints) and *Philo Supplement* 1-2 (trans. R. Marcus; LCL, Cambridge, Mass: Havard University Press, 1953).

Philo has a lengthy elaboration of Sarah's words in *Abr.* 247-53.

248 'Long have we lived together in mutual goodwill. But the purpose for which we ourselves came together and for which nature formed the union of man and wife, the birth of children, has not been fulfilled, nor is there any future hope of it, through me at least who am now past the age. 249 But do not let the trouble of my barrenness extend to you, or kind feeling to me keep you from becoming what you can become, a father, for I shall have no jealousy of another woman, whom you will take not for unreasoning lust but in fulfilment of nature's inevitable law. 250 And therefore I shall not defer to lead to you a bride (νυμφοστολεῖν) who will supply you with what is lacking in myself. And if our prayers for the birth of children are answered, the offspring will be your legitimate children (γνήσια), but surely mine also by adoption (θέσις).

251 'But to avoid any suspicion of jealousy on my part, take (marry) if you will my handmaiden, bodily a slave (τὸ μὲν σῶμα δούλην), but free and noble (well-born) as to disposition (ἐλευθέραν δὲ καὶ εὐγενῆ τὴν διάνοιαν), proved and tested by me for many years from the day when she was first brought to my house, by birth an Egyptian (γένος μὲν Αἰγυπτίαν), by choice/rule of life a Hebrew (τὴν δὲ προαίρεσιν Ἑβραίαν).

252 'We have much substance and abundance of wealth, not on the usual scale of immigrants, for in this we now outshine those of the native inhabitants who are noted for their prosperity, but no heir (κληρονόμος) or successor has appeared, though there may be if you follow my advice.'

253 Abraham with increased admiration for the wifely love, which never grew old and was ever showing itself anew, and her careful forethought for the future, took the mate whom she had approved until she had borne a child (τοῦ παιδοποιή-σασθαι), or, as the surest exegetes say, only till she became pregnant, and when this occurred not long after he abstained from her through his natural continence and the honour which he paid to his lawful spouse (ἀπένεμε τῇ γαμετῇ). 254 So a son was born just at that time to the handmaiden, but long afterwards the wedded pair, who had despaired of the procreation of children, had a son of their own, a reward for their high excellence, a gift from God the bountiful, surpassing all their hopes.

Here as elsewhere, Philo states explicitly that Hagar is a pagan Egyptian woman by birth. Since Hagar belonged to the household of Abraham and Sarah, she is a person on the borderline. In this passage she is brought so far into the Hebrew side that her role is largely that of a Hebrew woman. Sarah led Hagar as a bride to Abraham and he married her. Sarah characterizes Hagar as a person who is Hebrew by choice and by way of life. Sarah says to her husband: "But to avoid any suspicion of jealousy on my part take if you will my handmaiden (θεράπαινα), bodily a slave, but of free and noble race as to disposition (τὴν διάνοιαν, thought, notion, intention) proved and tested by me for many years from the day when she was first brought to my house, *an Egyptian by birth* (γένος), *but a Hebrew by her choice/rule of life* (τὴν δὲ προαίρεσιν)," *Abr.* 251. The word προαίρεσις means "choice" and "purpose". It may refer to the purpose or motive of some particular action (see *Contempl.*

29 and 79; *Jos.* 150) or the choice, motives and principles which regulate a lifetime or a career. Here in *Abr.* 251 it means that Hagar, although being an Egyptian by birth, based her way of life on Hebrew principles and rules.[12] Hagar lived as a law-abiding Jew. A similar understanding of Hagar is found in *Gen. Rab.* 61.4 (where she is identified with Keturah): "she united the practice of doing religious duties with the work of good deeds".[13]

With such exegesis of Hagar as background, Paul's points made in Gal 4.21-5.1 receive force in the overall argument of the letter: The Judaizers who require that the Galatian converts must become Jews and follow the Laws of Moses, they copy the pattern of Hagar, the pagan slave who turned Hebrew by way of life, and was married to Abraham as a substitute for Sarah.

Gal 4.21-31

Against this background, let us turn to Gal 4.21-31. The passage can be analysed as follows:

The scriptural "quotation" (a summary of LXX Gen 16.15; 21.2-3.9):

22 γέγραπται γὰρ ὅτι
'Αβραὰμ δύο υἱοὺς ἔσχεν,
ἕνα ἐκ τῆς παιδίσκης καὶ ἕνα ἐκ τῆς ἐλευθέρας.

Commentary:
a) Characterization of the different births of the two sons:
23 ἀλλ' ὁ μὲν ἐκ τῆς παιδίσκης κατὰ σάρκα γεγέννηται,
ὁ δὲ ἐκ τῆς ἐλευθέρας διὰ τῆς ἐπαγγελίας.

b) The deeper, typological meaning:
24 ἅτινά ἐστιν ἀλληγορούμενα.
Two covenants, the one from Sinai:
αὗται γάρ εἰσιν δύο διαθῆκαι.
μία μὲν ἀπὸ ὄρους Σινά, εἰς δουλείαν γεννῶσα,
ἥτις ἐστὶν 'Αγάρ.
25 τὸ δὲ 'Αγὰρ Σινὰ ὄρος ἐστὶν ἐν τῇ 'Αραβίᾳ.

---

12. See also *Contempl.* 2 and 17; *Hypoth.* 11.2; *Agr.* 60; *Ebr.* 46; *Fug.* 204; *Sacr.* 11; *Mos.* 1.161; *Spec.* 4.194. The distinction between Egyptians and Hebrews is found in several places in Philo, such as in *Mut.* 117: they call Moses an Egyptian (Exod 2.19), Moses who was not only a Hebrew, but of that purest Hebrew blood; *Jos.* 42. "we children of the Hebrews (οἱ 'Εβραίων ἀπόγονοι) follow laws and customs which are especially our own."
13. Translation by J. Neusner, *Genesis Rabba. The Judaic Commentary to the Book of Genesis. An American Translation*, 2 (Atlanta Scholars, 1985) 334. According to Targum Pseudo-Jonathan, *Gen.* 12.5, and other sources (*Gen. Rab.* 39.14; 84.4, etc.) Abraham and Sarah converted many pagans and made them proselytes.

The Sinai covenant and the present Jerusalem:
συστοιχεῖ δὲ τῇ νῦν ᾽Ιερουσαλήμ, δουλεύει γὰρ μετὰ τῶν τέκνων αὐτῆς.
26 ἡ δὲ ἄνω ᾽Ιερουσαλὴμ ἐλευθέρα ἐστίν,
ἥτις ἐστὶν μήτηρ ἡμῶν.
27 γέγραπται γάρ,
εὐφράνθητι...

c) Expository application: 28-31.

In the Commentary, part a), Gal 4.23, words from the Old Testament "quotation" (v 22) are interpreted by supplementary words "was born according to the flesh" (κατὰ σάρκα γεγέννηται) and "through promise" (διὰ τῆς ἐπαγγελίας). In the "allegory", part b), Paul follows in v 24 and 25a the very common expository method of equating a word or phrase with another word or phrase by using ἐστὶν/εἰσιν as the connecting word.[14] It is also a common exegetical formula to repeat a word or phrase from a text by introducing it by the neuter definite article το.[15] See Eph 4.9. τὸ δὲ "ἀνέβη", repeating a word from Ps 68.19, cited in Eph 4.8. This formula has the function of placing the word or phrase in quotation marks. Thus τὸ δὲ ᾽Αγάρ repeats the word ᾽Αγάρ at the end of v 24, and Paul has given the sentence the form of an explanatory gloss which refers back to v. 24. The gloss can be translated as "now 'Hagar' here (in v 24) is Mount Sinai in Arabia". Then in v 25b and 26 there is an expanding exegesis as indicated by the verb "stand in the same line with" (συστοιχεῖ). Finally, there is an expository application in 4.27-31 in the form of 2nd person plural in v 28, and 1st person plural in v 31.

Let us first turn to Gal 4.24.25. In his discussion of Gal 4.24-25 H. Schlier discusses various possible interpretations of these verses, but without finding a satisfactory understanding: "Dass Hagar aber allegorisch mit dem Testament vom Sinai identisch ist, geht daraus hervor, dass das Wort Hagar... in Arabien den Berg Sinai bedeutet. V. 25 erscheint auf alle Fälle eine Begründung für die Zusammengehörigkeit von ᾽Αγάρ und Σινά geben zu wollen. Doch ist der Sinn nicht mehr klar und die Auslegung schwierig... So muss m.E. der genaue Sinn des Sätzchens V. 25a und damit der Grund und Anlass, der es Paulus ermöglichte, Hagar mit der Diatheke vom Sinai zu verbinden, dunkel bleiben."[16] As for the association of Hagar with the present Jerusalem, Schlier explains it on the basis of the formal similarity: both represent slavery. He defines that the

14. Cf. the formular phrases for direct exegesis listed in P. Borgen, "Philo of Alexandria. A Critical and Synthetical Survey of Research since World War II," in *ANRW*, II:21.1, (Berlin, 1984) 138.
15. See for example Philo, *Leg. all.* 1.65,67; *Migr.* 7; *Congr.* 172; *Mut.* 27,29; *Opif.* 27; The Greek fragments of *QG* 1.1; 55; 93; 100; 2.54; 3.23; 40; 4.73; 99; 188.
16. H. Schlier, *Der Brief an die Galater*, 219-20.

slavery of Hagar corresponds to the slavery of Jerusalem: "Sie entspricht dem jetzigen Jerusalem."[17]

F. Mussner believes that Paul's allegorical comparison of Hagar with Mount Sinai, v. 24, which is based on the idea of "slavery" needed v. 25a causal foundation: "Hagar ist *'Sklavin'*, der Berg Sinai *'gebiert zu Sklaverei'*, das gegenwärtige Jerusalem *'liegt mit seinen Kindern in Sklaverei'*."[18]

H.D. Betz finds it difficult to see the basis for Paul's argument in Gal 4.24-25. "Paul's aim is clearly to discredit the 'old covenant' as the pre-Christian condition before salvation came. What he offers as proof, however, has strained the credulity of the readers beyond what many people can bear...At least Paul's intentions are easy to detect... 'one from Mount Sinai' refers to the 'Sinai covenant.' It is represented by the slave woman Hagar, whose children's destiny is slavery... Those who belong to this covenant of Judaism, are in the situation of 'slavery under the Law'..."

Betz also translates συστοιχεῖ in v. 25 with its general meaning "correspond". He then follows Lietzmann who has pointed out that in Gal 4.22-30 we do have a kind of correspondence of concepts, subjected to the names of Hagar and Sarah.[19]

These interpretations by Schlier, Mussner and Betz are largely based on a formal understanding of slavery. The focus on the theme of Jewish proselytism is then lacking. This focus seems essential, however, in an argument against the Judaizers who were making the gentile Christian converts into Jewish prose-lytes. Thus, one must raise the question how the pagan Hagar and Jerusalem, the center of Judaism, might represent the same kind of slavery. This is the case if Hagar and Ishmael are to be seen within the context of Jewish prose-lytism. Actually, Gal 4.24 expresses this view, when it is said that the slave Hagar represents the covenant which came from Sinai, i.e. the covenant of the Law of Moses. Against the background of ideas like those in *Abr.* 251, this covenant meant that gentile Christian converts should comply to the Laws of Moses and become Jews. This was the case with Hagar according to Philo: *an Egyptian by birth* (γένος), *but a Hebrew by choice and rule of life* (τὴν δὲ προαίρεσιν).

What then is the meaning of the gloss in Gal 4.25a: τὸ δὲ ʼΑγὰρ Σινὰ ὄρος ἐστιν ἐν τῇ ʼΑραβίᾳ, "now Hagar is Mount Sinai in Arabia"?

There are two main approaches to the interpretation of τὸ δὲ ʼΑγάρ. 1) The phrase may be translated as "the name Hagar", and imply an etymological interpretation, or a play on the name. The problem is that no Hebrew or Greek etymology makes sense in the context. It has been suggested that Paul, who spent some time in Arabia, may have interpreted "Hagar" etymologically from

17. Ibid., 220-21.
18. F. Mussner, *Galaterbrief*, 323.
19. H.D. Betz, *Galatians*, 244-45.

Arabic *hadjar*, which means "rock".[20] It seems improbable that Paul uses an etymological exegesis from Arabic in a letter to Christians in Galatia. It has been suggested that the name Hagar is understood by Paul as a word-play on the geographical name Hagra, which is found in Targum Pseudo-Jonathan and Targum Onqelos on Gen 16.7.[21] This geographical name does not give any direct connection with Mount Sinai, however. 2) Another possibility is to look for a similarity of kind, character and quality between the words Hagar and Sinai in Gal 4.25. It is referred to above how Mussner finds the key in the formal similarity expressed in the theme of slavery: Hagar is a slave and Sinai is bearing children for slavery. There is need to go beyond this formal similarity, however.

The exegesis of Gal 4.25a should rather find its starting-point in the observation that Paul's exegetical 'quotation mark' τὸ δὲ ʾΑγάρ refers back to the name Hagar in v. 24, where the slave girl Hagar is seen as the covenant from Sinai. Thus, "Hagar" as type, i.e. the Hagar-covenant of the Law, is Mount Sinai in Arabia. M.-J. Lagrange touched this interpretation, when he omitted the word Hagar in v. 25 and thought that the figure of Hagar, as the "Sinaidiatheke", made Paul to think of Sinai, because the main tribe of the Arabs should come forth from Ishmael.[22]

Paul's exegetical gloss in v. 25a refers back to v. 24 and Hagar as the covenant from Sinai. The equation in v. 25a "Now 'Hagar' is Mount Sinai in Arabia," is then based on the similar nature of Hagar's identification with the covenant/the Law and Mount Sinai's identification with the Law of Moses.[23] As seen from Philo, Hagar was the type of pagan who was characterized as a Hebrew because she chose the Law of Moses as her way of life. Similarly, Mount Sinai, which was part of the pagan Arabia, became the Mountain of the Law of Moses. This understanding of Arabia is in accordance with Gal 1.16-17 where Paul says that he was commissioned to preach the gospel among the Gentiles and that he then immediately went to Arabia. The meaning of Gal 4.25 is then: the pagan born slave Hagar, who became a law-abiding Hebrew meant typologically the Mountain of the Law located in the pagan country of Arabia.

In this way, Paul has made two important points of argument against the Judaizers: they were making slave-proselytes out of the Christian gentile

---

20. So M.-J. Lagrange, *Saint Paul, Épître aux Galates*, (Paris: Lecoffre, 1918, 2nd ed. 1925) ad loc. H. Schlier, *an die Galater*, ad loc. H.D. Betz, *Galatians*, ad loc. F. Mussner, *Galaterbrief*, ad loc.

21. See M.G. Steinhauser, "Gal 4.25a: Evidence of Targumic Tradition in Gal 4.21-31?", *Biblica*, 70 (1989) 234-40.

22. M.-J. Lagrange, *aux Galates*, ad loc.

23. Paul's exegesis of Gen 15.6 in Gal 3.6-7 is also built on similarity of nature and character:"As [it is written], 'Abraham had faith in God, and it was reckoned to him as righteousness.' Recognize, therefore, that the ones of 'faith', these are the sons of 'Abraham'."

converts, and these slave-proselytes were the result of the Law of Sinai, which similarly came into being on a mountain in a pagan country.

In the rank and line with Jerusalem

The Hagar and Sinai-covenant stands in the rank and line with the Jews of the Law, whose center is Jerusalem: "it also stands in the same line as the present Jerusalem" (Gal 4.25). Gal 4.25a was, as already seen, a gloss, which served as a parenthesis. The verb συστοιχέω, v 25, continues therefore ἥτις ἐστὶν Ἁγάρ at the end of v 24, and the run of thought is:"24 these are two covenants, one from Mount Sinai...which is Hagar. 25... it [the Sinai/Hagar-covenant] stands in the same line as the present Jerusalem." The verb συστοιχέω has its proper meaning "to stand in the same rank or line" and not only the general meaning "to correspond": The Judaizers who maintain that the Gentile Christians must comply with the Law of Moses and become Jews, make them join the Hagar-Sinai-covenant, the model of which is the pagan slave girl Hagar, who became Hebrew with regard to way of life and became Abraham's substitute wife. This Hagar-Sinai covenant stands in the same rank and line as Jerusalem, the center of the Jews of the Law.

As for Paul's thoughts on slave and free, a few comments should be made. As he interpreted these concepts, his use of slavery as a connecting link among Hagar, Sinai and the present Jerusalem, is not just of a formal nature. Since Hagar, although a pagan, was a Hebrew according to choice and way of life, she represents slavery under the Law. Thus, Paul in Gal 4.24-25 continues the same line of thought as also expressed in Gal 3.22-25.28; 4.1-10.

For Paul, Hagar was a slave, while Sarah was the free woman.

For Philo in *Abr.* 251 Hagar although bodily a slave, was, on the basis of being tested in a Hebrew home, free and noble relative to her disposition. Thus, Philo identifies freedom with being a Hebrew under the Law of Moses, while Paul makes Hagar remain a slave also as a type of the covenant from Sinai.

Both Paul and Philo see Hagar as a prototype of slavery. Thus, according to Philo, Hagar needs to realize that "of free and really high-born souls He who is free and sets free is the Creator, while slaves are makers of slaves" (*Fug.* 212). And according to Paul, the slave girl Hagar, the type of the Sinai covenant, gives birth to slaves, as well as Jerusalem, the center of the people of the Law, lives in slavery together with her children. The way of thinking about slavery is the same, although the applications are sharply different. To Philo, the Hebrew life, founded on the Law of Moses, is freedom, while to Paul it is slavery.

Two births

Hagar is compared with Sarah by Paul. In v. 23 he contrasts the birth of the son by Hagar and the birth of the son by Sarah, supplementing in v. 23 the Old Testament words cited in v 22 with the phrases κατὰ σάρκα γεγέννηται and διὰ τῆς ἐπαγγελίας. When Paul refers to the "promise", it is in accordance with his interest in this concept in Galatians, as seen from 3.14.17-29; 4.1-7. It also fits the story about Isaac in Genesis, as seen in Gen 17.15-19; 21.1-7.

When Paul in Gal 4.29 renders the two births as a contrast between flesh and spirit (ὁ κατὰ σάρκα γεννηθείς and τὸν κατὰ πνεῦμα) then it becomes more evident that he draws on expository traditions. In support of this understanding, one can refer to the corresponding contrast between body and soul made by Philo in the exposition of Gen 16.3 in QG 3.21. "For with the concubine the embrace was of bodies (Greek fragment, μίξις ἦν σωμάτων) for the sake of begetting children. But with the wife the union was one of the soul harmonized by heavenly (Greek fragment: divine) love (Greek fragment, ἕνωσις ψυχῆς ἁρμοζομένης ἔρωτι θείῳ).[24] A similar and more elaborate view is expressed in *Migr*. 141 where Sarah speaks (Gen 21.7): "For I bare a son," she continues, not as Egyptian women do in their bodily prime (κατὰ τὴν τοῦ σώματος ἀκμήν) but as the Hebrew souls do, "in my old age (ἀλλ᾽ ὡς αἱ Ἐβραῖαι ψυχαί, ἐν τῷ γήρᾳ μου), at a time, that is, when all things that are mortal and objects of sense-perception have decayed, while things immortal and intellectually discerned have grown young again, meet recipients of honour and esteem."

The similarities between Paul and Philo in this respect are probably due to expository traditions which each develops in his own way. There is evidence for a broad Jewish tradition about Isaacs' miraculous birth, as can be seen from the passages quoted in Str-B 3.216f.

Ishmael and Isaac

As shown above, Hagar is a figure on the borderline. Philo even can see her as a slave who is Egyptian by birth, but Hebrew on the basis of choice and way of life. Sarah gave Hagar as substitute wife to Abraham, and Ishmael was born.

From Paul's perspective in Galatians, how can Ishmael serve as argument against the Judaizers?

In the passage cited above from Philo's *Abr*. 250, Sarah said: "the offspring will be your legitimate children (γνήσια), but surely mine also by adoption (θέσις)." Philo here gives a positive interpretation of the status of children of mixed marriages, with reference to Ishmael. Ishmael was Abraham's legitimate child, and Sarah's by adoption. In *Mos*. 2.193 (see Lev 24.10-16) he mentions a

---

24. Cf. *QG* 3.60. "...moreover, it is said that 'in the other year' she will bear Isaac, for that birth is not one of the life of the time which now exists but of another great, holy, sacred and divine one..."

child of a mixed marriage where the father was an Egyptian and the mother a Jewess. In *Mos.* 1.147, there is an important elaboration of Exod 12.38. "A mixed multitude also went up with them..": "They were accompanied by a promiscuous, nondescript and menial crowd, a bastard (νόθος) host, so to speak, associated with the legitimately born (γνήσιος) multitude. These were the children of Egyptian women by Hebrew fathers into whose families they had been adopted (assigned, προσνεμηθέντες), also those who, reverencing the divine favour shewn to the people, had become proselytes, and such as were converted and brought to a wiser mind by the magnitude and the number of the successive punishments."

Philo lists here the children of mixed marriages being adopted into the Hebrew fathers' families, together with gentiles who became Jewish proselytes.

Being a figure on the borderline, Ishmael can, according to context, be seen as a person or a principle placed inside Judaism or outside. This dual possibility is expressed in the etymological meaning of the name Ishmael, according to Philo: "Ishmael" means by interpretation "hearing God", and the divine truths are heard by some to their profit, by some to the harm of themselves and others (*Mut.* 202). Among those who do not hear with an honest mind the holy instructions, whom Moses absolutely forbade to resort to the *ekklesia* of the Ruler of all, are those who extol their own mind and senses as the sole cause of what happens amongst men, and those who hold that gods are many.

The positive alternative Philo finds in Abraham's prayer according to Gen 17.18. "Let this Ishmael live before thee" (*Mut.* 201). He emphasizes the formulation "*this* Ishmael": When Abraham prays that *this* Ishmael may live, it means that what he hears from God may abide and inflame him spiritually (*Mut.* 209), and that his may be the sum happines of living *before God* , knowing that God's eye is always watching over him (*Mut.* 216). He will then in fear and trembling fly from wrongdoing. It should also be added that Philo refers to the biblical statement that Ishmael was circumcised at the age of thirteen, Gen 17.22-25 drawn on in *Sobr.* 8 and *QG* 3.61.

Thus, in Paul's argumentation in Gal 4.21-31, Ishmael, just as his mother Hagar, belong to the context of Jewish proselytes, and in the eyes of Paul, the Judaizers then follow the model of Hagar and Ishmael.[25]

Gal 4.21-31 and the situation reflected in Paul's Letter to the Galatians

At several points in the present study, the situation presupposed in Paul's

---

25. The birth of Isaac belongs to the realm of soul and heaven, according to Philo, and to the realm of promise and spirit, according to Paul. In Gal 4.25-26 Paul also explicitly mentions the heavenly realm, "the Jerusalem above" in contrast to the (earthly) "present Jerusalem". With regard to the Jewish traditions about the heavenly Jerusalem, references can be found in commentaries.

Letter to the Galatians has been drawn into the analysis. Some further remarks should be added, however.

As quoted at the beginning of this study, C.K. Barrett maintains that the Judaizers championed a certain exegesis of the Old testament story about Abraham, Sarah, Hagar, Isaac and Ishmael, and Paul rebuts their views. Paul's opponents, according to Barrett, followed the view expressed in Jewish writings such as *Jubilees* 16.17ff. and the Targum of Pseudo-Jonathan. Barrett concludes (note 7):

The Judaizing argument is clear. The true descendants of Abraham are the Jews, who inhabit Jerusalem. Here are the true people of God, now called the church. Those who are not prepared to attach themselves to this community by the approved means (circumcision) must be cast out; they cannot hope to inherit promises made to Abraham and his seed.

Barrett's suggestion is possible. In that case our study has shown that Paul rebuts the Judaizers by drawing on other Jewish expository traditions, traditions which see the slave girl Hagar and her son with Abraham within the context of Jewish thought about gentiles who become proselytes and live under the Law of Moses.

Another suggestion is made by Gijs Bouwman. He stresses the fact that Ishmael, as well as Isaac, was a son of Abraham. The argument of Paul's opponents were: "Auch die Nachkommenschaft Ismaels gehørt zu den Söhnen Abrahams und hat Anteil an dem Segen, der ihm zugesprochen wurde: 'Ja, ich segne ihn, lasse ihn Fruchtbar und überaus zahlreich werden ... und ich werde ihn zu einem grossen Volke machen' (Gen 17.20). Bedingung ist aber, dass diese Söhne Abrahams sich beschneiden lassen, den auch Ismael wurde beschnitten, sogar *vor* Isaak (Gen 17.23)."[26] Bouwman's view has some affinities with the interpretation given in the present study. It does not adequately take into consideration however the several points in the Letter to the Galatians that indicate that the basic issue was whether or not a gentile Christian convert should become a Jewish proselyte or not.[27] Against that background it seems insufficient to refer to blessings which could be claimed by Ishmaelites as Ishmaelites.

Finally, a suggestion should be made with regard to the importance of the ideas of 'the present Jerusalem' and 'the Jerusalem above'for the situation of the letter. The question of the role which Jerusalem played in the under-standing and teachings of the Judaizers might be brought more to the fore-

26. See P. Borgen, *'Paul Preaches Circumcision and Pleases Men' and Other Essays on Christian Origins* (Trondheim: Tapir, 1983) 15-42.
27. G. Bouwman, "Die Hagar und Sara-Perikope (Gal 4.21-31). Exemplarische Interpretation zum Schriftbeweis bei Paulus," *ANRW* II:25.4 (Berlin, 1987) 3147-48.

ground in the discussion. When the Judaizers claimed that the Christian gentile converts had to take circumcision and become Jewish proselytes, then these proselytes were to become members of the Jewish nation who had Jerusalem as its religious and political center. To be a proselyte under the Law of Moses meant also to be under the religious jurisdiction of Jerusalem. Both Paul and the Judaizers agreed on this central role of Jerusalem. Paul rebuts the view of the Judaizers by drawing a sharp distinction between the (Judaizers') present Jerusalem, "who" is in slavery with her children, and the Jerusalem above, "who" is free.

The general conclusion is: Gal 4.21-31 plays a central role in Paul's argument against the Judaizers who have unsettled the converts in Galatia.

Does Paul Argue Against Sacramentalism and Over-Confidence in 1 Cor 10.1-14?

Karl-Gustav Sandelin

Introduction

In the standard commentaries on Paul's first Epistle to the Corinthians it is often assumed that some of the Corinthians were over-confident in the effects of the sacraments.[1] The Corinthian "sacramentalists"[2] maintained that baptism and eucharist gave them protection against everything that threatened their future salvation. Therefore they did not see any danger in, for instance, sexual immorality (1 Cor 6.12,15; 10.8) or participation in pagan cultic activities (1 Cor 8.1,4; 10.14-22).

It was this Corinthian sacramentalism, so the theory goes, which motivated Paul to give such a lengthy description of what befell the fathers in the desert (1 Cor 10.1-10). These had been baptized into Moses (1 Cor 10.2) and had received spiritual food and drink (1 Cor 10.3-4). But God was not pleased with them (1 Cor 10.5) and they were punished for sins they had committed, like idolatry (1 Cor 10.7) and fornication (1 Cor 10.8). The over-confident sacramentalists in Corinth should understand that something similar could happen to themselves. The events in the desert were written down in order to set a warning example to those who are confronted with the end of times (1 Cor 10. 11). As a matter of fact the gift of the sacraments did not give such

---

1. H. Lietzmann and W.G. Kümmel, *An die Korinther I, II.* (HNT, Tübingen: Mohr [Siebeck], 1969) 45-47, J. Weiβ, *Der erste Korintherbrief* (KEK, Göttingen: Vandenhoeck & Ruprecht, 1925) 250, 254, C.K. Barrett, *A Commentary on the First Epistle to the Corinthians* (BNTC, London: Black, 1968) 25, 220, 227, H. Conzelmann, *Der erste Brief an die Korinther* (KEK, Göttingen: Vandenhoeck & Ruprecht, 1969) 28, 30, 194, 197, C. Wolff, *Der erste Brief des Paulus an die Korinther. Zweiter Teil: Auslegung der Kapitel 8-16* (THNT, Berlin: Evang. Verlagsanstalt) 39, F. Lang, *Die Briefe an die Korinther* (NTD Göttingen: Vandenhoeck & Ruprecht, 1986) 6, 26, 122-24, H.-J. Klauck, *1. Korintherbrief* (NEB, Würzburg: Echter, 1987), 71.
2. Such a term is used by G. Bornkamm, "Herrenmahl und Kirche bei Paulus," *ZTK* 53 (1956) 317. Bornkamm refers to H.v. Soden, Sakrament und Ethik bei Paulus, *Urchristentum und Geschichte, Gesammelte Aufsätze und Vorträge I* (Tübingen: Mohr [Siebeck], 1951) 245-46 (cf. 259), who interprets Paul with the words: "God does not allow that he be used like a talisman". E. Käsemann, Anliegen und Eigenart der paulinischen Abendmahlslehre, *ET* 7 (1947/48) 270, and Bandstra, "Interpretation in 1 Corinthians 10.1-11," *CTJ* 6 (1971) 6 understand the Corinthian position in the same way.

protection as the over-confident Corinthians believed. Therefore Paul warns the one who thinks that he stands firm lest he should fall (1 Cor 10.12).

Now it cannot of course be denied that 1 Cor 10.12 may be seen as a warning against over-confidence comparable to what we find in Rom 11.20.[3] But even then, if the thought of 1 Cor 10.12 in the mind of Paul may imply that he thinks that his addressees feel too secure, this does not necessarily mean that he thinks that this security derives from "sacramentalism", because Paul does not explicitly say that the Corinthians rely for their security on the sacraments.

It may be asked whether it is necessary or even appropriate to postulate sacramentalism in Corinth in order to understand Paul's message to the Corinthians. Actually the analogy between the fathers and the Corinthians ought to imply that the former were also over-confident sacramentalists[4] in Paul's view, if he is really attacking such sacramentalism. But the fathers, i.e. some of them, are described as real apostates. Paul does *not* say that the fathers thought that God would save them even if they became idolaters or fornicators. He does not say that the fathers rose up to play (around the golden calf, Exod 32.6) and tried to remain faithful to God at the same time (1 Cor 10.7). But precisely this seems to be the alleged idea of the Corinthians: sexual freedom and participation in pagan cults are possible and harmless to one who has received the sacraments and therefore believes that he has an unbroken relationship to the Lord. Since there is no direct reference to over-confidence in 1 Cor 10.1-11, however, verse 12, if understood as implying over-confidence, seems somewhat surprising. On the other hand Paul's argument that the fathers received sacraments and nevertheless perished would be effective without the description of the fathers as over-confident. He could just be saying to the over-confident sacramentalists: "Do not rely so much on the sacraments! Even the fathers received sacraments. Still they sinned and perished." But would Paul himself have looked for models among the fathers for over-confident Corinthians without some basis for such an attitude among the fathers?

To interpret Paul without the assumption that he is attacking over-confident sacramentalism would mean seeing his point in an alternative way. Paul could, for instance, warn some of the Corinthians against participating in pagan cultic activities just because he wants to say that such behaviour means

---

3. Cf. Weiß, *Der erste Korintherbrief*, 254.
4. A. Robertson and A. Plummer, *First Epistle of St Paul to the Corinthians* (ICC Edinburgh: Clark, 1911), 199, interpret 1 Cor 10.12 in the following way: "Therefore if, like our forefathers, you think that you are standing securely, beware lest self-confidence cause you, in like manner, to fall". Barrett, *The First Epistle*, 228, states: "The Israelites, as God's elect, equipped with sacraments, fancied themselves secure".

idolatry. The reference to the beneficial experiences of the fathers could only imply that the appropriate response to the gifts of God should be obedience, not fornication and idolatry.

This article tries to argue for an exegesis of 1 Cor 10.1-13 of this alternative type. Since Paul's argument is based on Scripture, we shall investigate the way in which he argues with the help of Scriptural material. We shall look at details as well as schemes or patterns in the texts he seems to be referring to. On points where Paul goes beyond Scripture we shall ask if his ideas may be understood with the help of post-Biblical Jewish literature.

The guiding question will be: is Paul attacking the over-confident sacramentalists, or is he just warning the Corinthians against participating in pagan cultic activities? Two points will be of special interest: 1) does Paul in 1 Cor 10.2-4 refer to Christian sacraments, and 2) are the fathers described as over-confident? I am going to argue for a modified no on the first question and for a negative answer to the second.

The Scriptural and Jewish Background

The Biblical and Jewish background to 1 Cor 10.1-10 has been the subject of intense debate among scholars. We may here just point to the standard commentaries to First Corinthians mentioned in the introduction.[5] Let us start by looking at the individual statements in the text, and continue with formal and structural traits. With few exceptions the details of the events in the desert are found in either Exodus or Numbers, or in both.

The Blissful Events Recorded in 1 Cor 10.1-4.

Generally it may be said that the "blissful events" referred to by Paul in 1 Cor 10.1-4 are found in Exodus and Numbers, following the sequence of the former: the cloud (Exod 13.21-22; 14.19, 24; Num 14.14), the sea (Exod 14. 21-22; Num 33.8), the manna (Exod 16. 4, 15; Num 11.6), the drink from the rock (Exod 17:6; Num 20.8).

There are some traits in the presentation of these events which are not described in the Scripture in the same way as we have it in the text of 1 Cor 10, but which may nevertheless be derived with ease from the Old Testament accounts. Thus it is said that the fathers were "under" the cloud (1 Cor 10.1), which may point to Num 14.14, where it is stated that the cloud of God "stays

---

5. In addition we may refer to the detailed treatments of 1 Cor 10.1-11 by A. Bandstra, "Interpretation in 1 Corinthians 10.1-11," *CTJ* 6, 5-21 and W.L. Willis, *Idol Meat in Corinth. The Pauline argument in 1 Corinthians 8 and 10.* (SBDS 68, Chico Cal: Scholars, 1985), 125-53.

over" the people (cf. Ps 105.39).[6] Further it is said that the water-giving rock accompanied the fathers (1 Cor 10.4). This idea may be derived from a combination of Num 20.7-11 talking of the water-giving rock at Kadesh and later in Num 21.16 mentioning a well at Beer. Such a derivation is made in a Jewish midrash: *Tosephta Sukka* 3.11 (cf. *Siphre* to Num 11.22b). The idea that the well followed the people in the desert is also attested in Pseudo-Philo (*Ant. Bibl.* 10.7; 11.15).[7]

The statement that the fathers were "baptized into Moses in the cloud and in the sea" is, however, difficult to derive directly from the Biblical story. W.G. Kümmel states that it is still not known whether, when writing these words, Paul was dependent on particular traditions.[8] Some scholars think that Paul is here projecting his own Christian ideas onto an Old Testament situation.[9] Even so, such a baptism into Moses would be a rather exceptional idea within a Pauline perspective. For Paul Christian baptism means being baptized to the death of Christ (Rom 6.3). This thought can hardly be applied to the figure of Moses.[10] There does, however, exist a Jewish text which might show that the idea presented in 1 Cor 10.2 is at least to some extent dependent on the Jewish tradition. In my book *Wisdom as Nourisher* I have made an attempt to show that a passage from Philo contains Jewish ideas which may also lie behind 1 Cor 10.2, i.e. *Her.* 203f.[11]

6. Ps 105 (104 LXX).39 is often referred to in attempts to explain Paul's expression "under the cloud". Some authors also refer to Wis 19.7. See Lietzmann, *An die Korinther*, 44, Barrett, *The first Epistle*, 220, Conzelmann, *Der erste Brief*, 195, Lang, *Die Briefe*, 124.

7. Cf. Conzelmann, *Der erste Brief*, 196.

8. Kümmel, *An die Korinther* (HNT, Anhang) 180-181. Kümmel also refers to Rabbinic traditions according to which the people were surrounded by clouds. See also Conzelmann, *Der erste Brief*, 195. But these passages do not explain the idea of baptism. Nor does in Kümmel's or Conzelmann's view Jewish baptism of proselytes explain Paul's reference to baptism in the cloud and in the sea.

9. E.g. H. Conzelmann, *Der erste Brief*, 195 ; J.D.G. Dunn, *Christology in the Making. An Inquiry into the Origins of the Doctrine of the Incarnation* (London: SCM, 1980) 183; H.-J. Klauck, *Herrenmahl und hellenistischer Kult. Eine religionsgeschichtliche Untersuchung zum ersten Korintherbrief* (Münster: Aschendorff, 1982) 253.

10. Lietzmann writes: "When one follows out the Apostle's typological exposition, it is easy to understand how salvation was bound up with Moses for the Israelites in much the same way as for Christians it is bound up with Christ". Cited according to the English version of Conzelmann's commentary *1 Corinthians. A commentary on the First Epistle to the Corinthians*. Translated by J.W. Leitch. (Hermeneia — A Critical and Historical Commentary on the Bible. Philadelphia: Fortress, 1988), 166 n. 18. Cf. Lietzmann, *An die Korinther*, 45. Conzelmann utters the following comment against Lietzmann: "his expression 'for the Israelites' is not covered by the text".

11. K.-G. Sandelin, *Wisdom as Nourisher. A Study of an Old Testament Theme, its Development within Early Judaism and its Impact on Early Christianity* (Åbo: Åbo Akademi, 1986 [1987]) 166.

In *Her.* 201-6 Philo first cites the story of Aaron, i.e. for Philo the Logos, standing between the living and the dead (Num 16.47-48). He then comments upon the account of the cloud which divided the host of Egypt from Israel (Exod 14.20). He is lost in admiration, he says, when he listens to the oracles and learns

how the cloud entered in the midst between the hosts of Egypt and Israel. For the further pursuit of the sober and God-beloved race by the passion-loving and godless was forbidden by that cloud, which was a weapon of shelter and salvation to its friends, and of offence and chastisement to its enemies (ἐχθροί). For on minds of rich soil that cloud sends in gentle showers the drops of wisdom (ἠρέμα σοφίαν ἐπιψεκάζει), whose very nature exempts it from all harm, but on the sour of soil, that are barren of knowledge, it pours the blizzards of vengeance, flooding them with a deluge of destruction (κατακλυσμὸν φθορὰν οἰκτίστην ἐπιφέρουσα) most miserable. (*Her.* 203-4).[12]

The text exceeds the Exodus story in some respects of interest to us here. It is the cloud, not the water of the sea, that drowns the enemies. In the Wisdom of Solomon (Wis 10.19) it is said that Wisdom drowned (κατακλύζειν) the enemies (ἐχθροί). In the same context Wisdom is identified with the cloud from Exodus (Wis 10.17). Thus the cloud has the same function in Philo in *Her.* 204 as Wisdom in the pre-Philonic wisdom tradition of Alexandria.[13] From Philo we can also see that the tradition has been developed, so that the cloud sends snow and rain, which is not directly stated in the Wisdom of Solomon: blizzards on the enemies and gentle drops of wisdom on Israel. Perhaps the expression βαπτίζεσθαι is not the best one to describe such a process, but it would not be impossible, since the verb can mean to be "soaked" or "drenched" (Plutarch *Mor.* 9 C., Eubulus 68). Thus the idea in Paul that the fathers were *baptized in the cloud* may well reflect a Jewish tradition such as we find attested in Philo.

But is it also possible to explain the idea that the fathers were baptized into Moses by referring to *Her.* 203-204? The expression of Paul seems to be derived from the Pauline formula "baptized into Christ" (Rom 6.3; Gal 3.27). Paul no doubt uses the expression "baptized into Moses" in order to state that there existed a prefiguration (τύπος verse 6) of baptism into Christ among the fathers. But is it possible that some idea in Jewish tradition made such an

---

12. F.H. Colson and G.H. Whitaker, *Philo with an English Translation* (LCL, Cambridge, Mass.: Harvard University Press, 1929ff.) 4, 385.
13. Philo may be thinking of the *Logos* when he describes the cloud. See Colson-Whitaker, *Philo* 4, 277; Sandelin, *Wisdom*, 107.

expression more natural than the strained analogy to the baptism into Christ, which implies a baptism into the death of the Lord?[14]

According to *Her.* 204 the cloud sends "heavenly drops of wisdom". Now the heavenly nourishment given by the heavenly figure of Wisdom is, according to Philo, identical with instruction (*Opif.* 158; *Post.* 138; *Fug.* 166f.; *Somn.* 1.50; *Contempl.* 35), which in reality means the teaching of the Law (*Mut.* 258-60, cf. *Fug.* 166-67 and *Spec.* 2.61-64).[15] Thus the teaching mediated later through Moses on Mount Sinai was already actual in the drops of wisdom during the wandering through the Red Sea. For Paul, at least in 2 Cor 3.15, Moses signifies the Law. The Pauline idea that the fathers were baptized into Moses in the cloud may therefore reflect a Hellenistic Jewish idea that the cloud of Wisdom which drowned the enemies in the Red Sea also gave showers of heavenly teaching of the Law to the Israelites.

Can we also explain the words that the fathers were baptized "in the sea" by referring to the tradition found in Hellenistic Jewish texts? In fact the fathers walked on *dry ground* through the Red Sea (Exod 14.16, 21-22, 29), the water being driven away (v. 21) and forming walls on both sides of the people (vv. 22, 29). It was the Egyptian pursuers that were drowned when the waters came rushing back (v. 28). This seems to be the unanimous view of Jewish tradition (see, for example, the Hellenistic Jewish passages: Wis 10.18-19; 19.7; Philo: *Mos.* 1.177-79; 2.253-55; *Conf.* 70). The idea that the people went on *dry ground* also seems to be implied in a later Rabbinic Jewish passage which speaks of the Red Sea forming a kind of tunnel around the people (*Mek. Exod.* 14.16).[16] Thus the Pauline words that the fathers were *baptized "in the sea"* do not seem to receive an explanation as a manifestation of ideas in Jewish texts. But if not pressed, they may be understandable as just a reflection of the Exodus story referred to as the general context and mentioned here in the preceding verse 1 Cor 10.1. Or to paraphrase Paul: The Red Sea, which the fathers went through on dry ground, was the location where they were baptized into Moses in the cloud.

In addition to the statements in 1 Cor 10.2 concerning baptism, the words in the two verses that follow partly exceed the Old Testament account. The food, the drink and the rock are called "spiritual", an attribute which is not found in the Old Testament passages referred to. The word does not occur in

---

14. Cf. Barrett, *The first Epistle*, 221, who does not find the expression very unnatural: "Granted the analogy with which Paul was working it was natural for him to coin the phrase 'into Moses', not only because it had been Moses who (under God) had delivered his people at the time of the Exodus, but also because of the Jewish belief that the 'latter Redeemer' (the Messiah) would be as the 'former Redeemer' (Moses)."

15. See further Sandelin, *Wisdom*, 129-130.

16. See Conzelmann, *Der erste Brief*, 195.

the LXX, but is occasionally used by Philo, although not directly in passages talking of the manna and the water from the rock.

When Paul talks of spiritual food and spiritual drink, this is often understood as Christian sacramental terminology already established in Paul's time.[17] For this hypothesis the occurrence of the term spiritual in the eucharistic prayers of the Didache (*Did.* 10.3) is used as an argument.[18] But the Didache is probably much later than Paul and in addition its eucharistic prayers may originally have been used in a setting quite different from the Lord's supper.[19] It is of course quite reasonable to think that Paul, in describing the feeding of the people in the desert, uses sacramental terminology because he did so when he said that the people were "baptized into Moses". But what terminology can be expected if we take such terminology from Paul himself? In 1 Cor 11.20 Paul uses the expression κυριακὸν δεῖπνον (the Lord's supper) and in 1 Cor 10.16 he employs the word κοινωνία (sharing or communion). Thus Paul does not in 1 Cor 10.1-4 use such terminology as he uses when he mentions the eucharist elsewhere. Nevertheless he speaks of the Lord's supper in the same chapter where he deals with the feeding in the desert. Without denying Paul's intention to point to an analogy between the spiritual gifts in the desert (1 Cor 10.3-4) and the Lord's supper (1 Cor 10.16-17, 21), I think one should be cautious in pushing the analogy too far.[20] If we compare the passages 1 Cor 10.1-10 and 1 Cor 10.14-22, where Paul provides a glimpse of his understanding of the meaning of the bread and the cup, we may see that the analogies between the nourishment in the desert and the Lord's supper are not so clear. Terminologically there is very little that knits the passages together. The βρῶμα (food) and πόμα (drink) in 1 Cor 10.3-4 are not, like the ἄρτος (bread) and the ποτήριον (cup) in 1 Cor 10.16-17, said to be a κοινωνία (sharing or communion)[21] in something else. Moreover, the

---

17. For instance A. Wedderburn, *Baptism and Resurrection* (WUNT 44, Tübingen: Mohr 1987) 244, who suggests that Paul may pick up the usage of the term from the Corinthians.

18. Conzelmann, *Der erste Brief*, 196, Klauck, *Herrenmahl*, 255, cf. Lang, *Die Briefe*, 124.

19. See my book *Wisdom as Nourisher*, 168, 190-221. Cf. Broer, "Darum: Wer da meint zu stehen, der sehe zu, daß er nicht falle." 1 Kor 10, 12f im Kontext von 1 Kor 10, 1-13. *Neues Testament und Ethik. Für R. Schnackenburg.* Hrsg. H. Merklein (Freiburg: Herder, 1989), 311.

20. See my discussion in *Wisdom*, 162-63, 167-68.

21. In an article written in Swedish (K.-G. Sandelin, "Gemenskap med Kristi kropp. Realpresens hos Paulus?," *Teologinen Aikakauskirja — Teologisk Tidskrift* 95, 1990, 385-86) I have argued for an understanding of the word κοινωνία which comes close to that of W.G. Kümmel, *An die Korinther, Anhang*, 181-82. Paul does not speak of eating and drinking the body and the blood of the Lord, but of becoming a member of the church through partaking of the bread and receiving the benefits of the death of the Lord through drinking from the cup. Cognate interpretations are found in N.

expression τὸ αὐτό (the same) is in 1 Cor 10.3, 4 not used in connection with βρῶμα and πόμα in order to show that the fathers became one body like the Christians according to 1 Cor 10.17 because they partook of the same food and drink. Finally, πάντες (all) in 1 Cor 10.1-4 forms a contrast to οὐκ ἐν τοῖς πλείοσιν (not all of them) in 1 Cor 10.5 and to τινές (some) in 1 Cor 10.7-10. The word πάντες is not, as in 1 Cor 10.17, used to express the thought that they all became one, but that although all partook of the same food, some became idolaters and therefore perished.

As an alternative to the theory that the expressions *spiritual food* and *spiritual drink* derive from Christian eucharistic language one should, I think, consider that Paul uses the word *spiritual* to designate his own message (e.g. 1 Cor 9.11),[22] which should be accepted as the word of God (1 Thess 2.13). In Hellenistic Judaism the manna in the desert is often understood as the word of God. This interpretation is found already in the LXX translation of Deut 8.3, and Philo in *Leg. all.* 3.174-76 comments upon this Scriptural passage explaining the manna, i.e. the word of God, as nourishment for the soul.

Now Paul goes on speaking of Christ, the spiritual rock, from which the fathers received spiritual drink. This Pauline idea also has a parallel in Philo's thought, where the rocks mentioned in Deut 8.15 and 32.13 are understood as the heavenly figure of Wisdom (*Leg. all.* 2.86; *Det.* 115-18), giving her nourishment. Wisdom is a spiritual reality (*Gig.* 23-28, 47), her nourishment is meant for the soul (*Leg. all.* 2.86). In *Det.* 115-18 Wisdom, the water-giving rock, is in fact identified with the manna (*Det.* 118). It is commonly accepted that Paul, in describing Christ as the nourishing rock in the desert, is dependent on Hellenistic Jewish wisdom-tradition.[23] He may also allude to Deut 32, where God is seen as a rock (verses 4, 15, 18, 30, 31, 37). This is, however, uncertain since the LXX does not use the word πέτρα (rock).[24]

Instead of saying that it was Wisdom that, as the spiritual rock in the

---

Walter, "Christusglaube und heidnische Religiosität in paulinischen Gemeinden," *NTS* 25 (1979) 432, and Willis, *Idol Meat*, 204-9.

22. See further Sandelin, *Wisdom*, 169. This possibility is rejected by Weiß, *Der erste Korintherbrief*, 251, and only slightly touched on by Wedderburn, *Baptism*, 246 n. 29. Wedderburn on pp. 246-48 operates with ideas which may have existed among the Corinthians, about whom we know very little, however. Wedderburn nevertheless tries to see links with their thoughts and the previous teaching of Paul. Thus Christ may have been understood as the life-giving spirit (1 Cor 15.45) who bestows the spirit as the Christians "partake of the eucharistic bread wine" (246). Or it was thought that the spirit was mediated by the rite of the Lord's supper as it was mediated by the rite of baptism (247). The latter idea seems to have been the thought of Paul in 1 Cor 12.13 (see Wedderburn, *Baptism*, 62-63, cf. 246).

23. Lietzmann, *An die Korinther*, 45, Barrett, *The First Epistle*, 222-23, Conzelmann, *Der erste Brief*, 196-97.

24. Cf. Bandstra, *Interpretation*, 13, W.A. Meeks, "'And rose up to play': Midrash and Paraenesis in 1 Corinthians 10.1-22," *JSNT* 16 (1982) 72.

desert, nourished the Israelites with the word, Paul seems to use this idea, but to maintain that it was Christ who gave this nourishment. Conzelmann, who accepts the idea that Paul and Philo use the same tradition, at the same time maintains that Paul in contradistinction to Philo differentiates between the elements of food and drink because of his Christology.[25] This conclusion seems to be a result of reading eucharistic ideas into 1 Cor 10.3-4, which is not necessary. Instead it can be maintained that Paul does not differentiate in 1 Cor 10.3-4 more than Philo does since he uses the attribute "spiritual" for both the food, the drink and the rock[26] in contradistinction to 1 Cor 10.16-17, where the bread is seen as that which creates communion with the body of Christ, the church, whereas the cup gives a sharing in the blood of Christ, i.e. his death.

We have noticed that scholars very often assume that Paul wrote 1 Cor 10.1-4 in order to attack the Corinthian sacramentalists by implying that the fathers already had something like sacraments which did not, however, protect them from sin and punishment. Therefore Paul so to say fights against the Corinthians with their own weapons by applying Christian sacramental terminology to the events in the desert. That Paul uses Christian sacramental terminology when he says that the fathers were "baptized into Moses" seems to be above doubt. From that premise it looks natural to postulate that he also uses Christian sacramental terminology when he states that the food and drink in the desert were "spiritual", although there is no direct reference to such use of the words until we come to the time of the Didache (Did. 10.3). By this Paul would say that the fathers had spiritual food and drink in the desert just as the Christians receive such food in the eucharist. But by that he would in reality also say that the fathers already received the eucharist in the desert, not just a prefiguration of it, as he seems to suggest in 1 Cor 10.6.

Paul does not, however, seem to want to give the impression that the fathers received exactly the same things in the desert as Christians receive through the sacraments. Paul makes distinctions. If baptism into Moses is not the same thing as baptism into Christ, then the food and drink in the desert should not be the same thing as the food of the eucharist. Paul is therefore quite consistent when he does not use Christian eucharistic terminology (share, communion, the Lord's supper) but terminology taken from some other source.[27] But if Paul does not want to give the impression that the fathers in

---

25. This is how I interpret Conzelmann, Der erste Brief, 197 n. 28., who is rather brief at this point.

26. Bandstra, Interpretation, 12-13, thinks that Paul and Philo use the same tradition since both authors saw the spiritual rock as the source for the spiritual food as well as for the spiritual drink.

27. Cf. Broer, "Darum: Wer da meint...", 310, states that Paul has no interest in total identification of the Christian sacraments and the gifts in the desert. Therefore he speaks of a baptism into Moses. But Broer does not want to extend the argument to the spiritual drink, which came from Christ!

the desert received something very similar to the Christians through their sacraments, then this seems to mean that he cannot here be arguing against people who base their confidence upon the sacraments. Nor could his words have had a strong argumentative value against the sacramentalists, since such people could have concluded that the gifts in the desert were not real sacraments after all and therefore had no salvific effect.

Apostasy and punishment in 1 Cor 10.5-10.

Having discussed the obvious Biblical and the possible Jewish background to Paul's description of the events in the desert in 1 Cor 10.1-4, let us now turn to verses 5-10, where Paul admonishes the Corinthians not to behave like the apostate fathers, who were punished for their sins. In this passage we do not have to consult any passages other than Biblical ones in order to understand what Paul is saying in individual cases. Even now the references are to Exodus and Numbers, although the latter seems to be referred to more often than the former.

In 1 Cor 10.5 Paul to begin with states that God was not pleased with most of the fathers (οὐκ ἐν τοῖς πλείοσιν εὐδόκησεν ὁ θεός). We find similar expressions in the LXX. In Jer 14.10 we read: " The Lord speaks thus of his people: They love to stray from my ways, they wander where they will. Therefore God has no more pleasure in them (καὶ ὁ θεὸς οὐκ εὐδόκησεν ἐν αὐτοῖς)". (Cf. Ps 151.5 and Sir 34.19). The displeasure of God with the fathers according to Paul then became manifest: "for they were scattered over the desert" (κατεστρώθησαν γὰρ ἐν τῇ ἐρήμῳ). The word κατεστρώθησαν is a hapaxlegomenon in the New Testament. Paul here uses an expression for which we find the model in Num 14.16 LXX as part of a prayer of Moses, where the latter creates a fictitious utterance of the pagans describing such a fate of the Israelites. According to Num 14.28-30 the dead bodies of most of the Israelites actually remained in the desert. Only Kaleb and Joshua were promised entry into the promised land (cf. Num 32.11-12).[28]

In 1 Cor 10.6 Paul says that the events in the desert happened as examples (τύποι) to warn us us not to become "men craving for evil things" (ἐπιθυμηταὶ κακῶν) like the fathers. The word ἐπιθυμητής occurs in the LXX only twice: in Prov 1.22 and Num 11.34. 1 Cor 10.6 probably refers to the latter instance.[29] The people had desired meat (Num 11.4) and God sent them quails (cf. Exod 16.2). After that he almost immediately struck the people with plague (Num 11.31-33).

In 1 Cor 10.7 the admonition not to become idolaters is substantiated by a

---

28. Cf. Barrett, *The first Epistle*, 222, Conzelmann, *Der erste Brief*, 197, Lang, *Die Breife*, 124.
29. Cf. Barrett, *The first Epistle*, 224, Lang, *Die Briefe*, 125.

direct citation of a Scriptural expression from Exod 32.6. After the warning not to commit fornication (1 Cor 10.8) the act referred to is most probably the Phinehas episode found in Num 25.1-9, although the verb used here in v. 1 is ἐκπορνεύω instead of just πορνεύω as in the Pauline text, and the number of people who fell (23000) is probably by mistake[30] derived from Num 26.62 (cf. Exod 32.28) instead of from Num 25.9, where it is said that those who died were 24000.

The warning against putting Christ to the test which follows (1 Cor 10.9) is motivated by the episode in Num 21.4-9 where God sent snakes to punish the people but later ordered Moses to erect a bronze serpent which cured them.[31] The text does not, however, use the expression of "testing" the Lord. But the sin the people committed according to Num 21.5 was to complain at their fate of being in the desert without food and water, and a similar sin is seen as a testing of the Lord in Exod 17.1-7. The last warning (1 Cor 10.10) is against grumbling. The verb "grumble" (γογγύζω) is used in, for instance, Exod 17.3 and Num 16.11; 17.6. But the idea of the "destroyer" is found in Exodus only in Exod 12.23 and nowhere in Numbers. It could be that 1 Cor 10.10 refers to Num 14.36-37 (punishment of the explorers) and Num 16.11-35 (punishment of Korah, Dathan and Abiram, cf. 41-49), where διαγογγύζω is employed.[32]

The impact of Ps 78 and 106 on 1 Cor 10.1-10.

In the standard commentaries one finds occasional references to other texts from the Old Testament than those from Exodus and Numbers. Of these texts Ps 78 (LXX 77) and 106 (LXX 105) are most frequently referred to.[33] These psalms have so many individual features in common with 1 Cor 10.1-10 that one may suspect that these particular texts are consciously referred to by the author of the Pauline passage.[34] Both psalms use the phrase "our fathers" (Ps 78.3, 5; 106. 6-7). The cloud is mentioned in Ps 78.14, the sea in Ps 78.13; 106.7, 9, 22. In contradistinction to the latter psalm Ps 78 mentions both the manna (verse 24) and the rock which gave water (verses 15-16, 20). The manna is called ἄρτος (bread cf. Exod 16.4, 15) and not βρῶμα (food) as in 1 Cor 10.3. Nevertheless Ps 77.18 LXX uses the plural form of βρῶμα, a word which is

---

30. Lietzmann, *An die Korinther*, 47.
31. Cf. Barrett, *The first Epistle*, 225, Conzelmann, *Der erste Brief*, 198, Lang, *Die Briefe*, 125.
32. Lietzmann, *An die Korinther*, 47.
33. See Robertson & Plummer, *First Epistle*, 200, for 1 Cor 10.3, 205, for 1 Cor 10.9, Lietzmann, *An die Korinther*, 47, for 1 Cor 10.9, Barrett, *The first Epistle*, 220, for 1 Cor 10.1, Conzelmann, *Der erste Brief*, 195, for 1 Cor 10.1, 196, for 1 Cor 10.3, 197, for 1 Cor 10.5 and 198, for 1 Cor 10.9, Wolff, *Der erste Brief*, 40, for 1 Cor 10.1, Lang, *Die Briefe*, 124, for 1 Cor 10.5 and 125 for 1 Cor 10.8-9.
34. Cf. Sandelin, *Wisdom*, 171.

common in the LXX but does not occur elsewhere in the descriptions of the events in the desert. The episode in Num 11.4, 31-34, where the people crave meat and receive quails, and probably referred to in 1 Cor 10.6, is taken up in Ps 78.26-31 (cf. 106.14).

When we come to the sins of the fathers and the warnings not to follow their example (1 Cor 10.6-10) it is notable that Ps 78.8 of the descendants to the Isaraelites in the desert says that they should put their trust in God "in order not to become like their fathers" (ἵνα μὴ γένωνται ὡς οἱ πατέρες αὐτῶν). Idolatry is mentioned in Ps 78.58; 106.36-38. The Phinehas episode is mentioned in Ps 106.28-31. In Ps 105.39 LXX the same verb πορνεύω (to commit fornication) as we find in 1 Cor 10.8 is employed instead of ἐκπορνεύω as in Num 25.1. The context is similar in the Old Testament passages. Both deal with idolatry. We also find the idea of testing the Lord in our psalms (Ps 78.41, 56; 106.14). But in addition Ps 78.18, like 1 Cor 10.9, uses the rare word ἐκπειράζω (to test). This word is also found in Deut 6.16 LXX, where it refers to the episode when the people tested the Lord at Massa (Exod 17:1-5). Finally the "grumbling" is taken up in Ps.106.25. The word γογγύζω is used here as in 1 Cor 10.10. The rebellion and punishment of Dathan and Abiram is mentioned in Ps 106.16-18.

Structure and form of 1 Cor 10.1-13.

It is often maintained that in 1 Cor 10.1-13 Paul presents a midrash,[35] or even quotes a pre-existing one.[36] W. A. Meeks tries to show that the midrash in this case consists of an interpretation of the verse from Exod 32.6 which Paul cites in 1 Cor 10.7 according to the LXX version: "and the people sat down to eat and drink and rose up to play".[37] According to Meeks the eating and drinking refer to the spiritual food and drink in the desert, whereas the phrase "and rose up to *play*" receives five different explications: craving for evil things, idolatry, fornication, testing Christ and grumbling. Meeks finds in *Tosephta Sota* 6.6 both a model for this procedure of interpretation and two of the evil deeds just mentioned: idolatry and fornication. The remaining three explanations he finds in the LXX and in Philo. The Tosephta passage[38] tells us that R. Simeon b. Yochai presented four different interpretations of Gen 21.9, which tells us that Ishmael *played* with Isaac. R. Aqiba explained the word *played* as idolatry

---

35. Lietzmann, *An die Korinther*, 44, Weiß, *Der erste Korintherbrief*, 250.
36. Barrett, *The Firste Epistle*, 220. Critical towards such a view: Willis, *Idol meat*, 127, Broer, "*Darum: wer da meint...*", 307-310.
37. W.A. Meeks, *And rose up to play*, 68-71.
38. See J. Neusner, *The Tosefta Translated from the Hebrew. Third Division: Nashim (The Order of Women)* (New York: KTAV, 1979) 172-173.

with reference to Exod 32.6, whereas another rabbi explained it as fornication with reference to a verse in Genesis, and so on. R. Simeon b. Yochai concludes the sequence by presenting his own understanding, which is based on two Scriptural verses from Genesis and says that he prefers it to R. Aqiba's interpretation. It is not difficult to see that the procedure differs considerably from that of Paul. First we find the verse interpreted in *Sota* 6.6 at the very beginning, whereas the Exodus verse cited by Paul is in the middle of the text. Secondly it is clearly indicated that the text itself is a presentation of different interpretations attributed to different sages of a verse from Scripture. This trait has no counterpart whatsoever in the Pauline text. If we take the Tosephta passage as a model for what a midrash is, then it is difficult to see 1 Cor 10.1-13 as representative of that literary genre.[39]

What we have in 1 Cor 10.1-10 is a description of events which occurred in the desert, first blissful events, then examples of apostasy. The latter are used as warnings to the present readers not to act like the fathers. In order to find models for the formal structure of 1 Cor 10.1-13, we do not need to go to texts as late as the Tosefta, which was no doubt compiled long after Paul, and still less later Rabbinic texts. Even W. A. Meeks emphasizes that "there is no dearth" of earlier Jewish models for the kind of composition which we find in Paul.[40] In the first place we must consult the Old Testament.

W. A. Meeks and H.-J. Klauck[41] mention Deut 32.7-27,[42] Neh 9.6-37 (LXX: 2 Esdr 19.6-37) and Ps 78 as Old Testament texts which are comparable to our passage in Paul.[43] In all these texts one finds one feature which is characteristic of 1 Cor 10.1-10: the apostasy of the fathers is described against the background of the benevolent acts of God.

In the prophetic-like text of Deuteronomy 32, verses 7-14 first describe God's goodness towards Israel with hints at the wandering through the desert, then verses 15-18 describe the apostasy of "Jesurun", which basically consisted in abandoning God, its rock, in favour of strange gods, and thirdly verses 19-27 enumerate the acts of punishment which God will send upon his people. In the

---

39. Lang, *Die Briefe*, 123, does not believe that in 1 Cor 10.1-13 Paul is using an already existing Jewish-Christian midrash. Paul was able, however, according to Lang, to refer to singular ideas of interpretation having their source within hellenistic Judaism.

40. Meeks, *And rose up to play*, 66. W. Schrage, "Korintherbriefe," *TRE* 19 (Berlin, New York: de Gruyter, 1990) 629, applies terms taken from classical rhetoric to 1 Cor 10.1-22. *exemplum* (verses 1-5), *applicatio* in the form of a circular composition (verses 6-11), *peroratio* (verse 12), *exhortatio* (verses 14-22).

41. H.-J. Klauck, *1. Korintherbrief*, 70.

42. Cf. E. Schüssler Fiorenza, *1 Corinthians* (Harper's Bible Commentary, ed. J. L. Mays etc., San Francisco: Harper & Row, 1988) 1181.

43. Meeks, *And rose up to play*, 66, adds Hos 13.4-8 and Amos 2.9-16; 3.2.

prayer which is presented in Neh 9.6-37 we find a description of the blissful Exodus events in verses 9-15: the sea (v. 11), the cloud (v. 12), the laws (v. 13), the sabbath (v. 14), the bread from heaven and the water from the rock (v. 15). Then follows a description of the apostasy of "our fathers" (cf. verses 9 and 32) including the episode with the golden calf in verses 16-18. But in contradistinction to Deut 32 the text of Neh stresses the mercy of God in the desert and in the promised land (verses 19-25). The same themes are repeated in verses 26-31 telling about the apostasy but also the mercy of God during the history in the land, and the passage is concluded by a confession in verses 32-37.

Psalm 78 describes in subsequent sequences the acts of the Lord, the sins of the people and the punishment of God. The gracious acts of God are presented in verses 3-8 (in more general terms), 12-16 (Exodus events), 23-29 (Exodus events), 38-39 (God's mercifulness), 42b-55 (punishment of the Egyptians), 65-66 (God wakes up and punishes his enemies), 68-72 (the election of Judah and David), the sins are described in verses 9-11 (apostasy from God's covenant), 17-20 (testing the Lord in the desert), 32 (sin and disbelief), 40-42a (rebellion in the desert), 56-58 (rebellion and idolatry), the punishment in verses 21-22 (fire in Jacob), 30-31 (death), 33 (calamity), 59-64 (destruction and exile), 67 (the clan of Joseph despised). Verses 34-37 speak of the people's repentance, which nevertheless ends in hypocrisy. Psalm 106 also has descriptions of the benevolent acts of God at the Red Sea (verses 8-11) and on other occasions (verses 43-44), but most of the psalm describes apostasy, e.g. idolatry (verses 19-21, 28, 36, 38), and punishment (e.g. verses 15, 17-18, 26-27, 41-42). But God's forgiving grace towards the sinful people is also mentioned several times (verses 8, 23, 44-47).

The list of Old Testament texts showing the same pattern of God's acts, the apostasy of the people and the punisment of the Lord can be augmented by texts from the Pentateuch (Exod 32; Num 14.22-23), or by texts like the prophetic units of Hos 13.4-9, Am 2.6-16, the prayers and confessions of Jer 14.7-10 and Dan 9.15 and the admonition in Ps 95 (94 LXX).8-11. We may pay some special attention to the latter verses, since the text of 1 Cor 10.1-10 has the character of an admonition. The passage starts with the injunction: "Do not grow stubborn, ...as at the time of Massah in the wilderness (ἐν τῇ ἐρήμῳ)". Then comes a description of sin, which is contrasted to an act of God: "when your forefathers tested (ἐπείρασαν) me, tried me though they had seen what I did". Finally the punishment is announced with the following words: "They shall never enter my rest".

This pattern also survives in the apocryphal books. We find it in the prayer of Baruch (Bar 1.15-3.8), especially in 2.11-15, a confession of sins against God, who led the people out of Egypt, but who now shows his wrath. Since Philo refers to Exod 32 several times, it is not surprising that the pattern has left its mark in his writings. In *Mos.* 2.271, Philo says about the worship of the golden calf:

At this, Moses was cut to the heart to think that in the first place the whole people had suddenly been blinded who shortly before (πρὸ μικροῦ)[44] had excelled every nation in clearness of vision (ὁ λαὸς...ὁ... πάντων ἐθνῶν ὀξυωπέστατος), and secondly, that a fable falsely invented (πλάσμα μύθου) could quench the bright radiance of truth (αὐγὴν...τῆς ἀληθείας) — truth on which no eclipse of the sun or of all the starry choir can cast a shadow, since it is illumined by its own light, the intelligible, the incorporeal, compared with which the light of the senses would seem to be as night compared with day.

According to this text the "fable" of the golden calf quenched something which the people had possessed, i.e. "the bright radiance of truth". This thought is paralleled in *Mos.* 2.167, where Philo says that Moses marvelled that the people had exchanged a great truth for a great delusion (ὅσον ψεῦδος ἀνθ᾽ ὅσης ἀληθείας ὑπηλλάξαντο). What exactly is Philo referring to by this idea of "truth"? Probably it is closely connected with the idea of the "true God" that the people had forgotten, an idea expressed immediately before the passage cited above (*Mos.* 2.270; cf. *Mos.* 2.161). Since Philo is dealing with the events at Sinai, he may also have the giving of the Law in mind (cf. *Dec.* 65). In any case Philo contrasts the apostasy of the people against a blissful past when they possessed the truth. He then goes on to describe the punishment of the people through the tribe of Levi (*Mos.* 2.168-173,272-274).

In the non-Pauline texts of the New Testament we find the pattern in Heb 3.8-11, where the admonition of Ps 75 (74 LXX).8-11 is cited, and in Jude 5.

We have thus been able to show that in his argument in 1 Cor 10.1-10 Paul employs a pattern which is well documented in many different kinds of texts, for instance stories and prophecies, but also in admonitions like Ps 95.8-11. But does Paul use this pattern in order to attack over-confident people in Corinth? He could of course do this, if the fathers themselves were described as over-confident in the texts that 1 Cor 10.1-10 refers to. Let us investigate this question.

Over-confidence among the fathers?

Do the texts from the Old Testament and Judaism referred to above contain the thought that the people of Israel sinned *because* they had the idea that nothing could harm them since God had saved them? Do we have hints of religious security of a similar kind as has been postulated in Corinth by those scholars who think that some of the Corinthians felt free to be sexually immoral or participate in pagan cults because the sacraments gave them protection against everything that threatened their relationship to God and their salvation?

---

44. Colson, *Philo* 6, 585, translates "a few hours ago". The French translation has "juste l'instant d'avant". See R. Arnaldez et al., *De vita Mosis 1-2, Introduction, traduction et notes*, Les Œuvres de Philon d'Alexandrie 22 (Paris: Cerf, 1967).

There are instances in these texts which show that the Israelites became too content with the gifts of God and became in a way secure. "Jacob ate and was well fed, Jeshurun grew fat and unruly" (Deut 32.15a). Similar expressions are found in Neh 9.25, Ps 78.29 and Hos 13.6. But this kind of security does not at all mean a security of the kind postulated in Corinth. On the contrary: when the Israelites grew fat, they forgot God! The verse just cited from Deuteronomy continues: "He forsook God who made him and dishonoured the rock of his salvation". And in Hos 13.6 we read: "So they were filled, and, being filled, grew proud; and so they forgot me" (cf. Neh 9.25-26).

I cannot find any instance in these texts bearing witness to the idea that the Israelites sinned because God had acted in their midst. According to Neh 9.17 the Israelites refused to obey and did not remember the miracles of God. A similar thought is found in Ps 78.11 and 106.7, 13. There is nothing that looks like over-confidence in God's acts here. On the contrary it is said in Ps 78.21-22 that God was filled with anger because the people did not believe and trust in him. When Ps 106 describes the episode of the golden calf, we do not find that the people wanted to honour God and the calf at the same time. Instead we read: "...They exchanged their Glory for the image of a bull that feeds on grass. They forgot God their deliverer, who had done great deeds in Egypt..." Having stated that the Israelites "sacrificed to foreign demons that are no gods", the song of Moses in Deuteronomy states: "You forsook your rock, who begot you" (Deut 32.17-18).[45] Similarly the book of Baruch confesses that the people have served other gods and sinned against the Lord (Bar 1.22; 2.5). Philo states that the Israelites who worshipped the golden calf "forgetting the reverence they owed to the Self-Existent, became zealous devotees of Egyptian fables" (*Mos.* 2.161). They forgot the true God and ruined "the high-born qualities inherited from their forefathers and fostered by piety and holiness" (*Mos.* 2.270). The apostates did not try to stick to the religious status they had before the lapse into the worship of the golden calf. On the contrary: they abandoned that status.

Instead of seeing the apostasy of the Israelites as a result of over-confidence in God, these texts understand the sins as results of distrust in him. The Israelites did not abandon God *because* he had acted graciously towards them, but *in spite of* this. Ps 78.16-17 seems to express this thought very well: "...he brought streams out of the cliff and made water run down like rivers. But they sinned against him yet again: in the desert they defied the Most High" (cf. Num 14.22; Ps 95.9).

If Paul wanted to see an analogy between over-confident Corinthians and over-confident Israelites, such an analogy finds no support at all in those Old

---

45. We may recall that in 1 Cor 10 Paul speaks both of demons and the rock, who was Christ (1 Cor 10. 4, 20, 21). Meeks, *And Rose up to Play*, 72, notes that Paul here probably alludes to Deut 32.

Testament texts which are referred to in 1 Cor 10.1-10. It is therefore difficult to imagine how Paul could have understood the fathers as having been over-confident. The texts give an unambiguous picture of quite a different kind. The sins, among these idolatry in its various forms, are signs of abandoning and forgetting God by a people who do not trust in him. In fact the picture Paul gives of the fathers does not have any feature of over-confidence either. Now, if Paul understood some Corinthians as over-confident, why would he refer to precisely these stories, which do not offer him the slightest argument to admonish such people?

Conclusion

The investigation of 1 Cor 10.1-13 presented in this article has been critical towards the common attempts to see the passage as directed against Corinthian over-confidence, especially if this is seen as based on the effects of the sacraments.

Paul's words are better explained as part of a traditional pattern, which the apostle uses. This pattern, found in several Old Testament and Jewish texts, sees the apostasy of the people against the beneficient acts of God. In spite of the blissful events, the people acted sinfully, for instance by turning to foreign gods, wherefore they were punished. By referring to this pattern Paul warns the Corinthians not to participate in pagan cults. Paul focusses in his text on the baptism and feeding of the people in the desert on the one hand and the idolatrous banquetting around the golden calf on the other. These events form prefigurations of the experiences in the present life of the Corinthian community, which Paul sees as an eschatological reality for which the Scriptures have been written (1 Cor 10.11). These realities are Christian baptism and the Lord's supper on the beneficial side and pagan cultic practices on the sinister and seductive side. Although the events in the desert are seen as prefigurations of the Christian sacraments, Paul at the same time describes them in a different way from baptism into Christ and the Lord's supper.

Just as the fathers were baptized into Moses and received spiritual food and drink, so the Corinthians have become baptized into Christ and have participated in the Lord's supper. These events have been gifts from God. Now the Corinthians should take warning and not participate in pagan cults, because this in turn would mean apostasy from faith, as in the case of the fathers. Let the man who thinks that he stands in faith (cf. 1 Cor 15.1; 16.13; 2 Cor 1.24) beware lest he should fall (1 Cor 10.12). The focus of the passage is not, according to our view, a warning against over-confidence, which scholars have often read into 1 Cor 10.12. The passage is instead a warning not to participate in idolatrous practices. Paul's words show the impossiblity of being a member of the Christian community with its sacramental meetings and a participant in the pagan cults at the same time (cf. 1 Cor 10.21). Instead of a warning of over-confident sacramentalism, the main point in Paul's argument is his injunction to flee idolatry (1 Cor 10.14), which follows like a conlusion immediately after 1 Cor 10.1-13.[46]

---

46. According to H.-D.Wendland, *Die Briefe an die Korinther* (ATD Göttingen: Vandenhoeck & Ruprecht, 1978) 77, it is 1 Cor 10.14 which motivates the preceding Scriptural proof in 1 Cor 10.1-10. Nevertheless Wendland postulates over-confidence among the Corinthian "Gnostics" (77-78). W. F. Orr and J. A. Walther, *I Corinthians. A New Translation, Introduction with a Study of the Life of Paul, Notes, and Commentary* (AB Garden City: Doubleday, 1976), 247, state that 1 Cor 10.14-15 "summarize the diverse preceding material as it relates to idolatry". According to Willis, *Idol Meat*, 141, the concern of Paul's "argument is not sacramentalism...but the danger of idolatry". In 1 Cor 10.14 Paul "draws the conclusion from his argument in 1.1-13".

Paul's Use of Deut 30,12-14 in Jewish Context.
Some Observations

Per Jarle Bekken

The Aim of the Present Study

In this essay we will make some observations on the following two aspects of
Paul's use of Deut 30.12-14 in Romans 10. (1) the Jewish context of Paul's
exegetical treatment involving the issues of exegetical techniques and forms; (2)
the Jewish context of Paul's eschatological application. In spite of the vastness
of the literature, these aspects have not received enough attention — at least
not against the background material offered by the poem of Baruch and the
writings of Philo. It is the purpose of this study to indicate that this material
can provide help in establishing a Jewish referential background, against which
these aspects of Paul's christological use of Deut 30.12-14 can be understood
and become more intelligble. However, for the purpose of clarity some basic
deliberations are necessary as to what we mean by referential background.

By referential background we think of features of a syntactic, semantic and
pragmatic nature, which, without necessarily being explicitly referred to in a
text, form the background of the text, in such a way that it should be known
in order to catch the full implications of the text. We can imagine cases in
which such features and implications of a text are fully shared by the author
and the readers, in such a way that the sender's and receiver's horizons
coincide. Here we will assume the view that a receiver has a correct
understanding of a text, when the sender and receiver fully share features of
the background to which the message of the text refers. The aim of
interpretation is then to specify and grasp the text's referential background as
far as possible.[1]

The evidence of parallels in literary independent texts can provide the
scholar with help in reconstructing the various features of a referential
background in a certain text. In such cases these parallel texts must satisfy the
following two criteria: 1. It must be possible to situate the parallel text
chronologically, historically, culturally and ideologically so that it becomes
probable that the sender and receiver of the text under consideration are aware
of and share the same presuppositions 2. The text under consideration must
be possible to explain and understand against the background of the alleged
parallels.

---

1. Cf. L. Hartman, *Asking for a Meaning* (Uppsala: Almqvist & Wiksell, 1979) 123-24.

For the purpose of further discussion it is it is first requisite to place this text within the argument of Rom 9-11 and then to give an outline of the argumentative structure in Rom 10.1-21.

After a brief introduction in which Paul expresses his dismay over his own people (9.1-5), Paul makes a statement which covers the following discussion in Rom 9-11. "It is not as though the word of God failed" (9.6a). This theme is followed by two subthemes which are treated in reversed order. Paul proves from Scripture that "not all are children of Abraham because they are his descendants" (Rom 9.7-13). Then he develops the theme which was introduced first: "Not all who are descended from Israel belong to Israel" (9.6b; 9.22-29). This theme is summarized by the statement in Rom 9.30-31 about the contemporary situation, and functions as a transition to the following section of the letter: "Gentiles who did not pursue righteousness have grasped righteousness, the righteousness from faith, but Israel, pursuing a law of righteousness, did not attain to the law".

The following section of Rom 10.1-21 clarifies the background as to how this paradox came to be. The argument ends with a recapitulation of the situation of the Gentiles and Israel (Rom 10.18-21). In chapter 11, Paul affirms that Israel is God's people despite their unbelief and disobedience towards the gospel, and that God in the end will effect Israel's eschatological restoration according to what he has always promised. In short, Rom 10.1-21 has a parenthetical place in the logic of the argument, and serves as an explanation and description of how Israel and the Gentiles came to switch roles in the history of election, and how Israel failed to grasp the true message of the law.

Outline of the argumentative structure in Rom 10.1-21.

1   Paul's plea to God on behalf of the Jews that they may be saved
2   (motivation($\gamma\dot{\alpha}\rho$) for the plea): they have zeal for God
     (negative contrast, $\dot{\alpha}\lambda\lambda$' o$\dot{\upsilon}$): but not in accordance with knowledge
3   (explanation, $\gamma\dot{\alpha}\rho$, of not in accordance with knowledge): for, being ignorant of the righteousness that comes from God, and seeking to establish their own
     (negative statement): they did not submit to God's righteousness
4   (explanation of God's righteousness, $\gamma\dot{\alpha}\rho$, and thesis): Christ is the end of the law to righteousness for all who believe
5   (motivation, $\gamma\dot{\alpha}\rho$)
     (background about righteousness of the law): the one who does shall live (Lev 18.5)
6   (contrast, $\delta\dot{\epsilon}$): but the righteousness of faith says: (negative statement) do not say in your heart (Deut 8.17; 9.4)
     (exegetical paraphrase of Deut 30.12-13): Who will ascend into heaven? that is, in order to bring Christ down
7   or: Who will descend into the abyss? that is, in order to bring Christ up from the dead

8   (positive statement) but what does it say? (exegetical paraphrase of Deut 30.14):
     The word is near you in your mouth and in your heart that is, the word of
     faith which we preach

9   (explanation, ὅτι, and exegetical paraphrase of "mouth" and "heart") because,
     if you confess with your mouth that Jesus is Lord and believe with your heart
     that God raised him from the dead, you will be saved

10   (explanation, γάρ, and repetition in chiastic order of the exegetical paraphrase
     of "mouth", and repetition, without explanation, of the exegetical paraphrase
     of "heart") for with the heart one believes to righteousness, and with the
     mouth one confesses to salvation

11   (explanation, γάρ, by quotation, of "belief" leading to "salvation") for, all who
     believe shall not be put to shame

12   (explanation, γάρ, of "all") for there is no distinction between Jew and Greek
     (explanation, γάρ, of the abolition of the distinction) for the same is Lord of all,
     generous against all who call upon him

13   (explanation, γάρ, by quotation, of generous against all who call upon him) for,
     all who call upon the name of the Lord will be saved

14   (application, οὖν, exception of the Jews from "all") they should "call upon" if
     they believed if they heard if anyone preached

15   if anyone had been sent (instance by quotation to support that the last two
     conditions had been fulfilled) beautiful are the feet of those who preach the
     gospel about the good things

16   (negative statement) but not all the Jews obeyed the gospel explanation, γάρ,
     by quotation) not all of them believed the message they heard from us

17   (recapitulation, ἄρα, of the preceding statement and a conclusion of the unit
     vv. 8-17; cf. the exegetical paraphrase of the term ῥῆμα from v.8) faith comes
     from the message which is heard, and what is heard comes through the word
     of Christ

18   (proceding statement, ἀλλὰ λέγω) have the Jews not heard? yes, indeed
     (instance by quotation)

19   (further proceding statement, ἀλλὰ λέγω) did Israel not understand? no
     (instance by quotation: "a foolish nation")

20   (further proceding statement, δὲ; quotation) others have instead found God

21   (contrast, δὲ; quotation) Israel is a disobedient people

Paul's Use of Exegetical Techniques and Forms

Point of departure

In the discussion of Paul's treatment of Deut 30.12-14 the following basic
questions have been raised: (a) Is there an exegesis? (b) Is Paul's exegesis
honest?

(a) The fact that Paul imposes on Deut 30.12-14 a meaning different from the
original one, has brought several scholars to the conclusion that Paul did not

actually intend to interpret Scripture at all.[2] For example, W. Sanday/A.C. Headlam even go so far as to think that Paul neither intended to quote Deut 30.12-14 nor to deliver an exposition of the scripture, but only that he was simply applying some of its language and imagery to make his point:

The Apostle does not intend to base any argument of the quotation from the O.T., but only selects the language as being familiar, suitable, and proverbial, in order to express what he wishes to say.[3]

Now most scholars have abandoned this standpoint for the following main reasons:

a. The text is too close to that of the Deuteronomy passage, and the deviations of Paul's rendering of Deut 30.12-14 from known textual versions are not significant enough to say that he only makes use of proverbial sayings.

b. Paul's explanatory notes, introduced by the exegetical phrase τοῦτ' ἔστιν, and inserted between the quotations from Deut 30.12-14, seem to indicate that Paul was offering an exegesis of a scriptural text.

c. Moreover, it has been observed that Paul carries the explanation further in vv. 9-10, where he picks up terms from Deut 30.14 and interprets them.[4]

(b) In any case, there is a commonly-held view that Paul in Rom 10.5-8 sets two texts from the Torah, Lev 18.5 and Deut 30.12-14 in antithesis to each other, both of which emphasize the necessity of keeping and acting according to the law; both using in the Greek translation the same verb (ποιεῖν).

You shall observe my institutions and my laws: the man who keeps (ποιήσας) them shall have life through them. (Lev 18.5.)

It is not in heaven, that you should say, Who will go up for us to heaven, and fetch it for us, that we may hear and do (ποιήσομεν) it?
Nor is it beyond the sea, that you should say, Who will cross to the other side of the sea for us, and fetch it for us, that we may hear and do (ποιήσομεν) it?

---

2. See e.g. W. Sanday & A.C. Headlam, *Romans* (Edinburgh, 1902) 289; C.K. Barrett, *Romans* (London: A & C Black, 1957) 199; O. Kuss, *Römer* (Regensburg, 1978) 3.758-61; see further R. Badenas, *Christ the End of the Law* (Sheffield: JSOT Press, 1985) 125-26 with bibliography.
3. W. Sanday & A.C. Headlam (note 2) 289.
4. Cf. the survey of current research in J.D.G. Dunn, "'Righteousness from the Law' and 'Righteousness from Faith'," in: *Paul's Interpretation of Scripture in Romans 10.1-10, Tradition and Interpretation in the New Testament* (ed. G.F. Hawthorne; Tübingen: Mohr-Siebeck, 1987) 216-28.

The word is very near to you, in your mouth and in your heart, so that you can do (ποιειν) it. (Deut 30.12-14.)

The former Paul takes as a description of "the righteousness which is from the law" and the latter as a reference to "the righteousness from faith", "Christ" and "the word of faith". There is a prevailing opinion that this exegesis of Deut 30.12-14 not only seems startling to a modern reader, but it must even have startled Paul's first audience.[5] Thus, one has found the interpretation "purely fanciful",[6] "especially crass"[7] and "arbitrary".[8]

However, can any more be said to characterize, explain and even justify Paul's exegetical treatment of Deut 30.12-14? It is the purpose of the next lines to show that Paul's handling of Deut 30.12-14 is not arbitrary, but follows accepted techniques and forms, even when it is shaped by his theology. We further presume that such techniques and forms were recognized — at least by the competent reader in the Roman congregations — to be characteristic signals of Jewish exegesis in that time.

The technique of exegetical paraphrase

Paul's exposition of Deut 30.12-14 has not received sufficient attention as a sample of conventional exegetical paraphrase of a biblical text, in which words, phrases and sentences from the Old Testament are either quoted, repeated or replaced by interpretive terms and fused together and supplemented with other qualifying terms.[9] An understanding of Paul's treatment of Deut 30.12-14 on the basis of this accepted exegetical method can not only explain the textual form of reference to Deut 30.12-14, but also the exegetical reasoning behind Rom 10.6ff., and thus to some extent justify his fresh exposition of Deut 30.12-14.

The following outline of the text can display the way Paul has paraphrased the Old testament quotation (the words from the Old Testament are underscored):

6   ἡ δὲ ἐκ πίστεως δικαιοσύνη οὕτως λέγει· μὴ εἴπῃς ἐν τῇ καρδίᾳ σου· Τίς
     ἀναβήσεται εἰς τὸν οὐρανόν; τοῦτ᾽ ἔστιν Χριστὸν καταγαγεῖν·

---

5. So e.g. R.B. Hays, *Echoes of Scripture in the Letters of Paul* (New Haven: Yale University Press, 1989) 1-5.
6. C.H. Dodd, *The Epistle of Paul to the Romans* (London, 1932) 166.
7. E. Gaugler, *Der Brief an die Römer* (Zürich, 1952) 2.124.
8. A.T. Hanson, *Studies in Paul's Technique and Theology* (London, 1974) 147.
9. This definition of an exegetical paraphrase is deduced from the empirical data provided by the texts themselves. Thus, we have attempted to avoid a definition which can be assumed to be too mechanical and too abstract.

(But the righteousness on faith says, Do not say in your heart, Who will ascend
into heaven? that is to bring Christ down)

7   ἢ Τίς καταβήσεται εἰς τὴν ἄβυσσον; τοῦτ᾽ ἐστιν Χριστὸν ἐκ νεκρῶν
ἀναγαγεῖν·
(or Who will ascend into the abyss? that is to bring Christ up from the dead)

8   ἀλλὰ τί λέγει; ἐγγύς σου τὸ ῥῆμά ἐστιν ἐν τῷ στόματί σου καὶ ἐν τῇ καρδίᾳ
σου, τοῦτ᾽ ἐστιν τὸ ῥῆμα τῆς πίστεως ὃ κηρύσσομεν.
(But what does it say? The word is near you on your lips and in your heart,
that is the word of faith which we preach)

9   ὅτι ἐὰν ὁμολογήσῃς ἐν τῷ στόματί σου κύριον Ἰησοῦν καὶ πιστεύσῃς ἐν τῇ
καρδίᾳ σου ὅτι ὁ θεὸς αὐτὸν ἤγειρεν ἐκ νεκρῶν, σωθήσῃ·
(because, if you confess with your mouth that Jesus is Lord and believe with
your heart that God raised him from the dead, you will be saved)

10 καρδίᾳ γὰρ πιστεύεται εἰς δικαιοσύνην, στόματι δὲ ὁμολογεῖται εἰς σωτηρίαν.

(For man believes with his heart and so is justified, and he confesses with his
mouth and so is saved.)

17 ἄρα ἡ πίστις ἐξ ἀκοῆς, ἡ δὲ ἀκοὴ διὰ ῥήματος Χριστοῦ
(So faith comes from what is heard, and what is heard comes by the preaching
of Christ.)

These verses feature some characteristic elements as to the method of exegetical
paraphrase. Within the context of Rom 10.4-17 Deut 30.12-14 is divided into
parts and interpreted in a succesive sequence. Thus, Deut 30.12 is given an
exposition in v. 6, Deut 30.13 in v. 7 and Deut 30.14 in vv. 9-10 and v. 17.

In vv. 6-8 a rendering of the biblical text is fused together with interpretive
sentences which can be bracketed out as detachable paraphrastic expansions.
Thus the paraphrase is organized as 1) a series of three partial quotations, 2)
expanded by an interpretive clause following each citing, and each introduced
by an exegetical expression(τοῦτ᾽ ἐστιν). Fortunately, Philo's paraphrastic
rendering and exposition of Deut 30.12-14 in *Praem*. 80 provides us with an
important parallel, since it can illustrate the same way of paraphrasing an Old
Testament text and the same exegetical structure. The following outline of
Praem. 80 can display the similarities to Rom 10.6-8 (the words from the Old
Testament are underscored):

1) Paraphrase of the partial quotation of Deut 30.13:
    ἢ πέραν θαλάττης ἢ ἐν ἐσχατιαῖς γῆς (either beyond the sea or at the
    end of the sea), expanded by an
2) interpretive clause introduced by the exegetical phrase ὡς·

ὡς δεῖσθαι πολυχρονίου καὶ καματηρᾶς ἀποδημίας (so that it requires of you a lingering and wearisome exile),

1) Paraphrase of the partial quotation of Deut 30.12:
   οὐδ' ἐξαίφνης ἐστείλατο τὴν ἐνθένδε εἰς οὐρανὸν ἀποικίαν (nor has it suddenly left this earth to settle in heaven), expanded by an
2) interpretative clause introduced by the epexegetical phrase ἵνα:
   ἵνα τις μετέωρος καὶ πτηνός ἀρθεὶς μόλις ἐφικέσθαι τούτων δυνηθῇ (so that one can scarce reach them though he soar on high and wing his way thither):

1) Paraphrase of the quotation of Deut 30.14:
   πλησίον δ' ἐστὶ καὶ ἐγγύτάτω, τρισὶ μέρεσι τῶν καθ' ἕκαστον ἡμῶν ἐνιδρυμένον, στόματι καὶ καρδίᾳ καὶ χερσί (But it is close by and very near, firmly set in three of the parts of whic h each of us is constituted, mouth and heart and hand), expanded by an
2) interpretative clause introduced by the exegetical phrase τροπικώτερον· τροπικώτερον λόγῳ καὶ διανοίᾳ καὶ πράξεσιν (representing in a figure speech and thought and action).

As we shall see below, the context of *Praem.* 80 provides more important material, since it can illustrate how Deut 30.12-14 is interpreted within the framework of exegetical forms and applied in an eschatological perspective comparable to Romans 10.

The hermeneutical freedom of Paul's reading of Deut 30.12-14 has been set into relief and highlighted by comparing Paul with Philo and Baruch.[10] All three appeal to the same scripture as a warrant for very different contents and meanings. In general, Philo's interpretations demonstrate freedom and flexibility in the interpretation of Deut 30.12-14. I t has been pointed out that Philo takes Deut 30.11-14 to refer to "the good" (*Praem.* 80-81; *Somn.* 2. 180; *Post.* 84ff.), to the subject of "conversion" (*Virt.* 183) and ethical virtues in general (*Prob.* 67ff.). Likewise, Baruch demonstrates free use of this text, since here Deut 30.12-14 is taken to refer to the divine wisdom (Bar 4.1). Against the background of a flexibility in the interpretation of this scripture, we should evaluate the possibility that such a flexibility might facilitate an application of Deut 30.12-14 in other contexts or combinations with new motifs or elements. Accordingly, the way Paul takes the same scripture to refer to "the righteousness of faith", "Christ" and "the word of faith", could of course have been controversial, but not surprising to his readers, since as compared with Philo and Baruch, his free and creative use of the text represented no idiosyncracy, but instead puts him in good Jewish company.[11]

In addition, we can now make the observation that despite their free use

10. Cf. J.D.G. Dunn (note 4) 220.
11. See J.D.G. Dunn (note 4) 220.

of the text, the interpretations by Paul and Baruch fall within the framework
of the method of exegetical paraphrase. In Rom 10.6-7 the words from Deut
30.12-13 are followed and interpreted by two paraphrastic expansions: τοῦτ'
ἐστιν Χριστὸν καταγαγεῖν (that is to bring Christ down) (v. 6) and τοῦτ' ἐστιν
Χριστὸν ἐκ νεκρῶν ἀναγαγεῖν (that is to bring Christ up from the dead) (v. 7).
The question to be asked then is: Do some of the words and phrases in these
expansions replace and interpret words and phrases in Deut 30.12-13? The
answer seems to be in the affirmative. In Rom 10.6-7 the phrases Χριστὸν
καταγαγεῖν (to bring Christ down) and Χριστὸν ἀναγαγεῖν (to bring Christ up)
are probably an interpretation and replacement of the purpose clause λήμψεται
αὐτήν in Deut 30.12-13.[12] The following observations seem to support this
suggestion: In combination with τοῦτ' ἐστιν the constructions Χριστὸν
καταγαγεῖν and Χριστὸν ἀναγαγεῖν must be understood as final infinitive
constructions that state the purpose and meaning of the quoted questions from
Deut 30.12-13:

Τίς ἀναβήσεται εἰς τὸν οὐρανόν; (Who will ascend into heaven?)
Τίς καταβήσεται εἰς τὴν ἄβυσσον; (Who will descend into the abyss?)

The phrase Χριστὸν probably interprets and replaces αὐτήν in Deut 30.12-13
which refers back to the commandment, ἡ ἐντολή in Deut 30.11. The exegetical
reasoning behind this exposition and replacement is obviously stated in Rom
10.4, which makes an explicit identification of Christ and the law (τέλος γὰρ
νόμου Χριστὸς).

Moreover, the Deuteronomic verb λήμψεται (take) in Deut 30.12-13 has
been altered and changed to καταγαγεῖν and ἀναγαγεῖν. Thus, Paul has
adjusted the vocabulary so that Deuteronomy 30.12-13 is conformed to a new
context, viz. the Christ-event.

An important parallel which can illustrate Paul's treatment of scripture in
Rom 10.6-7 is provided by the paraphrase of Deut 30.12-13 within the context
of Bar 3.9-4.4. The paraphrase of Deut 30.12-13 appears in Bar 3.29-30 (the
words from the biblical text are underscored):

(29) τίς ἀνέβη εἰς τὸν οὐρανὸν καὶ ἔλαβην αὐτὴν
     καὶ καταβίβασεν αὐτὴν ἐκ τῶν νεφελῶν
(30) τίς διέβη πέραν τῆς θαλάσσης καὶ εὗρεν αὐτὴν
     καὶ οἴσει αὐτὴν χρυσίου ἐκλεκτοῦ
     (Who has gone up into heaven and taken her,
     and brought her down from the clouds?

---

12. The method of replacing words from the Old Testament with interpretive words is
    commonplace in an exegetical paraphrase, see P. Borgen, *Bread from Heaven* (Leiden:
    Brill, 1981) 98.

Who has gone over the sea, and found her
and acquired her with choice gold?)

In a corresponding way to Paul, the use of Deuteronomy 30 is characterized by selective citation, alteration in vocabulary and additional complementary statements. Thus, the writer has conformed the Deuteronomic material to a new, specifically wisdom context. For example, in v 29, in the place of the Deuteronomic purpose clause the verbal idea of "taking it" has been supplemented by the sequential activity of "bringing" wisdom "down from the clouds". In v 30 the Deuteronomic verb "take her" likewise has been changed to "find her". Moreover, in the light of the immediate context, in which the author reproaches Israel for deserting and not seeking the wisdom (cf. vv. 12; 20-22; 31), we see that the author has taken αὐτὴν in Deut 30.12-13 not to refer to the commandment, but to the Wisdom. The point of the allusion to Deut 30.12-13 appears to be stated in the following verses: Israel had no reason to set out on a search for Wisdom, since it was already available: "for God gave it to Jacob his servant and to Israel whom he loved"(3.37). At the conclusion of the prose, wisdom is identified with "ἡ βίβλος τῶν προσταγμάτων τοῦ θεοῦ καὶ ὁ νόμος ὁ ὑπάρχων εἰς τὸν αἰῶνα" (the book of the commandments of God and the Torah which endures forever). Thus, Bar 3.29f. echoes Deut 30.12-13 to make the point that God's Wisdom is accessible and ready to hand in the law.

The method of supplementing words from an Old Testament quotation with other interpretative words is a characteristic feature of an exegetical paraphrase.[13] In Rom 10, vv. 8-10; 17 words from the quotation of Deut 30.14 in Rom 10.8 are repeated and paraphrased by supplementary terms. In v. 8 the terms τὸ ῥῆμα are repeated and qualified by the genitive construction τῆς πίστεως and the relative clause ὃ κηρύσσομεν. Another sample of a supplementary qualification of the same term is given in v. 17. There the qualification of the repeated term is represented by the genitive Χριστοῦ. Rom 10.9-10 reads:

9   ὅτι ἐὰν ὁμολογήσῃς ἐν τῷ στόματί σου κύριον Ἰσοῦν καὶ πιστεύσῃς ἐν τῇ καρδίᾳ σου ὅτι ὁ θεὸς αὐτὸν ἤγειρεν ἐκ νεκρῶν, σωθήσῃ· (because, if you confess with your mouth that Jesus is Lord and believe with your heart that God raised him from the dead, you will be saved)

10 καρδίᾳ γὰρ πιστεύεται εἰς δικαιοσύνην, στόματι δὲ ὁμολογεῖται εἰς σωτηρίαν. (For man believes with his heart and so is justified, and he confesses with his mouth and so is saved.)

13. Cf. P. Borgen (note 12) 66-7.

In v. 9 we can observe how Paul picks up and builds each of the phrases "ἐν τῷ στόματί σου" (in your mouth)and "ἐν τῇ καρδίᾳ σου" (in your heart) into an exegetical paraphrase. In v. 10 he repeats the terms καρδίᾳ and στόμα, and at the same time motivates and elaborates the paraphrase from v. 9. Again Philo's paraphrasing exegesis of Deut 30.14 offers a parallel. In *Virt.* 183 the rendering of Deut 30.14 is followed by a suplementary clause which explains the meaning of the key terms στόματι, καρδίᾳ and χερσί without repeating them. Then follows a proposition which repeats the same key terms of Deut 30.14 and at the same time serves as a motivation and elaboration of the preceding explanation. The result can be diagrammed as follows:

Philo, *De Virtutibus* 183.
Paraphrasing quotation of Deut 30.14:
> ἀλλ' ἔστιν ἐγγυτάτω, τρισὶ μέρεσι τῶν καθ' ἡμᾶς
> ἐνδιαιτώμενον, στόματι καὶ καρδίᾳ καὶ χερσί,
> (but is very near, residing in three parts of our being, mouth, heart
> and hands)

Explanation:
> διὰ συμβόλον λόγοις καὶ βουλαῖς καὶ πράξεσι·
> (symbolizing words and thought and actions)

Expanded explanation:
> λόγου μὲν γὰρ στόμα σύμβολον, καρδία δὲ βουλευμάτων,
> πράξεων δὲ χεῖρες, ἐν οἷς τὸ εὐδαιμονεῖν ἐστιν.
> (for the mouth is a symbol of speech, the heart of intentions, the hand of
> actions)

The next paragraph will further show that Paul's fresh exegetical paraphrase of Deut 30.12-14 is shaped within the framework of conventional exegetical forms.

Exegetical Forms

In this essay, we will use the term *form* to refer to what has been labelled both "specific" form and "general" form.[14] In addition, by "specific" form we mean the specific shape of a given text and by "general" form we think of the

---

14. A useful survey of the problems related to the concept of "form" among Biblical scholars can be found in W.G. Doty, *The Concept of Genre in Literary Analysis*, SBL Seminar Papers 1972 (ed. L.C. McGaughy; Missoula, 1972) 413-48. See also L. Hartman, "Survey of the Problem of Apocalyptic Genre," *Apocalypticism in the Mediterranean World and the Near East* (ed. D. Hellholm; Tübingen: Mohr-Siebeck, 1983) 329-43.

structure, that is an inner organizational coherence of a bounded entity, that occurs in several literary pieces and that manifests itself in the shape of a given text.[15] From a linguistic point of view this distinction between "general" form and "specific" form corresponds to the distinction between language and speech made by F. de Saussure. To use Saussure's terms, the "general" form belongs to a wider linguistic system, *langue*, which can manifest itself in individual "specific" forms, *parole*, within that system.[16] The aspects of form such as langue and parole make clear that when an author uses a fixed conventional form on the level of *langue*, he is the sovereign master of how to give it shape on the level of *parole*. This means that the "general" forms can manifest themselves in the "specific" forms in a fluid and flexible way.

Illustrations of "general" forms are manifested in Rom 10.6-7 with regard to the form of the exegetical praphrase of Deut 30.12-13. Paul paraphrases Deut 30.12-13 by 1) a series of two partial quotations, 2) with an epexegetical clause inserted and added to each citing, each explanation introduced by an exegetical expression (τοῦτ' ἐστιν). As we observed above, this exegetical structure, which does not appear elsewhere in the Pauline writings, is paralleled by Philo's use of Deut 30.12-13 in *Praem.* 80. Moreover, in a similar way to Paul in Rom 10.6-7, Philo here supplements the paraphrases of Deut 30.12-13 with final infinitive clauses which indicate their meaning. This interpretative form of a paraphrase of or a quotation from an Old Testament passage supplemented by means of a final clause, represents a "general" form, since St. John's gospel as well as rabbinic writings provide more examples of it.[17] In the examples given the words from the Old Testament quotation are underscored.

Rom 10.6. "Who will ascend into heaven? that is to bring Christ down."
Praem. 80. "...nor has it suddenly left this earth to settle in heaven, so that one can scarce reach them though he soar on high and wing his way thither."
John 6.38. "For I have come down from heaven, not to do my own will, but the will of him who sent me."
Mek. Exod. 19.7: " Do not read thus, but read: The Lord came to Sinai, to give the Torah to Israel."

Another example of a "general" form is provided by Paul's exegetical paraphrase of Deut 30.14 in Rom 10.9-10. Analysing Rom 10.8-10, we can observe that Paul's exegetical paraphrase of each of the expressions "ἐν τῷ στόματί σου" and "ἐν τῇ καρδίᾳ σου" from Deut 30.14 follows the exegetical structure of a basic exposition of an Old Testament quotation succeeded by an elaboration of the exposition. In fact, in all of the texts in which Philo deals

15. Cp. W.G. Doty (note 14) 434.
16. Cf. F. de Saussure, *Cours de linguistique generale* (Paris, 1916) 23-54.
17. Cf. P. Borgen (note 12) 71-2.

with the same part of Deut 30.14, he parallels this form. In this context we will restrict ourselves to indicating this form in two of these texts, e.g. *Virt*. 183 and *Praem*. 80-81. In addition it can be demonstrated that John 6.31b-33 also illustrates the same form. The underlining indicates the quotation from the Old Testament and the paraphrasing of words from this quotation in the exposition.

Philo, *De Virtutibus* 183.
Quotation:
    ἀλλ᾽ ἔστιν ἐγγυτάτω, τρισὶ μέρεσι τῶν καθ᾽ ἡμᾶς
    ἐνδιαιτώμενον, στόματι καὶ καρδίᾳ καὶ χερσί,
    (but is very near, residing in three parts of our being, mouth, heart and hands)

Explanation:
    διὰ συμβόλον λόγοις καὶ βουλαῖς καὶ πράξεσι·
    (symbolizing words and thought and actions)

Rationale and expanded explanation:
    λόγου μὲν γὰρ στόμα σύμβολον, καρδία δὲ βουλευμάτων,
    πράξεων δὲ χεῖρες, ἐν᾽ οἷς τὸ εὐδαιμονεῖν ἐστιν.
    (for the mouth is a symbol of speech, the heart of intentions, the hand of actions)

Philo, *Praem*. 80-81.
Quotation:
    πλησίον δ᾽ἐστὶ καὶ ἐγγυτάτω, τρισὶ μέρεσι τῶν
    καθ᾽ ἕκαστον ἡμῶν ἐνιδρυμένον, στόματι καὶ καρδίᾳ
    καὶ χερσί.
    (But it is close by and very near, firmly set in three of the parts of which each of us is constituted, mouth and heart and hand,)

Exposition:
    τροπικώτερον λόγῳ καὶ διανοίᾳ καὶ πράξεσιν.
    (representing in a figure speech and thought and action.)

Rationale and expanded exposition:
    ἐὰν γὰρ οἷα τὰ βουλεύματα τοιοῦτοι οἱ λόγοι καὶ οἷα
    τὰ λεγόμενα τοιαίδε αἱ πράξεις ὦσι, καὶ ταῦτα ἀλλήλοις
    ἀντακουλουθῇ δεθέντα ἁρμονίας ἀλύτοις δεσμοῖς
    εὐδαιμονία κρατεῖ........
    (For if our words correspond with our thoughts and our actions with our words and the three mutually follow each other, bound together with indissoluble bonds of harmony, happiness prevails.....)

John 6.31b-33.
Quotation:

ἄρτον ἐκ τοῦ οὐρανοῦ ἔδωκεν αὐτοῖς φαγεῖν.
(He gave them bread from heaven to eat.)

Exposition:

εἶπεν οὖν αὐτοῖς ὁ 'Ιησοῦς· ἀμὴν ἀμὴν λέγω ὑμῖν,
οὐ Μωῦσῆς δέδωκεν ὑμῖν τὸν ἄρτον ἐκ τοῦ οὐρανοῦ,
ἀλλ' ὁ πατήρ μου δίδωσιν ὑμῖν τὸν ἄρτον ἐκ τοῦ οὐρανοῦ
τὸν ἀληθινόν
(Jesus the said to them, Truly, truly, I say to you, not Moses gave you the
bread from heaven, but my Father gives you the true bread from heaven.)

Rationale and expanded exposition:

ὁ γὰρ ἄρτος τοῦ θεοῦ ἐστιν ὁ καταβαίνων ἐκ τοῦ οὐρανοῦ
καὶ ζωὴν διδοὺς τῷ κόσμῳ.
(For the bread of God is that which comes down from heaven
and gives life to the world.)

These texts unquestionably follow the same literary convention as Rom 10.8-10.
The agreements between them justify the following contention: 1) The Old
Testament is quoted. 2) The quotation is given an exposition which is signalled
and introduced by an exegetical expression. 3) Then follows a sequence,
introduced by the conjunction γὰρ, which gives the rationale and expands the
exposition.

In the remaining part of this discussion of traditional expository forms
given to Paul's use of Deut 30.12-14, we shall turn to forms of smaller range.
According to F. de Saussure the linguistic system, *langue*, includes all kinds of
signs, whether they be the structure of signs as those outlined above, or the
simplest clause, or just single words such as will now be considered.

In Rom 10.9 the exegetical paraphrase of στόμα and καρδία from Deut
30.14 is cast in the form of a conditional clause. In *Praem.* 81, in which Philo
interprets this part of Deut 30.14, we can find the same form used.

Rom 10.9:

ὅτι ἐὰν ὁμολογήσῃς ἐν τῷ στόματί σου κύριον 'Ιησοῦν καὶ
πιστεύσῃς ἐν τῇ καρδίᾳ σου ὅτι ὁ θεὸς αὐτὸν ἴγειρεν ἐκ νεκρῶν,
σωθήσῃ·
(because, if you confess with your mouth that Jesus is Lord and believe with
your heart that God raised him from the dead, you will be saved)

Praem 81:

ἐὰν γὰρ οἶα τὰ βουλεύματα τοιοῦτοι οἰ λόγοι καὶ οἶα
τὰ λεγόμενα τοιάδε αἱ πράξεις ὖσι, καὶ ταῦτα ἀλλήλοις

ἀντακουλουθῇ δεθέντα ἁρμονίας ἀλύτοις δεσμοῖς,
εὐδαιμονία κρατεῖ .... (For if our words correspond with our thoughts and
our actions with our words and the three mutually follow each other, bound
together with indissoluble bonds of harmony, happiness prevails.....)

The conditional clauses are introduced by the conjunctions ὅτι ἐάν (Rom 10.9)
and ἐάν (*Praem.* 81). The subjunctive mood expresses the aspect of eventuality:
if the condition is met, the consequence is within reach. With Philo the
condition is that there is correspondence and harmony between the mind, the
words and the actions. When this harmony occurs, the consequence of
happiness is fulfilled. In Rom 10.9 the condition is confession to Jesus as Lord,
and the belief that God has raised Jesus from the dead. If this condition is met,
the consequence of salvation is within reach. Expositions cast in a similar
conditional style are not unusual, and the New testament, Philo's writings and
other Jewish expository literature can provide us with further examples.[18]

An examination of Paul's and Philo's use of exegetical terminology within the
contexts of their expositions of Deut 30.12-14, reveals a variety of forms.
Nevertheless, some specific points of agreement between Paul and Philo can
be noticed: Both Paul (Rom 10.7-8) and Philo (*Praem.* 80; *Somn.* 2.180) can use
the disjunctive conjunction ἤ to introduce the partial quotation from Deut 30.13
and the adversative conjunction ἀλλὰ-δὲ to introduce the partial quotation of
Deut 30.14.

Rom 10.7-8:

7 ἤ τίς καταβήσεται εἰς τὴν ἄβυσσον; τοῦτ' ἐστιν Χριστὸν ἐκ νεκρῶν
   ἀναγαγεῖν· (or Who will ascend into the abyss? that is to bring Christ up from
   the dead)

8 ἀλλὰ τί λέγει; ἐγγύς σου τὸ ῥῆμά ἐστιν ἐν τῷ στόματί σου καὶ ἐν τῇ καρδίᾳ
   σου, τοῦτ' ἐστιν τὸ ῥῆμα τῆς πίστεως ὃ κηρύσσομεν.
   (But what does it say? The word is near you on your lips and in your heart, that
   is the word of faith which we preach)

18. See Chr. Köhler, *Studien zur Form-und Traditionsgeschichte der biblischen Makarismen*
    (typed diss, Jena, 1974 (abstract in *TLZ* 101 [1976], 77-80); P. Borgen (note 12) 88-90;
    K. Beyer, *Semitische Syntax im Neuen Testament* (Göttingen, 1968) 75-229.

Praem 80:

ἢ πέραν θαλάττης..... (either beyond the sea....)
.....πλησίον δ' ἐστὶ καὶ ἐγγύτατω, τρισὶ μέρεσι τῶν
καθ᾽ ἕκαστον ἡμῶν ἐνιδρυμένον, στόματι καὶ καρδίᾳ
καὶ χερσί,
(But it is close by and very near, firmly set in three of the parts of which each
of us is constituted, mouth and heart and hand,)

Often Jewish practise of exposition reflected adapted forms of the common usage of the Graeco-Roman world.[19] This fact applies to Paul's and Philo's appropriation of exegetical notes with the formula τοῦτ᾽ ἔστιν. This exegetical expression has been seen parallel to the demonstrative pronoun of 3.p.sg. or pl. used in the Qumran expositions to introduce an interpretation.[20] A commentator such as O. Michel chooses to view Paul's use of the formula in what seems a one-sided way when set against this background: "τοῦτ᾽ ἔστιν stammt nicht aus der hellenistischen retorik, sondern aus der exegetischen Terminologie des Judentums."[21] This view of the Jewish background may be regarded as one-sided, since the formula has also been found to introduce an interpretation in Hellenistic literature, as evidenced in the writings of Plutarch and Homer.[22] Accordingly, there is no reason either to consider Paul's and Philo's use of τοῦτ᾽ ἔστιν mainly in the light of the exegetical phraseology of the Qumran writings, or to make too sharp a distinction between Jewish and Hellenistic methods of exegesis. In our context it is of further interest to notice that both Paul (Rom 10.6-8) and Philo (*Praem.* 81) can use this exegetical expression in their exposition of Deut 30.12-14.

Paul's Eschatological Use of Deut 30.12-14

If we presuppose that Paul intended to contrast Lev 18.5 and Deut 30.12-14 as expressions of two different principles of righteousness, we must ask for his reasons for so doing. It is our suggestion that Philo can provide help in finding an answer to this question. A comparison of *Praem.* 79ff. with Roman 10.4ff. makes clear that both passages expound Deut 30.12-14 in an eschatological perspective within the framework of the principle of the law. By principle of the law, we are here thinking of the obedience to the demands of the law by action. Such a use of Deut 30.12-14 illustrated by Philo we thus consider to be an important component part of the referential background, which probably

19. See E. Ellis, *Biblical Interpretation in the New Testament Church, Mikra* (ed. M.J. Mulder; Philadelphia: Fortress Press, 1988) 691-725.
20. See E. Käsemann, *A Commentary on Romans* (Grand Rapids: Eerdmans, 1980) 284.
21. O. Michel, *Der Brief an die Römer* (Göttingen: Vandenhoeck & Ruprecht, 1978) 328-29.
22. For references, see D.-A. Koch, *Die Schrift als Zeuge des Evangeliums* (Tübingen: Mohr [Siebeck], 1986) 28.

has determined both Paul's appeal to Deut 30.12-14 as a warrant for eschatological salvation, and the reception of it in the Roman congregations where the letter would have been read.

Briefly, the literary context of *Praem.* 79-84 is as follows: The wider context is the group of writings that we denote as "Exposition of the Laws of Moses", where Philo follows the sequence of the Pentateuch. De Praemiis ends Philo's "rewriting" of the Law of Moses. The closer context is made up of the two parts of *Praem.* 1-78 and 79-172. The first part deals with rewards and punishments of individuals and houses in the biblical past. This section is for the most part a rewriting of the narrative of Genesis. A transitional passage which is missing has served as a conclusion of the first part and as an introduction to the second part, which for the most part is based on the sequences of blessings and curses in biblical covenant texts such as Lev 17-26, Exod 23 and Deut 28-30. *Praem.* 79-172 is made up of the sections on eschatological blessings (79-126) and eschatological curses (127-62), while the last part is dominated by a looking forward to the final eschatological restoration of the Jewish nation (163-72). The immediate context of *Praem.* 85-126 deals with the blessings of victory over human and natural enemies (85-97), wealth (98-107), long and good life (108-17) and exemption from disease (118-26).

It is noticeable that as in the law codes of the Pentateuch itself, Philo's exhortations to law obedience are sandwiched between his exposition of the Mosaic law code and its sanctions. In *Praem.* 79-84 Philo expresses the positive claim for law-obedience, which is a condition for the fulfilment of the eschatological blessings. The principle of the law is conveyed in *Praem.* 79 by an amplification of Deut 28.1 in the following way:

If, he says, you keep (φυλάττητε) the divine commandment in obedience to his ordinances (τοῖς προστάγμασι) and accept his precepts, not merely to hear them but to carry them out by your life and conduct (ἀλλὰ διὰ τῶν τοῦ βίου πράξεων ἐπιτελῆτε), ...

Parallels to the topos of hearing as well as acting according to the law are documented in Rom 2.13, Jas 1.22-25 and in rabbinic writings (Str-B 3,84ff.). The function and aim of the law, that it should be carried out, is further repeated throughout *Praem.*, cf. 82, 98, 101, 108, 110, 119, 126. Thus, the aim of the whole section of *Praem.* 79-126 seems to be to exhort the Jews to follow the law in order to prepare for the inauguration of the eschatological age of blessings. The first eschatological blessing attendant upon adherence to the law, is in *Praem.* 79 taken to be the victory over the enemies. Philo's biblical bases for this idea are Lev 26.8 and Deut 28.7. We will return to this issue below.

Praem. 80-82 (cf. γὰρ in 80) demonstrates that Philo interprets Deut 30.11-14 as a further elaboration on the principle of the law which comes to expression in 79. He takes Deut 30.11 to refer to both the commandments of the law and to "the good" (τὸ ἀγαθόν), while he takes Deut 30.12-14 to mean "the good". *Post.* 84, *Mut.* 236f. and *Somn.* 2.180 highlight the fact that Philo in his exposition of Deut 30.14 identifies "the good" and the commandments of the law. Thus, by the reference to Deut 30.11-14 about the commandments which are neither too huge nor heavy for the strength of those to whom they will apply, but close by and near, Philo will exhort to adherence to the law. Moreover, Philo's exposition of Deut 30.14 in *Praem.* 80-82 serves to clarify the condition for such an adherence to the law: when mouth, heart and hand, representing in a pictorial form word, thought and action, corresponds with eachother and these aspects of life mutually follow each other, happiness will prevail. In *Praem.* 82 Philo further applies his interpretation of Deut 30.11-14 to the issue of a total carrying out of the law: not only acceptance of the law by words is demanded, but one must "add thereto deeds which follow in their company, deeds shown in the whole conduct of our lives". In *Praem.* 83-84 Philo elaborates further on the outcome and manifestation of such an realization of the law. Such a lawobservant nation will manifest itself and be recognized by others as a wise nation and as great nation by its worship of God (cf. Deut 4.6-7).

In *Praem.* Philo's use of Deut 30.11-14 is located within the context of the eschatological expectations of blessing for the Jewish nation and "messianic" conquest of the Gentile nations. These eschatological expectations were widespread within post-biblical Judaism and can be evidenced in several sources.[23] In *Praem.* 79 we find the thought that if the Jewish nation heeds the law, it shall have victory over its enemies as blessing. After having emphasized by means of Deut 30.11ff. the necessity of carrying out the law in 80-84, Philo develops the theme of victory over the enemies in 85-97. The content of these latter paragraphs will here be summarized briefly: In 85-92 Philo describes these enemies to be of two kinds, wild beasts and men. When men become what they should be, the beasts will be tamed and men will stay away from war with each other (cf. Isa 11.6-9). Then he proceeds in 93-97 stating that war will either never come (cf. Lev 26.6) because the enemy will dissolve and fall to pieces when they recognize the virtues of the Jewish nation, or if some enemies attack, they will be defeated. The defeat can take place in various ways: 1. The enemy will be forced back by the superior strength of the Jewish nation (cf. Lev 26.8 and Deut 28.7), 94. 2. Some will flee due to fear caused by the military leader, 95. In this context Num 24.7 is quoted and elaborated upon:

23. See E. Schürer, *The History of the Jewish People in the Age of Jesus Christ*, (A new English version revised and edited by G. Vermes, F. Miller and M. Black; Edinburgh, 1979) 2. 527-29.

For there shall come forth a man, says the oracle, and leading his army and doing battle, he will subdue great and populous nations, because God has sent to his aid the reinforcement which befits the godly, and that is dauntless courage of soul and all-powerful strength of body, either of which strikes fear into the enemy and the two if united are quite irresistible.

As the eschatological emperor of many nations, the "man" carries some of the features of the Messiah, in accordance with the messianic interpretation of Num 24.7 elsewhere in Judaism.[24] 3. Others are described as unworthy to be defeated by men, and these will be conquered by swarms of wasps (cf. Exod 23.28; Deut 7:20), *Praem.* 96. In *Praem.* 97 Philo concludes that the Jewish nation, besides victory, will also gain ruling power over the enemies after the war. A catalogue of three virtues, dignity, strictness and benefaction is then listed to characterize the quality of the Jewish nation which makes the other peoples obedient to them as rulers. This expectation of the Jewish nation as the future world rulers of all nations is found also elsewhere in Philo's books (cf. *Mos.* 1.289-91), and comes also to expression later in *Praem.* 125 with the thought that the Hebrew nation will become the head of the other nations.

Information within the context of Rom 10.1-21 indicates that Paul's eschatological application of Deut 30.12-14 works within a frame of reference analogous to the one just illustrated by Philo. It is beyond the scope of this article to elaborate on thise information in detail. Here we will just give a few hints and present a preliminary sketch that can make Paul's choice and use of Deut 30.12-14 even more intelligible against such a referential background.

In a corresponding way to Philo, *Praem.* 79-97, Paul interprets Deut 30.12-14 in an eschatological perspective within the framework of the principle of the law. In Rom 10.5 Paul takes Lev 18.5 as a scriptural support for his statement of the principle of the law: "Moses writes that the one who does (ὁ ποιήσας) them [sc. the regulations (τὰ προστάγματά) and statues (τὰ κρίματά) of the law] shall live by them". This scripture, which could be summarized by the the the words — "do and live" — , was a typical expression of Israel's understanding of its obligations and promises under the covenant (cf. e.g. Deut 4.1; 5.32-33; 8.1; Deut 30.15-20; Neh 9.29; Ezek 18.9, 21; 20.11; 33.19).[25] The place of Lev 18.5 within the context of Rom 9.30-10.21 speaks in favour of the view that he could have taken the phrase "shall live by them" as a reference to eschatological salvation-life equivalent with righteousness, cf. the term of salvation in Rom 10.1, 9, 10 (equivalent to righteousness), 13; and also Paul's

---

24. See G. Vermes, *Scripture and Tradition in Judaism* (Leiden: Brill, 1961) 159.; W.A. Meeks, *The Prophet-King* (Leiden: Brill, 1967) 71-2; J. Neusner, *Messiah in Context* (Philadelphia: Fortress Press, 1984) 241-47.
25. Cf. J.D.G. Dunn (note 4) 219.

use of Lev 18.5 in Gal 3.12 within the context of Gal 3.1-14. A similar interpretation of Lev 18.5 is found in *Tg. Onq.* Lev 18.5, *Tg. Ps.-J.* Lev 18.5 and
Siphre Lev 18.5.

Regarding Rom 10.5 within the line of thought of vv. 1-5 and as an
introduction to vv. 6ff., the significance of the reference to Lev 18.5 can be
summed up briefly in the following points: 1. In v. 1 Paul states that he prays
for the salvation of his kinsmen. In v. 2 Paul motivates this request by his
characterization of the Jews: they have a zeal for God. In v. 3 he makes the
statement that they sought to establish their own righteousness. In v. 5 Paul
accordingly explains the understanding of the law of such typically devout
Jews, who by obedience to the law hoped for the fulfillment of the promises
of the law in the eschatological age to come. We have pointed out how Philo
can illustrate such an expectation based on his understanding of the principle
of the law in *Praem.* 79. 2. Reading telos in v. 4 as both end and intent, v. 5
explains the kind of law to which Christ both meant a termination and a
replacement, performing more perfectly the purposes it was intended to serve.
3. Moreover, v. 5 clarifies the background of Paul's interpretation of Deut
30.12-14.

The way Paul takes Deut 30.12-14 in vv. 6ff. as a reference to "the
righteousness of faith" and "Christ", and sets it in antithesis to Lev 18.5 (v. 5),
in order to explain Christ as the telos of the law expressed in v.4, makes it
highly probable that he presupposes a use of Deut 30.12-14 similar to the one
attested by Philo. As we have just observed Philo interpreted Deut 30.11-14 as
a further elaboration of the principle of the law within an eschatological
perspective about the "messianic" victory of the Jewish nation over the nations.
Thus, Philo provides us with an analogy which makes it possible to situate
Paul's eschatological application of Deut 30.12-14 in juxtapposition with his use
of Lev 18.5 within a roughly contemporary Jewish context. However, the
contrast Paul made between Lev 18.5 and Deut 30.12-14 states the difference
between Philo's and Paul's understanding of Deut 30.12-14. Differing from
Philo, Paul has found that Deut 30.12-14 could no longer be taken to speak in
terms of the principle of the law. This principle expressed by Lev 18.5 (v. 5)
Paul regarded as abolished because of the Christ-event. However, in a
corresponding manner as Philo, Paul probably still continued to see Deut 30.14
as a token of a kind of rule of eschatological inauguration (cf. the conditional
form in v. 9), when approached in the light of the Christ-event. The deeds
element of the law was terminated by Christ, though not the requirement
expressed by Deut 30.14 that men both should and could be obedient to God
by mouth and heart. In light of the Christ-event, Paul further qualified the
eschatological principle of Deut 30.14 to refer to the "word of faith", i.e. the
gospel, of which he and other Christians were spokesmen (v. 8). Accordingly,
participation in the eschatological salvation was conditioned by obedience to
the gospel by mouth and heart, which Paul expounded to mean to confess the

lordship of Christ and to believe in Christ's resurrection (vv. 9-10). In this way the gospel was proclaimed on a scriptural basis as an entrance requirement for admission to the eschatological salvation (cf. Rom 10.8-10, 15). In short, Paul's use of Deut 30.12-14 within the context of Rom 10.1-10 is at the center of his attempt to broaden the significance of the law from what he perceived to be a too narrowly defined understanding. Thus, the eschatological effect of the Christ-event meant for Paul also a redrawing of the boundaries between the people of God and other peoples. The membership of the people of God was still defined by righteousness, but no longer understood as Jewish national righteousness(what he calls "their own righteousness" in Rom 10.3), but a righteousness from faith in Christ, which is the obedience the law now calls for. It corresponds with this that Paul declares that there is no distinction between Jew and Greek in Rom 10.12.

According to Philo, the eschatological restoration of the Jewish nation would include their victory over the nations by the "Messiah" as world emperor. Also this perspective has parallels in Romans 10. We can presuppose with some confidence that Paul assumed that the eschatological age had been inaugurated by the resurrection of Christ. The appearance of Jesus as Kyrios meant that the "Hebrew world emperor" had come who would complete the blessing of Israel and the "conquest" of the nations. Now the eschatological time had come when these events were to take place. As the apostle of Christ to both Jews and the nations (Rom 1.5; 10.15; 11.13ff.), Paul regarded himself as sent to announce the gospel and its promise of salvation to both the Jews and all the nations. At the time Paul wrote the letter to the Romans he presupposed that the eschatological goods of salvation had been offered through the gospel to Israel (cf. Rom 10.16, 18). Accordingly, they have had the possibility to respond positively to the gospel, and thus to get a share in salvation. Instead Paul had been witness to the fact that the overwhelming majority of Israel, despite its advantages, had proven to be disobedient to the gospel and therefore closed to salvation (vv. 16, 21), while the Gentiles representing all the nations had proved to be faithful and so open for the salvation (vv. 19-20). This fact must have been a theological problem and at least a paradox for both Paul and many of his readers. In Romans 9-11 Paul addressed the problem. In that case Rom 10.1-21 and his interpretation of Deut 30.12-14 served as an explanation of the factors which caused the problem.

Concluding Remarks

This conference has concentrated among other topics on the following themes: 1. Eschatological expectations in the Jewish Diaspora and in the New Testament; 2. Philo and the New Testament; 3. The interpretation of the Old Testament in the Jewish Diaspora and in the New Testament. In this article we have focused on a topic which combines these three themes. The purpose of the essay has been to establish a Jewish referential background against which it can be demonstrated that Paul's christological interpretation of Deut 30.12-14 in Romans 10 falls within the context of Jewish exegetical techniques, forms and eschatological application.

Paul and Hellenistic Judaism in Corinth

Niels Hyldahl

Our task will be to concentrate, not upon the social and philosophical conditions prevailing among the Christians in Corinth, but upon the way in which Paul treats these conditions. By doing so, we may hope to discover important structures in Paul's complicated relations with Hellenism.

Before doing this it should, however, be brought to mind that Paul already lived in the Hellenistic world. As a Jew, he had long ago experienced the Hellenistic influence upon Judaism, both in Palestine and in the diaspora. The Palestinian Jews had come to know Hellenism as early as the beginning of the second century BC, under Seleucid rule, and even when certain limits were fixed for Jewish acculturation into and assimilation with the non-Jewish world, the Jewish people was nonetheless open to both Greek language and Greek literature.[1] Paul did not, therefore, enter a totally new world when, as an apostle for the Gentiles, he came to Asia Minor, to Macedonia and to Greece, and he did not turn into a Hellenistic writer when or because he, in his letters, made use of Greek language and Greek rhetorics. He was already a Hellenistic Jew even before he became an apostle.

It should also be noticed beforehand how fascinating the literary genre of Greek and Latin letter-writing is.[2] The interesting aspect here is not the usually adopted definition of a letter as one half of a dialogue, the other half of which has to be reconstructed by the modern reader who does not know in advance the circumstances of the correspondence. Rather, what is of interest is the mostly unrecognized fact that the letter itself is one event in a whole series of many events which the story of the letter is about.[3] After the writing, the dispatch and the reception of a letter, the world is no longer the same as it was

---

1. Cf. Niels Hyldahl, "The Maccabean Rebellion and the Question of 'Hellenization'," *Religion and Religious Practice in the Seleucid Kingdom* (Studies in Hellenistic Civilization 1, ed. Per Bilde/Troels Engberg-Pedersen/Lise Hannestad/Jan Zahle; Århus 1991) 188-203.
2. Cf. Norman R. Petersen, *Rediscovering Paul: Philemon and the Sociology of Paul's Narrative World* (Philadelphia, 1985) 53-65: 'On the Sociology of Letters'; Abraham J. Malherbe, *Paul and the Thessalonians: The Philosophic Traditions of Pastoral Care* (Philadelphia, 1987) 68-78: 'Paul's Pastoral Letter'; idem, *Ancient Epistolary Theorists* (Society of Biblical Literature Sources for Biblical Study 19; Atlanta, 1988).
3. See Petersen, *Rediscovering Paul*, passim; Niels Hyldahl, *Die paulinische Chronologie* (Acta Theologica Danica XIX; Leiden, 1986), passim; Malherbe, *Paul and the Thessalonians*, 61-67: 'Nurturing the Community'.

before. To comprehend the letter as an event taking its own place in a sequence of events covered by the letter itself is the important thing. A visit is postponed, or the plan of a visit is abandoned, and a letter is written as a — perhaps only preliminary — substitution. The postponement, or the abandonment, of a visit as well as a letter written instead of the visit are in themselves events. What a loss it would have been had Paul not postponed his visit to Corinth!

1 Corinthians as a Written Solution of the Crisis

The first observation to be made is the fact that, in spite of his promise of a visit (1 Cor 4.18-21), Paul refrains from turning up personally to meet the Corinthian crisis face to face. On the contrary, he writes a letter, 1 Corinthians, in which he attempts to solve the problems from a distance, with the disadvantage of not knowing whether he will be successful or not; this he will only know when Titus returns from his visit and joins him in Macedonia (cf. 2 Cor 2.13; 7.6-7, 13-15).

Paul's not-coming in person to Corinth entails yet another disadvantage: that he exposes himself as being in desperate need of personal authority and power and, at least for the time being, must admit his own weakness to his church in Corinth (cf. 1 Cor 4.10; 2 Cor 11.21, 30; 12.5, 9-10) relating to the Corinthian situation. He who, as the founder of the Corinthian church, was its superordinate has, by writing instead of coming, against his will declared himself a subordinate to the Corinthian Christians. He has become a spectacle to all (1 Cor 4.9), and he knows it. How is he to gain authority and power again?

Form and primary contents of 1 Corinthians

It is hardly accidental that where Paul, in 1 Corinthians, first mentions his promise and his original plan of visiting Corinth, 1 Cor 4.18-21, is also where he is on the very point of revealing or disclosing that he is going to alter the plan and that he will not come at once: "As if I am not coming to you some have blown themselves out; but I shall come speedily to you ..." (4.18-19).[4] When he wrote these words, indeed, when he wrote the letter as such, Paul had already altered his travel plans. But because he must keep his readers and/or listeners in suspense until he has finished writing, the virtual alteration of his travel plan is only announced at the end of the letter (16.5-9).

This means that Paul's reference to his promise of a visit — a promise that

---

4. I have elsewhere drawn attention to the fact that 1 Cor 4.19 is chronologically identical with Phil 2.24 and relates to one and the same travel plan — there as a promise, here as a threat: Hyldahl, *Chronologie*, 43, n. 27.

turns out to be a threat[5] — and to his original travel plan in 1 Cor 4.18-21 occur at a very crucial point in the letter as a whole: at the end of the first part of the letter (1.10-4.21) and at the transition (5.1-6.20) to that part of the letter where he starts answering the questions contained in the letter from the Corinthians (7.1). Everything else in the letter apart from the first four chapters Paul might more or less easily have told the Corinthians orally (cf. perhaps already 5.3-4: "absent in body, but present in spirit, ... when you and my spirit have come together"). The contents of chapters 1-4 he could only commit to writing, and it would not be fair to say that this part of the letter contains what Paul would have said had he been present; it is not a substitute for his presence, but for his absence. In other words: 1 Cor 4.18-21 marks the end of that part of the letter that contains the reason why he refrained from coming and chose to write instead. The reason is evidently the divisions within, or rather: the division of, the Corinthian church.

The form of this part of the letter corresponds perfectly to its contents: "But I admonish you, brethren, through the name of our Lord, Jesus Christ, ..." (1.10; cf. the almost identical words in 2 Cor 10.1), which means that 1 Corinthians, or at least its first part, takes the form of a severe παρακαλῶ-letter — otherwise it would be difficult to find a proper name for it, as it is at any rate not a friendly letter, of the φιλικὸς τύπος.

There is no other letter in the *corpus Paulinum* similar in form to 1 Corinthians. It starts with admonitions and ends with announcing a postponement of a visit. There is nothing in 1 Corinthians to indicate the existence of a preconceived plan of writing that might point to a dual arrangement of *a*) theology, instruction or theory first and *b*) *parainesis*, exhortation or practice next, such as may be found e.g. in Romans (Romans 1-8 or 11 and 12-15) or in Greek popular philosophy. On the contrary, Paul's strategy in writing 1 Corinthians is a strategy of desperation. The Corinthian crisis was, as it seems, far more serious than the Galatian crisis — at least he intended to visit the Galatian churches, though he did not succeed in doing so.[6] The Corinthian church he did not dare to visit until its members had submitted to his will, and it took him two whole letters, 1 and 2 Corinthians, to make them do so.

Form and contents of 2 Corinthians

Just as 1 Corinthians begins with a severe admonition, so 2 Corinthians ends in the same manner. And in exactly the same way as 1 Cor 1.10-4.21 was not written as a substitute for Paul's failing presence, but as a substitute for his intentional absence, so 2 Cor 10.1-13.13 is also written as a substitute for his

5. Cf. n. 4, above.
6. Cf. Hyldahl, *Chronologie*, 64-75: 'Paulus und die Galater'.

consciously intended absence. This is evident from his words at the end of the letter: "I write this in absence in order not to be forced, when I am present, to use severity according to the authority which the Lord has given me for edification, not for demolition" (2 Cor 13.10; cf. 10.8). Paul could hardly have expressed himself more clearly! He just does not dare to appear in Corinth without being sure that he will not have to expel a substantial number of members from the community, thereby running the risk of declaring the Corinthian church to be no longer existent. For what would he gain by that? On the contrary, he would have lost almost everything. He therefore makes every possible effort to submit the Corinthians to his will before he himself arrives. Perhaps he hopes that Titus, who also in this case carries the letter to Greece, can effect that quantity of reconciliation which Paul seems unable to establish.[7] At any rate, Titus and his two travelling companions (2 Cor 8.18, 22; 9.3) may be imagined to have worked as buffers between Paul's letter and the church in Corinth.

The primary contents of 2 Corinthians are, as their literary form has demonstrated, to be found in 2 Cor 10.1-13.13. These last four chapters are therefore also that part of the letter which caused the letter as a whole to be written, and which could not have been told face to face, but had to be committed to writing. That this is in fact the important result of the analysis is strongly corroborated by the other parts of 2 Corinthians. The whole of 2 Corinthians 1-7 is "only" a prelude or introduction and does not in itself constitute a letter.[8] And even with the inclusion of 2 Corinthians 8-9 no proper

---

7. Cf. Petersen, *Rediscovering Paul*, 117.
8. As an analogy to 2 Corinthian 1-7 it is worth mentioning 1 Thessalonians 1-3. In both cases we are dealing with preludes or introductions to letters not yet brought to an end, and in both cases the preludes take up more than half of the letter. Only after the conclusions of the preludes come those parts of the letters containing the decisive contents — in 1 Thessalonians chapters 4-5, in 2 Corinthians chapters 10-13. Besides, in both cases Paul, in these preludes, draws the historical line from the very foundation of the community through the moment of writing. Finally, in both cases Paul has, on his own behalf, sent one of his fellow workers who returns with good news — in 1 Thessalonians: Timothy (1 Thess 3.1-5, 6-10), in 2 Corinthians: Titus (2 Cor 7.6-7; 8.6); cf. esp. 1 Thess 3.6 and 2 Cor 7.7. An indication of the correctness of this analysis of 1 Thessalonians may be found in Paul's use of the triad 'faith — love — hope' in 1 Thess 1.3 (cf. Col 1.4-5), disrupted in 3.6: 'faith — love' (cf. 3.10: "the insufficiencies of your faith"), and in 4.13: bereft of 'hope', but reestablished in 5:8: 'faith — love — hope'; cf. Niels Hyldahl, "Auferstehung Christi — Auferstehung der Toten (1 Thess. 4.13-18)," *Die Paulinische Literatur und Theologie. Anlässlich der 50.jährigen Gründungs-Feier der Universität von Aarhus* (Teologiske Studier 7, ed. Sigfred Pedersen; Göttingen, 1980) 119-35, esp. 123; the occurrence of this triad in 1 Thess 1.3 and 5.8 has not been fully recognized by Malherbe, *Paul and the Thessalonians*, who writes (73): "faith, hope, and love ([1 Thess] 1.3)" — but this is the sequence of 1 Cor 13.13. As to *Teilungshypothesen* relative to 2 Corinthians I refer

letter has as yet been either formed or finished, since it is evident that a letter cannot possibly end with these two chapters about the collection for Jerusalem, least of all when chapters 1-7 are prefixed as their prelude. Only with chapters 10-13 does the letter come to its conclusion.

Interim Conclusions

In their totality 1 and 2 Corinthians constitute a literary unit. 1 Corinthians 1-4 and 2 Corinthians 10-13 contain the words that could not possibly have been expressed face to face, but could only be written in letters. These parts of the two letters, the beginning of the first and the end of the second, correspond to each other in regard to form, contents and literary strategy. These observations strongly urge the exegete to reconsider the more usual views on Paul's Corinthian correspondence and to think anew in a way different from the traditional historical-critical exegesis. Even the literary, rhetorical and sociological aspects should be taken more seriously — and more precisely — than has been done in earlier studies.

The Social Conditions

What is most at stake in Paul's Corinthian letters is his own status within the Corinthian church.[9] He just cannot cope with the social conditions prevailing among the Christians in Corinth. But of what nature exactly were these social conditions?

Since Gerd Theissen's sociological studies were published in the years after 1974, the sociology of the Corinthian church has often been looked upon as indicating the existence of a conflict between rich and poor, between socially weak and socially strong persons.[10] Paul's statement in 1 Cor 1.26 that there were not many wise, powerful and noble among the Corinthian Christians was understood very literally, in the sense that the wise, powerful and noble were

to Hyldahl, *Chronologie*, 88-102: 'Die Reisen des Titus nach Korinth'.
9. Cf. Petersen, *Rediscovering Paul* 142.
10. Gerd Theissen, *Studien zur Soziologie des Urchristentums* (WUNT 19, 2. erweiterte Aufl.: Tübingen, 1983), cf. Theissen, *The Social Setting of Pauline Christianity: Essays on Corinth* (ed. and trans. John H. Schütz: Philadelphia, 1982); idem, *Sociology of Early Palestinian Christianity* (trans. J. Bowden: Philadelphia, 1978). I refer especially to the following *Studien* or *Essays*: 'Legitimation und Lebensunterhalt: ein Beitrag zur Soziologie urchristlicher Missionare' (1975, 201-30), 'Soziale Schichtung in der korinthischen Gemeinde. Ein Beitrag zur Soziologie des hellenistischen Urchristentums' (1974, 231-71), and 'Die Starken und Schwachen in Korinth. Soziologische Analyse eines theologischen Streites' (1975, 272-89), all of which are translated by Schütz into English in: Theissen, *The Social Setting of Pauline Christianity*.

indeed only few in number, but the fact that they were mentioned indicated, on the other hand, their actual presence, importance and influence. In what seems to be at odds with the whole church in Corinth, Paul points to their prudence, power and respectability (1 Cor 4.9-13); but a closer view reveals that these characteristics are almost exactly the same as were spoken of earlier in the letter: wisdom, power and nobility (1.26). Paul is, therefore, not addressing the whole church, but only the wise, powerful and noble who are also those responsible for the division of the Corinthian church.[11]

In other words: Paul's underlining of the Christians' low social standing was taken to mean the almost opposite of what was clearly intended and to prove that there were in fact quite a few rich and influential Christians in Corinth.[12] One of these was, according to Theissen, the *quaestor*, and later *aedile*, Erastus who is known inscriptionally as living in Corinth; Theißen identifies him with the Corinthian Erastus of Romans 16.23.[13] The conflict between the weak (cf. 1 Cor 8.7, 9, 11, 12; 9.22) and the strong (1.26; 4.10) was considered as a social conflict between poor and rich.[14] Only the rich people were owners of houses where the believers might gather (11.22), and only the rich members of the congregation allowed themselves to eat the flesh offered to idols (8.9-12). The whole conflict was caused by the existing social stratification inside the Corinthian church.

It is, of course, not to be denied that at the time of Paul's writing 1 (and 2) Corinthians a serious conflict with apparently social implications was taking place in the Corinthian church, and that the delicate question of money was involved, both in the collection for Jerusalem and in the financial support for Paul — though he refused to receive it — and for the super-apostles.

There are, however, at least four sets of problems not touched upon nor solved through Gerd Theissen's admirable pioneer studies.[15] *1)* Theissen does

---

11. Cf. Theissen, *Studien zur Soziologie* 228: "In der Parteienfrage sind die wenigen 'Weisen, Einflußreichen und Hochangesehenen' (i. 26) die Adressaten des Paulus. Und wenn er in I Cor. iv. 9-13 seine eigene Situation mit der der Korinther kontrastiert — genauer mit derjenigen der 'klugen', der 'starken' und 'angesehenen' Korinther (iv. 10) — so führt er wohl nicht zufällig auch seine Handwerksarbeit auf, als gebe es unter den angeredeten Korinthern Christen, die sich nicht mit eigenen Händen ihren Lebensunterhalt verdienen mußten. Wie aus dem Kontext (I Cor. iii. 18 — iv. 9) hervorgeht, sind die für die Parteibildungen Verantwortlichen angeredet."

12. Theissen, *Studien zur Soziologie* 234: "Wenn Paulus nun sagt, es gebe nicht viele Weise, Einflußreiche und Vornehme in der korinthischen Gemeinde, so steht ja eins fest: daß es einige gegeben hat." Cf. Dieter Säger, "Die *dynatoí* in 1 Kor 1,26," *ZNW* 76 (1985) 285-91: the 'powerful' as the rich people.

13. Theissen, *Studien zur Soziologie* 236-45.

14. Cf. Theissen, *Studien zur Soziologie* 272-89.

15. Cf. also T. Engberg-Pedersen, "The Gospel and Social Practice according to 1 Corinthians," *NTS* 33 (1987) 557-84, esp. 559-60 about Theissen.

not account for the fact that Paul, in contrast to the Corinthians, calls himself weak (1 Cor 4.10; cf. 2.3) — Paul is here not contrasting a weak wing in Corinth with a strong one, but himself as a weak person with the Corinthians as strong persons (cf. also 2 Cor 11.21). 2) Theissen does not explain the fact that the Corinthians had become divided or how this had come about (1 Cor 1.10-4.21) — it should be obvious, however, that the division did not exist when Paul, with Silvanus and Timothy as his fellow workers (2 Cor 1.19), founded the Corinthian church and left the city; the division had only arisen afterwards; it had not been a constitutive factor from the beginning. 3) Theissen's description of the conflict as a socio-economic clash between rich and poor does not correspond very well with the facts about Stephanas. Stephanas and his house (1 Cor 1.16; 16.15-18) evidently belonged to the influential and relatively prosperous wing of the church — but Stephanas was, as expressly stated by Paul (16.15; cf. Rom 16.5 about Epaenetus), the person who had first become a Christian in Greece and had been baptized by Paul personally; he cannot, therefore, have been responsible for the division in Corinth, and the existence of "poor" and "rich" must have been apparent already at the foundation of the Corinthian church. 4) Theissen gives no convincing explanation of Paul's remarkable use of the important concept 'riches' ($\pi\lambda o\hat{u}\tau o\varsigma$: 1 Cor 1.5; 4.8) — though obviously, it is not only a question of material or economic wealth, but also of spiritual richness; it is, therefore, highly questionable whether the strong and powerful persons in Corinth, responsible for the division, were in fact also wealthy or even rich.

I suggest that the Corinthian church founded by Paul did not yet suffer from the effects of division. These only turned up later. Paul planted, he laid the foundation stone (1 Cor 3.6, 10). His converts were for the greater part less important people, including slaves and their masters, won from the workshop, but also more influential persons, e.g. Stephanas, Gaius (cf. Rom 16.23), Crispus and Sosthenes, were converted by Paul to the new faith.[16] No serious social difficulties arose in Paul's own time in Corinth. But in his absence, after he had left, Apollos and his fellow workers arrived, and their mission in Corinth had a rather amazing effect in the form of numerous new converts who did not live up in every respect to the expectations Paul — and rightly so — would have of Christians.[17] The new Christians won by Apollos had, for instance, quite non-Pauline ideas about marriage, divorce and sexual behaviour, about intercourse with gentiles, and about congregational gatherings, including the

16. Cf. Malherbe, *Paul and the Thessalonians'* 17-20: 'Paul in the Workshop', giving an impressive picture of Paul's missionary strategy in Thessalonica and Corinth.
17. This is probably the reason why Paul, in 1 Cor 1.14-17, seems to diminish the significance of baptism; but see also Petersen's excellent comments, *Rediscovering Paul*, 120-22.

Lord's Supper. First and foremost, they did not know Paul whom they had never seen or met, and, therefore, they did not acknowledge him as their apostle — which from their point of view was perfectly understandable.[18]

In this way a social, but not necessarily a socio-economic chasm arose between Paul's people and Apollos' people, and as the latter were in all probability the more numerous group, Paul had to keep away until he, through his letters, had regained control and authority, or had gained control and authority also over the Apollos wing of the Corinthian church.

But who were Apollos and his fellow workers?

The Philosophical Conditions

A certain distance seems to have existed between Paul and Apollos.[19] Paul had probably only met Apollos once or twice, and Apollos had plainly refused to comply with Paul's appeal that he, in company with the brethren (1 Cor 16.12), visit the Corinthians. The fact, as it seems to be, that Paul and Apollos never worked together in Corinth and that Paul did not send Apollos, is also important; Apollos had worked in Corinth without the consent of Paul, and he arrived at a time when Paul and his fellow workers had already left the new community. "I planted, Apollos watered," as Paul writes (3.6), also describes the chronological sequence of Paul's and Apollos' activities in Corinth.[20]

Quite a few scholars have long ago recognized that Paul's opponents in 1 Corinthians 1-4 were the Corinthian adherents of Apollos. Especially clear in

---

18. Cf. Petersen, *Rediscovering Paul*, 115: "Paul's role as the initiator of action is evident, even in the interesting case of Apollos, who may well be the exception which illustrates the rule. For despite Paul's questioning of this fellow worker's work in 1 Corinthians 1-4, Apollos apparently enjoyed a sufficient independence from Paul to decline his appeal (*parakalo*) that he visit Corinth (1 Cor 16.12). If so, Paul's authority may not have been acknowledged by Apollos, and Paul's identification of him as a fellow worker in 3.5-23 may reflect Paul's attempt to get the Corinthians to view Apollos as *his* subordinate."

19. Apollos did not go to Corinth alone, he had adherents travelling with him. It is remarkable that only Sosthenes, not Apollos, is the co-author of 1 Corinthians and that there is no greeting from Apollos to the Corinthians, which indicates some personal distance between Paul and Apollos at the time of writing the letter. Later, in 2 Corinthians, Apollos is no longer mentioned by name; it is not plausible that he was one of the two unknown brethren accompanying Titus on his second visit to Corinth. On his first visit Titus, who brought 1 Corinthians (= the Letter of Tears) to Corinth, was not accompanied by Apollos either (1 Cor 16.12); Apollos is therefore not to be identified with the one unknown brother mentioned in 2 Cor 12.18.

20. Cf. John Coolidge Hurd, *The Origin of 1 Corinthians* (London, 1965 [Reprinted with Corrections and a New Preface; Macon, 1983]) 98.

this respect are the studies of Gerhard Sellin and Simone Pétrement.[21] They have convincingly shown that the entire text 1 Cor 3.1-23 is directed against the influence of Apollos, not, as some have suggested, against Cephas.[22] Nothing indicates that Paul should have changed the address of his words completely when he warns against those who build upon the foundation stone laid by Paul himself. This is of fundamental importance since the text of 3.1-23 is inextricably connected with the foregoing material and, in this way, secures the inner coherence of the central parts of 1 Corinthians 1-4.

Perhaps more important still is the observation that it is Apollos and his fellow workers Paul refers to in 2 Corinthians 10-13 when he, in his sarcastic way, mentions the 'super-apostles' (2 Cor 11.5; 12.11) or — what is the same — the 'pseudo-apostles' (11.13).[23] Clearly, these have nothing to do with Jerusalem or with the Judaizing movement known from Galatians; the super-apostles are not the Jerusalem apostles, and the pseudo-apostles not their emissaries. On the contrary, the rival apostles in Corinth are of the Hellenistic type. They are also called 'servants of Satan' (2 Cor 11.15), and they are, in

---

21. Gerhard Sellin, "Das 'Geheimnis' der Weisheit und das Rätsel der 'Christuspartei' (zu 1 Kor 1-4)," *ZNW* 73 (1982) 69-96; idem, *Der Streit um die Auferstehung der Toten. Eine religionsgeschichtliche und exegetische Untersuchung von 1. Korinther 15* (FRLANT 138; Göttingen, 1986); idem, "Hauptprobleme des Ersten Korintherbriefes," *ANRW* II/25.4 (Berlin, 1987) 2940-3044; Simone Pétrement, *Le Dieu séparé. Les origines du gnosticisme* (Paris, 1984 [= *A Separate God: The Christian Origins of Gnosticism*; London, 1991]) 343-63: 'Les "gnostiques" de Corinthe' (here also 358-63: 'Sur quelques interprétations récentes') and 365-71: 'Les sources possibles de l'enseignement d'Apollos'. Cf. also Hyldahl, "Den korintiske krise — en skitse [The Corinthian crisis — a sketch]," *DTT* 40 (1977) 18-30; idem, "The Corinthian 'Parties' and the Corinthian Crisis," *ST* 45 (1991) 19-32, for exegetical details; idem, "Paul and Apollos: Exegetical Observations to *1 Cor.* 3,1-23," *Apocryphon Severini presented to Søren Giversen* (ed. Per Bilde/Helge Kjær Nielsen/Jørgen Podemann Sørensen; Aarhus, 1993) 68-82.
22. E.g., Philipp Vielhauer, "Paulus und die Kephaspartei in Korinth," *NTS* 21 (1974-75) 341-52 (= Vielhauer, *Oikodome. Aufsätze zum Neuen Testament* 2, ed. G. Klein, Theologische Bücherei 65; München, 1979 169-82), esp. 347-48. But cf. already my remarks, *DTT* 40 (1977) 23-24; also Petersen, quoted n. 18, above. I am sorry not to be able to find any other place than here for mentioning Michael D. Goulder, "*Sofía* in 1 Corinthians," *NTS* 37 (1991) 516-34; Goulder regrets that there has, to his knowledge, been no 'Tübingen' view of 1 Corinthians since Wilhelm Lütgert's exposition of its weaknesses in 1908, but he is evidently not aware of Vielhauer's 'Tübingen' thesis. Cf. M.D. Goulder, *A Table of Two Missions* (London, 1994).
23. Cf. Pétrement, *Le Dieu séparé*, 343-63: 'Les "gnostiques" de Corinthe'; Hyldahl, *ST* 45 (1991) 27-29. Petersen, Rediscovering Paul, 122-25, has correctly pointed out that, according to 1 Corinthians, Paul is the only person called apostle to the Corinthians. The fact that rival apostles had been operating before the time of Paul's writing 2 Corinthians may, therefore, be understood as indicating that Apollos and his fellow workers actually did apply the title to themselves.

addition, apparently also called 'servants of Christ' (11.23) — a characterization which seems to be contradictory when compared to the one indicating them as 'servants of Satan'. This has, as is well known, caused much exegetical trouble. The solution to this difficulty seems to be that Paul, in 2 Cor 11.22-23, bluntly denies that these 'apostles' and 'servants' are Christians at all. To the last of Paul's four — not three — rhetorical questions in 11.22-23: "Are they servants of Christ?" he answers differently from what he does to the three other questions: "I am even more".[24] But this answer does in fact mean: 'No, they are not servants of Christ, but I am.' Here Paul exceeds them, and the Corinthian Christians have in Paul's person more than they would ever find in these foreign "apostles".

It is consequently clear that both in 1 Corinthians 1-4 and in 2 Corinthians 10-13 Paul has Apollos and his fellow workers and their adherents in Corinth in mind. The importance of this observation is to be seen in the inference that Apollos and the other rival apostles are 1) of Jewish Hellenistic origin 2) 2 Cor 11.22: Hebrews, Israelites, seed of Abraham) and 3) representatives of a philosophical kind of σοφία-ideology (1 Cor 1.17-3.23).

One of the persuasive characteristics of the philosophy which Apollos brought to Corinth was its rhetorical form and style. In apparent contrast to Paul, Apollos made use of adorned speech, λόγος, as an instrument to win his hearers (1 Cor 1.5, 17; 2.1, 4, 13; 4.19-20; 2 Cor 10.10-11; 11.6).[25] This in itself should not be condemned as a morally bad thing. Everybody who appeared publicly, with the possible exception of Paul, performed rhetorical speeches, and was expected to do so; and perhaps Paul in 1 Corinthians, in his indirectly expressed condemnation of the eloquence of Apollos, set a fashion that spread among Christian writers — at any rate, Justin makes a virtue of Jesus' and the apostles' lack of eloquence (*Apol.* 14.5 — actually almost a paraphrase of 1 Cor 1.18-25!). Or, to quote Abraham J. Malherbe in order to understand the method made use of by Apollos — and by Paul himself:

---

24. There seems to be a consciously intended play on words between the expressions 'I am even more' and 'super-apostles' — which means that Paul, in contrast to the false ones, is a *true* 'super-apostle'. References should also be made to Josef Zmijewski, *Der Stil der paulinischen "Narrenrede". Analyse der Sprachgestaltung in 2 Kor 11,1-12,10 als Beitrag zur Methodik von Stiluntersuchungen neutestamentlicher Texte* (BBB 52; Köln, 1978) 236-43, and to Karl-Wilhelm Niebuhr, *Heidenapostel aus Israel. Die jüdische Identität des Paulus nach ihrer Darstellung in seinen Briefen* (WUNT 62; Tübingen, 1992) 127-33, who both maintain that Paul claims exclusive superiority over the rival apostles in their assumed status as "servants of Christ". But even Zmijewski and Niebuhr have, in my view, underestimated the significance of the dramatic shift in tone and content in 2 Cor 11.23a.

25. Cf. Acts 18.24. I would, however, here and in the following warn against drawing too heavily on the evidence of Acts; cf. *ST* 45 (1991) 32, n. 31.

The preferred way of instructing was through speech. Writers like Seneca regarded letters as the next best. Philosophers liked to emphasize that they were different from orators, whom they accused of playing to their audiences, yet even in their letters they frequently commented on the appropriate rhetorical style of the philosopher and criticized those whose eloquence had become an end in itself (cf. 1 Cor 2.1-5). With a possible few exceptions (e.g., Hebrews; 1 John; 2 *Clement*), the early Christian writings that have been preserved were not originally speeches. Nevertheless, that they were dictated (cf. Rom 16.22) and intended to be read aloud to congregations (cf. 1 Thess 5.27; Rev 1.3), thus functioning like speeches or sermons, meant that the writers were conscious of oral style.[26]

As to the contents of Apollos' philosophy we have almost only the hints found in 1 Corinthians 1-4. A dominant feature was presumably γνῶσις (1 Cor 1.5, 21; 2.8, 11, 14; cf. 8.1, 2, 3, 7, 11; 12.8; 13.2, 8, 12; 2 Cor 11.6), and it seems that Apollos was proud of calling his philosophy 'wisdom', σοφία (1 Cor 1.17, 20, 21, 22; 2.1, 4, 5, 6, 7, 13; 3.18, 19, 20). According to this wisdom, human beings were pneumatic, psychic or sarcic (2.10-16; 3.1-3), a distinction that relates to ontological differences between individuals: some were pneumatic, others were psychic, and others again were only sarcic. The sarcic ones were definitely lost and could never hope to acquire γνῶσις and, through that, perfection and immortality; the πνεῦμα-possessing already were gnostic, and the psychic might possibly become pneumatic, or they would sink for ever into the status of the sarcic. The πνεῦμα-possessing gnostic was, in all probability, convinced of being immortal and of being morally and cognitively perfect, τέλειος (1 Cor 2.6-7; cf. 13.10, 12).

These features are admittedly few, and they do not allow the exegete to determine, with any reasonable certainty, the details of the philosophy of Apollos. However, they do make it clear enough that his philosophy was most likely akin to the philosophy of Philo of Alexandria.[27]

It is worth noting that the recognizable traits of Apollos' philosophy, however scanty they may be, do not in the least betray whether he was a Christian or not. Even if Paul calls him brother (1 Cor 16.12) he was probably not baptized, but knew only the baptism of John the Baptist (cf. Acts 18.25). That he was versed in the Scriptures (cf. Acts 18.24), i.e., the Greek Septuagint, does not make him a Christian; rather, it would explain why Paul is forced — predominantly in 2 Cor 3.4-18, in his sweeping midrash on Exodus 34 — to engage in a counter-attack against those who, like Apollos and his followers,

---

26. Malherbe, *Moral Exhortation, A Greco-Roman Sourcebook* (Library of Early Christianity 4; Philadelphia, 1986) 68.
27. Cf. Pétrement, *Le Dieu séparé*, 343-63; Sellin, *Der Streit um die Auferstehung*, 95-171: 'Anthropologie, Ontologie und Soteriologie Philos' — a complete compendium of Philo's philosophy.

believed themselves well versed in the Scriptures; it would also explain why Paul, in the end, does not consider these same people as Christians at all.

With Apollos a genuine piece of Hellenistic philosophy made its way from Alexandria (cf. Acts 18.24) to Corinth and entered successfully the scene of Paul's Christian community there. The Pauline church in Corinth was not prepared to accept, or to reject, this foreign thinking. Had it been prepared to handle the problems which arose from the new ideology it would probably not have been so overwhelmed by it as it evidently was.

The question therefore arises: How would Paul react to this unforeseen situation?

Paul's Reaction to Apollos' Philosophy

It is clear that the gospel which Paul had preached in Corinth was not a philosophy or philosophical system. This statement is not a conclusion reached on the basis of what Paul himself writes in 1 Cor 2.1-5, since these words are adjusted to the situation in which he writes the letter. On the contrary, it follows from the whole story of 1 and 2 Corinthians. On the other hand it is explicitly said by Paul in 1 Cor 1.18-25 that the gospel is not a philosophy: contrary to the wisdom of this world the gospel is foolishness to this world, and only to the truly "perfect" does it reveal itself also as wisdom (2.6-16).

There can hardly be any serious doubt that Paul's argumentation in 1 Cor 1.18-3.23 is formed as an indirect refutation of Apollos' wisdom. Certainly, the most urgent task is, as Troels Engberg-Pedersen says, to try to follow the train of thought in the text as it stands.[28] But if 'as it stands' means that Paul's narrative world, which the text itself is part of, is disregarded or ignored, then Paul's train of thought is not followed; at any rate no attempt is made at following it as the Corinthian readers were able to do. The text is not a philosophical essay on the relation between theory and practice, put down in writing independently of the concrete circumstances, but a desperate refutation of Apollos' Corinthian influence.

It follows that there is no sharp break in 1 Cor 2.6 where Paul, in contrast to his preceding words about the gospel as foolishness, admits that there is in fact a wisdom that belongs to the perfect. Paul has not moved from faith to understanding: from *faith* as the only possible 'positive' reaction to the word of the cross (1.18-2.6) to an *understanding* of its meaning in the form of a specific Christian wisdom (2.6-16), an understanding which is made into the theoretical basis of a social practice, as Engberg-Pedersen maintains.[29] Christian wisdom is not a thing or quantity that transcends Christian faith;

28. Engberg-Pedersen, *NTS* 33 (1987) 564.
29. Engberg-Pedersen, *NTS* 33 (1987) 565.

there is no 'surplus' in Christian wisdom compared with Christian faith.[30] Christian wisdom is, according to Paul, foolishness to those who do not have faith, i.e., to Apollos and his followers who are, therefore, not representatives of Christianity, but of Hellenistic philosophy.

The 'break' in 1 Cor 2.6 does not indicate a move in Paul's thought from pure faith to rational understanding, but must be understood as provoked by the 'wisdom' of Apollos. The word of the cross *is* foolishness to the world. But at the same time it is also, as the wisdom of God (1.18-25), the only true philosophy — by far surpassing Apollos' so-called "philosophy". If that is a "break", it is a break with traditional Hellenistic moral philosophy, not with Paul's own logical thinking. But Paul was hardly aware that he, when proclaiming this polemical thought, became the source of an important current in Christian thinking and theology; Christianity as the only true philosophy, only revealed to the true philosopher, is a structure unmistakeably underlying, e.g., the philosopher's cloak which Justin wore in his capacity as a Christian philosopher (*Dial.* 1.1-2; 8.1-2) and the scholastic idea of philosophy as being only the *ancilla theologiae*.

What Paul *was* aware of was that he, temporarily subordinated to Apollos' impressive wisdom as he was, would have to subordinate this very wisdom to the gospel he preached. There is, however, more to it than just this formalistic subordination of philosophy to Christianity. Paul's reaction to Apollos was also a genuine *Zurückweisung* of the contents of his philosophical thinking, and there are two aspects: sociology and anthropology.

As we have seen, Apollos distinguished between three kinds of human beings, the pneumatic, the psychic and the sarcic. Paul declares this distinction null and void — or, to put it in Paul's own words coloured by the terminology of Apollos: all three classes are at one and the same time declared as belonging to one class only — the sarcic (1 Cor 3.1-3)! The believer, on the other hand, is declared to be pneumatic (2.16; cf. 7.40).

This annulment of Apollos' distinction has important sociological consequences. Paul's rejection of the anthropological distinction — a distinction which clearly implied a profiled élitist sociology, including claims to super- and subordination (cf. 4.8 about the πνεῦμα-possessing as being kings) — means that Apollos and his followers will have to give up their philosophically based anthropology and submit to Paul's 'democratic' thoughts about what a Christian congregation should look like, or leave the congregation altogether.

If Paul, therefore, was compelled to think philosophically this was due to the influence of the Hellenistic philosopher Apollos of Alexandria.

---

30. Against Engberg-Pedersen, ibid.

The Catalogues of Hardships in the Pauline Correspondence: Background and Function

Niels Willert

Introduction

Once Paul was a persecutor of the Christians in Palestine and Syria. But on his way to Damascus, he was called by the Lord to be his apostle. In Acts 9.4 it is told that Paul was addressed with these words: "Saul, Saul, why are you persecuting me?" In Gal 1.13 and Phil 3.6 Paul refers to the time when he, as a pharisaic Jew, persecuted the Christians. Paul must have realized that by becoming a Christian, he would be subject to persecutions. And from the beginning, Paul was undoubtedly persecuted by his Jewish compatriots.

In this paper I will examine the testimony of Paul on his sufferings, in particular the so-called peristasis catalogues, which is the name given to the Pauline texts where Paul reports on his hardships and sufferings in such a way that literary models seem obvious. These catalogues occur in Rom 8. 35; 1 Cor 4.10-13; 2 Cor 4.8-9; 6.4-10; 11.23-33; 12.10 and Phil 4.12. Together with other texts, especially in 1 Thess, they give testimony of the importance given to the sufferings in the presentation by Paul of himself as a Christian and as an apostle.

A great research effort has been made concerning the question of cultural background of the catalogues in Graeco-Roman philosophy and in literature of Old Testament and Antique Judaism.[1] However, it is not enough to examine the catalogues in the light of their cultural background. I think that many scholars have focused too much on the question concerning cultural background instead of examining the function these catalogues have in their literary and theological context. In my opinion the texts in which Paul speaks of his hardships and sufferings, must also and not least be viewed in the light of the Christian passion tradition.

When I talk about Christian passion tradition I understand primarily the tradition behind the Passion narratives in the Gospels. The Gospels were, as it is known, written at a later date than the letters of Paul, but we may not forget

---

1. Cf. the survey of research in J.T. Fitzgerald, *Cracks in an Earthen Vessel. An Examination of the Catalogues of Hardships in the Corinthian Correspondence* (Atlanta, Georgia: Scholars Press, 1988) 7ff. Cf. also the "Nachwort" in K.T. Kleinknecht, *Der leidende Gerechtfertigte* (Tübingen: Mohr [Siebeck], 1984, reprinted 1988) 391ff.

that the Passion narrative in the Gospels constitutes the culmination of a
tradition development that may be traced back to an early passion tradition,
which pertains to the oldest cohesive legend material. The attempts to reconstruct a passion narrative before the Gospels will not be discussed here.[2]
I only presuppose that Paul possessed knowledge of a tradition of the passion
and death of Jesus. And it is my contention, that it was also important for him
to maintain this tradition. In that connection it has to be underlined that the life
on earth of Jesus together with his passion was important to Paul. He did not
only give importance to the tradition about the death and resurrection of Jesus.
One of the objects in my paper is to show how Paul reinterpreted the tradition
of the life and the passion of Jesus Christ.[3]

First we may ask: What importance did the passion of Jesus Christ have on
Paul's description of himself as a Christian and an apostle? Here, the peristasis
catalogues may hold a central place. For it is precisely in connection with these
texts that the correlation between the christology of Paul and his presentation
of himself as a Christian and an apostle appears clearly. It is in fact a question
whether the christology of Paul and his presentation of himself can be
separated in any way.

Then, the next question may be: What are the intentions of Paul when he
presents himself as one who follows the suffering Jesus Christ? And: Does Paul
defend himself against opponents who hold another opinion on being a
Christian and an apostle, or does Paul quite simply announce Jesus Christ as
the suffering precursor by whose life the Christians are to orient their own
lives? In considering relevant texts I find it most obvious, as will be shown,
that the presentation of Paul himself primarily serves a paraenetic and not a
polemic purpose. My contention is that the christology and the paraenesis are
correlated. In presenting himself Paul correlates christology and paraenesis. The
suffering Jesus Christ is made present in the person of Paul. My purpose in this
paper is not to discuss the questions, who are the opponents of Paul, or in
which way Paul's intention is apologetic. I will show instead that it is possible

---

2. See the classics of the Form and Tradition criticism by M. Dibelius and R. Bultmann:
   M. Dibelius, *Die Formgeschichte des Evangeliums* (Tübingen: Mohr [Siebeck], 1919,
   reprinted 1971) 178-218; R. Bultmann, *Die Geschichte der synoptischen Tradition*
   (Göttingen: Vandenhoeck & Ruprecht, 1921, reprinted 1970) 282-308. See also W.H.
   Kelber (ed.), *The Passion in Mark* (Philadelphia: Fortress, 1976, especially J.R.
   Donahue's article: "Introduction: From Passion Traditions to Passion Narrative" (1-
   20).
3. Therefore, the interpretation by Paul of the death and resurrection will not be
   discussed in this article. Instead I will concentrate on the suffering Jesus as a model
   to be imitated. The soteriological question has been investigated not least in the
   careful study of M.L. Gubler, *Die frühesten Deutungen des Todes Jesu. Eine
   motivgeschichtliche Darstellung aufgrund der neueren exegetischen Forschung* (Freiburg,
   1977).

to read Paul's presentation of himself as a christologically founded paraenesis.

Before we look at the texts, it will be convenient to discuss the question as to which background has been the basis of Paul's thought. Surely, Paul may have been influenced by themes both from a Graeco Roman and a Jewish tradition. But here we may ask whether it is at all possible to solve the problem of background by an either-or. As a Hellenistic diaspora Jew, Paul has been influenced both by Graeco-Roman philosophy and by Jewish religious thought. Therefore, I will begin with a critical survey of research into the peristasis catalogues. Against this background then, I shall carry on with the question of the relation of Paul to the tradition of the life and passion of Jesus Christ. Then, I shall examine some texts, especially the peristasis catalogues, in order to indicate how Paul, in presenting himself, becomes a link between christology and paraenesis. Perhaps the cultural background of the peristasis catalogues can offer part of the explanation of this interconnection between christology and paraenesis, although just a christologically founded paraenesis makes the Pauline thought original.

Survey of Research

R. Bultmann in particular is responsible for the use of the term peristasis catalogue concerning the texts of Paul on his adversities and sufferings. And it is not only the terminology but also the underlying interpretation of the catalogues. Their background is, according to Bultmann, to be found in Graeco-Roman culture.[4] Before Bultmann attention had been drawn to a stylistic connection between the Cynic-Stoic diatribe and the method of Paul consisting of parallelisms and anti-theses.[5] For Bultmann the peristasis catalogues are textual passages in which the writer recites the various sufferings imposed by fate, then boasting of being able to resist them. Like the Greek philosopher, Paul recites the adversities and sufferings to which he is subjected, just as at the same time he demonstrates his superiority above them.[6] With Bultmann the peristasis catalogues became a literary phenomenon in line with catalogues of virtues and vices.

Bultmann's work has been continued, not least by the fact that more background source material has been involved, and altogether it has been

---

4. R. Bultmann, *Der Stil der paulinischen Predigt und die kynisch-stoische Diatribe* (Göttingen:Vandenhoeck & Ruprecht, 1910), especially 17-19.
5. Especially J. Weiss, a teacher of Bultmann, may be mentioned here. See his: "Beiträge zur Paulinischen Rhetorik," in: *Theologische Studien. B. Weiss zu seinem 70. Geburtstage,* (ed. C.R. Gregory; Göttingen: Vandenhoeck & Ruprecht, 1902).
6. Bultmann refers to texts of Epictetus, Musonius Rufus, Horace and Seneca. Moreover, Bultmann made a comparison between the Greek philosopher whose condition is described by means of paradoxical antitheses, and the corresponding descriptions of Paul by himself (*Der Stil*, 19 and 71).

indicated how extensive the genre peristasis catalogue has been in the Graeco-Roman world.[7] Thus H. Windisch drew attention to relevant texts from for example Cicero, Ovid and Plutarch, but also from the Hellenistic diaspora Jew Philo of Alexandria and the Jewish apocalyptic literature.[8] This is important, for it means that Hellenistic Jewry has been included as a factor of importance. But a long time was to pass before a serious attempt to involve Jewish material was made. The tendency in the continuing research was an understanding of Paul's texts against the background of Graeco-Roman material.

Thus A. Fridrichsen in two articles from 1928-29 examined the background of 2 Cor 11.23-33.[9] He claimed that Paul consciously imitated the style from the so-called cursus honorum, for instance the inscription on the Monumentum Ancyranum, where the exploits of the emperor Augustus are listed. According to Fridrichsen, Paul has imitated these res gestae, which stated the various office functions and honorary titles of a person, as well as his exploits and virtues in service of the State. These res gestae also have oriental parallels, having the official propaganda function of combining a self-presentation and a self-praising presentation. The thesis of Fridrichsen is an example showing that focusing on specific parallels narrows the field of view and easily excludes other possible parallels. In addition, the thesis may be critizised on several points. For in fact there are more differences than similarities between the res gestae of Augustus and 2 Cor 11, for instance the res gestae contain a number of time statements for events, whereas 2 Cor 11 only mentions the Aretas episode in Damascus (2 Cor 11.32-33). But most problematic is the fact that Fridrichsen concentrates exclusively on stylistic criteria and leaves out the point of contents. Res gestae is in the first place a listing of services for the State, whereas Paul states his adversities and sufferings.[10]

The tendency was still to focus on the Graeco-Roman background, which can be seen in the studies of D. Georgi on the opponents of Paul in 2 Cor.[11] According to Georgi, the peristasis catalogues of Paul have the purpose of underlining the basic divine power. The opponents made use of recom-

7. See Fitzgerald, *Cracks*, 13f.

8. H. Windisch, *Der zweite Korintherbrief*. Meyer K. 6 (Göttingen: Vandenhoeck & Ruprecht, 1924).

9. A. Fridrichsen, "Zum Stil des paulinischen Peristasenkatalogs, 2 Cor 11," *SO* 7 (1928) 25-29; A. Fridrichsen, "Peristasenkatalog und Res gestae," *SO* 8 (1929) 78-82.

10. For good reasons the thesis of Fridrichsen has not gained ground, but he has inspired to further parallel studies, for instance those of R. Höistad, who made comparisons between the Cynical description by Dio Chrysostomus of the suffering philosopher (*Oratio* 8.15-16) and Paul's description of God's suffering servants in 2 Cor 6.3-10. See R. Höistad: "Eine hellenistische Parallelle zu 2. Kor. 6.3ff," *Con NT* 9 (1944) 20-27.

11. D. Georgi, *Die Gegner des Paulus im 2. Korintherbrief. Studien zur religiösen Propaganda der Spätantike* (Neukirchen-Vluyn:Neukirschener Verlag, 1964).

mendation letters by which they confirmed their pneumatic power and called attention to their own powerful actions as signs of that divine power. While Paul saw the divine power as being present in weakness and sufferings, the opponents saw it, on the contrary, in their powerful deeds. Ironically Paul imitates the self-presentation of the opponents. But in connection with Georgi's reconstruction of the background of 2 Cor, it is necessary to ask whether the opponents also mentioned adversities and sufferings, so that Paul legitimated himself, just by exceeding them on this point. Georgi does not think that the opponents made use of peristasis catalogues. But I think, this may very well have been the case.[12] The difference between Paul and his opponents is probably not that he suffered and they did not, but that he considered his adversities and sufferings as signs of God's power, whereas they saw that same power manifest only in "signs, miracles and mighty deeds" (2 Cor 12.12).

The study of Georgi is an example of the fact that inquiries have also been made about the function of the peristasis catalogues. This is very important. For Georgi they have a legitimating function. Another scholar, H.D. Betz, follows Georgi, when he understands the peristasis catalogues against the background of the Cynic Stoic diatribe.[13] In fact, boasting about adversities and sufferings is not unique to Paul. In Hellenistic literature the connection between peristasis catalogues and self-praise is frequent, and, according to Betz, this is very important for the understanding of Paul's self-presentation.

In his book "Cracks in an Earthen Vessel" J.T. Fitzgerald continues this line, when he also compares Paul and the Cynic-Stoic wise man.[14] It is in fact the only monography which deals exclusively with the peristasis catalogues, but it is done on a narrow basis. Fitzgerald has thus cemented a tendency in the research to interpret in a one-sided way the peristasis catalogues against the background of the Graeco-Roman philosophy and literature. With the statement "The sage and his sufferings provide the backdrop for the analysis of Paul's Corinthian catalogues" Fitzgerald ends in a certain way on the point, where Bultmann started! [15]

A quite different — and later — tendency in the research has been to understand the peristasis catalogues against the background of Old Testament

---

12. Here I agree with O. Wischmeyer and J.T. Fitzgerald in their critical comments of Georgi's view. See O. Wischmeyer, *Der höchste Weg*. SNT 13 (Gütersloh: Mohn, 1981) 85f; J.T. Fitzgerald, *Cracks* 24f.

13. H.D. Betz, *Der Apostel Paulus und die sokratische Tradition*. BHT 45 (Tübingen: Mohr [Siebeck], 1972), especially 97-100.

14. In his careful but one-sided study, Fitzgerald ought to have examined other texts in the Pauline correspondance concerning suffering. And unfortunately Fitzgerald has in his book refrained from analysing the very important catalogue in 2 Cor 11.23-33 and its context.

15. In his survey of research Fitzgerald also begins with the studies of Bultmann. See *Cracks*, 7f.

and Antique Jewish literature. Here scholars as W. Schrage, K.T. Kleinknecht, J.S. Pobee and R. Hodgson have to be mentioned.

In an article "Leid, Kreuz und Eschaton" W. Schrage has included Late Jewish material from the apocalyptic literature, in order to demonstrate parallels and the importance of the apocalyptic thought to the understanding of the peristasis catalogues of Paul.[16] Schrage claims that the earlier reference to Stoic parallels is not sufficient. It is rather misleading, because one is thereby inclined to the opinion that adversities and sufferings also for Paul are the reason to prove his invincibility and superiority. Schrage writes here:

Die θλῖψις ist für Paulus also weder eine rein innerliche, geistig-seeliche Aporie noch aber auch ein rein äusserliches Geschehen, das den Menschen in seinem innersten Kern gar nicht berührt (vgl. auch 2.Kor. 2.13), sondern es handelt sich um Anfechtung, die den totus homo trifft.

Schrage's understanding of the peristasis catalogues of Paul is concentrated on these points: The sufferings of Paul are viewed in combination with his apostolic service for others. This combination is especially visible in 2 Cor. The sufferings of the Christian arise primarily because of his service. On the other hand, according to Schrage, the apostolic character of the sufferings must not be over-emphasized, for as is the case, in 2 Cor 2.14-7.3 e.g., Paul presents himself also as exemplary in order to make suffering specific to the Christian existence.[17] Schrage is against an imitatio interpretation because an imitation of the sufferings of Christ does not hold a meaning, "weil die im Tod Jesu als eschatologischem Heilsereignis geschehene Begründung des Heils nicht zu imitieren ist".[18] But on the other side, Schrage maintains that a conformity between the sufferings of Christ and of the Christians is not excluded. At the same time, adversities and sufferings are signs of an affiliation with Christ. But more than that: Because the last days have broken through with the death and resurrection of Jesus, then the Christians have been co-included in the sufferings and glorification of Christ. Their adversities and sufferings are indication that they still live in the old world, but that they will soon be glorified with Christ. Paul's understanding is, according to Schrage, apocalyptical-eschatological, but he is not, as in the traditional apocalyptical thought, interested in the actual order of the apocalyptic events. Nor is it stated that sufferings are followed up by life and glory, but, on the contrary, suffering

---

16. W. Schrage, "Leid, Kreuz und Eschaton. Die Peristasenkataloge als Merkmale paulinischer theologia crucis und Eschatologie," *EvT* 34 (1974) 141-75.

17. Especially p. 158f. I agree with Schrage in his critical comments on E. Güttgemann (*Der leidende Apostel und sein Herr. Studien zur paulinischen Christologie* (Göttingen, 1966). Another important study is E. Kamlah, "Wie beurteilt Paulus sein Leiden? Ein Beitrag zur Untersuchung seiner Denkstruktur," *ZNW* 54 (1963) 217-32.

18. Ibid., 162.

and glory; death and life are viewed paradoxically together in Paul's thought.[19] On the other hand Schrage agrees with D. Georgi that in the peristasis catalogues an anti-enthusiastic polemic is contained. Schrage emphasizes the christology as central: "Christus und sein Kreuz sind Grund und Ursache des Leidens des Christen".[20]

Against Schrage the objection has to be made that the christology is emphasized so strongly that theology is left out of consideration, and furthermore that the peristasis catalogues are much too generalized with basis in 2 Cor 4.8-11, so that nuances and differences vanish. Finally the references to the Jewish apocalyptic texts before and after Paul are uncertain in some cases.[21] The study of Schrage is once more an example of an one-sided understanding of the provenance of the peristasis catalogues. For Schrage it is mostly an either-or, Stoic or Jewish background; an alternative which in my opinion is untenable.

We find the same tendency in the study of K.T. Kleinknecht. He maintains a general interpretation of the view of Paul on his adversities and sufferings on the basis of the Old Testament passio justi-theme.[22] After a careful examination of the Jewish material, which is mainly based on L. Ruppert's studies, he analyses the Pauline texts and indicates a structure corresponding to the passio justi-theme.[23] It is a structure that, according to Kleinknecht, also has its roots in the Jesus tradi-tion and especially in the Passion tradition. Here a pre-Marcan passion tradition may, according to Kleinknecht, have been created on the basis of the passio justi-theme. On the basis of that theme, Jesus has been viewed as God's representative who meets resistance from the enemies of God and finally suffers death, but is then saved by God. The theme may also be characterized as a theme of abasement-elevation, such as exists in the pre-Pauline hymn in Phil 2.6-11. According to Kleinknecht, Paul is faithful to this entire tradition, but he integrates it into his self-understanding, the point of departure of which is the christology. The Crucified is, with his sufferings, not only a model of the community. The Crucified is, as Messiah and the righteous, also the soteriological point which produces the position of the Christian as righteous:

Als Leiden des Gerechtfertigten haben die Leiden des Paulus keine grundsätzlich

---

19. Ibid 171f.
20. Ibid 162.
21. See Fitzgerald's critical comments in: *Cracks* 30.
22. K.T. Kleinknecht, *Der leidende Gerechtfertigte*.
23. The studies of L. Ruppert are: *Der leidende Gerechte. Eine motivgeschichtliche Untersuchung zum Alten Testament und zwischentestamentlichen Judentum* (Würzburg, 1972); *Der leidende Gerechte und seine Feinde. Eine Wortfelduntersuchung* (Würzburg, 1973); *Jesus als der leidende Gerechte? Der Weg Jesu im Lichte eines alt- und zwischentestamentlichen Motivs* (Stuttgart, 1972).

besondere Qualität, durch die sie als apostolische Leiden von denen anderer Christen unterschieden waren, wohl aber ist ihnen eine besondere Intensität und ein besonderes Mass eigen.[24]

Paul does not suffer especially because he is an apostle, but because he is a Christian. Only in 2 Cor 10-13 do his sufferings seem to be apostolic, which is caused by the situation of the letter. Otherwise Paul presents himself as a model of the communities, so that the sufferings of the Christians do not differ substantially from the sufferings of Paul. Kleinknecht has, in drawing atttention to the passio justi-theme, undoubtedly pointed at something central for the provenance of the peristasis catalogues, but he makes the same mistake as many other scholars, when he in a too one-sided way, underlines just one theme as the key for understanding the Pauline texts.

Another example of a narrow interpretation of the self-understanding of Paul is J.S. Pobee, who understands the passion evidence of Paul in the light of Jewish martyr literature.[25] He limits himself to this literature from the persecutions of the Maccabaean period, and thus he excludes other streams of tradition, both Jewish and Graeco-Roman. It has undoubted consequences both for the christology and the self-understanding of Paul. But Pobee is right in emphasizing the eschatological-apocalyptical point that "the sufferings of Paul constitute a part of the cosmic battle between the forces of God and the forces of Satan."[26]

Finally let me mention R. Hodgson, who claims that the religious background is "broader than the one generally found in relevant modern commentaries, monographs and articles."[27] As opposed to Bultmann and Schrage, Hodgson shows that the peristasis catalogues of Paul "stem from a widespread literary convention of the first century which served a Hellenistic Jewish history writer like Josephus, the pharisaic Judaism of the Mishnah, and the incipient Gnosticism that appeared full-blown in the Nag Hammady library."[28] Whatever one may think of the individual sources that are involved, Hodgson has at any rate broken down the dividing wall, according to which the provenance of the peristasis catalogues are claimed to be either Graeco-Roman or Jewish. And it is furthermore worth noting the insistence of Hodgson on not overlooking differences and nuances between the single peristasis catalogues. But when Hodgson rightly points, for instance, to parallels between the Graeco-Roman myth about Heracles, who has to pass

---

24. Kleinknecht, Der leidende, 372.
25. J.S. Pobee, Persecution and Martyrdom in the Theology of Paul. JSNT Suppl. Ser. 6 (Sheffield: JSOT Press, 1985).
26. Ibid., 106.
27. R. Hodgson, "Paul the Apostle and First Century Tribulation Lists," ZNW 74 (1983) 59-80.
28. Ibid., 60.

through adversities in order to become divine, and thereafter the placing by Paul of the adversities of the Christians on their way from the old world to the filial existence in the new world (Rom.8), then one may hesitate.[29] For the adversities and sufferings of the Christians are just a sign of their filial situation, just as they constitute their conformity with the Crucified when they suffer.

After this survey of research I may join the objections of Hodgson against previous either-or-standpoints. I find it necessary to emphasize that it is impossible to discern between Graeco-Roman or Jewish background. As a Hellenistic Jew, Paul was primarily influenced by Jewish thought. On the other side he makes use of a terminology from Graeco-Roman philosophy. But we ought to be cautious not to over-emphasize that influence when interpreting the Pauline texts. I find the contributions by scholars as Schrage, Kleinknecht and Pobee fruitful, although they are far too generalizing when understanding the texts against the background of some specific Jewish themes.

They also isolate the texts from their concrete social situation, for they do not take into account the different situations which have caused Paul to write a letter. It is my contention, as will be shown, that a paraenetic intention lies behind Paul's emphasizing his suffering. It is not least caused by the fact that his Greek and Roman audience is not able to understand suffering as a part of Christian life. Here we may also be aware that Paul as a Christian understood himself as a true Jew.

The paraenetic intention has to be seen together with the christology. And I will here show that in Paul's thought the suffering and death of Jesus Christ are coherent with his earthly life. For Paul the earthly life of Jesus Christ is much more important than often assumed. In fact it is the foundation of his paraenesis. Therefore Paul's reference to the life and passion of Jesus Christ will be discussed, before I examine some relevant texts concerning suffering.

2. Paul and the Passion Tradition

In 1 Thess reference is very often made to the suffering and death of Jesus Christ (1.6; 1.10; 2.15; 4.14; 5.10). Especially 2.14-16 in this oldest letter of Paul is interesting, as reference is here not only made to the death of Jesus, but responsibility for it is also imposed: The Jews alone killed the Lord Jesus, it is said. Paul says in 2.14-16 that the Thessalonians with their adversities have had the communities in Judaea as patterns, because they also have been objects of persecutions on the part of their compatriots. And when the Jews have persecuted the Christian compatriots in Judaea, then they repeat what they did against Jesus when they killed him, just as they had in former times killed the

---

29. Ibid., 79-80.

prophets.[30] Now the Jews are also persecuting Paul, and thus they are preventing the Gospel being preached to Gentiles and salvation coming to them.
What Paul repeats time and again is that compatriots persecute their own
people. The statement that the Jews killed Jesus does not concern the soteriological significance of his death, but emphasizes that it was his compatriots
who killed him.

Now we may ask: Does this statement correspond to the passion tradition
of the Gospels? In some ways it does. However, in some of the Gospels, Pilate
causes the sentence of death to be executed in full accordance with Roman
legal practice in Judaea.[31] But Pilate is in the Gospels portrayed as a weak
and hesitating procurator who prefers to avoid being responsible for the
sentence pronounced against Jesus. It is the Jewish leaders who compel him to
allow Jesus to be crucified. And in all four Gospels there is a tendency to
attribute to the Jews the responsibility for the death of Jesus. On the other side,
this is a reflection of the conflict between Jews and Christians in the period
when the Gospels were written. But it also corresponds to the historical fact:
The conflict between Jesus and the Jewish leaders in Jerusalem is the
background of the death of Jesus.[32] Thus in 1 Thess there is not only
accordance between Paul and the Gospels, but also between Paul and a
supposed historical reality. The tradition in 1 Thess that Paul not only had
knowledge of a passion tradition but also maintained that the Jews were
responsible for the death of Jesus. For that reason too we may accept 2.14-16
as a Pauline text.

That Paul knew and stressed the importance of a passion tradition is also
confirmed in 1 Cor. Here we find references to a passion tradition in 2.6-8; 11.
23-26 and not least 15.3-5.

In 15.3-5 Paul refers to a tradition about the death, burial and resurrection
of Jesus according to the Scriptures. In some way it corresponds to the narrative in Mark's gospel (15.22-16.8), where crucifixion, burial and resurrection
(empty tomb) follow each other, and where in particular the crucifixion scene
is marked by allusions to the Scripture.

---

30. I prefer to read 2. 14-16 as an original Pauline text not least because of its coherence
    with other parts of the letter. And it is completely wrong to understand the text in
    an antisemitic way. N. Hyldahl has rightly argued against such a view in: "Jesus og
    jøderne ifølge 1.Tess 2, 14-16," SEÅ 37-38 (1972) 238-74.
31. In the gospels of Mark and Matthew the Jews pass sentence of death on Jesus (Mark
    14.64; Matt 26.66). In the Gospels of Luke and John it is Pilate, who does it (Luke
    23.24; John 19.13). In my book: Pilatusbilledet i den antike jødedom og kristendom
    (Århus: Aarhus University Press, 1989) I have examined the portrait of Pilate in
    Christian and Jewish texts. In my opinion it is most probable that Luke and John are
    correct in making Pilate responsible for the sentence of death, while Matthew and
    Mark are more tendentious in an antijudaic way.
32. This I have maintained in my book: Pilatusbilledet, especially 185ff.

In 1 Cor 11.23 the tradition of the Last Supper (11.23-26) is opened with the statement that it happened when the Lord was betrayed. It shows a knowledge of the development of events preceding the death of Jesus corresponding to what we are told in the passion narrative of the Gospels (Mark 14.17-52 parr.) Here attention is drawn to Luke's text in particular, as there are some agreements between Paul's and Luke's Last Supper tradition (cf. Lk 22.19-23). We may suppose that Luke did use the passion narrative of Mark, but possibly he used another tradition of the Last Supper, a tradition which perhaps is the same as the tradition used by Paul. And when Paul knows that Jesus was betrayed in the night, he probably also knows who betrayed Jesus, and who arrested him. Paul does not mention exactly who arrested Jesus. Perhaps he presupposes a knowledge of that fact.

That Paul presupposes who crucified Jesus, can also be seen in 1 Cor 2.6-8. Here Paul speaks about the rulers of this world who do not know the wisdom of God, for if they had known it, they would not have crucified the Lord. Paul places the wisdom of God not with the rulers of the world and the powerful in general, but, on the contrary, with the Crucified and those who followed him in weakness and in powerlessness. The rulers of the world existed in a contrary way to the wisdom of God, whom in their ignorance they arranged to be crucified. They did not understand that the wisdom of God manifested itself in the abasement of the crucifixion.

Now our question is: Who are these rulers? Mostly they are viewed as demonic powers.[33] But some scholars regard them as historical persons. In the latter case it may be historical persons such as Pilate, the Jewish leaders and Herod Antipas.[34] In any case, it is not necessary to maintain one of two possibilities. For they are at one and the same time historical persons and mythical persons.[35] The mythical drama manifests itself in a historical event which thus receives eschatological character. Paul can quite well have thought both of the Roman power and the Jewish leadership. The decisive point is to note that he does not hold only the Roman power responsible for the death of Jesus. This is confirmed by the context, especially 1 Cor 1.22-24. In 2.6-8 we thus have another example of the use made by Paul of a passion tradition. And

---

33. See for instance M. Dibelius: *Die Geisterwelt im Glauben des Paulus* (Göttingen, 1909) 90; U. Wilckens: *Weisheit und Torheit. Eine exegetisch-religionsgeschichtliche Untersuchung zu 1.Kor 1 und 2* (Tübingen, 1959) 62f. Later on he recalled that opinion; see the next note.

34. Herod Antipas is mentioned in *Luke* 23.7-15 and 4.27. That the rulers are historical persons is maintained by e.g. W. Carr, "The Rulers of this age — 1 Corinthians II.6-8," *NTS* 23 (1976-77) 20-35; U. Wilckens, "Zu 1 Kor 2.1-16," in: *Theologia crucis — signum crucis, FS E. Dinkler* (ed. C. Andresen und G. Klein; Tübingen, 1979) 501-37, especially 508f.

35. For this opinion see G. Theissen, *Psychologische Aspekte paulinischer Theologie.* FRLANT 131(Göttingen: Vandenhoeck & Ruprecht, 1983) 364f.

the text 1.18-2.16 shows that for Paul the historical event of the crucifixion is not without importance.

The next question is then, whether the historical event of the crucifixion is attached by Paul to the life of Jesus on earth. This seems to be the case. In a central text, the pre-pauline hymn in Phil 2.6-11, the mythical drama manifests itself in the historical event that Jesus humbled himself and was obedient until the death on a cross. With the addition made by Paul about the death on the cross, the connection is clarified between the life lived and the death.[36] Paul is not only interested in the death of Jesus, however important it is in a soterio-logical way. For Paul life and death cannot be separated. This is seen in Phil 2.6-11, where the death alone is not even given a soteriological interpretation. It is the life of Jesus together with his death, which is given a soteriological interpretation: Jesus humilated himself until death and was therefore exalted as the Lord of the world. In this soteriological reality the Christians participate.

We find the same thought in Rom 5.12-21, where in a typology the life of Jesus in obedience with justification as a result is opposed to the life of Adam in disobedience with death as a result. And as the life of Adam has constituted a pattern for human beings until Christ, so the Christians are now to live their life with Jesus Christ as the ideal pattern, in which they participate.

This is in fact seen in Rom 8, which deals with the Christian life under the Spirit. The Christians are made in equal form with Jesus Christ, which implies that as children of God they are to live a life corresponding to the life lived by Jesus Christ, which means a life that implicates adversities and persecutions with death as a consequence. But as children of God, they may also be convinced that the sufferings in the old world are as nothing compared with the coming glory (Rom 8.18). Here Jesus Christ has made a pattern of his life, which is described at the beginning of the chapter as an incarnation in the figure of a sinful man. For the sake of sin he was sent, and he thus condemned the sin in the flesh in order that the demands of the Law might be met with those who live in obedience to the Spirit (Rom 8.3-4).

That Jesus, according to Paul, lived a life on completely human terms is also seen in Gal 4.4-5. "When the time came God sent his son, born of a woman, born under the Law, so that we might become as children". The life of Jesus is seen as a pattern of a life as God's children in obedience.

After having observed the importance of the life of Jesus Christ in the letters of Paul, I will now proceed to find out in some letters of Paul, in which way the life of Jesus in adversities and sufferings constitutes the pattern of the corresponding life that Paul lives, and which the communities are to live.

---

36. The importance of the life and death of Jesus is rightly seen by Chr. Wolff, "Niedrigkeit und Verzicht in Wort und Weg Jesu und in der apostolischen Existenz des Paulus." NTS 34 (1988) 183-96.

3. The First Letter to the Thessalonians

A climax in 1 Thess is the passage 4.3-18, where Paul argues for the Parousia of Christ. That the Parousia is imminent, is a theme which runs through the letter. This eschatological-apocalyptical theme characterizes the entire letter (1.10; 2.12; 2.16; 2.19-20; 3.13; 4.13; 5.11). And the reason is not least that there is a crisis between Paul and the community.

The community has apparently lost the hope of the Coming of Christ (3.6; 4.13) and must therefore harbour doubt as to the mission of Paul. But why has hope disappeared? Hardly because the Parousia has been postponed! The cause has more probably been that the Thessalonians have been exposed to persecutions (1.6; 2.14; 3.3). Here we must not forget that Paul confronts himself with a Graeco-Roman audience without an understanding of sufferings and persecutions as unavoidable in Christian life. I will leave out of consideration here the argumentation of Paul in favour of the Parousia and I will concentrate instead on his argumentation for the place of suffering in Christian life.

Paul places the sufferings of the community caused by persecutions not only in relation to his own sufferings, but also to the sufferings of Christ. The Christians in Thessalonica have become μιμηταί of Paul and of Christ by the fact that they have accepted the Word in great adversity (1.6). They have also become μιμηταί of God's communities in Judaea, who have also been persecuted (2.14).

Paul makes use of the substantive μιμητής here (1.6 and 2.14) and in 1 Cor (4.16 and 11.1). This substantive and its corresponding verb μιμέομαι have in Greek culture the sense of imitating. Very often they are used in an ethical context when for example pupils and children are imitating their teacher and their parents respectively. We find the same sense in Antique Judaism when for example martyrs are imitated (4 Macc 9.23; 13.9). That is summary the background against which we may understand the use Paul makes of the same words. Therefore I disagree with Michaelis when he writes: "Die Forderung einer imitatio Christi hat in den paulinischen Aussagen keine Stütze".[37] Of course the matter is not, as Michaelis writes at the same place, "eine Nachahmung des irdischen Lebens Jesu in einzelnen Zügen". However, it may not be neglected that for Paul the exemplary way of the life and suffering of Jesus is not without importance .

Michaelis understands the use of the substantive in 1.6 and 2.14-16 as a comparison.[38] That is not correct. In 1.6 the context shows that the Thessalonians have followed the exemplary way of suffering of Paul and Jesus and now have been τύπος for other Christians. In 2.14-16 the Thessalonians are said to have suffered in the same way as their brethren in Judaea. That means that

---

37. W. Michaelis, "μιμέομαι, μιμητής, συμμιμητής," TWNT 4. 661-78, here p. 676. Cf. Willis P. de Boer, The Imitation of Paul (Amsterdam: J.H. Kok, 1962), especially 206ff.
38. Michaelis, 668, 672f.

they have imitated a pattern of life in which suffering is included. It is not a comparison, but instead it is a question of fellowship of experience as a consequence of following the Lord. The Christians, both in Judaea and in Thessalonica, have in common with Paul and Jesus the fact that they suffer but persevere throughout it. In 2.15, Paul compares the suffering Christian with the Old Testament prophets, who also suffered because of their compatriots. To Paul, suffering because of one's compatriots constitutes a Christian as a true Jew. The decisive factor to Paul is to insist that suffering constitutes the Thessalonians as Christians and thereby as true Jews. If they are Christians they are also exposed to adversities and sufferings when they are persecuted by their compatriots, just as Paul is persecuted and Jesus too. Paul reminds them that they have borne their sufferings, but it is obvious that their perseverance has reached a limit.

In the climax of the letter, which has already been prepared, Paul repeats his preaching of the Parousia, which is intended to convince the Christians that adversities and sufferings will be of short duration and will be substituted by glory. But Paul does not only console the community by maintaining that the present situation will have an end. He also insists on suffering as a constituent part of the life as a Christian. And he does so in two ways: Partly he presents himself as a model for the community, and partly he turns his own sufferings and those of the community into time-identifying signs that the end of the world and the Parousia of Christ are near. Let us first look at his presentation of himself: If the preaching of Paul has been doubted by the community, then it is understandable when in 2.1-12 Paul gives a detailed description of his way of living as an apostle. It is probably not a question of defense towards opponents or polemic against them, but on the contrary it is an attempt to reestablish the relations between the community and himself by means of reminders of his way of living as an apostle.[39]

A.J. Malherbe has compared the text with Cynical-Stoic material.[40] From speeches by Dio Chrysostomos (about AD 40-120) Malherbe finds parallels to the Pauline text. In these speeches the true philosopher is contrasted with false sophists. Paul is expected, according to Malherbe, to have made use of the same pattern of argumentation: As the true philosopher Paul acts with παρρησία, his speech is not κενός. The false philosophers cheat their audience and mislead them, while the true philosopher speaks purely and without ruse.

---

39. I find no reason for understanding the text in a polemic way, such as it is very often interpreted e.g. by W. Schmithals, *Paulus und die Gnostiker. Untersuchungen zu den kleinen Paulusbriefen* (Hamburg, 1965) 89ff. For Schmithals, Paul is fighting against a Jewish Christian gnosticism.

40. A.J. Malherbe, "'Gentle as a Nurse'. The Cynical Background to I Thess II". *NT* 12 (1970) 203-17. See further Malherbe, *Paul and the Thessalonians: The Philosophic Traditions of Pastoral Care* (Philadelphia, 1987).

He speaks neither for the sake of honour or money, and neither does he flatter. In the same way Paul neither acted with flattery nor hidden cupidity (2.5-6). Both the true philosopher and Paul speak on God's behalf (2.4). The true philosopher is not hard, but gentle as a nurse. Paul might have burdened the Christians, but he preferred to act as ἤπιος. Malherbe rightly concludes that "This is the context within which Paul describes his activity in Thessalonica".[41] But Malherbe narrows the field in viewing the texts as texts, whose only purpose is to contrast the true and the false preacher.

In my view the text has a paraenetic intention. The context seems to indicate that it is so. Both before and after 2.1-12 Paul mentions the Thessalonians as μιμηταί of himself, and this is so both on account of their sufferings and of their way of being Christians and passing on the Word (1.6-8). The style in 2.1-12 also points in the direction of paraenesis when Paul refers all the time to the memory of the Thessalonians (2.1-2; 2.5; 2.9-11). Paul intends not only to reinstitute the relation of trust from the time when he once came to them. Just by maintaining that he could have avoided sufferings, if he had acted like false philosophers, he reminds them about their own situation, where they likewise might be tempted to avoid persecutions. Finally the use made by Paul of the father-child metaphor is to be noted, as it is done in 2.7; 2.11 and 2.17. As a father, Paul is a model for the community.

Now let us look at the place of suffering in history. Besides presenting himself as the apostle who does not avoid sufferings, Paul views the sufferings as time-identifying signs. They are an important part of the drama of the end-of-time which is already at work, and moreover had its beginning with the death of Christ (1.10; 4.13; 4.17). In 2.1-12 Paul includes a motive of judgment by a quotation from Jer 11.20 (1 Thess 2.3-4) and thus places his action in an eschatological frame, which is also confirmed by the end of the text (2.12). The action of Paul, which implies preaching in sufferings, is thus a sign that the last time is approaching. And when Paul in 3.3 says that εἰς τοῦτο κείμεθα and in 3.4 that μέλλομεν θλίβεσθαι, then the suffering is viewed as a necessary part of history. Paul is influenced by the Jewish apocalyptic thought where sufferings precede the end of history and are even a sign of its end. In the apocalyptic discourse in the Gospels (Mark 13 parr.) preaching and sufferings are connected (Mark 13.9-13 parr). This is also the case in 1 Thess, where Paul views himself in the centre of the drama of the end of time, when he states that Satan placed obstacles in the way (2.18) and when he fears that the Tempter might have tempted the Thessalonians. The sufferings are interpreted in a time-identifying manner as signs of the final struggle between God and Satan.

Finally we may ask, whether in this letter Paul makes a connecting link of himself between Jesus Christ and the community, or in other words whether christology and paraenetic intention are combined? It is my contention that it

---

41. Ibid., 217.

is the case: In the first place Paul maintains that the Christians are μιμηται of Jesus Christ, which has been caused by Paul himself. They are called to imitate their Lord, which is only possible when imitating Paul. And to this may be added that by his presentation of himself, Paul places himself on a line with the disciples of Christ, who renounced possessions, work and family, and wandered without any firm base. It is obvious to draw parallels between Paul in 1 Thess 2.1-12 and the Gospel tradition concerning Jesus and his disciples on wandering. When Paul makes use of the word μιμητής he not only draws attention to suffering, but also to a way of life which causes adversities and persecutions. To imitate Paul is to imitate the apostle who acts exactly as an apostle of Christ in renouncing everything. The text has a paraenetic function, just as is the case in Paul's reminding the Thessalonians about their Christian life in the first 3 chapters of the letter.

4. The First and Second Letter to the Corinthians

In the letters of Paul to the Corinthians we must also be aware that Paul is confronting himself with a Graeco-Roman audience. There are, as previously mentioned, peristasis catalogues in 1 Cor 4.10-13; 2 Cor 4.8-9; 6.4-10; 11.23-33 and 12.10. The first question must be whether Paul in these catalogues attached himself to the earthly Jesus, whose apostle he is.

At first let me draw attention to some parallels between the peristasis catalogues and the Gospel tradition. In 1 Cor 4.10-13 Paul talks about hunger, thirst and bareness, and he mentions further that he is ill-treated (κολαφι-ζόμεθα) and constantly moving from place to place without a permanent residence (ἀστατοῦμεν); he is abused and persecuted, just as evil words are spoken about him. The catalogue is framed of statements which make of Paul a person sentenced to death (ἐπιθανατίους) and expelled (ὡς περικαθάρματα). Although only a few words appear directly in the Gospel tradition, there are nevertheless similarities between the form of life of Paul and his experience of sufferings, and the wandering form of the life of Jesus and his disciples and their sufferings. Both parts suffer from wants, renounce possessions (cf. 1 Cor 9.15f) and they are exposed to persecutions and made outcasts (see for example Mark 8.34ff; 10.28ff; 13.9ff).

A similar comparison may be made between the peristasis catalogues in 2 Cor and the Gospel tradition. Here too Paul mentions himself as the one who suffers hunger (6.5; 11.27), is poor and owns nothing (6.10). In 8.9 he refers to Jesus Christ, who for our sake made himself poor, although rich.

Chr. Wolf has examined the presence of the Jesus tradition in the letters of Paul, and he gives this general comment:

Paulus versteht seine Lebensweise als eine von Christus, und d.h. in erster Linie: vom Gekreuzigten und Auferstandene bestimmte; die Niedrigkeit des Gekreuzigten und das wahrhaft neue Leben des Auferstandenen machen sich in seinem Gesandten geltend. Dies zu betonen is gerade das Anliegen der Peristasenkataloge.[42]

The words in 2 Cor 8.9 that Jesus made himself poor for our sake are undoubtedly valid also in relation to the life of Jesus and not only to his death on the Cross. It is the life of Jesus, and not only the death on the Cross, which is for Paul the sign of abasement and renunciation, just as it is expressed in Phil 2. 6-11. In the same way as in the hymn, the life and death of Jesus are viewed altogether, as death is viewed as the final consequence of the abasement of Jesus. Here too we have to ask whether there are concrete parallels between Paul and the passion tradition. We have previously noted that Paul had knowledge of the passion events, but does he view himself as the one in whom these events gain presence? The peristasis catalogues contain statements which, as in 1 Cor 4.9 and 4.13 point to the passion events. In 2 Cor there are also noteworthy statements in 1.5 (cf. Gal.6.7); 11.24f, and not least 4.10f, where Paul maintains that he has constantly the νέκρωσις of Christ on his body, that he is constantly surrendered to death for the sake of Jesus. Particularly the use of the verb παραδίδωμι points to the passion tradition, where it appears frequently.[43]

Very important is the use of the word νέκρωσις, which means the death process, both before and after the death.[44]The use of the word advocates a wider sense than the fact of death. As an apostle Paul presents not only the Crucified, but the man who abased himself and was finally surrendered to death on the Cross. In Paul, the passion events gain presence.

The next question then must be whether the peristasis catalogues have a paraenetic function. First let us look at 1 Cor 4.10-13. The peristasis catalogue in 1 Cor 4.9-13 is to be viewed as part of the whole text 1.18-4.21. The point of departure in this text is the Cross preaching of Paul (1.18-25), in which the wisdom of God is manifested only. Towards those who act with conceit, self-praise and worldly wisdom, Paul declares that the wisdom of God is only to be found in the crucifixion, where God revealed himself in abasement and powerlessness. From this point it is verified by a reference in the first place of the social composition of the community, where especially the socially weak were summoned (1.26-31), and then to Paul's own appearance in weakness (2.1-5). In his subsequent speech of wisdom (2.6-16) the thought is developed upon the destruction by the Cross of worldly wisdom. Here Paul speaks about the archons who crucified the Lord of Glory (2.8). They represent the worldly

---

42. Chr. Wolf, *Niedrigkeit*, 185.
43. Undoubtedly this verb is used in the Passion tradition before Mark. In Mark it is very often used, both in the predictions of passion (9.31; 10.33) and in the Passion narrative (for example 14.21,41,42). See W. Popkes, *Christus traditus. Eine Untersuchung zum Begriff der Dahingabe im Neuen Testament* (AThANT 49; Zürich, 1967).
44. See the careful analysis of the word by Fitzgerald in *Cracks*, 177f.

wisdom which did not acknowledge God's wisdom in the Crucified. Similar tendencies are now prevailing in the Corinthian community, whose unity is exposed. This critical situation is the background of Paul's insistence on the foundation of the community on the death of Christ. Those who appear with arrogance, selfpraise and worldly wisdom, probably believe in Christ as exalted only. In the christology of Paul, Jesus Christ Crucified is emphasized. Paul teaches and admonishes the Corinthians on this basis. And the whole text 1.18-4.21 may be viewed as a paraenetic text.[45] It is seen clearly in 3.1ff; 4.6; 4.14-15 and 4.16-17. With a father-child metaphor Paul reminds in 4.1 the community both of its basis and of its founder. The community must, with the words in 4.16(μιμηταί μου γίνεσθε), live with Paul as a model and follow him(cf. τὰς ὁδούς μου in 4.17) instead of allowing themselves to be conceited.

In the peristasis catalogue Paul ironically addresses the community, which has already anticipated the eschatological glory. The Corinthians are said to be already satisfied, rich and kings, while Paul presents himself together with Apollos as hungry, poor and an outcast, who is condemned to death. Fitzgerald has compared the text with Stoic-Cynical material, in which he finds the same terminology.[46] Against that background, Paul's description of himself can be seen as a description of the true sage, whom God has exhibited through poverty and hardships, so that the sage becomes a spectacle to the world. Undoubtedly Paul is influenced by that Graeco-Roman tradition, in which Paul makes understandable what it means to be an apostle of Christ. However, Fitzgerald's interpretation is too narrow in two ways. Firstly while one may follow him, when he understands the text and its context as a paraenetic text, one may at the same time draw attention to the christological point of departure in the whole text 1.18-4.21. First of all Paul is presenting himself as an apostle of Christ. Paul sets forth his apostolic life as a paradigm for Christian life. He admonishes the Corinthians to imitate him. That means that there is no Christian community in Corinth, unless the Corinthians follow Paul. Fitzgerald has neglected the importance of the christology, in which the Cross is the centre. He has also forgotten the ecclesiology, when he is not aware of the critical situation of the community as an entity. Secondly, Fitzgerald has also neglected the Jewish background of Paul. Here one may emphasize that as a Jew Paul was familiar with both Jewish and Graeco-Roman cultural tradition.

45. This view is maintained also by Fitzgerald, who rightly argues against an interpretation of the text as an apologetic text. See *Cracks*, 117ff.
46. Especially the synkrisis in which Paul compares himself with the Corinthians can be seen as influenced by a Cynic-Stoic tradition, in which poor and rich, hungry and satisfied, weak and strong are opposed to one another. In examining the text against that background Fitzgerald is following an old exegetical tradition, which interprets the peristasis catalogues against the background of Graeco-Roman material (see for example H. Conzelmann, *Der erste Brief an die Korinther*. Meyer K 5 (Göttingen: Vandenhoeck & Ruprecht, 1969. Reprinted 1981) 114ff. See Fitzgerald, *Cracks*, 132ff.

He was living in a Hellenistic world and knew very well that Judaism had long ago been influenced by the Graeco-Roman culture. To Paul it was not a problem to speak like a Greek philosopher or a pharisaic Jew. He was influenced by Graeco-Roman and Jewish culture at one and the same time.

Then we may ask, in which way the peristasis catalogue is influenced by Jewish tradition. Firstly we may look at the difficult statement in 4.6 τὸ μὴ ὑπὲρ ἃ γέγραπται. For me there can be no doubt that the statement concerns the Scriptures.[47] In the preceding chap 3 Paul has presented himself together with Apollos as God's servants, who are not boasting of own wisdom, but instead work on the basis of God's acting in Jesus Christ. Paul has, with the example of himself and Apollos, shown (μετεσχημάτισα) what the Cross preaching means. At the same time their example shows what is God's will, as it is written in the Scriptures. In 1.18-4.21 we find allusions to the Scriptures in 1.19; 1.31; 2.9 and 3.19. These quotations have God's destruction of worldly wisdom and power in common. And that is exactly the central theme in 1.18-4.21. In the Crucified God has destroyed worldly wisdom and power and turned upside-down, what is weak and mighty, poor and rich. And this is shown by Paul in his peristasis catalogue. In Paul, God is acting (cf. 4.9,13). Here we may be aware too that the statement in 4.6 shows that Paul presents himself as a Jew in line with Old Testament prophets. As a suffering Christian, he is a true Jew.

Kleinknecht has emphasized the importance of Jewish tradition behind the text.[48] But firstly he is wrong in maintaining the passio justi-theme behind the quoted Old Testament texts (Isa 29.14; Jer 9.22-23; Job 5.12).[49] These texts have first of all the destruction of worldly wisdom and power in common and not a tradition of the righteous who suffers. Secondly Kleinknecht's attempt to show the passio-justi theme behind the text is not convincing.[50] In my view Paul is influenced by the Old Testament texts and the Gospel tradition at the same time.

Let me give some examples: Paul and Apollos are like the ἐλάστιχοι in Matt 25.31-46, who are hungry, thirsty and naked. Paul and Apollos λοδορού

---

47. The interpretation by Fitzgerald (*Cracks*, 124f.)is not convincing. He finds the background in the instruction given to young children in how to draw or write correctly (cf. Seneca *Ep.* 94.51). They must imitate their teacher in drawing and writing. Fitzgerald's interpretation may be seen as one more attempt to understand the text against the background of Graeco-Roman culture and at the same time to emphazise the paraenetic intention behind the text. However, Fitzgerald does not look at the text against the background of its context, and he completely neglects the possibility of allusion to the Scriptures.

48. Kleinknecht, *Der leidende*, 208ff.

49. Kleinknecht, *Der leidende*, 213ff.

50. Kleinknecht finds parallels in *T. Juda* 25.4; *T. Benj.* 4; Ps 44.15; Ps 69.12; Jer 20.7-8; 1 *Enoch* 103.

μενοι εὐλογοῦμεν, as in Mt 5.44 Jesus admonished to love one's enemies. Paul endures while persecuted (διωκόμενοι ἀνεχόμεθα) as the disciples are admonished to do (Mark 4.17; 13.9-13). Paul endures because he is sure of salvation.

Here I am going to draw attention to the eschatological-apocalyptical thought in the text. As in 1 Thess the suffering is viewed as a time-identifying sign. Still the Christians live in the world (cf. ἄρτι in 1 Cor 4.11,13). Paul addresses the Corinthians, who have anticipated the eschatological glory. For Paul the paraenetic purpose is primarily, on the basis of his christology, to give the Corinthians the right understanding of the end of time. They must still suffer as Paul because of adversities and persecutions. So the peristasis catalogue also intends to make clear that the Corinthians may expect the end of time and the Parousia of Christ. In fact Paul is in 1.18-4.21 (especially 4.1-5) preparing his teaching about resurrection and Parousia of Christ in chap 15.

Now let us look at 2 Cor. Firstly we must ask, whether the peristasis catalogues have a paraenetic function. In the catalogue in 4.8-9 Paul describes his situation in four antithetic sentences, which are framed by the statement in 4.7 that he has a treasure in earthen vessels, and in 4.10 that he always wears the death of Jesus on his body. Mostly the whole context 2.14-7.4 is viewed as an apology.[51] But Paul is not defending himself. Moreover, he is recommending himself to the Corinthians, as is seen especially in 3.1ff, where Paul compares the Old and the New Covenant. As a servant of the New Covenant, which means the life-giving Spirit, Paul represents the life and death of Jesus Christ. He shows that it is the power of God, which is at work in him. This is seen in the catalogue of 4.8-9, but that does not mean that "his catalogue of hardships is thus a catalogue of God's power at work in him", as Fitzgerald maintains.[52] Moreover the intention of the catalogue is to demonstrate, that in Paul's service the suffering Christ is present. Paul's ministry and his willingness to suffer is itself a proclamation of the Crucified. To the Corinthians Paul presents himself as a model(cf. 5.20). At the same time Paul reminds the Corinthians of the Parousia of Christ (1.14; 4.14). The peristasis catalogue may be seen in the eschatological-apocalyptical context: It is for the sake of the Corinthians that Paul suffers. As a Christ letter (3.3) they will be the fruit of his suffering (cf. 4.15). That means that the Corinthians may imitate Paul as their father (cf 6.13,18).

In the catalogue of 6.4-10 Paul presents himself as a servant of reconciliation in a context concerning reconciliation between God and the world (5.18ff). Again Paul is not defending himself, but instead he maintains his role as a servant of reconciliation. He represents God, who in Jesus Christ became reconciled with the world. And Paul wants to become reconciled with the

---

51. See for example Kleinknecht, *Der leidende*, 250ff; Fitzgerald: *Cracks*, 160ff.
52. Fitzgerald, Cracks, 171.

Corinthians, who are then admonished to follow him. The paraenetic purpose of Paul's catalogue in 6.4-10 is seen in its paraenetic context, especially in 5.20, 6.1 and 6.13. Fitzgerald writes "that 6.3-10 is primarily paraenetic in function, and the apologetic aim is only secondary".[53] I agree with him, but as in his analysis of 1 Cor in maintaining the Cynic-Stoic tradition he has completely overlooked the Jewish background. Again we may emphasize that Paul is a Hellenistic Jew, who is influenced both by Jewish and Graeco-Roman tradition.

In his drawing attention to the Jewish passio justi-theme Kleinknecht has shown that details in the peristasis catalogue in 4.8-9 have parallels in Old Testament Psalms, especially Ps 115 (LXX).[54] In 6.4-10 there is an explicit quotation from Isa 49.2. The promise of Jahve about help to those in need is here eschatologically interpreted (6. 2).The peristasis catalogue has, according to Kleinknecht, parallels in Late Jewish apocalypticism, as can be seen in 6.7 e.g. with reminiscences of the dualistic fight. However, the allusions to Old Testament texts are not very much evident, and when Kleinknecht mentions some Antique Jewish texts, one can not be sure, whether the texts have been written before or after Paul.[55] Probably Paul has been influenced by this widespread basic theme in Jewish thought, but he does not use it in a deliberate way.

However, when we arrive at the last peristasis catalogue in 11. 23-33, it is evident that Paul presents himself against the background of an Old Testament notion. But that is not the passio-justi theme. Rather, it is the notion of boasting. The catalogue may be interpreted on the basis of the greater context 2 Cor 10-13, where in 10. 17 a quotation is taken from Jer 9.23 about boasting. This exact quotation dominates the entire section where Paul, in a kind of a "fool speech", settles with the so-called "head-apostles" (11.13; 12.11). They boast of their Jewish descendancy (11.22), whereas Paul boasts of his same Jewish descendancy together with his many adversities and sufferings, to which he as a Jew is exposed from the side of his compatriots. Indirectly Paul compares himself with the suffering prophet fighting against his compatriots. Because he is a servant of Christ (11.23), he is persecuted. But then he can boast of his weakness, for when he is weak he is strong (12.10).

The notion has to be viewed in the light of Jer 9. 23, which also dominates the first chapters in 1 Cor. To me, this is more important than drawing attention to the widespread passio justi-theme in such a way as Kleinknecht does it. But it is more problematic that Kleinknecht has overlooked the paraenetic function in 2 Cor 10-13. As in 1 Cor 1.18-4.21 Jer 9.23 marks the paraenetic intention, so also in 2 Cor 10-13. It can be seen especially in 10.1f

---

53. Fitzgerald, *Cracks*, 188.
54. Kleinknecht, *Der leidende*, 244 and 257ff.
55. Kleinknecht draws attention to Wis 7.4; Ezra 4.11, 7.88; 2 *Enoch* 66.6; *T. Jos.* 1f. (*Der leidende*, 257ff.).

(παρακαλῶ), which introduces the last part of the letter. Paul admonishes the Corinthians to follow him as an apostle who represents Jesus Christ, instead of listening to the so-called "head apostles".

Talking about the paraenesis in 2 Cor, one ought to look at the preceding chap 8-9 too, where Paul admonishes the Corinthians concerning the collection. As Jesus Christ became poor for our sake although he was rich, the Corinthians may give of their wealth (8.9; 9.7f). 2 Cor 8-9 shows how in Paul's thought christology and paraenesis are linked together.

As a difference from 1 Cor it may be admitted, that the eschatological apocalyptical vocabulary is not present to the same extent in 2 Cor. However, it is present (4.14; 6.2; 10.3f; 12.1f). It also characterizes the way in which Paul presents himself. Here an essential point is the opening eulogy in 1.3-11, where Paul mentions his adversities in Ephesos. He clearly makes use of the Jewish tradition of the righteous who suffers, but is liberated by God from his enemies. In 1.3-7 an expression is made of a general connection between suffering and consolation with Paul and the community on the basis of the sufferings of Christ, whereas 1.8-11 describes this connection based on the concrete experiences of Paul in Ephesos. In 1.10 Paul applies the verb ῥύομαι 3 times about the liberation by God of the distressed, a verb which often appears in Old Testament psalms containing the passio justi-theme as Pss 22; 70 and 93 e.g.[56] Paul combines a similar experience of liberation with an eschatological consciousness that both suffering and consolation come to him in full measure (1.5), and that in future he will be liberated (1.10). The notion is also combined with the apostle service of Paul, as the sufferings to which he is exposed as an apostle are for the benefit of the communities (1.6-7).[57]

It is true that in 2 Cor suffering is viewed to a special extent as a consequence of the apostle service, but that is due to the special cause of the letter, where Paul needs to re-establish the close relation of trust. In fact, there is really a crisis between Paul and his community. The Christ identification is markedly present in the effort of Paul to maintain the community firmly on the fact that only he, and not the so-called head-apostles, represents Christ. The suffering of Paul is not apostolic, but as an apostle he is exposed to sufferings to a special degree. Wolf writes:

Aber für den Apostel ist das besondere Ausmass der Leiden kennzeichnend das seine umfassende missionarische Tätigkeit mit sich brachte. Durch diese einzigartige Nähe zur Passion Jesu ist er in unverwechselbarer Weise der Bevollmächtigte, Gesandte des Christus.[58]

---

56. In fact Kleinknecht is most convincing in his analysis of 2 Cor 1.3-11 on the background of the passio justi-theme.
57. See Schrage, *Leid*, 157f.
58. Wolf, *Erniedrigung*, 190.

This is exactly the case for the so-called "head-apostles", and here I find it most probable that both parts are suffering and have experienced persecutions. In his study of the opponents of Paul in Corinth D. Georgi finds these opponents boasting of their pneumatic power and powerful actions. In Georgi's opinion their christology was a theios aner-christology, and they did not emphasize suffering as Paul did.[59] As I have earlier maintained, I find it most probable that the opponents too may have talked about sufferings as experienced by the disciples of Jesus. Perhaps they also made use of peristasis catalogues. An examination by G. Theissen suggests two different types of missionaries: The wandering charismatics and the organizers of communities, among whom Paul is one.[60] Both parts are, according to Theissen, legitimating themselves by charismatic, traditional and functional legitimation. The difference between them is the question of support: The wandering charismatic renounce everything and are supported by the communities, while Paul does not receive support and instead works as an artisan. In defending himself he shows himself exceeding the other apostles: He renounces support in accordance with a Jesus-word, he presents himself as following Christ and his law, he emphasizes his Jewish descendancy, and finally his missionary work has resulted in much more than others. Theissen rightly looks at the conflict between Paul and the "head-apostles" in a way other than the traditional theological way. But what is lacking in his examination, is the suffering as an apostolic legitimation. It is my contention that Paul also and not least legitimates himself when he is talking about his adversities and sufferings. In fact he is surpassing the "head-apostles" in suffering, which means that he is surpassing in Christ identification. Maybe the difference between the two parts is a question of having followed Jesus or not. While the first disciples experienced persecutions in following Jesus, Paul at the beginning did not. Instead he was a persecutor, and it may have given him problems. That the difference between Paul and the other apostles might have given him problems, can be seen in 1 Cor 9 and 15.1-11.

5. The Letter to the Philippians

Finally I shall discuss a letter in which the suffering constitutes the central theme to a higher extent than in any other letter by Paul. It is hardly exclusively due to the fact that Phil is written in captivity.

---

59. Georgi: *Die Gegner*, 295. He writes: "Rühmte sich Paulus seiner Leiden, so die Gegner ihrer geistlichen Erfahrungen und Machttaten und sahen sie im Gegensatz zu Paulus als Beweise für die Echtheit und Lebendigkeit ihrer Christusrepräsentation an."

60. G. Theissen, "Legitimation und Lebensunterhalt: ein Beitrag zur Soziologie urchristlicher Missionare," *NTS* 21 (1975) 192-221.

It also has its explanation in the fact that Paul must admonish the community in its attitude to sufferings. It is partly done by the thought of rejoicing in suffering in the certainty of salvation, and partly by admonitions where the identity of the community is placed in relation to the world outside, from where persecutions and attacks come (3.2,18-19). Finally it occurs in the central hymn 2.6-11, which constitutes the point of departure for the presentation of Paul himself (3.3-16), which for its part presents an ideal character for the community.

N. Walter has rightly maintained that there is no agreement between Paul and the Philippians concerning suffering as constituting Christian life. He writes:

So fremd für den aus hellenistischer Tradition kommenden Menschen der Gedanke des Leidens um Gottes und seines Ausschliesslichkeitsanspruches willen sein musste, so sehr war es einem Paulus aus der Tradition des Judentums seit der Zeit der Makkabäer und Hasidim geläufig, dass Leiden um Gottes willen Freude sein könne. [61]

I agree with Walter in this general view of the religious background of the Greeks and Romans, who converted to Christianity in Philippi. However, I do not agree with him when he, as many other scholars, maintains that the letter is composed of 3 different letters. For example it is Walter's view that 3.2-4.1 is a polemic letter. But in my view there is no polemics in that part of the letter. Paul is not polemizing but instead he warns the community against dangers from outside and he gives an account of himself as a pattern of Christian life. He does so in connecting this account with the hymn. That is a reason too for viewing the letter as originally one letter. The coherence of the letter is also seen in the fact that Paul both in chap. 1 (1.12-26) and in chap. 3 (3.2-16)gives an account of his own situation in such a way that his presentation of himself has an indirectly paraenetic character.

As written above, the hymn in chap. 2 constitutes a point of departure of Paul's presentation of himself. It may be emphasized that in the letter Paul makes use of this prepauline hymn in a paraenetic way. In fact as a prepauline hymn it has also a paraenetic intention. As U.B. Müller rightly writes:

Es zeigt sich, dass die Struktur des Traditionsstückes einem verbreiteten paränetischen Schema entspricht, in dem Selbsterniedrigung und Erhöhung einander gegenüberstehen. Man könnte deshalb den Schluss ziehen: An Jesus Christus

---

61. N. Walter, "Die Philipper und das Leiden," *Die Kirche des Anfangs: FS H. Schürmann* (ed. R. Schnackenburg, J. Ernst, J. Wanke; Freiburg, 1978) 417-34.

realisiert sich die ursprünglich weisheitliche Heilsansage, dass Gott den erhöht, der sich selbst erniedrigt.[62]

In the hymn Jesus Christ is described as the one who abased himself and was humbly obedient until death on the Cross, after which he was elevated to Lord. This is the content of faith by which the Philippians have to orient their life, not in a narrow form of imitatio Christi, but in the consciousness that they have received as a gift both the fact of faith in Christ and of suffering for him.

In 3.17 the Philippians are admonished with the words: σύμμιμεταί μού γίνεσθε. They shall have Paul as a τύπος. What this implies, Paul has extensively described in the preceding self-presentation (3.2-16), which constitutes at the same time a pattern of Christian life. As written above, Paul alludes to the hymn in many ways. His speech of being perfect consists of a consciousness of having not yet reached the goal. And to this consciousness belongs the fact of seeing suffering as a fellowship with Christ and as a similitude with his death (3.10). It precedes the aim that is hinted at in 3.12 and is later on clarified in 3.20-21. Both in 3.10 and 3.20-21 Paul maintains a similitude with Christ, as he is described in the hymn. Just as in the hymn and in the preceding paraenesis(2.3-5) it was a question of ταπεινοφροσύνη, so here also: Paul renounces everything that has until now given him identity. He considers it as a loss (ζημία in 3. 7-8; cf. 2.6), an attitude that he generalizes by speaking about renouncing everything for the sake of Christ. Presenting himself as a model, Paul must keep the Philippians to the fact that suffering belongs to Christian life, which is a life with citizenship (πολίτευμα) in Heaven and in expectation of conformity with the resurrected Lord.

Later on Paul once more points to himself as the one who understands ταπεινοῦσθαι (4.12). In an antithetic peristasis catalogue Paul presents himself as αὐτάρκης both in relation to hunger and to abundance. In using a Stoic term he claims to be just as independent of the monetary gift of the Philippians as he is persevering in sufferings. The decisive point is not that he is attached to a Stoic thought of independence of all exterior things, but that he identifies himself with Christ and immediately afterwards reminds the Philippians that they have participated in his adversities.[63]

The reason for writing the letter is on the surface to give thanks for their help, but Paul profits at the same time from the opportunity to keep an

---

62. U.B. Müller, "Der Christushymnus Phil 2 6-11," ZNW 79 (1988) 17-44. In this article Müller gives a survey of research. Among modern scholars it has been a *sensus communis* that it is a pre-pauline hymn. That is also Müller's view, but in contradiction to modern German scholars in particular Müller rightly maintains the paraenetic character of the pre-pauline hymn. That does not mean that the hymn invites to imitatio Christi. As Müller writes: "Eine solche Auslegung übersieht jedoch das Aussergewöhnliche des Geschehens, von dem der Hymnus handelt" (43).

63. See J. Gnilka, *Der Philipperbrief.* HTK (Freiburg, 1987) 174f.

apparently wealthy community tied to the fact that adversities and sufferings pertain to Christian life. As a prisoner, he can to a special extent appear as an apostle of the Crucified. The Christ identification is more evident than in any other letter of Paul, just as the paraenetic intention is clearly allied to the christology.

In a comparison with 1 Thess, Walter writes that Paul, in his missionary work in Philippi, not as in Thessalonica, told the Philippians that suffering is a constituent part of Christian life.[64] I am not sure that it is the case. I can not imagine that Paul has preached the Crucified without talking about suffering. And one must not forget that once Paul himself was a persecutor of the Christians. What is a new situation to the Philippians is that Paul has now been imprisoned. That gives him the opportunity to emphasize the Christ identification. And this identification is more sharply formulated than in any other letter of Paul.

Therefore the letter may be viewed as one more example of how important it is for Paul to state the reason for his paraenetic matter in the christology. The letter may be read as a paraenetic letter.

Conclusion

In my survey of research concerning the peristasis catalogues I have emphazised that one may not discern between Graeco-Roman or Jewish background because Paul as a Hellenistic Jew thought as a Jew and made use of Greek language and philosophical terminology at one and the same time. Paul was already living in the Hellenistic world before he as an apostle confronted himself with Graeco-Roman people.

Now, my subject has been the theme of suffering in Paul's theology, and here my intention has been first of all to stress the paraenetic purpose in Paul's presentation of himself as suffering. Instead of interpreting some Pauline texts as polemical or apologetical, as very often happens, I have tried to show that Paul, in urging an imitation of himself, joined the communities to the suffering Jesus Christ. Paraenesis and christology are correlated with each other when Paul speaks about his hardships and adversities. Here it is not enough to understand the theme against the background of Graeco-Roman and Jewish thought. One may also ask, if Paul has been influenced by Jesus tradition. I have maintained that the earthly life of Jesus Christ, including suffering and death, was much more important for Paul than normally asserted.

Finally, it is mostly neglected that in speaking about suffering Paul refers to experiences of persecutions by his compatriots. That means that he portrays himself in some way as an Old Testament prophet who experiences resistance

64. Walter, *Die Philipper*, 423.

from his compatriots, just as Jesus was killed by the Jews. In that way Paul presents himself as a true Jew.

In this connection I may draw attention to the social reality behind Paul's speaking about suffering. Paul was confronting himself with a Graeco-Roman audience, which did not understand persecutions as unavoidable in Christian life. And again and again Paul interprets suffering in a time-identifying manner as signs of the end of world history. That means that Paul considers Christian communities as social realities clashing with the persecuting world outside. Therefore, when Paul presents himself as suffering, the purpose of his paraenesis is also to maintain the eschatological quality of Christian life. One ought to be much more aware of the theme of suffering as a social theme which serves identifying Christians as the true Israel.

The Structural Typology of Adam and Christ. Some Modal-Semiotic Comments on the Basic Narrative of the Letter to the Romans

Ole Davidsen

Introduction

Paul's Letter to the Romans is an overwhelmingly complex discourse. On the one side we are facing a real *letter* sent to the church in Rome, but undoubtedly written also with the forthcoming visit to Jerusalem in mind. This is evident from the letter's opening introduction (1.1-15) and closing conclusion (15.14-16.27).[1] On the other side the *corpus* of the letter (1.16-15.13) presents itself as an *epistle*, of which the addresser is certainly Paul, but in his capacity of apostle, i.e., as a preacher who is speaking on behalf of God, and of which the addressee is certainly the church in Rome, but only because it is part of a general addressee (1.6).

The Letter to the Romans can therefore be read in two principally different modes. The first one is *specifying*, considering every utterance in the light of that specific situation of communication (setting in life), which the opening and closing sections of the letter bear witness to. The second one is *generalizing*, considering every utterance in the light of that general situation of communication, which characterizes the Christian proclamation. The specifying reading asks why Paul wants exactly the Romans to be informed or reminded of (15.15), that ὁ δὲ δίκαιος ἐκ πίστεως ζήσεται (1.17). On the contrary, the generalizing reading is interested in that proclamation, which Paul is presenting, i.e., his development of the basic claim, that ὁ δὲ δίκαιος ἐκ πίστεως ζήσεται, — an utterance, which obviously is valid not only to the church in Rome.

Thus, whether intended or not, Paul's discourse appears as *literature* in a generalized perspective. By this is not meant, that the text simply manifests itself by means of characters on papyrus, parchment or paper, but that this discourse is characterized by a relative autonomy, which makes it able to function for other persons in other times and in other places. It is this fact, that the function is not bound to an original situation of communication, a specific chronological setting in life, that turns it into literature, i.e., into a discourse,

---

1. The literary problems of the last three chapters are not to be discussed here; cf. for example C.K. Barrett, *The Epistle to the Romans* (London: A. & C. Black, 1991) 9.

which loosens itself from a given anchorage and offers itself as relevant in a different situation.

The Letter to the Romans can and should be subject to specifying investigations, which consider it as a source leading to the understanding of a specific historical situation of communication. However, exegesis fails to appreciate essential sides of its object, unless it recognizes this letter's status of literature in the sense mentioned above, i.e., its character as kerygmatic epistle. It is an historical fact that this letter has been preserved and canonized as epistle. Therefore it should also be studied as such.

When the manuscript G (012, Boernerianus from the 9. century) in the vv. 7 and 15 erases ἐν ῾Ρώμῃ and in v. 7 replaces ἀγαπητοῖς θεοῦ with ἐν ἀγάπῃ θεοῦ, so that the discourse is now addressed to anyone who stands in the love of God and not only to the Romans, these changes bear witness to the fact, that the letter is read as an epistle.[2] This epistle, which is addressed to all Christians (even to those, who are only potential Christians), then clearly receives the status of *gospel proclamation* (The Gospel According to Paul), in so far as Paul, a servant of Christ Jesus and called to be an apostle (1.1), *in precisely this literary discourse*, is proclaiming the Gospel of God (1.1) and thereby revealing a mystery, which had been kept secret since the creation of the world.[3] This Gospel, and thereby *the epistolary discourse itself*, is God's power for the salvation of everyone who has faith (1.16).[4]

Epistolary and Narrative Discourse

Any meaningful discourse is on the one side directed towards an addressee and comes on the other side from an addresser. However, it would be wrong just to consider the given discourse as a message transferred from a sender to a receiver. Thus the apostle never reveals himself to his addressee; they do not

---

2. Cf. C.K. Barrett who writes that his variant probably 'reflects a desire to show that the epistle is of universal, and not merely local application' (ibidem 17). In this paper the word *letter* is used to designate the local (or specific) application of the discourse, while the word *epistle* refers to its universal (or general) use.

3. This is a matter of fact, even if the doxology in 16.25-27 was not formed by Paul himself.

4. L. Hartman rightly assumes, that Paul, when he wrote his letters, "had a wider usage in mind than we usually assume" ("On Reading Others' Letters," *HTR* 79 (1986) 137-46). But for fear of justifying the church's re-reading of others' letters, he tries to persist in an historical-philological point of view, which seeks to reconstruct those further ancient communication situations, in which the letters could have been read secondarily. The generalizing reading, semiotic or narrative criticism, could of course be seen as an exegetical counterpart to the dogmatic approach, but even in the science of religion's perspective such an one-sided concentration on the past is unfounded. The Letter to the Romans is read even today, and this historical fact can only be explained from this epistle's literary properties.

know him except from the discourse itself. Similarly the addressee is anyone who recognizes himself in that role given by the discourse. It is as communicative roles in the discourse, i.e., as discursive phenomena, addresser and addressee are designated *enunciator* and *enunciatee*.[5] The text itself is seen as a discourse, that comprises not only the *enunciate* (utterance, message), but the *enunciation* as well. It is the enunciation, understood as the production of a meaningful discourse (and this is not exactly the same as its realized communication), which articulates the discourse as a speech act. And this speech (or language) act is present in the discourse itself.

Semiotic (or narrative exegesis) now takes its point of departure in the following model of the enunciation of the discourse:

1) The enunciator seeks to give the enunciatee an idea of a state of being and/or an action.
2) The subject of being for this state/action is the enunciator, the enunciatee or a third person A.
3) The responsible subject of doing for this state/action is the enunciator, the enunciatee, the third person A or a fourth person B.

A *narrative discourse*, in the strict sense of this word, can then be defined as a story-telling discourse, where neither the enunciator nor the enunciatee is performing as subject of being and/or as subject of doing. The Gospel of Mark can be viewed as a narrative discourse in this sense, since neither the enunciator Mark (implied author) nor his enunciatee (implied reader), is performing in the enunciate of this text. None of these actors are performing in the narrative world, which is populated by third party persons (God, Jesus, disciples, etc.). For example it is Jesus, as subject of doing (the fourth person B), who heals the sick person as subject of being (the third person A). Neither Mark nor his presupposed reader is healing or being healed.

An *epistolary discourse*, again in the strict sense of the word, can then be defined as a discourse, where both the enunciator and the enunciatee are performing as subject of being and/or as subject of doing. The Letter to the Romans can be viewed as such a discourse, since both the apostle (1. person, I) and the presupposed reader (2. person, You) are acting in the enunciate of the text. The apostle is not telling a story about a third person, who, as subject of doing, is exhorting other third party persons, as subject of being, but he is himself exhorting a generalized second person (cf. 12.1-15.14).

The distinction, made by form criticism inside the gospel narrative, between

---

5. To the semiotic concepts, cf. A.J. Greimas and J. Courtés, *Semiotics and Language. An Analytical Dictionary* (Bloomington: Indiana University Press, 1982).

narrative material and discursive material is well known.[6] In the narrative material Jesus is profiled as proclaimed, while he is profiled as proclaiming in the discursive material. However, this division is only valid on a certain level. If we take a closer look at the narrative material, we will see that the narrated persons can of course talk. And it is not without interest, that Jesus is narrating in the discursive material. The parabolic discourse is certainly discourse, but in the form of a narrative.

We are facing a similar problem here. The gospels are certainly narratives, while the letters are discourses, but as the narratives comprise discourses, so the discourses comprise narratives.

The importance of these apparently pure formal observations becomes clear, when we — with a slight semiotic reformulation of Clifford Geertz's classical statement — formally define Christianity as:

1) a *discursivized system of significations* which acts to 2) establish powerful, persuasive, and longlasting moods and motivations in men by 3) formulating conceptions of a general order of existence and 4) clothing these conceptions with such an aura of factuality that 5) these moods and motivations seem uniquely realistic.[7]

The basis of Christianity is the gospel-discourse (the Word), whether it is spoken or written, but as religious practice it certainly not only comprises this semiotic dimension, but a psychological (basically faith) and sociological (basically as ritual community) dimension as well.

The Christian system of significations is manifested by two main types of discourses, the gospel narratives and the letters. The first ones deal primarily with the founding events of Christianity (the life, death and resurrection of Jesus), the second ones with the life "in Christ", and thereby with Christian community. Thus the *conceptions of a general order of existence* are of two kinds, the first ones dealing with the *constitution*, the second ones with the *persistency* of Christianity. However, constitution and persistency are structurally bound together. Even if for example the Gospel of Mark only contains a few allusions to the post-paschal Christian life, there can be no doubt that this narrative did function in a ritual community.[8] On the other hand we see, that Paul in his

---

6. Rudolf Bultmann, *Die Geschichte der synoptischen Tradition* (Göttingen: Vandenhoeck & Ruprecht 1970).

7. Clifford Geertz, "Religion as a Cultural System," *Anthropological Approaches to the Study of Religion* (ed. M. Banton; London: Tavistock, 1966) 4.

8. For example the cup and the baptism in Mark 10.38 (cf. 1.9-11; 14.22-24) refer to the eucharist and the baptism as ritual acts, which are justified by the narrative itself. It is reasonable to assume, that Mark lets Jesus speak of his death as a baptism, because the Christian baptism — beyond the resurrection — is a baptism to his death, cf. Rom 6.3.

Letter to the Romans cannot teach without referring to the constituent events, for example that Jesus "was handed over to death for our sins and raised to life for our justification" (4.25).

If we, as a heuristic hypothesis, define the Roman discourse itself as a discursivizated system of significations which formulates conceptions of a general order of existence, we should start by asking for the constituent events of this order. That would be the same as asking for the fundamental level of Paul's semiotics or theology.

The general order of existence, which Paul proclaims, is both Jewish and Hellenistic, and it would not be wrong to say, that he is a particular representative of Hellenistic Judaism.[9] On the one side we have one God, one World, and one People (Mankind). On the other side one History, one Plan of Salvation, and one Destiny, where Israel has played and is still playing a decisive part (chap. 9-11). The transition from particularity to universality does not imply the simple substitution of one God or history by another, but Paul insists that the God who raised Jesus, is the same God who expelled Adam and gave Abraham (chap. 4) the promise and Moses (5.14) the law (cf. 3.29).

Thus we would not be surprised, if someone told us, that Paul is a child of his age. On the contrary, today we would really be surprised if he were not. The comparative study of Hellenistic discourses is therefore essential, but a comparativism, which is not based on a typological model (in the semiotic sense), is often more confusing than illuminative.[10] Furthermore the comparative project does not relieve us from the task of studying the single discourse, and one should remember that narrative exegesis is working with models, which themselves are the result of previous comparative studies. Thus the concern is here to show how narrative exegesis is able to clarify our understanding of that *narrative rationality*, which characterizes the general order of existence in the Pauline universe of Hellenistic Judaism.

Text and Typology

The interest is concentrated on 5.12-21, which is quite complex in its structure. In v. 12 a comparison is commenced, but immediately interrupted by more parentheses; a first one about death's power over mankind before the arrival

9. See for example A.F. Segal, *Paul the Convert. The Apostolate and Apostasy of Saul the Pharisee* (New Haven: Yale University Press, 1990).

10. According to A.J. Greimas and J. Courtés, *Semiotics and Language. An Analytical Dictionary*, "Comparativism", "Comparativism is a set of cognitive procedures aiming at establishing formal correlations between two or more semiotic objects and eventually at constituting a typological model of these semiotic objects which then are only variables of this model". For example is Paul's comparison of Adam and Christ only significant, because they are both Son of God/representative Man — though in two variants.

of the law, vv. 13-14; a second one about the inequality between the fall of Adam and the grace of God, vv. 15-17. It is not until vv. 18-19 the comparison between Adam and Christ is brought to an end, and Paul finishes with some considerations concerning the role of the law, v. 20, before he gives his conclusion in v. 21.

The typologization must be considered as the main question to Paul. That digression, which concerns the law (vv. 13-14), has to be seen as the anticipation of the objection, that the law should disperse the typology. However, the law does not contradict the basic order of existence (v. 20). Neither is the digression, concerning the inequality between the fall and the grace, denying the comparison, but must be considered as a rhetorical articulation of certain aspects of the basic narrative, cf. 5.6-10. The digressions differentiate and articulate the typology, but without denying its integrity or transgressing its semantic framework.

The comparison is accomplished in vv. 18 and 19, which thus contain the most fundamental information about that general order of existence that Paul is proclaiming. And it is these verses, which will be taken into consideration in what follows, — using, naturally, information from the remaining verses.

The claim, that a given discourse (here the Letter to the Romans) is a *discursivizated system of significations* (an organized field of virtual significations brought into being as discourse), implies the hypothesis, that this discourse as (syntagmatic) process is characterized by a scattered and elliptic manifestation of signification structures, which can be reconstructed systematically. The discourse is a surface phenomenon that has to be analyzed structurally, and in one way the procedure includes the systematization of the information on the basis of a chosen level of relevance, in this case the narrative in vv. 18-19, that can be paraphrased in the form of presentic propositions:

1) One man's transgression brings condemnation and death to all humanity.[11]
2) One man's act of righteousness brings justification and life to all humanity.
3) By one man's disobedience all are made sinners.
4) By one man's obedience all are made righteous.

This typology opposes and compares two men, Adam (v.14) and Christ (vv. 15,17,21). The relationship between these persons is characterized by resemblance, since the acts of both have consequences for others, but also by

---

11. By a procedure of catalysis the utterances are filled out with other information in the text. For example 18a speaks of justification and life, whereas 18b mentions condemnation, but not death. The parallelism is underlined by the addition of death according to 5.12, 15, 17, 21. Cf. further that one = one man, and many = all; cf. 3.9-20.

difference, since the first one (*malefactor/malefaction*) is disobedient, which results in death, while the second one (*benefactor/benefaction*) is obedient, which results in life. "Type" and "anti-type" as they are usually characterized, but without recognizing the *structural relation* between these two entities.[12]

In fact we are facing a structural resemblance and a structural difference. The Adam/Christ-typology is a *structural typology*, which gathers together difference and resemblance and sets Adam and Christ as inter-defined by relations of reciprocal presupposition. In a syntagmatic perspective Adam is ὁ πρῶτος ᾿Αδάμ, while Christ is ὁ ἔσχατος ᾿Αδάμ (1 Cor 15.45), and it is evident, that the second one presupposes the first one. However, in a paradigmatic perspective these two persons presuppose each other reciprocally, and that is why Christ too is designated Adam. We cannot understand who Christ is without our knowledge of Adam. But neither do we really understand Adam without our knowledge of Christ. These persons interpret each other, and we should not be surprised, if Adam was called Christ, because that is exactly what he is (cf. Luke 3.38 and 3.22).

Thus this structural typology of Adam and Christ is not simply a comparison, but the fundamental structure of signification in the Pauline universe of meaning. As such we can expect, that this typology, given, as we shall see, as a double narrative, organizes all other information in the Pauline discourse. That is why we should focus on this basic narrative of the Letter to the Romans.

Narrative Typology

The four propositions that constitute the base of the typology, must be identified as an Adam/Christ-narrative, which contains two interrelated processes of action. The first one is the Fall, that can be designated δυσαγγέλιον. The second one is the Rising, i.e., the εὐαγγέλιον. The typology is a *narrative typology*.

This means that neither the subjects of doing, Adam or Christ, nor the subjects of being, the many or the all, are to be identified directly with the narrator (enunciator) or the narratee (enunciatee). The apostle is not describing an action, that he or his listener has done; neither is he simply giving information about his own or his readers being. Obviously both the apostle and his reader are members of the collective actor mankind, but nevertheless we must distinguish between the universe of the narrative, in which mankind is located, and the universe of narration where the apostle and his reader are present. It is only then that we will be able to see, that it is the universal quantification (all) of the narrative subject of being, which tends towards the anchorage of the narrative world in the world of narration (enunciation). We

---

12. Cf. for example C.K. Barrett, *The Epistle to the Romans*, 105.

must begin by identifying the subject of being as the third person A, i.e., mankind, and the subject of doing as the fourth person B, i.e., Adam/Christ.

It is now possible to differentiate between the general roles subject of doing and subject of being according to the given valorisation. The act of Adam implies a loss of value, since the subject of being involved undergoes the change of a positive state of being into a negative one, passing from abundance (life) to deficiency (death, — understood as the lack of life). Such a process can be designated *degression*; the responsible subject of doing is called *degressor*, and the subject of being is designated *victim*. On the contrary, the act of Christ implies the acquisition of value, the subject of being involved passing from deficiency (death) to abundance (life), since we have here the change of a negative state of being into a positive one. Such a process is designated *progression*; the responsible subject of doing is called *progressor*, and the subject of being in this case can be determined *beneficiary*.

Thus it appears that this narrative typology contains three fields of difficulty of which the first two are internal, belonging to the narrative world (the enunciate), while the third one is external, belonging to the world of narration (the enunciation):

1) The relation between the two subjects of doing, Adam and Christ.
2) The relation between the one subject of doing (Adam or Christ) and the many subjects of being.
3) The relation between the persons in the narrative world and the persons in the world of narration.

I cannot deal with 2) and 3) here, but can only say, that the acts of Adam and Christ are what the semiotician calls factitive acts.[13] Furthermore, that it is the basic narrative, which interprets the persons in the world of narration and imposes their being upon them.[14]

---

13. The factitive act is an act where a modalizing subject (Adam/Christ) does something so that, as a result of this doing, the modalized subject (Mankind) is instituted as a competent subject, either by increase (Christ, who opens up for new possibilities) or by decrease (Adam, who provokes a loss of given possibilities), cf. A.J. Greimas and J. Courtés, *Semiotics and Language*, "Factitiveness". Cf. καθίστημι (5.19) in the sense of doing someone to something.

14. This being has to be accepted, cf. Rom 5.11,17, and it appears to be in ritual (in this case in baptism, cf. 6.1-11), that this conviction that religious conceptions are veridical and that religious directives are sound, is somehow generated. It is in some sort of ceremonial form — even if that form be hardly more than the recitation of a narrative — that the moods and motivations which sacred systems of significations induce in men and the general conceptions of the order of existence which they formulate for men, meet and reinforce one another, cf. Clifford Geertz, "Religion as a Cultural System," *Anthropological Approaches to the Study of Religion*, 28, who further

Here I shall look at the relation between the two subjects of doing, Adam and Christ, but analytically. I want to underline the overlooked point, that Adam and Christ are not only subjects of doing, but are, of course, subjects of being as well. When we are told, that the disobedience of Adam implies death, it is first of all the death of Adam, that we are dealing with. And when we are told, that the obedience of Christ implies life, it is first of all the life of Christ, i.e., his eternal life, we should have in mind.

I am trying to elaborate a model for the underlying narrative rationality that organizes the basic narrative content of the Pauline discourse. And in this perspective it is decisive to concentrate upon the destinies of Adam and Christ, the degressive and progressive processes in which they undergo transformations of their being.

Life and Death

It is an advantage to consider Christ first. He is undergoing a narrative process, which consists of three states of being:

$$\text{Life1} \rightarrow \text{Death} \rightarrow \text{Life2}$$

His death is caused by the crucifixion, while Life2 is caused by the resurrection. So Life2 is an eternal life, and as such in opposition to Life1. According to 6.9 Christ has been raised from the dead and will never die again. So whatever else it may be, eternal life (v. 21) is a state of being, which cannot be changed by death. On the contrary, Life1 is a state of being, which can be changed by death, as shown by the crucifixion. In opposition to a definitive life (eternal life, Life2), located beyond, stands a provisional life (Life1) located under the reign of death. Furthermore it should be observed, that the Death of the Cross is a provisional death, since this state of being can be changed by life. So we have:

Provisional Life $\rightarrow$ Provisional Death $\rightarrow$ Definitive Life.

Paul does not give more definite information about Adam, but at least it should be clear, that at a given moment he is alive, but — sooner or later — bound to die. The life that immediately precedes the death is necessarily

---

writes: "Whatever role divine intervention may or may not play in the creation of faith — and it is not the business of the scientist to pronounce upon such matters one way or the other — it is, primarily at least, out of the context of concrete acts of religious observance that religious conviction emerges on the human plane". I think this is the religiological reason, why Paul is reflecting upon baptism in 6.1-11.

provisional, which in this case death cannot be. The death of Adam has to be determined as a definitive death, an eternal death, i.e., a death, that cannot be changed by life, since it is located beyond the reign of life. This definitive death is in opposition to the Death of the Cross, which is surely a temporary or provisional death.

So it develops that the fundamental semantics of the Adam-Christ-typology is constituted by an isotopic semantic universe, which consists of a network of interrelated terms:

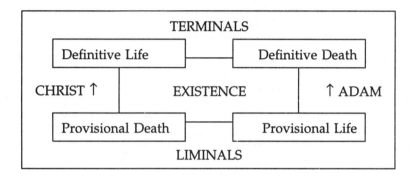

It should be observed that Provisional Life is the state of being in which Adam is located after the expulsion from the garden of Eden.[15] This state is not only oriented (↑) towards Definitive Death, but at that moment this terminal state of being is inevitable. On the other hand the Provisional Death is the state of being in which Christ is located by the Death of the Cross. Neither is this state only oriented (↑) towards Definitive Life, but by his realization of this being the terminal state becomes inevitable. The liminals are both states of being that cannot persist. So the problem presents itself as a question of modalities, and it seems appropriate to take the dynamic modalities of being into consideration.

Dynamic Modalities

In a given, possible world, the world of the narrative subject, this will be the subject of being susceptible to processes, which are either possible/evitable, impossible or inevitable. The being of the narrative subject is modalized by the dynamic (cf. δύναμαι, δύναμις) modalities of being:

---

15. I consider Gen 2-3 to be the most adequate intertextual point of reference for an understanding of the narrative rationality in Paul's Adam-theology.

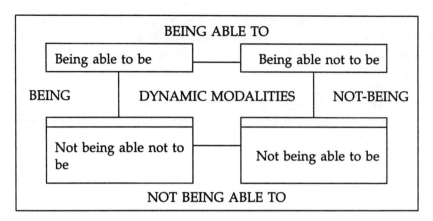

corresponding with:

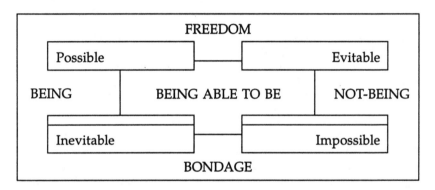

According to this modal category, a non-realized state of being can be given in four different dynamic modes:

— it can be *impossible*: the subject of being is powerless, kept in its initial state because of a fatal process of preservation (repression or protection);
— it can be *inevitable*: the subject of being is dependent and will enter the final state because of a fatal process of change (degression or progression);
— it can be *possible*: the subject of being is powerful, the initial state can be changed (progression or degression);
— it can be *evitable*: the subject of being is independent, the initial state can be preserved (protection or repression).

To a person, initially located in Provisional Life (here Adam after the expulsion), the state of being Definitive Death is inevitable. As subject of being this person is the future victim of a fatal degression. So an eschatological perspective appears here since the final state of being is, so to speak, *already/not yet* realized: here we speak of *condemnation* (κατάκριμα, 5.1,18; 8.1), since Definitive Death is inevitable, while Definitive Life is impossible.

To a person, initially located in Provisional Death (here Christ in and by the death on the Cross), the state of being Definitive Life is inevitable. As subject of being this person is the future beneficiary of a fatal progression. Here we speak of *justification* (δικαίωσις, δικαιόω), since Definitive Life is inevitable, while Definitive Death is impossible.

From a physiological/biological perspective death is inevitable, man is a mortal being, who sees his existence determined by this basic fact. However, the religious discourse gives an interpretation of this natural fact by inscribing it into a wider narrative context. The reality of death is not simply denied, but is given a narrative interpretation. Of course it can be said, that the narrative about Adam is an etiological myth, which seeks to explain the reality of death, but the religious discourse wants not only to give intellectual explanations, but existential understanding, and it is in this perspective the *narrative discourses* must be seen.

When we distinguish between beneficiary and victim, we are operating on a narrative level. It is only a human or anthropomorphized being, which — in his own or in other peoples eyes — is able to undertake these roles. The anthropocentrism is a constituent quality of narrativity. A given process is only significant, when it performs a function in the action, i.e., when it serves or harms a person's existential project. However, a goal-oriented project is only given in the cases where a human subject is inscribed into a system of values. A narrative integrates a succession of events into one action, and it is the narrative subject which is the symbol of unity. The events only have significance in relation to a human project. It is human beings (or at least anthropomorphized beings) who perform and undertake the processes founding the events, persons who ask for the meaning of these processes and their results. The religious discourse humanizes the world, "le monde se trouve justifié par l'homme, l'homme intégré dans le monde".[16]

Fall and Rise

The modal situation, that Death reigns, is in power (cf. that βασιλεύω 5.14, 17,21; 6.12 and κυριεύω 6.9,14 are used to express this modal reality), is not presented as a single fact, but as the result of Adam's disobedient action. The modal situation, that Provisional Life is fatally oriented towards Definitive Death, is due to Adam's παράβασις (5.14), παράπτωμα (5.15,17,18), ἁμαρτία (5.12,16), and παρακοή (5.19). Adam's doing, his performance, is a narrative pivotal point, which something precedes and something else follows.

Thus we here rediscover the narrative scheme, which organizes the action

---

16. A.J. Greimas, *Sémantique structurale* (Paris: Le Seuil, 1966) 213.

of the story. This concerns the interaction between a Destinator and a Destinatee, a Lord and a Servant, here God and Adam.[17] The first phase is a phase of influence or manipulation, where God sets a commandment for Adam, more precisely an interdiction. The second phase is a phase of performance, where Adam transgresses the interdiction. Third phase is a phase of sanction, where God partly evaluates and judges his servant, partly performs retribution, here in the shape of punishment:[18]

MANIPULATION	PERFORMANCE	SANCTION
Interdiction	Transgression	Judgement/ Punishment
ἐντολή	παράβασις/ παράπτωμα	κατάκριμα
νόμος	παρακοή/ἁμαρτία	θάνατος

Any narrative discourse gives information about the change or preservation of states of being, but we find different kinds of states of being. Beside the *somatic* (or *pragmatic*) states of being it is possible to distinguish what we could call *covenantal* states, which indicate whether a subject of being/doing is righteous or sinner. Thus to begin with, the transgression of Adam is a change of his covenantal being, from righteous to sinner. It is this being, which is subject to judgement, and then, in the case of the sinner, results in punishment, death penalty. The execution implies a pragmatic change of the somatic being, from life to death.

However, Adam does not die as an immediate consequence of his crime. The penalty consists in the first place of the expulsion from the garden of Eden, and this is much more than a simple move from one place to another, because it concerns the *modal existence* of Adam. The punishment consists in the first place of the change of his *modal* state of being.[19]

17. I suggest to translate Destinateur/Destinataire by Destinator/Destinatee instead of using Sender/Receiver or Addresser/Addressee; cf. A.J. Greimas and J. Courtés, *Semiotics and Language*, "Sender/Receiver".

18. I use νόμος in the scheme, since there is an evident analogy between the commandment given to Adam and the law given to Moses; cf. Egon Brandenburger, *Adam und Christus. Exegetisch-religionsgeschicthliche Untersuchung zu Röm 5.12-21 (1. Kor 15)* (Neukirchen: Neukirchener Verlag, 1962) 191, 250.

19. It is significant, that also the salvation of the Christian — as justification — in a first moment consists of a change of the modal being. To be the heir of eternal life does not mean that one have it, but that one inevitably will get it.

If the expulsion from the garden of Eden implies, that death becomes inevitable, then initially Adam must be located in a modal state of being, where death is neither inevitable nor impossible. Is this state of being eternal life? No, not exactly, since eternal life is defined — by Paul himself — as a state of being located beyond the power of Death, that is a state where death is impossible. So, initially Adam must be located in a state of being characterized by *freedom* (ἐλευθερία, cf. 6.18, 20, 22; 8.21), i.e., a state, where death at the same time is possible and evitable (modalized by being-able-to-be/being-able-not-to-be).

This liminal phase of transition can also be determined on the basis of Definitive Life. In the same way, eternal life is simultaneously possible and evitable in this modal state of being. That the expulsion implies a modal transformation becomes evident, when one remembers, that the great winged creatures are guarding the way to the Tree of Life (Gen 3.24). This is no longer at hand, no longer a possibility: Definitive Life has become impossible. However, at the same time Definitive Death has become inevitable.[20]

It is this modal change which makes Adam's act especially important, even from a cosmological perspective, since it establishes a new world, a new reality, a new age: a new order of existence.

This new world, the given world between the Fall and the Rising, is characterized by a particular modal nature or condition, since it, after Adam's transgression, is fatally oriented towards destruction. A world which is distinguished by such a *particular modal existence*, is called an *age* or an *era* (αἰών; 12.2; cf. Gal 1.4). This is not primarily a period of time, but a state of being characterized by a particular modal quality.[21]

The process of destruction itself is not modal, but pragmatic (somatic). However, this process is temporized. Between the judgement and the execution of the punishment a waiting period is given, which refers to God's kindness, tolerance and patience (2.4).

We have seen, that Adam in the garden of Eden was characterized by a particular modal situation. Definitive Life and Definitive Death were at the same time possible and evitable. We can give another interpretation of this situation on the basis of the dynamic modalities of doing:

---

20. Cf. J.G. Frazer's remarkable reading: "The gist of the whole story of the fall appears to be an attempt to explain man's mortality, to set forth how death came into the world. It is true that man is not said to have been created immortal and to have lost his immortality through disobedience; but neither is he said to have been created mortal. Rather we are given to understand that the possibility alike of immortality and of mortality was open to him, and that it rested with him which he would choose; for the tree of life stood within his reach, its fruit was not forbidden to him, he had only to stretch out his hand, take of the fruit, and eating of it live for ever." (*Folk-Lore in the Old Testament*, London: Macmillan, 1923) 16.

21. Time is an epiphenomenon, which can be seen from the fact, that it starts from zero, when the world enters into a new mode of being, cf. our chronology.

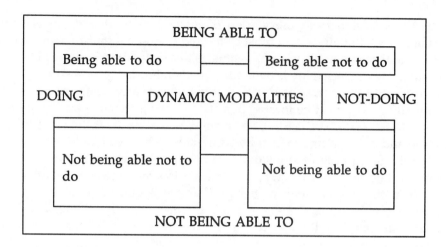

corresponding with:

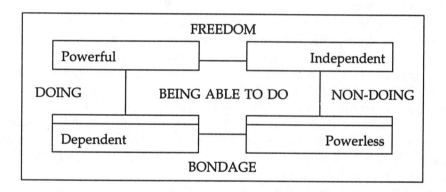

The disobedient act, the transgression of the interdiction, is not caused by the fact that Adam is under the reign of Sin, so that he should be unable not to sin. If the interdiction is to be meaningful, he must be located in a situation characterized by freedom. He must at the same time be modalized as powerful and independent. Without this dimension of freedom, the uniqueness of Adam's act becomes incomprehensible, — not only to modern man, but to anyone who reads this narrative and asks for its meaning, i.e., its narrative rationality.

One could conjecture, whether the eating from the Tree of Life would have implied a modal transformation, which located Adam in a modal state of being characterized by a positive *bondage* (δουλεία, cf. 6.19; 8.15, 21), not-being-able-to-sin.

However, it seems obvious, that the expulsion from the Garden of Eden implies a transformation into a negative bondage: from now on Adam is not-being-able-not-to-sin.[22] He is not only under the reign of Death (concerning his somatic being), but also under the reign of Sin (concerning his doing). We do not need to go into Augustinian speculations concerning the nature of sin here.[23] The main point is clear: Adam is in a situation characterized by dependence, since he is unable to change his state of being. He cannot preserve his (provisional) life, protection is impossible, and he cannot avoid (definitive) death; degression is inevitable.

We could look at this situation from another angle and say, that Adam is characterized by the covenantal state of being *sinner* and unable to change this being. He cannot justify himself, cannot regain the covenantal state of being *righteous*, which is impossible.

The disobedience of Adam is opposed to the obedience (ὑπακοή, v. 19) of Christ. Paul says nothing further about this obedience, but the narrative exegesis can systematically ask for its rationality.

Here too we must be dealing with a process that is organized as an interactive doing with two different subjects, a Destinator and a Destinatee, a Lord and his Servant, God and Christ.

The obedience as performance presupposes a phase of manipulation, where God confronts Christ with a commandment, in this case with a prescription.[24] By his observance of this prescription (by his δικαίωμα/δικαιοσύνη, vv. 18,21) Christ qualifies himself as upright or righteous (δίκαιος) and the phase of sanction must include recognition (δικαίωσις) and recompense (ἀπόδοσις) in the shape of eternal life (ζωὴ αἰώνιος, v. 21):

MANIPULATION	PERFORMANCE	SANCTION
Prescription	Observance	Judgement/ Recompense
ἐντολή	δικαίωμα	κρίμα/ἀνάστασις
νόμος	ὑπακοή/δικαιοσύνη	δικαίωσις/ζωή

22. Also Augustine thinks in a modal-semiotic way. Before the Fall Adam was characterized by freedom, by *posse peccare* and *posse non peccare*; after the Fall he is distinguished by bondage, by *non posse non peccare*. In eternity, however, the saints will be determined by *non posse peccare*; cf. for example *De Civitate Dei*, 22.30.

23. Cf. E. Brandenburger, *Adam und Christus*, 168-80.

24. Both interdiction and prescription alienate the desire of the Destinatee, but in different ways. The interdiction presupposes that the Destinatee wants to realize a state of being, which is possible, but forbidden, and thus points to *temptation*. On the contrary, the prescription presupposes that he does not want to realize a state of being, which is evitable, but ordered, and thus points to *trial* (test).

The performance of Christ can only be identified as the Death of the Cross, i.e., this event seen as an act for which Christ himself is the responsible subject of doing. In that case the Death of the Cross has been understood as a gift (a giving, cf. Mark 10.45), not as a take (a taking, execution or murder).

The sanction (cf. ὁρίζω, 1.4) is first of all God's recognition of Christ as righteous and his affirmation of this state of being, subsequently the resurrection of Christ to eternal life. The observance of the prescription is only significant, if it is presumed that Christ was liberated from the reign of sin, which is not exactly the same as being sinless. He must be able to observe the prescription, but also be able to disregard it. So he must be located in a situation, where Definitive Life is possible and evitable at the same time. The observance of the prescription, his obedience to the death on the Cross, must imply a modal transformation, since Definitive Life in and by this death becomes inevitable: God keeps his promises. The resurrection must be seen as an effect of the obedience, and the issue of the prescription must be seen in relation to a promising project, to which the goal is eternal life, the overcoming of the reign of Death.

One of the questions to be asked concerns the conditions that must be given for Christ to act in freedom. Paul says nothing about this, but Mark tells us, that it was the baptism, not the baptism of John, but the baptism by the spirit, i.e., the anointing by the Holy Spirit in continuation of the water baptism, which endowed Jesus in such a way that he became able to realize the project of salvation or justification, i.e., the Christ-project.[25]

He comes to John to be baptized, that is to get the forgiveness of sins, when suddenly the heavens tear apart, and God chooses one single person from among the baptized, one man, whose action (doing) is going to be of great importance to many (Mark 1.9-11). The temptation in the desert (1.12-13) as well as the trial in the Garden of Gethsemane (14.32-42) show, that Christ is not regarded as a robot or as an automat, i.e., as a subject of doing, which is modalized by not-being-able-not-to-do. The speaking of obedience refers to a subject of doing, that can observe the prescription but disregard it as well. As Adam, so is Christ free to act for or against God.

Justification

The righteousness of God is revealed in the Gospel (Rom 1.17). However, the Gospel is only given as *discourse*, spoken or written, so we can say as well, that the righteousness of God is revealed in the discourse of the apostle. This

---

25. I use here Mark as reference text, because an analysis of this gospel story's narrative organisation has revealed a modal structure which is exactly the opposite to what we find in Gen 2-3. Cf. Ole Davidsen, *The Narrative Jesus. A Semiotic Reading of Mark's Gospel* (Aarhus: Aarhus University Press, 1993).

righteousness (salvation) is given to every one who believes (10.4), i.e., to every one, who calls upon the name of the Lord (10.13). Though, how can a man call on the Lord Jesus in whom he does not believe? And how can he believe in him of whom he has not heard? And how can he hear without a preacher? And how can anyone preach if he is not sent? Faith comes from hearing the word (cf. 10.14-17), and to many that word has been the one apostle's Letter to the Romans.[26]

However, faith has a content, a general order of existence, and this investigation has been interested in the basic narrative of that content.

It is natural to understand Paul's teaching on justification in relation to the law, since he himself comments on it. A righteousness from God without law is now revealed (3.21), and Christ is the end of the law (10.4). Nevertheless I will suggest, that first of all we should define the righteousness of God in relation to the Adam/Christ-typology.

The narrative scheme is a covenant scheme. The relationship established between the Destinator and the Destinatee is a covenant between a covenantal Lord and his covenantal Servant. The Adam- and the Christ-covenant are the two arch-covenants in relation to which all other covenants in the history of salvation are defined.[27]

The covenant establishes an *ordinance* (δικαίωμα, cf. 1.32; 8.4), and both the Lord and the Servant are then under an obligation. When Adam transgresses the interdiction, he is breaking the covenant and becomes worthy of punishment. When God punishes Adam, he is doing so because he is righteous, i.e., acting according to the present ordinance.

On God's part, the establishment of the covenant with Jesus is an act of grace. Nevertheless, and this should not be neglected, it is the founding of a new ordinance. If Jesus keeps the commandment, then God is obliged, according to his own ordinance, to raise Jesus up to eternal life. Since God is righteous, the upright Jesus is really raised in the narrative, and a new modal reality is given. From now on eternal life is inevitable to all who believe in the message. Death is no longer definitive, but provisional and will necessarily be followed by Definitive Life. If there is an asymmetry in the Adam/Christ-

---

26. Rom 10.14-17 is clear evidence, that Paul himself was aware that the Letter to the Romans — as an apostolic discourse — is gospel proclamation.

27. "Die Vorstellung von der Restitution des alten Bundes war nicht geeignet, die universale Wirklichkeit des Christusgeschehens voll auszuschöpfen", writes E. Brandenburger. That is why Paul did not use this tradition in his mission to the gentiles, but choose to use "die gnostische Anthropos-Kategorie mit ihrer Zuordnung von εἷς ἄνθρωπος und πάντες ἄνθρωποι", *Adam und Christus*, 240. He may be right, but we are nevertheless facing two arch-covenants here, and the idea of an Adam-covenant is known at least from *Apoc. Mos.* 8.2 (cf. even 23.3 and *Adam and Eve* 26.2; 34.1). See *The Old Testament Pseudepigrapha* (Vol. 2; ed. J.H. Charlesworth; London: Darton, Longman & Todd, 1985) 249.

typology, it can only be due to the fact, that Christ realized that eternal life, which Adam never had except as a possibility.

According to the Romans general Christian order of existence God's, Man's, and World's destiny depends upon the acts of two men, Adam and Christ. The Christian God renounces his almightiness and lets the realization of his project of creation depend upon man. Adam fails and the righteous God hands him over to destruction. The God of love remains behind however, disappointed in his hopes, seeing his act of creation rejected and denied.

However, the disappointment is overcome and God gives man another chance by the establishment of a new covenant with Jesus, and this time it works. In this manner the way is prepared for the final realization of the eschatological-apocalyptical kingdom of God.

This is the narrative rationality in Paul's Adam-Christology. Eternal life is now as certain as eternal death was in the old age. Because the degression of Man's being was also a degression of God's being. When his project of creation failed, God nevertheless acted righteously according to his own ordinance and death became inevitable. It is then much more to expect (cf. 5.6-10), that eternal life is inevitable in the new order of existence, since the righteous God — thanks to the obedience of his covenantal servant Christ — has now finally the possibility of realizing his project of creation in accordance with his own δικαίωμα.

Abbreviations

AB	Anchor Bible
ABRL	Anchor Bible Reference Library
ANET	Ancient Near Eastern Texts Relating to the Old Testament
ANRW	Aufstieg und Niedergang der römischen Welt
ATD	Das Alte Testament Deutsch
ATDan	Acta theologica danica
BETL	Bibliotheca ephemeridum theologicarum lovaniensium
BFCT	Beiträge zur Förderung christlicher Theologie
BJS	Brown Judaic Studies
BNTC	Black's New Testament Commentaries
BWANT	Beiträge zur Wissenschaft vom Alten und Neuen Testament
ConB	Coniectanea biblica
CRINT	Compendia Rerum Iudaicarum ad Novum Testamentum
CTJ	Calvin Theological Journal
DTT	Dansk teologisk Tidsskrift
EKKNT	Evangelisch-katholischer Kommentar zum Neuen Testament
ET	Evangelische Theologie
FRLANT	Forschungen zur Religion und Literatur des Alten und Neuen Testaments
HNT	Handbuch zum Neuen Testament
HTK	Herder theologischer Kommentar zum Neuen Testament
HTR	Harvard Theological Review
HUCA	Hebrew Union College Annual
ICC	International Critical Commentary
JBL	Journal of Biblical Literature
JSHRZ	Jüdische Schriften aus hellenistisch-römischer Zeit
JSJ	Journal for the Study of Judaism in the Persian, Hellenistic and Roman Period.
JSNT	Journal for the Study of the New Testament
JSNTSup	Journal for the Study of the New Testament — Supplement Series
JSOT	Journal for the Study of the Old Testament
JTS	Journal of Theological Studies
KEK	Kristisch-exegetischer Kommentar über das Neue Testament
LCL	Loeb Classical Library
NEB	Die Neue Echte Bibel
NedTTs	Nederlands theologisch tijdschrift
Neot	Neotestamentica
NovT	Novum Testamentum

NTD	Das Neue Testament Deutsch
NTS	New Testament Studies
ÖTK	Ökumenischer Taschenbuch-Kommentar zum Neuen Testament
OTP	J.H. Charlesworth (ed.), The Old Testament Pseudepigrapha
PVTG	Pseudepigrapha Veteris Testamenti graece
RAC	Reallexikon für Antike und Christentum
SANT	Studien zum Alten und Neuen Testament
SBB	Stuttgarter biblische Beiträge
SBL	Society of Biblical Literature
SBLDS	SBL Dissertation Series
SBLSCS	SBL Septuagint and Cognate Studies
SBT	Studies in Biblical Theology
SEÅ	Svensk exegetisk årsbok
SNT	Studien zum Neuen Testament
SNTSMS	Society for New Testament Studies Monograph Series
ST	Studia theologica
SUNT	Studien zum Umwelt des Neuen Testaments
SVTP	Studia in Veteris Testamenti pseudepigrapha
TD	Theology Digest
THNT	Theologischer Handkommentar zum Neuen Testament
ThR	Theologische Rundschau
TLZ	Theologische Literaturzeitung
TRE	Theologische Realencyklopädie
TTZ	Trierer theologische Zeitschrift
TU	Texte und Untersuchungen
TWNT	G. Kittel and G. Friedrich (eds.), Theolgisches Wörterbuch zum Neuen Testament
VC	Vigiliae christianae
VT	Vetus Testamentum
VTSup	Vetus Testamentum, Supplements
WMANT	Wissenschaftliche Monographien zum Alten und Neuen Testament
WUNT	Wissenschaftliche Untersuchungen zum Neuen Testament
ZAW	Zeitschrift für die alttestamentiche Wissenschaft
ZEE	Zeitschrift für evangelische Ethik
ZNW	Zeitschrift für die neutestamentiche Wissenschaft
ZTK	Zeitschrift für Theologie und Kirche

Index of Names

Aaron 35, 169
Abraham 30, 60, 151-56, 159, 161-63, 175-76, 184, 213, 248
Achilles 93
Achtemeier, P.J. 107
Adam 60-61, 122, 228, 248-62
Aeschylus 24
Agamemnon 92
Agar 154
Alexandria 35, 56, 95, 112, 169, 215
Alexandros 42
Alexandros Polyhistor 45
Alexiares 94
Altmann, A. 42
Altwell, J. 44
Amersfoort, J. van 65
Amir, Yehoshua 42-43
Ancyra 220
Anderson, H. 76-77, 85
Andresen, C. 227
Anicetus 94
Antiochien 54
Antiochus 27
Antiochus IV Epiphanes 96
Antipas, Herod 227
Apollodorus 94
Apollonius of Tyana 108, 110
Apollos 211-12, 214-16, 235
Aqiba 38, 176-77
Arabia 157-58
Aretas 220
Aristeas 9, 11, 20, 94, 125, 132, 138
Aristobulus 9, 19, 20, 24, 27, 49, 56
Arnaldez, R. 179-80
Artapanus 9, 20, 26, 29, 45, 112
Artemis 92
Aseneth 22-24, 28, 32, 45, 139
Asmodeus 80
Athena 94
Athos 69
Atrahasis 91

Attridge, H. 44
Auer, A. 123
Augustus 220
Aune, David E. 100
Avigad, N. 73
Awgerean, B 45

Babel 32
Badenas, R. 186
Bandstra 165, 167, 172-73
Banton, M. 247
Barnabas 9, 14, 16, 17
Barnanas 54
Barrett, C.K. 152-53, 163, 165-66, 168, 170, 172, 174-75, 186, 244-45, 250
Bartimaeus 72, 74, 76-77, 79, 83, 85-86
Baruch 12, 180, 183, 189
Baumgarten, A.I. 63
Baur, F.C. 40
Becker, J. 40, 125-27, 142
Beelzebul 118
Begg, Christopher 95
Behnisch, M. 132, 134-35
Bekken, Per Jarle 12, 183
Beniot, P. 90
Benoît, A. 60
Bensly, R.L. 67
Berger, K. 129, 142
Bergren, Theodore 67-68
Berossus 95, 99
Betz, H.D. 103-5, 107, 113, 115, 152, 158, 221
Betz, O. 103, 145
Beyer, K. 196
Bibelerk, L. 107
Bickerman, E. 56
Bieler, L. 101, 104
Bilde, Per 204, 212
Bilezikian, Gilbert G. 94

Index Locorum

Rabbinica and related literature